LINGUISTICS AND LITERARY STYLE

To the memory of Whitney Marshall Duer
1967–1969

PREFACE

The essays in this book have been assembled for two main purposes: to serve the needs of those graduate and undergraduate courses now devoted wholly or in part to the connections between modern linguistics and the study of literature, and to represent the several different approaches that scholars in this developing field have found fruitful. Users of this book should read the essays in such other collections as Seymour Chatman and Samuel R. Levin, *Essays on the Language of Literature* (Boston, 1967); and Glen A. Love and Michael Payne, *Contemporary Essays on Style* (Chicago, 1969).

I am grateful to the authors and publishers of these essays for permission to reprint them here, and particularly to the authors who consented to have portions of their books excerpted in the following pages. Hopefully the excerpts will lead readers to the books in their entirety. The most obvious candidate for reprinting in a collection of this sort, Roman Jakobson's "Linguistics and Poetics," is absent from *Linguistics and Literary Style*. Professor Jakobson is publishing a revised and expanded version of this seminal essay in Volume V of his *Selected Writings* next year.

Though they bear no responsibility for whatever shortcomings there may be in what follows, I should like to thank Walker Gibson, Paul Kiparsky, Samuel R. Levin, John Thompson, and Seymour Chatman for suggestions and advice; Morris Halle for the encouragement and measured criticism he gives everyone who passes through M.I.T.; Richard A. Demers, Margaret H. Rawson, and Wyatt E. F. James for assistance with various aspects of the manuscript, and most of all my colleague Peter H. Salus for contributing the translation of Manfred Bierwisch's "Poetik und Linguistik."

Amherst, Massachusetts   D.C.F.
January 1970

CONTENTS

LINGUISTICS
AND
LITERARY
STYLE

INTRODUCTION

I

1. LINGUISTIC APPROACHES TO LITERATURE

Donald C. Freeman

1

Recent work in linguistics and the increased interest in linguistic approaches to literary studies have led to the emergence of modern linguistic theory as a contributory discipline to literary criticism. Most of the current approaches are represented in this book. As such, linguistics is as much entitled to a place in the baggage of the literary critic as history, biography, bibliography, or psychology—all disciplines which contribute new facts, new ways of looking at facts, and new kinds of theoretical commitments to the craft of studying, explaining, and evaluating literary art. Viewed in this way—as a contributing but not a controlling body of theory—linguistics gives literary criticism a theoretical underpinning as necessary to that undertaking as mathematics is to physics. A good critic is perforce a good linguist.

Nearly twenty years ago, Harold Whitehall asserted (in a remark which caused outrage in some quarters) that "no criticism can go beyond its linguistics." [1] Developments in linguistics since that time—in particular, the interest generated by Noam Chomsky and his followers in learning theory, cognitive psychology, language acquisition, and philosophy of mind—have confirmed Whitehall's judgment. The business of linguistics is to inquire into what Chomsky has called the "close relation between innate properties of the mind and features of linguistic structure"; [2] the business of literary criticism in at least one of its modern versions is the relation between the organization of the human esthetic and the features of *literary* structure and language. I should like to make a case for linguistics in literary studies by reviewing briefly the most important recent work in what M. A. K. Halliday has called "linguistic stylistics." [3] Two kinds of "borderline" studies will not be considered here: work which is in some ways linguistically oriented but not directly related to literary explication (for example, computer-oriented studies of authorship), and work which, although dealing with "style," does not make use of linguistic fact and theory. This distinction is one of subject matter, not of value. The achievement of linguistically oriented studies of literature will be measured for some time against the high standard of such "nonlinguistic" books as Richard Bridgman's *The Colloquial Style in America* and Richard Poirier's *A World Elsewhere: The Place of Style in American Literature* (to take only two recent examples); nevertheless, I omit consideration of them here. Perhaps this is the place to say that I by no means hold that important insights about literary style can be gained only through formal linguistics, and that I do not share the disdain for "impressionism" prevalent in some linguistically oriented studies (a disdain rightly castigated as contrary to the spirit of humane inquiry). In this last, if "impressionism" is understood as a respect for intuition (and the object of scholarship as an accounting for intuition), I stand with, not against, most modern linguists.

Recent work in linguistic stylistics may be divided into three types: style as deviation from the norm, style as recurrence or convergence of textural pattern, and style as a particular exploitation of a grammar of possibilities. These distinctions are easily discernible in the work of the last decade; curiously, they are also discernible in the currents of both literary criticism and linguistics during this century. Criticism has moved from the anthropocentric and biographical work of men like A. C. Bradley through the text-centered, autotelic studies of John Crowe Ransom, Cleanth Brooks, and the "New Criticism," to attempts to reconstruct an author's conscious and unconscious motives in the work of Northrop Frye, Kenneth Burke, and Norman N. Holland. In like manner, modern linguistics has moved from anthropologically and philologically oriented study (Eduard Sievers, Franz Boas) to data-restricted empiricism and taxonomy (the so-called structural linguistics) to the concern of transformational-generative linguists with how the surface form of language arises from deeper, more universal forms, and what the processes of producing sound from meaning and understanding meaning from sound reveal about innate intellectual capacities, language acquisition, and the structure of the mind.[4]

2

Hugh Kenner has written of the "game" of empiricism that its "central rule forbids you to understand what you are talking about." [5] Early work in linguistic stylistics was rigorously empirical and at times nearly behavioristic. In its rejection of "impressionism" and its adherence to an objectivity and quantification alleged to be scientific, the "style as deviation" school occasionally let methodology overwhelm its subject. Such a misconception of the nature of literary study exists, in my opinion, in some aspects of Michael Riffaterre's work in stylistics,[6] which is strongly influenced by a behaviorist philosophy of science. Riffaterre's criticism of Leo Spitzer for succumbing to the "strong temptation to be subjective" [7] ignores the fact that literary criticism is not laboratory work (see Spitzer's definition of the "philological circle" in Selection 1). Criticism does not proceed from a *tabula rasa*. Spitzer's philological circle depends upon a critical mind and a sense of cultural values. To refer to a given literary effect as a "stimulus," [8] with the philosophical commitments inherent in such a term, is to do violence to the very nature of literature.

Another difficulty in the work of the "style as deviation" school of linguistic stylistics is its definition of the norm from which an author's style is supposed to differ in certain ways. For example, Bernard Bloch defines style as "the message carried by the frequency distributions and transitional probabilities of [a discourse's] linguistic features, especially as they differ from those of the same features in the language as a whole." [9] This definition is a chimera. The "frequency distributions and transitional probabilities" of natural language are not known and never will be, and even if they could be ascertained they would constitute no particularly revealing insight into either natural language or style.

These difficulties aside, the questions asked by the "style as difference" school are of the following sort: what does the language of a literary text convey in addition to information? what does a writer's language do in addition to what the rules of grammar require it to do? what are a writer's typical patterns of syntactic and lexical choice where he has an option?

These questions are most fruitfully considered in the work of the Linguistic Circle of Prague, particularly in Jan Mukařovský's famous essay, "Standard Language and Poetic Language" (reprinted here, Selection 2). Mukařovský characterized poetic (that is, literary) language as an esthetically purposeful distortion of standard language: to varying degrees, different kinds of literature make a business of violating the rules of grammar. Poetic language deliberately breaks the rules in order that a given passage be noticed *as language:* the hallmark of literary language is *foregrounding.*

The opposite of foregrounding Mukařovský wrote, is automatization: a change in literary taste can be characterized as the gradual automatization of previously foregrounded linguistic elements in a literary text and the (perhaps sudden) de-automatization and foregrounding of different linguistic elements. A case in point might be the fate of Miltonic diction in the eighteenth century—heavily Latinate, deliberately archaic in lexis and syntax, laden with classical allusion. The sure cadence of

> Thee I revisit now with bolder wing,
> Escaped the Stygian pool, though long detained
> In that obscure sojourn, while in my flight,
> Through utter and through middle darkness
>   borne,
> With other notes than to th'Orphean lyre
> I sung of Chaos and eternal Night;
> Naught by the Heavenly Muse to venture down
> The dark descent, and up to reascend,
> Though hard and rare.

PARADISE LOST, BOOK III

degenerates slightly as, in the following passage, the elevation of the subject—a prospect of nature—falls short of the elevation of the style, which relies heavily upon derived adjectives ("lawny," "misty," "bladed," "soon-clad," "mossy,") and syntactic inversions:

> Young day pours in apace,
> And opens all the lawny prospect wide.
> The dripping rock, the mountain's misty top
> Swell on the sight and brighten with the dawn.
> Blue through the dusk the smoking currents
>   shine;
> And from the bladed field the fearful hare
> Limps awkward; while along the forest glade
> The wild deer tip, and often turning gaze
> At early passenger. Music awakens,
> The native voice of undissembled joy;
> And thick around the woodland hymns arise.
> Roused by the cock, the soon-clad shepherd
>   leaves
> His mossy cottage, where with peace he dwells,
> And from the crowded fold in order drives
> His flock to taste the verdure of the morn.

> James Thomson
> THE SEASONS, "SUMMER"

At length these lexical abstractions, personifications, and inversions become poetic cliché in the pre-Romantic odes:

> How sleep the brave who sink to rest
> By all their country's wishes blest!
> When Spring, with dewy fingers cold,
> Returns to deck their hallowed mold,
> They there shall dress a sweeter sod
> Than Fancy's feet have ever trod.
>
> By fairy hands their knell is rung,
> By forms unseen their dirge is sung;
> There Honor comes, a pilgrim gray,
> To bless the turf that wraps their clay,
> And Freedom shall awhile repair,
> To dwell a weeping hermit there!

> William Collins
> "ODE WRITTEN IN THE BEGINNING OF THE YEAR 1746"

The bold innovations of Milton have become part of the background noise, stale and attenuated, not the essence of poetry and poetic language but their accidents, which Wordsworth was to stigmatize as "arbitrary and capricious habits of expression" in the preface to the *Lyrical Ballads.* The automatization of Miltonic diction by Wordsworth's time is the background against which Wordsworth's return to "the real language of men" becomes idiosyncratic and stylistically significant.

The same kind of theoretical assumption—that style is best viewed as a differentiation from a norm, and that linguistics is best able to assist literary studies by gathering facts about these differentiations—underlies what Roger Fowler has called "structural metrics." This work, which began with Whitehall's review of George Trager and Henry Lee Smith's *Outline of English Structure* (see note 1), argues that metrical analysis depends upon a "tension" between the abstract metrical pattern, which is bipolar, and the observed speech stress of the language, which actualizes that pattern. Speech stress is, according to Trager and Smith, based on four differentiated levels; thus a speech stress of level three (´) can constitute metrical ictus if it is surrounded by syllables which are stressed at level four (˘); secondary speech stress (ˆ) is not a metrical ictus if it is surrounded by syllables with primary speech stress (´). Edmund L. Epstein and Terence Hawkes outlined the possibilities for metrical analysis using this system in *Linguistics and English Prosody,*[10] and showed that, in theory, 6236 different kinds of iambic foot were possible in English verse.

In *The Founding of English Metre* (London and New York, 1961), John Thompson argued that the liberation of English metrical style from the rote punctilio of Gascoigne, Googe, and Turberville and their immediate contemporaries occurred when poets became aware of the distinction between metrical form and speech rhythm. In a later study, Seymour Chatman's *A Theory of Meter* (The Hague, 1965), syllabic weights were classified according to their stress and vowel quantity, and on the basis of this classification thirty-two different iambic foot-types were isolated. Using eleven recorded readings of Shakespeare's "Sonnet 18," and checking his conclusions against those of twenty-one professors of English literature, Chatman showed that lexical stress always marks metrical ictus unless phrase accent overrides it. He argues elsewhere in the book and in other articles that metrical ictus and the varying degrees of lexical stress which actualize ictus are relevant to the study of metrical style. These observations have been extended in several articles by Fowler,[11] who also has argued that another important characteristic of metrical style is a poet's exploitation, or avoidance, of coincidence between metrical units (feet and lines) and linguistic units (words and phrases).

The most important aspect of this work is its raising of the possibility that surface phenomena (in this case, the rhythms of speech stress) and the deep form underlying them (the abstract metrical pattern) can differ, and that a proper object of scholarly investigation is the system of rules which relates the two levels.

A body of work in linguistic stylistics which depends on a different definition of "norm" and a different concept of deviation is that of the so-called London or neo-Firthian school of linguistics. Language—including literary language—cannot, this work argues, be viewed apart from its *context of situation;* language can be considered under the rubrics of register (language according to use), and dialect (language according to user). A literary text must be described not so much against the background of the entire language as against the typical characteristics of its register (the set of linguistic choices typical to a given use of language, as the ode, the short story, the essay) and against the dialect of the writer. Keats's "verdurous glooms and winding mossy ways," while highly idiosyncratic from the point of view of general English ("gloom" normally is an abstract, unpluralizable noun; it never collocates with "verdurous," which is itself quite low in frequency of occurrence) is not at all untypical of the register (late Romantic poetry, and, at a more delicate level, the ode) or of Keats's poetic dialect.

These studies have brought to linguistic stylistics the concepts of *lexical set* and *collocation.* A lexical set is a group of words that occur in similar semantic situations, that "have a similar range of collocation." [12] One kind of figure that can be systematically examined is a poet's strategic exploitation of what Geoffrey Leech has called a "collocative clash," [13] when in such lines as Dylan Thomas's "broke the grape's joy" the poet violates customary patterns of collocation.

From neo-Firthian work in linguistic stylistics has arisen the important theoretical concept that literature, even individual literary texts, must be construed as a microlanguage with a microgrammar. This microgrammar must describe as a unity the characteristics of the microlanguage at all levels—phonology, syntax, and lexis—and it must go beyond the text itself.

3

The notion of style as a recurrence of convergence of textural pattern has stemmed in large part from Roman Jakobson's famous dictum: "The poetic function projects the principle of equivalence from the axis of selection into the axis of combination." [14] Poetic language, Jakobson argued, seeks in its *chain,* or combinatory relationships—its syntactic elements—the same properties of close coherence that are to be found among the individual members of a *choice* relationship, or paradigm.

Consider, for example, the octave of Sidney's first *Astrophil and Stella* sonnet:

> Loving in truth, and fain in verse my love to show,
> That she, dear she, might take some pleasure of my pain,
> Pleasure might cause her read, reading might make her know,
> Knowledge might pity win, and pity grace obtain,
> I sought fit words to paint the blackest face of woe:
> Studying inventions fine, her wits to entertain,
> Oft turning others' leaves, to see if thence would flow
> Some fresh and fruitful showers upon my sunburnt brain.

At the level of phonology, Sidney systematically exploits paradigms (classes) of sounds at different points in the syntagmatic (horizontal) pattern, and interrelates these classes in an extraordinarily complex way. In one class are *fain, pain,* and *paint;* these are at the same time related to other classes: *fain* with *fine,* hence also with *fit* and thence to *pity* (itself related by alliteration to the *pain, pity,* and *paint* class); *pain* both phonologically and semantically with *pleasure* (hence both phonologically and syntactically with *pity*). At the level of syntax, the five included sentences which follow "that" (line 2) are structured so that the subject noun of each sentence recapitulates the "object" (whether verb ["read," "know"] or noun ["pleasure," "pity"]) of the main verb. The relationship of each of these units to the other is as natural, in poetic language, as that among members of a paradigm, a natural class, in ordinary language.

These principles generally are followed out in Walter A. Koch's curious and at times opaque monograph, *Recurrence and a Three-Modal Approach to Poetry.*[15] Koch's three modes are *topic* (roughly, semantic sames), *meter,* and *styleme* (differentiation from the linguistic norm). His essay attempts to correlate pattern (constellations of different items) and figure (constellations of similar items) with syntagm (chain) on the one hand and paradigm (choice) on the other. Poetic language typically organizes figures along the chain and violates pattern at a point of choice (most typically, for example, in Dylan Thomas's poetry). Poetic analysis involves consideration both of the elements that are present in the poetic text and their relationships (syntagmatic analysis) and of the elements that are strategically omitted (paradigmatic analysis).

A third view of style as the coherence and convergence of patterns is to be found in the work of M. A. K. Halliday and Geoffrey Leech on *cohesion,* which Halliday has characterized as a grouping of descriptive categories organized around the lexical and grammatical means of unifying a literary text.[16] Cohesion, which is realized at different ranks of linguistic structure,[17] is a syntagmatic or chain relationship. Cohesion can be grammatical (such items as anaphoric [pointing backward] determiners, pronouns, demonstratives, and certain adverbs [*such, so*]) or lexical (repetition of lexical items or sequential occurrence of items from the same lexical set). Halliday has shown, for example, that in Yeats's "Leda and the Swan," determiners which normally would be construed as cataphoric (pointing forward)—"the dark webs," "the feathered glory"—are in fact anaphoric: their only referent is backward to the "swan" in the poem's title, which appears nowhere else, a stylistic feature that contributes to the poem's sense of mysterious power.

Cohesion, or lack of it, can be an important factor in the tone of literary prose. In the opening paragraphs of *The Mayor of Casterbridge,* Hardy carefully controls the gradual, sequential unfolding of the picture of Michael and Susan Henchard as they enter the stage of the novel on their plodding journey to Weydon-Priors. Hardy achieves this control through a careful attention to cohesion:[18]

> One evening of late summer, before the nineteenth century had reached one-third of *its* span, a young man and woman, *the latter* carrying a child, were approaching the large village of Weydon-Priors, in Upper Wessex, on foot. *They* were plainly *not ill* clad, though the thick hoar of dust *which* had accumulated on *their* shoes and garments from an *obviously* long journey lent a disadvantageous shabbiness to *their* appearance just now.
>
> The man was *of fine figure, swarthy,* and *stern in aspect;* and *he* showed *in profile* a *facial angle* so slightly inclined as to be almost *perpendicular. He* wore a short jacket of *brown corduroy,* newer than the remainder of his suit *which* was a *fustian waistcoat* with white horn buttons, *breeches* of the same, tanned *leggings,* and a *straw hat* overlaid with black glazed canvas. At *his* back *he* carried by a looped strap a rush basket, from *which* protruded at *one end* the crutch of a hay-knife, a wimble for haybonds being *also* visible in *the* aperture. *His* measured, springless walk was *the walk* of the skilled countryman as distinct from *the desultory shamble* of the general laborer; while in *the turn and plant of each foot* there was, further, a dogged and cynical indifference personal to *himself,* showing *its* presence even in the regularly interchanging *fustian* folds, now in *the left leg,* now in *the right,* as *he* paced along.

In the first paragraph of Conrad's *Lord Jim,* however, where sequential time is deliberately violated from the outset, we see Jim for the first time *after* his trial and disgrace but *before* his retreat to Patusan, and we see him not as a figure in time but as a man deliberately sequestered from all contexts, at once a donnée. Conrad achieves this effect by deliberately minimizing cohesion:

> He was an inch, perhaps two, under six feet, powerfully built, and *he* advanced straight at you with a slight stoop of the shoulders, head forward, and a fixed from-under stare *which* made you think of a charging bull. *His* voice was *deep,*

loud, and *his* manner displayed a kind of dogged self-assertion which had nothing aggressive in *it. It* seemed a necessity, and *it* was directed apparently as much at *himself* as at anybody *else. He* was spotlessly *neat, apparelled* in immaculate white from shoes to hat, and in the various Eastern ports where *he* got his living as ship-chandler's water-clerk *he* was very popular.

As Halliday and Leech have shown, cohesion can be an important device in the linguistic description of literary texts.

Samuel R. Levin's work—*Linguistic Structures in Poetry*[19] and a number of later articles[20]—uses a transformational-generative theoretical framework in an attempt to characterize the peculiar unity of poetic language in terms of what he calls "coupling": the convergence of a pair of semantically related elements and a pair of syntagmatic (that is, positional) patterns. In a line such as Pope's "A Soul as full of Worth as void of Pride," "full" and "void" are semantically related (antonymous) and occur in identical parallel positions. Poetic language, Levin argues, maximizes the use of such figures or "couples." In his later work, Levin shows that poetic language has both idiosyncratic restrictions and idiosyncratic licenses in its exploitation of the grammatical rules in ordinary language. This deviation from grammaticalness is formalizable in transformational-generative linguistics as a grammar that both characterizes the "microgrammar" of the language of a particular poem and is predictive, that is, goes beyond the data. An explicit grammar of a particular poem must not only characterize its language but must show what language is possible (even if not chosen) for a particular poem and poet.

4

This last concept is more fully developed in a body of work that can be considered under my third major heading: the view of style as a particular exploitation of a grammar of possibilities. The notion of a grammar that goes beyond the literary text, that accounts for the data and predicts the "grammatical" language of a given poem or poet, implies that certain typical expressive characteristics (that is, selections from these possibilities) are indicative of what Richard Ohmann has called a writer's "cognitive orientation."

The basic precepts of transformational-generative grammatical theory, Ohmann shows,[21] can characterize more exactly Buffon's famous statement, *le style est l'homme même*. According to this theory of grammar, language can be characterized at two levels of representation: deep and surface syntactic structure. Semantic interpretation proceeds from deep structure; only phonetic interpretation proceeds from surface syntactic structure. The two levels are related by an ordered set of transformations, which are *meaning-preserving* (since semantic interpretation functions before transformations begin). Given this theoretical framework, then, a writer's typical exploitation of particular kinds of transformations (particularly optional transformations) may be said to constitute his syntactic style. With a number of transformational patterns available to him to express a given deep structure (roughly, a set of semantic relationships), he prefers certain patterns over others.

Much the same set of assumptions is embodied in what has been called generative metrics, which has sought to formalize a poet's metrical options, his grammar of metrical possibilities, in terms of modern phonological theory. Morris Halle and Samuel J. Keyser's "Chaucer and the Study of Prosody" [22] shows that the so-called permissible licenses in iambic pentameter are not accidental but arise from a concept of the metrical pattern as a set of linguistically assigned potential stress contrasts (in their terms, stress maxima). Halle and Keyser argue that deep and surface form must be distinguished in meter as well as in natural language; iambic pentameter as a form consists of lines of ten *metrical positions* each, but iambic pentameter verse consists of lines of from nine to twelve *syllables* each, and what Joseph C. Beaver calls the "grammar of prosody" consists in part of a set of rules relating metrical position and syllable. A study of metrical style in sixteenth-century verse shows that the metrical norm in the iambic pentameter verse of the period shifted from a line with four actualized stress maxima (that is, stress contrasts assigned by the rules of the language) to a line with three; Beaver shows that while Donne tended to write lines with actualized stress maxima at the beginning and end of lines, Shakespeare tended to actualize stress maxima at the middle and end.[23] All of this work has attempted to characterize the set of possibilities native to English poetry and to account for a poet's typical selections from these possibilities.

A little-known article by Manfred Bierwisch (translated into English in this book for the first time) considers this general question of style as choice from a grammar of possibilities in the broader context of general linguistic theory. His conclusions have important consequences for literary studies. Bierwisch argues, quite simply, that our sense of "poeticality," our recognition of a sequence as a piece of poetry, is analogous to, though not identical with, our sense of "grammaticality" by which we immediately recognize a sequence of discourse as natural language. A "poetic grammar," then, must characterize two phenomena: our ability to distinguish poetic from nonpoetic discourse, and our assigning of a "scale of poeticality" to different kinds of poetic language.

Bierwisch formalizes this grammar as two selectional mechanisms that operate on abstract surface structural descriptions in natural language. The first of these has as its input *two* structural descriptions, one poetic (characterized in terms of the "rules" of poetic language), one nonpoetic. This mechanism would distinguish poetic from nonpoetic structures. The other selectional mechanism would assign a scale of poeticality according to a literary text's exploitation of certain poetic devices.

The content of these mechanisms—for the first, a set of linguistic characteristics which uniquely specifies *poetic* language as opposed to *nonpoetic* language; for the second, a valued ranking or hierarchy of these characteristics—is the business of poetics, not linguistics. Just such a distinction and hierarchy is now actively being developed in generative metrics; the work of Ohmann, Curtis Hayes, and James Peter Thorne has pointed the way for similar work in syntactic aspects of style.

One must conclude from this work, I believe, that the study of style (defined in the restricted way proposed above) is in essence inspired mind-reading: that is, the study of "a *way* of saying *it*" (Ohmann's brief definition of style) should attempt to recapitulate formally the mental processes and the set of esthetic priorities that issue in the literary text. This ideal never can be realized, of course. I hold no brief for computer-composed, or, for that matter, linguist-composed, poetry. Art without mystery is not art. But the essays that follow assert in various ways that modern linguistics, with its increasing interest in those characteristics of mind which underlie aspects of natural language, can make substantive theoretical and factual contributions to our understanding of the poetic process.

NOTES

1. Whitehall, "From Linguistics to Criticism," *Kenyon Review*, XIII (1951), p. 713.

2. Chomsky, *Language and Mind* (New York, 1968), p. 81.

3. Halliday, "The Linguistic Study of Literary Texts," in *Proceedings of the IXth International Congress of Linguists*, ed. Horace G. Lunt (The Hague, 1964), pp. 302–307. I have some misgivings about the use of the word "style" as a cover term for linguistically oriented studies of literature. "Poetics" (in the root sense, as used by Roman Jakobson) seems to me a much more accurate term. But since "style" and "stylistics" seem to have acquired the cachet of popular usage, I have used these terms throughout.

4. The most cogent recent summary of this last concern is Chomsky's "The Formal Nature of Language," an appendix to Eric Lenneberg's *Biological Foundations of Language* (New York, 1967), pp. 397–442.

5. Hugh Kenner, *The Counterfeiters: An Historical Comedy* (Bloomington, 1968), p. 173.

6. See Riffaterre, "Criteria for Style Analysis," *Word*, XV (1959), 154–174, and "Stylistic Context," *Word*, XVI (1960), 207–218.

7. Riffaterre, "Criteria for Style Analysis," p. 164.

8. "Criteria," p. 162.

9. Bloch, "Linguistic Structure and Linguistic Analysis," *Georgetown University Monograph Series on Languages and Linguistics*, IV (1953), 42.

10. Epstein and Hawkes, *Studies in Linguistics*, Occasional Papers, 7 (Buffalo, N. Y., 1959).

11. See Roger Fowler, " 'Prose Rhythm' and Metre," in *Essays on Style and Language*, ed. Fowler (London, 1966), pp. 82–99 [reprinted in this volume], and "Structural Metrics," *Linguistics*, no. 27 (1966), 49–64.

12. M. A. K. Halliday, Angus McIntosh, and Peter Strevens, *The Linguistic Sciences and Language Teaching* (London, 1964), p. 33.

13. Leech, " 'This Bread I Break': Language and Interpretation," *Review of English Literature*, VI (1965), 66–75 [reprinted in this volume].

14. Jakobson, "Closing Statement: Linguistics and Poetics," *Style in Language*, ed. Thomas A. Sebeok (Cambridge, Mass., and New York, 1960), p. 358.

15. The Hague, 1966.

16. See Halliday, "Descriptive Linguistics in Literary Studies," in this volume, Selection 4, and Leech's essay referred to earlier. Ruqaiya Hasan of University College London has done some important work on cohesion which is still unpublished.

17. For a general discussion, see Halliday, "The Linguistic Study of Literary Texts," p. 303 ff.

18. In the following passages, words and phrases that are anaphorically cohesive are italicized.

19. The Hague, 1962.

20. "Poetry and Grammaticalness," *Ninth Congress Papers,* pp. 308–314; "Deviation—Statistical and Determinate—in Poetic Language," *Lingua,* XII (1963), 276–290; "Two Grammatical Approaches to Poetic Analysis," *College Composition and Communication,* XVI (1965), 256–260, and "Internal and External Deviation in Poetry," *Word,* XXI (1965), 225–237.

21. In "Generative Grammars and the Concept of Literary Style," reprinted here, Selection 15, and "Literature as Sentences," *College English,* XXVII (1966), 261–267.

22. Reprinted here, Selection 21.

23. See Joseph C. Beaver, "A Grammar of Prosody," and Donald C. Freeman, "On the Primes of Metrical Style," in this volume, Selections 22 and 23.

LINGUISTIC STYLISTICS: THEORY

2. LINGUISTICS AND LITERARY HISTORY

Leo Spitzer

Leo Spitzer's essay, "Linguistics and Literary History," is one of the classic studies in what might be called philological stylistics. In this article Professor Spitzer propounds the doctrine of the "philological circle": the process of stylistic analysis from one group of superficial details to the "inward life-center," the artist's creative principle, and then back to an integration of other details of the analysis. Like modern transformational-generative linguists, Professor Spitzer was deliberately and frankly "mentalist"; he sought psychologically sound explanations for aspects of style and regarded with disdain mere accumulation and classification of data. "Linguistics and Literary History" is a typical example of the richness of Spitzer's scholarly style; his footnotes are a classical education in themselves. Leo Spitzer was professor of Romance languages at The John Hopkins University. He died in 1960.

. . . Since the best document of the soul of a nation is its literature, and since the latter is nothing but its language as this is written down by elect speakers, can we perhaps not hope to grasp the spirit of a nation in the language of its outstanding works of literature? Because it would have been rash to compare the whole of a national literature to the whole of a national language (as Karl Vossler has prematurely tried to do) I started, more modestly, with the question: "Can one distinguish the soul of a particular French writer in his particular language?"

Leo Spitzer, *Linguistics and Literary History,* Princeton University Press, 1948, pages 10–20, 27–29. Reprinted by permission of Princeton University Press.

It is obvious that literary historians have held this conviction, since, after the inevitable quotation (or misquotation) of Buffon's saying: *"Le style c'est l'homme,"* they generally include in their monographs a chapter on the style of their author. But I had in mind the more rigorously scientific definition of an individual style, the definition of a linguist which should replace the casual impressionistic remarks of literary critics. Stylistics, I thought, might bridge the gap between linguistics and literary history. On the other hand, I was warned by the scholastic adage: *individuum est ineffabile;* could it be that any attempt to define the individual writer by his style is doomed to failure? The individual stylistic deviation from the general norm must represent a historical step taken by the writer, I argued: it must reveal a shift of the soul of the epoch, a shift of which the writer has become conscious and which he would translate into a necessarily new linguistic form; perhaps it would be possible to determine the historical step, psychological as well as linguistic? To determine the beginning of a linguistic innovation would be easier, of course, in the case of contemporary writers, because their linguistic basis is better known to us than is that of past writers.

In my reading of modern French novels, I had acquired the habit of underlining expressions which struck me as aberrant from general usage, and it often happened that the underlined passages, taken together, seemed to offer a certain consistency. I wondered if it would not be possible to establish a common denominator for all or most of these deviations; could not the common spiritual etymon, the psychological root, of several individual "traits of style" in a writer be found, just as we have found an etymon common to various fanciful word formations? [1] I had, for example, noticed in the novel *Bubu de Montparnasse* of Charles-Louis Philippe (1905), which moves in the underworld of Parisian pimps and prostitutes, a particular use of *à cause de,* reflecting the spoken, the unliterary language: "Les réveils de midi sont lourds et poisseux. . . . On éprouve un sentiment de déchéance *à cause des* réveils d'autrefois." More academic writers would have said "en se rappelant des réveils d'autrefois . . . ," "à la suite du souvenir. . . ." This, at first glance, prosaic and commonplace *à cause de* has nevertheless a poetic flavor, because of the unexpected suggestion of a causality, where the average person would see only coincidence: it is, after all, not unanimously accepted that one awakes with a feeling of frustration from a noon siesta *because* other similar awakenings have preceded; we have here an assumed, a poetic reality, but one expressed by a prosaic phrase. We find this *à cause de* again in a description of a popular celebration of the 14th of July: "[le peuple], *à cause de* l'anniversaire de sa délivrance, laisse ses filles danser en liberté." Thus, one will not be surprised when the author lets this phrase come from the mouth of one of his characters: "Il y a dans mon coeur deux ou trois cent petites émotions qui brûlent *à cause de toi*." Conventional poetry would have said "qui brûlent pour toi"; "qui brûlent *à cause de toi*" is both less and more: more, since the lover speaks his heart better in this sincere, though factual manner. The causal phrase, with all its semipoetic implications, suggests rather a commonplace speaker, whose speech and whose habits of thought the writer seems to endorse in his own narrative.

Our observation about *à cause de* gains strength if we compare the use, in the same novel, of other causal conjunctions, such as *parce que:* for example, it is said of the pimp's love for his sweetheart Berthe: "[il aimait] sa volupté particulière, quand elle appliquait son corps contre le sien. . . . Il aimait cela qui la distinguait de toutes les femmes qu'il avait connues *parce que* c'était plus doux, *parce que* c'était plus fin, et *parce que* c'était sa femme à lui, qu'il avait eue vierge. Il l'aimait *parce qu'*elle était honnête et qu'elle en avait l'air, et pour toutes les raisons qu'ont les bourgeois d'aimer leur femme." Here, the reasons why Maurice loved to embrace his sweetheart (*parce que c'était doux, fin, parce que c'était sa femme à lui*) are outspokenly classified or censored by the writer as being *bourgeois;* and yet, in Philippe's narrative, the *parce que* is used as if he considered these reasons to be objectively valid.

The same observation holds true for the causal conjunction *car*: in the following passage which describes Maurice as a being naturally loved by women: "Les femmes l'entouraient d'amour comme des oiseaux qui chantent le soleil et la force. Il était un de ceux que nul ne peut assujettir, *car* leur vie, plus forte et plus belle, comporte l'amour du danger."

Again, it can happen that a causal relationship is implied without the use of a conjunction, a relationship due to the gnomic character adherent, at least in that particular milieu, to a general statement—the truth of which is, perhaps, not so fully accepted elsewhere: "Elle l'embrassa à pleine bouche. *C'est une chose hygiénique* et bonne entre un homme et sa femme, qui vous amuse un petit quart d'heure avant de vous endormir." (Philippe could as well have written "car . . . ," "parce que c'est une chose hygiénique. . . .") Evidently this is the truth only in that particular world of sensuous realism which he is describing. At the same time, however, the writer, while half-endorsing these bourgeois platitudes of the underworld, is discreetly but surely suggesting his criticism of them.

Now I submit the hypothesis that all these expansions of causal usages in Philippe cannot be due to chance: there must be "something the matter" with his conception of causality. And now we must pass from Philippe's style to the psychological etymon, to the radix in his soul. I have called the phenomenon in question "pseudo-objective motivation": Philippe, when presenting causality as binding for his characters, seems to recognize a rather objective cogency in their sometimes awkward, sometimes platitudinous, sometimes semipoetic reasonings; his attitude shows a fatalistic, half-critical, half-understanding, humorous sympathy with the necessary errors and thwarted strivings of these underworld beings dwarfed by inexorable social forces. The pseudo-objective motivation, manifest in his style, is the clue to Philippe's *Weltanschauung*; he sees, as has also been observed by literary critics, without revolt but with deep grief and a Christian spirit of contemplativity, the world functioning wrongly with an appearance of rightness, of objective logic. The different word-usages, grouped together (just as was done with the different forms of *conundrum* and *quandary*) lead toward a psychological etymon, which is at the bottom of the linguistic as well as of the literary inspiration of Philippe.

Thus we have made the trip from language or style to the soul. And on this journey we may catch a glimpse into a historical evolution of the French soul in the twentieth century: first we are given insight into the soul of a writer who has become conscious of the fatalism weighing on the masses, then, into that of a section of the French nation itself, whose faint protest is voiced by our author. And in this procedure there is, I think, no longer the timeless, placeless philology of the older school, but an explanation of the concrete *hic et nunc* of a historical phenomenon. The to-and-fro movement we found to be basic with the humanist has been followed here, too: first we grouped together certain causal expressions, striking with Philippe, then hunted out their psychological explanation, and finally, sought to verify whether the element of "pseudo-objective motivation" [2] concorded with what we know, from other sources, about the elements of his inspiration. Again, a belief is involved —which is no less daring than is the belief that the Romance languages go back to one invisible, basic pattern manifest in them all: namely, the belief that the mind of an author is a kind of solar system into whose orbit all categories of things are attracted: language, motivation, plot, are only satellites of this mythological entity (as my antimentalistic adversaries would call it): *mens Philippina*. The linguist as well as his literary colleague must always ascend to the etymon which is behind all those particular so-called literary or stylistic devices which the literary historians are wont to list. And the individual *mens Philippina* is a reflection of the *mens Franco-gallica* of the twentieth century; its ineffability consists precisely in Philippe's anticipatory sensitivity for the spiritual needs of the nation.

Now, it is obvious that a modern writer such as Philippe, faced with the social disintegration of humanity in the twentieth century, must show more patent linguistic deviations, of which the philologist may take stock in order to build up his "psycho-gram" of the individual artist. But does Philippe, a stranded being broken loose from his moorings, transplanted, as it were, into a world from which he feels estranged—so that he must, perforce, indulge in arbitrary whimsicality—represent only a modern phenomenon? If we go back to writers of more remote times, must it not be that we will always find a balanced language, with no deviations from common usage?

It suffices to mention the names of such dynamic writers of older times as Dante or Quevedo or Rabelais to dispel such a notion. Whoever has thought strongly and felt strongly has innovated in his language; mental creativity immediately inscribes itself into the language, where it becomes linguistic creativity; the trite and petrified in language is never sufficient for the needs of expression felt by a strong personality. In my first publication, "Die Wortbildung als stilistisches Mittel" (a thesis written in 1910), I dealt with Rabelais' comic word-formations, a subject to which I was attracted because of certain affinities between Rabelaisian and Viennese (Nestroy!) comic writing, and which offered the opportunity of bridging the gap between linguistic and literary history. Be it said to the eternal credit of the scholarly integrity of Meyer-Lübke that he, in contrast to the antimentalists who would suppress all expressions of opposition to their theories, recommended for publication a book with an approach so aberrant from his own. In this work I sought to show, for example, that a neologism such as *panta-gruélisme,* the name given by Rabelais to his stoic-epicurean philosophy ("certaine gayeté d'esprict, conficte en mépris des choses fortuites") is not only a playful outburst of a genuine gaiety, but a thrust from the realm of the real into that of the unreal and the unknown—as is true, in fact, of any nonce-word. On the one hand, a form with the suffix *-ism* evokes a school of serious philosophic thought (such as *Aristotelianism, scholasticism,* etc.); on the other, the stem, *Pantagruel,* is the name of a character created by Rabelais, the half-jocular, half-philosophical giant and patriarchal king. The coupling of the learned philosophical suffix with the fanciful name of a fanciful character amounts to positing a half-real, half-unreal entity: "the philosophy of an imaginary being." The contemporaries of Rabelais who first heard this coinage must have experienced the reactions provoked by any nonce-word: a moment of shock followed by a feeling of reassurance: to be swept toward the unknown frightens, but realization of the benignly fanciful result gives relief: laughter, our physiological reaction on such occasions, arises precisely out of a feeling of relief following upon a temporary breakdown of our assurance. Now, in a case such as that of the creation *pantagruélisme,* the designation of a hitherto unknown but, after all, innocuous philosophy, the menacing force of the neologism is relatively subdued. But what of such a list of names as that concocted by Rabelais for the benefit of his hated adversaries, the reactionaries of the Sorbonne: *sophistes, sorbillans, sorbon-*

agres, sorbonigenes, sorbonicoles, sorboniformes, sorboniseques, niborcisans, sorbonisans, saniborsans. Again, though differently, there is an element of realism present in these coinages: the Sorbonne is an existing reality, and the formations are explainable by well-known formative processes. The edition of Abel Lefranc, imbued with his positivistic approach, goes to the trouble of explaining each one of these formations: *sorboniforme* is after *uniforme, sorbonigene* after *homogène,* while *niborcisans, saniborsans* offer what, in the jargon of the linguists, is called a metathesis. But by explaining every coinage separately, by dissolving the forest into trees, the commentators lose sight of the whole phenomenon: they no longer see the forest—or rather the jungle which Rabelais must have had before his eyes, teeming with viperlike, hydralike, demonlike shapes. Nor is it enough to say that the scholarly Rabelais indulges in humanistic word lists with a view to enriching the vocabulary—in the spirit of an Erasmus who prescribed the principle of *copia verborum* to students of Latin—or that Rabelais' rich nature bade him make the French language rich; the aesthetics of richness is, in itself, a problem; and why should richness tend toward the frightening, the bottomless? Perhaps Rabelais' whole attitude toward language rests upon a vision of imaginary richness whose support is the bottomless. He creates word-families, representative of gruesome fantasy-beings, copulating and engendering before our eyes, which have reality only in the world of language, which are established in an intermediate world between reality and irreality, between the nowhere that frightens and the "here" that reassures. The *niborcisans* are as yet an entity vaguely connected with the *sorbonisans,* but at the same time so close to nothingness that we laugh—uneasily; it is *le comique grotesque* which skirts the abyss. And Rabelais will shape grotesque word-families (or families of word-demons) not only by altering what exists: he may leave intact the forms of his word material and create by juxtaposition: savagely piling epithet upon epithet to an ultimate effect of terror, so that, from the well known emerges the shape of the unknown—a phenomenon the more startling with the French, who are generally considered to inhabit an orderly, clearly regulated, well-policed language. Now, of a sudden, we no longer recognize this French language, which has become a chaotic word-world situated somewhere in the chill of cosmic space. Just listen to the inscription on the *abbaye de Thélème,* that Renaissance convent of his shaping, from which Rabelais excludes the hypocrites:

> Cy n'entrez pas, hypocrites, bigots,
> Vieux matagotz, marmiteux, borsoufles,
> Torcoulx, badaux, plus que n'estoient les Gotz,
> Ny Ostrogotz, precurseurs des magotz,
> Haires, cagotz, cafars empantouflez,
> Gueux mitoufles, frapars escorniflez,
> Befflez, enflez, fagoteurs de tabus;
> Tirez ailleurs pour vendre vos abus.

The prosaic commentators of the Lefranc edition would explain that this kind of rather mediocre poetry is derived from the popular genre of the *cry* (the harangue of a barker), and over-loaded with devices of the *rhétoriqueur* school. But I can never read these lines without being frightened, and I am shaken in this very moment by the horror emanating from this accumulation of *-fl-* and *-got-* clusters—of sounds which, in themselves, and taken separately, are quite harmless, of words grouped together, bristling with Rabelais' hatred of hypocrisy—that greatest of all crimes against life. A *cry,* yes, but in a more extensive meaning of the word: it is the gigantic voice of Rabelais which cries to us directly across the gulf of the centuries, as shattering now as at the hour when Rabelais begot these word-monsters.

If, then, it is true that Rabelais' word-formation reflects an attitude somewhere between reality and irreality, with its shudders of horror and its comic relief, what of Lanson's famous statement on Rabelais in general, which is repeated in thousands of French schools and in most of the Lanson-imbued seminars of French throughout the world: "Jamais réalisme plus pur, plus puissant et plus triomphant ne s'est vu"? Well, it is simply wrong. I have not time to develop here the conclusions which would round out the utterly antirealistic picture of Rabelais that stands out in his work; it could be shown that the whole plot of Rabelais' epic, the fantastic voyage of fantastic people to the oracle of the priestess Bacbuc (whose ambiguous response: "*Trinc!*" is just a nowhere word) as well as the invention of detail (e.g. Panurge's speech on debtors and lenders, in which the earthy Panurge drives forward, from his astute egoistic refusal to live without debts, to a cosmic, utopian vision of a paradoxical world resting on the universal law of indebtedness) —that everything in Rabelais' work tends toward the creation of a world of irreality.

Thus, what has been disclosed by the study of Rabelais' language, the literary study would corroborate; it could not be otherwise, since language is only one outward crystallization of the "inward form," or, to use another metaphor: the lifeblood of the poetic creation[3] is everywhere the same, whether we tap the organism at "language" or "ideas," at "plot" or at "composition." As regards the last, I could as well have begun with a study of the rather loose literary composition of Rabelais' writings and only later have gone over to his ideas, his plot, his language. Because I happened to be a linguist it was from the linguistic angle that I started, to fight my way to his unity. Obviously, no fellow scholar must be required to do the same. What he must be asked to do, however, is, I believe, to work from the surface to the "inward life-center" of the work of art: first observing details about the superficial appearance of the particular work (and the "ideas" expressed by a poet are, also, only one of the superficial traits in a work of art);[4] then, grouping these details and seeking to integrate them into a creative principle which may have been present in the soul of the artist; and, finally, making the return trip to all the other groups of observations in order to find whether the "inward form" one has tentatively constructed gives an account of the whole. The scholar will surely be able to state, after three or four of these "fro voyages," whether he has found the life-giving center, the sun of the solar system (by then he will know whether he is really permanently installed in the center, whether he finds himself in an "excentric" or peripheric position). There is no shadow of truth in the objection raised not long ago by one of the representatives of the mechanist Yale school of linguists against the "circularity of arguments" of the mentalists: against the "explanation of a linguistic fact by an assumed psychological process for which the only evidence is the fact to be explained."[5] I could immediately reply that my school is not satisfied with psychologizing one trait but bases its assumptions on several traits carefully grouped and integrated; one should, in fact, embrace *all* the linguistic traits observable with a given author (I myself have tried to come as close as possible to this requirement of completeness in my studies on Racine, Saint-Simon, Quevedo . . .). And the circle of which the adversary just quoted speaks is not a vicious one; on the contrary, it is the basic operation in the humanities, the *Zirkel im Verstehen* as Dilthey has termed the discovery, made by the Romantic scholar and theologian Schleiermacher, that cognizance in philology is reached not only by the gradual progression from one detail to another detail, but by the anticipation or divination of the whole—because "the detail can be understood only by the whole and any explanation of detail presupposes the understanding of the whole." [6] Our to-and-fro voyage from certain outward details to the inner center and back again to other series of details is only an application of the principle of the "philological circle." After all, the concept of the Romance languages as based on one Vulgar Latin substratum, and reflected in them although identical with none—this has been reached by the founder of Romance philology, Diez, the pupil of the Romantics, precisely by means of this "philological circle," which allowed him to sit installed in the center of the phenomenon "Romance Languages," whereas Raynouard, his predecessor, by identifying one of the Romance varieties, Provençal, with Proto-Romance, found himself in an excentric position, from which point it was impossible to explain satisfactorily all the outward traits of Romance. To proceed from some exterior traits of Philippe's or Rabelais' language to the soul or mental center of Philippe and Rabelais, and back again to the rest of the exterior traits of Philippe's and Rabelais' works of art, is the same *modus operandi* as that which proceeds from some details of the Romance languages to a Vulgar Latin prototype and then, in reverse order, explains other details by this assumed prototype—or even, from that which infers from some of the outward, phonetic and semantic appearances of the English word *conundrum* to its medieval French soul, and back to all its phonetic and semantic traits. . . . A very understanding but critical ex-student of mine, an American, once wrote me: "To establish a behavioristic technique which would reveal the application of your method is, it seems to me, beyond your possibilities. You know the principles that motivate you, rather than any 'technique' that you rigorously follow. Here, it may be a memory from boyhood, there an inspiration you got from another poem; here, there and every-where it is an urge in you, an instinct backed up by your experience, that tells you immediately: 'this is not important; this is.' At every second you are making choices, but you hardly know that you make them: what seems right to you must be immediately right. And you can only show by doing; you see the meaning as a whole from the beginning; there are almost no steps in your mental processes; and, writing from the midst of your thoughts, you take it for granted that the reader is with you and that what is self-evident to you as the next step (only, it's not the next step, even: it's already included, somehow) will also be so to him."

These words, obviously, offer a picture of the limitations of a particular individual temperament. But much of what my correspondent says is given with the operation of the circle—when this is applied, not to routine reading, on the one hand, or to the deductions of schematic linguistics on the other, but to a work of art: the solution attained by means of the circular operation cannot be subjected to a rigorous rationale because, at its most perfect, this is a negation of steps: once attained, it tends to obliterate the steps leading up to it (one may remember the lion of medieval bestiaries who, at every step forward, wiped out his footprints with his tail, in order to elude his pursuers!).

Why do I insist that it is impossible to offer the reader a step-by-step rationale to be applied to a work of art? For one reason, that the first step, on which all may hinge, can never be planned: it must already have taken place. This first step is the awareness of having been struck by a detail, followed by a conviction that this detail is connected basically with the work of art; it means that one has made an "observation,"—which is the starting point of a theory, that one has been prompted to raise a question—which must find an answer. To begin by omitting this first step must doom any attempt at interpretation—as was the case with the dissertation . . . devoted to the "imagery" of Diderot, in which the concept "imagery" was based on no preliminary observation but on a ready-made category applied from without to the work of art.

Unfortunately, I know of no way to guarantee either the "impression" or the conviction just described: they are the results of talent, experience, and faith. And, even then, the first step is not to be taken at our own volition: how often, with all

the theoretical experience of method accumulated in me over the
years, have I stared blankly, quite similar to one of my beginning students, at a page that would not yield its magic. The only
way leading out of this state of unproductivity is to read and
reread,[7] patiently and confidently, in an endeavor to become, as it
were, soaked through and through with the atmosphere of the
work. And suddenly, one word, one line, stands out, and we
realize that, now, a relationship has been established between
the poem and us. From this point on, I have usually found that,
what with other observations adding themselves to the first, and
with previous experiences of the circle intervening, and with
associations given by previous education building up before me
(all of this quickened, in my own case, by a quasi-metaphysical
urge toward solution) it does not seem long until the characteristic "click" occurs, which is the indication that detail and whole
have found a common denominator—which gives the etymology
of the writing.[8] And looking back on this process (whose end, of
course, marks only the conclusion of the *preliminary* stage of
analysis), how can we say when exactly it began? (Even the "first
step" was preconditioned.) We see, indeed, that to read is to
have read, to understand is equivalent to having understood.[9]

I have just spoken of the importance of past experience in
the process of understanding the work of art—but as only one of
the intervening factors. For experience with the "circle" is not,
itself, enough to enable one to base thereupon a program
applicable to all cases. For every poem the critic needs a separate
inspiration, a separate light from above (it is this constant need
which makes for humility, and it is the accumulation of past
enlightenments that encourages a sort of pious confidence). Indeed, a Protean mutability is required of the critic, for the device
which has proved successful for one work of art cannot be applied
mechanically to another: I could not expect that the "trick of the
five *grands*" (which I shall apply to an ode of Claudel's) would
work for the "récit de Théramène," or that proper names, which
will serve as a point of departure in my article on Cervantes,
would play any part in the study on Diderot. It is, indeed, most
trying for the experienced teacher to have to watch a beginner
re-use, and consequently mis-use, a particular clue that had
served the teacher when he was treating a quite different writer
—as though a young actor were to use the leer of Barrymore's

Richard III for his performance of Othello. The mutability required of the critic can be gained only by repeated experiences with totally different writers; the "click" will come oftener and more quickly after several experiences of "clicks" have been realized by the critic. And, even then, it is not a foregone conclusion that it will inevitably come; nor can one ever foretell just when and where it will materialize ("The Spirit bloweth . . .").

The reason that the clues to understanding cannot be mechanically transferred from one work of art to another lies in the fact of artistic expressivity itself: the artist lends to an outward phenomenon of language an inner significance (thereby merely continuing and expanding the basic fact of human language: that a meaning is quite arbitrarily—arbitrarily, at least, from the point of view of the current usage of the language—associated with an acoustic phenomenon); just *which* phenomena the literary artist will choose for the embodiment of his meaning is arbitrary from the point of view of the "user" of the work of art. To overcome the impression of an arbitrary association in the work of art, the reader must seek to place himself in the creative center of the artist himself—and re-create the artistic organism. A metaphor, an anaphora, a staccato rhythm may be found anywhere in literature; they may or may not be significant. What tells us that they are important is only the feeling, which we must have already acquired, for the whole of the particular work of art.

And the capacity for this feeling is, again, deeply anchored in the previous life and education of the critic, and not only in his scholarly education: in order to keep his soul ready for his scholarly task he must have already made choices, in ordering his life, of what I would call a moral nature; he must have chosen to cleanse his mind from distraction by the inconsequential, from the obsession of everyday small details—to keep it open to the synthetic apprehension of the "wholes" of life, to the symbolism in nature and art and language. I have sometimes wondered if my "explication de texte" in the university classroom, where I strive to create an atmosphere suitable for the appreciation of the work of art, would not have succeeded much better if that atmosphere had been present at the breakfast table of my students.

NOTES

1. Perhaps the transition from a particular historical line in language, as traced by an etymology, to the self-contained system of a work of literature, may seem violent to the reader: in the first case the "etymon" is the "soul of the nation" at the moment of the creation of the word; in the second, it is the "soul of one particular author." The difference, as Professor Singleton has pointed out to me, is that between the unconscious will of the nation that creates its language, and the conscious will of one member of the nation who creates willfully and more or less systematically. But, apart from the fact that there are rational elements in popular linguistic creations, and irrational ones in those of the creative artist—what I would point out here is the relationship, common to both, between the linguistic detail and the soul of the speaker(s), and the necessity, in both cases, of the to-and-fro philological movement.

Perhaps a better parallel to the system of a work of art would be the system of a language at a definite moment of its evolution. I attempted just such a characterization of a linguistic system in my article on Spanish in *Stilstudien*, I.

2. This study has been published in *Stilstudien*, II. The method I have been describing in the text is, of course, one that is followed by all of us when we must interpret the correspondence of someone with whom we are not well acquainted. For several years I had been in correspondence with a German emigrant in France whom I did not know personally and whose letters had given me the impression of a rather self-centered person who craved a cozy and congenial environment. When she was finally rescued to another country, she published a book of memoirs, a copy of which was sent me. On the cover of the book I saw pictured the window of the room she had occupied in Paris; behind this window, in the foreground, was a great cat looking out upon the Cathedral of Notre Dame. A great part of the book itself was taken up with this cat, and I had not read far before I found—without great surprise—several sentences such as "blottie dans un fauteuil, j'éprouvai un tel bonheur, je me sentis si bien à mon aise sous ce soleil doux qui me faisait ronronner à la manière des chats." Evidently a catlike existence was the deep-felt aspiration of this emigrant who, in the midst of world catastrophe, had lost the feeling of protectedness and had had to seek protection in herself.

3. We could here also be reminded of Goethe's simile (in *Die Wahlverwandtschaften*, II, 2): "We have learned about a special arrangement of the English Navy: all ropes of the Royal Fleet, from the strongest to the thinnest, have a red thread woven into them in such a way that it cannot be taken out without completely raveling the rope, so that even the smallest particle is stamped as the property of the Crown. Similarly, Ottilia's diary is pervaded by a thread of affection and attachment which connects every part and characterizes the whole of it." In this passage Goethe has formulated the principle of inner cohesion as it exists in a sensitive writer. It is the recognition of this principle which enabled Freud to apply his psychoanalytical finds to works of literature. While I do not wish to disavow the Freudian influence in my earlier attempts at explaining literary texts, my

aim today is to think, not so much in terms of the all-too-human "complexes" which, in Freud's opinion, are supposed to color the writing of the great figures of literature, but of "ideological patterns," as these are present in the history of the human mind.

Mr. Kenneth Burke, in his book *Philosophy of Literary Form* (Baton Rouge, La., 1941), has worked out a methodology of what he calls the "symbolic" or "strategic" approach to poetry—an approach which comes very close to the Freudian one (and to my own, as far as it was influenced by Freud), and which consists of establishing emotional clusters. When Mr. Burke finds such clusters in Coleridge, for example, he will claim to have found a factual, observable, irrefutable basis for the analysis of the structure of the work of art in general.

What I would object to in this method is that it can, obviously, be applied only to those poets who do, in fact, reveal such associational clusters—which is to say, only to those poets who do allow their phobias and idiosyncrasies to appear in their writing. But this must exclude all writers before the eighteenth century, the period in which the theory of the "original genius" was discovered and applied. Before this period, it is very difficult to discover, in any writer, "individual" associations, that is to say, associations not prompted by a literary tradition. Dante, Shakespeare, Racine are great literary "individuals," but they did not (or could not) allow their style to be permeated by their personal phobias and idiosyncrasies (even Montaigne, when portraying himself, thought of himself as "l'homme"). When a student of mine, working on the style of Agrippa d'Aubigné, was influenced by Professor Burke's book to apply the method of "emotional clusters" to that sixteenth-century epic poet, and was able, indeed, to find a series of antithetical associations, such as "milk-poison," "mother-serpent," "nature-unnatural" used in reference to pairs represented by the Catholic Catherine de Médicis and her Protestant opponents, I had to point out to him that these particular associational patterns (which had reminded him of Joyce) were all given by classical and Scriptural tradition: D'Aubigné merely gave powerful expression to age-old ideological motifs that transcended his personal, nervous temperament: the starting point for his "mère non-mère" was, obviously, the Greek μήτηρ ἀμήτωρ. Recently, I have had occasion also to point out the same truth in regard to the sixteenth-century poet Guevara, whose style has been explained by Freudian frustration.

4. Under the noble pretext of introducing "history of ideas" into literary criticism, there have appeared in recent times, with the approval of the departments of literary history, academic theses with such titles as "Money in Seventeenth-Century French (English, Spanish, etc.) Comedy," "Political Tendencies in Nineteenth-Century French (English, Spanish, etc.) Literature." Thus we have come to disregard the philological character of the discipline of literary history, which is concerned with ideas couched in linguistic and literary form, not with ideas in themselves (this is the field of history of philosophy) or with ideas as informing action (this is the field of history and the social sciences). Only in the linguistico-literary field are we philologians competent qua scholars. The type of dissertations cited above reveals an unwarranted extension of the (in itself commendable) tendency toward breaking down departmental barriers, to such a degree that literary history becomes the gay sporting ground of incompetence. Students of the department of literature come to treat the complex subjects of a philosophical, political, or economic nature with the same self-assurance that once characterized those Positivists who wrote on "The Horse in Medieval Literature." But while it

is possible for the average person to know "what a horse is" (if less so what "a horse in literature" is), it is much more difficult for a student of literature to know "what money is" (and still more so what "money in literature" is). In fact, this new type of thesis is only an avatar of the old positivistic thesis; but, while the original positivism was motivated by a sincere respect for competence, the neopositivists now would administer the death-blow to scholarly competence.

5. Cf. my article in *Modern Philological Quarterly*: "Why Does Language Change?" and the polemics resulting therefrom in *Language*, xx (1944), 45, 245.

6. Cf. Schleiermacher, *Sämtl. Werke*, iii, no. 3, p. 343. "Über den Begriff der Hermeneutik mit Bezug auf F. A. Wolfs Andeutungen und Arts Lehrbuch" —a speech delivered in 1829. Schleiermacher distinguishes between the "comparative" and the "divinatory" methods, the combination of which is necessary in "hermeneutics," and since hermeneutics falls into two parts, a "grammatical" and a "psychological" part, both methods must be used in both parts of hermeneutics. Of the two methods, it is the divinatory which requires the "Zirkelschluss." We have been dealing here with the *Zirkelschluss* in the "divination" of the psychology of authors; as for "grammatical divination," any college student who attempts to parse a Ciceronian period is constantly using it: he cannot grasp the construction except by passing continuously from the parts to the whole of the sentence and back again to its parts.

Dr. Ludwig Edelstein has called my attention to the Platonic origin of Schleiermacher's discovery: it is in *Phaedo* that Socrates states the importance of the whole for the cognition of the parts. Accordingly, it would appear that I err in adopting Schleiermacher's "theological" approach and that I am undiplomatic in asking for an approach so at variance with that which is traditional in the humanities (when Dewey reproved the Humanists for the residues of theology in their thinking, they made haste to disavow any theological preoccupation—while I take the stand of saying: "Yes, we Humanists are theologians!"); would it not, I am asked, be better to show the irrationalism inherent in any rational operation in the humanities, than to demand the overt irrationalism of religion which our secular universities must thoroughly abhor? My answer is that Socrates himself was a religious genius and that, through Plato, he is present in much of Christian thought. As concerns the necessity, for the scholar, of having recourse to religion, cf. the conclusive reasoning of Erich Frank in his book *Philosophical Understanding and Religious Truth* (1945).

The traditional view of the "viciousness" of the philological circle is unfortunately held in an otherwise brilliant attack against "the biographical fashion in literary criticism" (University of California Publications, in *Classical Philology*, xii, 288) by Professor Harold Cherniss: in his argument against the philologians of the Stefan George school who, though not dealing with the outward biography of artists, believe that the inner form of the artist's personality can be grasped in his works by a kind of intuition, Cherniss writes: "The intuition which discovers in the writings of an author the 'natural law' and 'inward form' of his personality, is proof against all objections, logical and philological; but, while one must admit that a certain native insight, call it direct intelligence or intuition as you please, is required for understanding any text, it is, all the same, a vicious circle to intuit the nature of the author's personality from his writings and then to interpret those writings in accordance with the 'inner necessity' of that intuited personality. Moreover, once the intuition of the individual critic is accepted as the ultimate basis of all interpretation, the comprehension of a literary work becomes a completely private affair, for the intuition of any one interpreter has no more objective validity than that of any other."

I believe that the word "intuition" with its deliberate implication of extraordinary mystic qualities on the part of the critic, vitiates not only the reasoning of the Stefan George school but also that of their opponents. The "circle" is vicious only when an uncontrolled intuition is allowed to exercise itself upon the literary works; the procedure from details to the inner core and back again is not in itself at all vicious; in fact, the "intelligent reading" which Professor Cherniss advocates without defining it (though he is forced to grant rather uncomfortably that it is "a certain native insight, call it direct intelligence or intuition as you please") is based precisely on that very philological circle. To understand a sentence, a work of art, or the inward form of an artistic mind involves, to an increasing degree, irrational moves—which must, also to an increasing degree, be controlled by reason.

Heidegger, in *Sein und Zeit*, I, 32 ("Verstehen und Auslegung"), shows that all "exegesis" is circular, i.e., is a catching up with the "understanding," which is nothing else than an anticipation of the whole that is "existentially" given to man: "Zuhandenes wird immer schon aus der Bewandtnisganzheit der verstanden. . . . Die Auslegung gründet jeweils in einer *Vorsicht*, die das in Vorhabe Genommene auf eine bestimmte Auslegbarkeit hin 'an-schneidet.' . . . Auslegung ist nie ein voraussetzungsloses Erfassen eines Vorgegebenen. . . . Alle Auslegung, die Verständnis beistellen soll, muss schon das Auszulegende verstanden haben. . . . *Aber in diesem Zirkel ein vitiosum sehen und nach Wegen Ausschau halten, ihn zu vermeiden, ja ihn auch nur als unvermeidliche Unvollkommenheit 'empfinden,' heisst das Verstehen von Grund aus missverstehen* [the italics are the author's]. . . . Das Entscheidende ist nicht aus dem Zirkel heraus-, sondern in ihn nach der rechten Weise hineinzukommen. . . . In ihm verbirgt sich eine positive Möglichkeit ursprünglichsten Erkennens, die freilich in echter Weise nur dann ergriffen ist, wenn die Auslegung verstanden hat, dass ihre erste, ständige und letzte Aufgabe bleibt, sich jeweils Vorhabe, Vorsicht und Vorgriff nicht durch Einfälle und Volksbegriffe vorgeben zu lassen, sondern in deren Ausarbeitung aus den Sachen selbst her das wissenschaftliche Thema zu sichern. Der 'Zirkel' im Verstehen gehört zur Struktur des Sinnes, welches Phänomen in der existenzialen Verfassung des Daseins, im aus-legenden Verstehen verwurzelt ist."

This "Vorsicht," this anticipation of the whole, is especially necessary for the understanding of philosophical writing. Franz Rosenzweig, "Das neue Denken" (in *Kleinere Schriften*, 1937) writes: "The first pages of philosophical books are held by the reader in special respect. . . . He thinks they [such books] ought to be 'especially logical,' and by this he means that each sentence depends on the one that precedes it, so that if the famous one stone is pulled, 'the whole tumbles.' Actually, this is nowhere less the case than in philosophical books. Here a sentence does not follow from its predecessor, but much more probably from its successor. . . . Philosophical books refuse such methodical ancien-régime strategy; they must be conquered à la Napoleon, in a bold thrust against the main body of the enemy; and after the victory at this point, the small fortresses will fall of themselves." (I owe this quotation to Kurt H. Wolf's article, "The Sociology of Knowledge" in *Philosophy of Science*, x; Wolf calls the anticipatory understanding of wholes a "central attitude": "In our everyday social interaction we constantly practice the central-attitude approach without which we could not 'know' how to behave toward other persons, or how to read a book, to see a picture, or to play or listen to a piece of music. . . .") What Heidegger, Rosenzweig, and Wolf describe is the method of the humanities which Pascal has called the "esprit de finesse" (as contrasted to the "esprit géométrique").

For the students in Romance Gröber formulated the idea of the philological circle (without mentioning the "circle" itself) in *Gröber's Grundriss* 1/3 (1888): "Absichtslose Wahrnehmung, unscheinbare Anfänge gehen dem zielbewussten Suchen, dem allseitigen Erfassen des Gegenstandes voraus. Im sprungweisen Durchmessen des Raumes hascht dann der Suchende nach dem Ziel, mit einem Schema unfertiger Ansichten über ähnliche Gegenstände scheint er das Ganze erfassen zu können, ehe Natur und Teile gekannt sind. Der vorschnellen Meinung folgt die Einsicht des Irrtums, nur langsam der Entschluss, dem Gegenstand in kleinen und kleinsten vorsichtigen Schritten nahe zu kommen, Teil und Teilchen zu beschauen und nicht zu ruhen, bis die Uberzeugung gewonnen ist, dass sie nur so und nicht anders aufgefasst werden müssen."

It is also true of the comparative linguist who establishes his "phonctic laws" on the basis of "evident etymologies," which themselves are based on those "phonetic laws," that he moves in a circle, in the words of Zupitza, *Zeitschr. f. vergl. Sprachwissenschaft*, XXXVII (1904), 387: "Unsere wissenschaft kommt aus einem kreislauf nicht heraus: sie geht von evidenten gleichungen aus, entnimmt diesen ihre gesetze und prüft an diesen gesetzen jene gleichungen, die ihre grundlage bilden." And even elementary language teaching must move in a circle: R. A. Hall in *Bulletin of the American Association of University Professors,* XXXI, no. 6, advocating the modern "direct method" as preferable to the old "reading method," writes: "When he [the student] has learnt a sufficient number of examples, the linguistic analysis becomes simply a series of obvious deductions from what he has learned; it helps him to perceive the patterns inherent in what he already knows, and tells him how far he can go in extending these patterns to new material." The inference from "patterns" is nothing but an anticipation of a whole deduced from the known examples.

7.   If I were to give one piece of advice to our students of literary history, it would be substantially the same as that which Lanson, touring the United States forty years ago, gave to the students of his time who were then, as they are now, only too eager to rush to their big libraries to find in the many books of "secondary literature" an alibi for getting away from the "primary" texts they should study: *"Read your texts!"* My "circular method" is, in fact, nothing but an expansion of the common practice of "reading books": reading at its best requires a strange cohabitation in the human mind of two opposite capacities: contemplativity on the one hand and, on the other, a Protean mimeticism. That is to say: an undeflected patience that "stays with" a book until the forces latent in it unleash in us the re-creative process.

8.   Sometimes it may happen that this "etymology" leads simply to a characterization of the author that has been long accepted by literary historians (who have not needed, apparently, to follow the winding path I chose), and which can be summed up in a phrase which smacks of a college handbook. But, to make our own way to an old truth is not only to enrich our own understanding: it produces inevitably new evidence, of objective value, for this truth—which is thereby renewed. A *comédie-proverbe* of Musset is based, after all, on a commonplace saying: was it a waste of

time to illustrate so wittily "il faut qu'une porte soit ouverte ou fermée"?

9. The requirement at St. John's for the Hundred Great Books is good, I believe, insofar as it may encourage the "click" to repeat itself in an accelerated manner—if, of course, it has come about in the first experiences: to have read these hundred books "without click" would be equivalent to not having read a single book.

3. STANDARD LANGUAGE AND POETIC LANGUAGE

Jan Mukařovský

Edited and translated by Paul L. Garvin

The concept of *foregrounding* has been central to much recent work in stylistics. These studies have sought to establish what methods a writer of poetry or prose uses to make particularly prominent—more prominent than in ordinary, nonliterary language—certain aspects of texture in a given literary work. Foregrounding, first postulated by Jan Mukařovský in the essay reprinted here, is at issue in such questions as the definition of poetic language, the effect of poetic language upon ordinary or "standard" language, the aesthetic freshness of metaphor and other figures, the significance of certain metrical patterns. "Standard Language and Poetic Language" is a typical product of the Cercle Linguistique de Prague—the famous "Prague School"—both in subject and method: it seeks to establish a firm theoretical basis for an important differentiating factor in an area of linguistics, in this case, between poetic and nonpoetic language. Jan Mukařovský, one of the founding members of the Prague Linguistic Circle, is professor of aesthetics at Charles University in Prague. The editor and translator of this essay, Dr. Paul L. Garvin, is manager of language analysis and translation, Bunker-Ramo Corporation, Canoga Park, California.

The problem of the relationship between standard language and poetic language can be considered from two standpoints.

Reprinted from *A Prague School Reader on Esthetics, Literary Structure, and Style*, selected and translated by Paul L. Garvin. Georgetown University Press, 1964, pages 17–30.

The theorist of poetic language poses it somewhat as follows: is the poet bound by the norms of the standard? Or perhaps: how does this norm assert itself in poetry? The theorist of the standard language, on the other hand, wants to know above all to what extent a work of poetry can be used as data for ascertaining the norm of the standard. In other words, the theory of poetic language is primarily interested in the differences between the standard and poetic language, whereas the theory of the standard language is mainly interested in the similarities between them. It is clear that with a good procedure no conflict can arise between the two directions of research; there is only a difference in the point of view and in the illumination of the problem. Our study approaches the problem of the relationship between poetic language and the standard from the vantage point of poetic language. Our procedure will be to subdivide the general problem into a number of special problems.

The first problem, by way of introduction, concerns the following: what is the *relationship* between the extension of *poetic language* and that of the *standard,* between the places of each in the total system of the whole of language? Is poetic language a special brand of the standard, or is it an independent formation?—Poetic language cannot be called a brand of the standard, if for no other reason than that poetic language has at its disposal, from the standpoint of lexicon, syntax, etc., all the forms of the given language—often of different developmental phases thereof. There are works in which the lexical material is taken over completely from another form of language than the standard (thus, Villon's or Rictus' slang poetry in French literature). Different forms of the language may exist side by side in a work of poetry (for instance, in the dialogues of a novel, dialect or slang, in the narrative passages, the standard). Poetic language finally also has some of its own lexicon and phraseology as well as some grammatical forms, the so-called poetisms such as *zor* [gaze], *oř* [steed], *pláti* [be aflame], 3rd p. sg. *můž* [can; cf. English *-th*] (a rich selection of examples can be found in the ironic description of "moon language" in [Svatopluk] Čech's [1846–1908, a realist] *Výlet pana Broučka do měsíce* [Mr. Brouček's Trip to the Moon]). Only some schools of poetry, of course, have a positive attitude towards poetisms (among them the Lumír Group including Svatopluk Čech), others reject them.

Poetic language is thus not a brand of the standard. This is not to deny the close connection between the two, which consists in the fact that, for poetry, the standard language is the background against which is reflected the esthetically intentional distortion of the linguistic components of the work, in other words, the intentional violation of the norm of the standard. Let us, for instance, visualize a work in which this distortion is carried out by the interpenetration of dialect speech with the standard; it is clear, then, that it is not the standard which is perceived as a distortion of the dialect, but the dialect as a distortion of the standard, even when the dialect is quantitatively preponderant. The violation of the norm of the standard, its systematic violation, is what makes possible the poetic utilization of language; without this possibility there would be no poetry. The more the norm of the standard is stabilized in a given language, the more varied can be its violation, and therefore the more possibilities for poetry in that language. And on the other hand, the weaker the awareness of this norm, the fewer possibilities of violation, and hence the fewer possibilities for poetry. Thus, in the beginnings of Modern Czech poetry, when the awareness of the norm of the standard was weak, poetic neologisms with the purpose of violating the norm of the standard were little different from neologisms designed to gain general acceptance and become a part of the norm of the standard, so that they could be confused with them.

Such is the case of M. Z. Polák [1788–1856, an early romantic], whose neologisms are to this day considered poor neologisms of the standard. . . .

A structural analysis of Polák's[1] poem would show that [Josef] Jungmann [a leading figure of the Czech national renascence] was right [in evaluating Polák's poetry positively]. We are here citing the disagreement in the evaluation of Polák's neologisms merely as an illustration of the statement that, when the norm of the standard is weak—as was the case in the period of national renascence, it is difficult to differentiate the devices intended to shape this norm from those intended for its consistent and deliberate violation, and that a language with a weak norm of the standard therefore offers fewer devices to the poet.

This relationship between poetic language and the standard, one which we could call negative, also has its positive side which is, however, more important for the theory of the standard language than for poetic language and its theory. Many of the linguistic components of a work of poetry do not deviate from the norm of the standard because they constitute the background against which the distortion of the other components is reflected. The theoretician of the standard language can therefore include works of poetry in his data with the reservation that he will differentiate the distorted components from those that are not distorted. An assumption that all components have to agree with the norm of the standard would, of course, be erroneous.

The second special question which we shall attempt to answer concerns the different *function* of the two forms of language. This is the core of the problem. The function of poetic language consists in the maximum of foregrounding of the utterance. Foregrounding is the opposite of automatization, that is, the deautomatization of an act; the more an act is automatized, the less it is consciously executed; the more it is foregrounded, the more completely conscious does it become. Objectively speaking: automatization schematizes an event; foregrounding means the violation of the scheme. The standard language in its purest form, as the language of science with formulation as its objective, avoids foregrounding [aktualisace]: thus, a new expression, foregrounded because of its newness, is immediately automatized in a scientific treatise by an exact definition of its meaning. Foregrounding is, of course, common in the standard language, for instance, in journalistic style, even more in essays. But here it is always subordinate to communication: its purpose is to attract the reader's (listener's) attention more closely to the subject matter expressed by the foregrounded means of expression. All that has been said here about foregrounding and automatization in the standard language has been treated in detail in Havránek's paper in this cycle;* we are here concerned with poetic language. In poetic language foregrounding achieves maximum intensity to the extent of pushing communication into the background as the objective of expression and of being used for its own sake; it is not used in the services of communication,

* Bohuslav Havránek, "The Functional Differentiation of the Standard Language," in *A Prague School Reader*, pp. 3–16.—Ed.

but in order to place in the foreground the act of expression, the act of speech itself. The question is then one of how this maximum of foregrounding is achieved in poetic language. The idea might arise that this is a quantitative effect, a matter of the foregrounding of the largest number of components, perhaps of all of them together. This would be a mistake, although only a theoretical one, since in practice such a complete foregrounding of all the components is impossible. The foregrounding of any one of the components is necessarily accompanied by the automatization of one or more of the other components; thus, for instance, the foregrounded intonation in [Jaroslav] Vrchlický [1853–1912, a poet of the Lumír Group, see above] and [Svatopluk] Čech has necessarily pushed to the lowest level of automatization the meaning of the word as a unit, because the foregrounding of its meaning would give the word phonetic independence as well and lead to a disturbance of the uninterrupted flow of the intonational (melodic) line; an example of the degree to which the semantic independence of the word in context also manifests itself as intonational independence can be found in [Karel] Toman's [1877–1946, a modern poet] verse. The foregrounding of intonation as an uninterrupted melodic line is thus linked to the semantic "emptiness" for which the Lumír Group has been criticized by the younger generation as being "verbalistic."—In addition to the practical impossibility of the foregrounding of all components, it can also be pointed out that the simultaneous foregrounding of all the components of a work of poetry is unthinkable. This is because the foregrounding of a component implies precisely its being placed in the foreground; the unit in the foreground, however, occupies this position by comparison with another unit or units that remain in the background. A simultaneous general foregrounding would thus bring all the components into the same plane and so become a new automatization.

The devices by which poetic language achieves its maximum of foregrounding must therefore be sought elsewhere than in the quantity of foregrounded components. They consist in the consistency and systematic character of foregrounding. The consistency manifests itself in the fact that the reshaping of the foregrounded component within a given work occurs in a stable direction; thus, the deautomatization of meanings in a certain work is consistently carried out by lexical selection (the mutual interlarding of contrasting areas of the lexicon), in another equally consistently by the uncommon semantic relationship of words close together in the context. Both procedures result in a foregrounding of meaning, but differently for each. The systematic foregrounding of components in a work of poetry consists in the gradation of the interrelationships of these components, that is, in their mutual subordination and superordination. The component highest in the hierarchy becomes the dominant. All other components, foregrounded or not, as well as their interrelationships, are evaluated from the standpoint of the dominant. The dominant is that component of the work which sets in motion, and gives direction to, the relationships of all other components. The material of a work of poetry is intertwined with the interrelationships of the components even if it is in a completely unforegrounded state. Thus, there is always present, in communicative speech as well, the potential relationship between intonation and meaning, syntax, word order, or the relationship of the word as a meaningful unit to the phonetic structure of the text, to the lexical selection found in the text, to other words as units of meaning in the context of the same sentence. It can be said that each linguistic component is linked directly or indirectly, by means of these multiple interrelationships, in some way to every other component. In communicative speech these relationships are for the most part merely potential, because attention is not called to their presence and to their mutual relationship. It is, however, enough to disturb the equilibrium of this system at some point and the entire network of relationships is slanted in a certain direction and follows it in its internal organization: tension arises in one portion of this network (by consistent unidirectional foregrounding), while the remaining portions of the network are relaxed (by automatization perceived as an intentionally arranged background). This internal organization of relationships will be different in terms of the point affected, that is, in terms of the dominant. More concretely: sometimes intonation will be governed by meaning (by various procedures), sometimes, on the other hand, the meaning structure will be determined by intonation; sometimes again, the relationship of a word to the lexicon may be foregrounded, then again its relationship to the phonetic structure of the text. Which of the possible relationships will be foregrounded, which will remain automatized, and what will be the direction of foregrounding—whether from component A to component B or vice versa, all this depends on the dominant.

The dominant thus creates the unity of the work of poetry. It is, of course, a unity of its own kind, the nature of which in esthetics is usually designated as "unity in variety," a dynamic unity in which we at the same time perceive harmony and disharmony, convergence and divergence. The convergence is given by the trend towards the dominant, the divergence by the resistance of the unmoving background of unforegrounded components against this trend. Components may appear unforegrounded from the standpoint of the standard language, or from the standpoint of the poetic canon, that is, the set of firm and stable norms into which the structure of a preceding school of poetry has dissolved by automatization, when it is no longer perceived as an indivisible and undissociable whole. In other words, it is possible in some cases for a component which is foregrounded in terms of the norms of the standard, not to be foregrounded in a certain work because it is in accord with the automatized poetic canon. Every work of poetry is perceived against the background of a certain tradition, that is, of some automatized canon with regard to which it constitutes a distortion. The outward manifestation of this automatization is the ease with which creation is possible in terms of this canon, the proliferation of epigones, the liking for obsolescent poetry in circles not close to literature. Proof of the intensity with which a new trend in poetry is perceived as a distortion of the traditional canon is the negative attitude of conservative criticism which considers deliberate deviations from the canon errors against the very essence of poetry.

The background which we perceive behind the work of poetry as consisting of the unforegrounded components resisting foregrounding is thus dual: the norm of the standard language and the traditional esthetic canon. Both backgrounds are always potentially present, though one of them will predominate in the concrete case. In periods of powerful foregrounding of linguistic elements, the background of the norm of the standard predominates, while in periods of moderate foregrounding, that of the traditional canon. If the latter has strongly distorted the norm of the standard, then its moderate distortion may, in turn, constitute a renewal of the norm of the standard, and this precisely because of its moderation. The mutual relationships of the components of the work of poetry, both foregrounded and unforegrounded, constitute its *structure,* a dynamic structure including both convergence and divergence and one that constitutes an undissociable artistic whole, since each of its components has its value precisely in terms of its relation to the totality.

It is thus obvious that the possibility of distorting the norm of the standard, if we henceforth limit ourselves to this particular background of foregrounding, is indispensable to poetry. Without it, there would be no poetry. To criticize the deviations from the norm of the standard as faults, especially in a period which, like the present, tends towards a powerful foregrounding of linguistic components, means to reject poetry. It could be countered that in some works of poetry, or rather in some genres, only the "content" (subject matter) is foregrounded, so that the above remarks do not concern them. To this it must be noted that in a work of poetry of any genre there is no fixed border, nor, in a certain sense, any essential difference between the language and the subject matter. The subject matter of a work of poetry cannot be judged by its relationship to the extralinguistic reality entering into the work; it is rather a component of the semantic side of the work (we do not want to assert, of course, that its relationship to reality cannot become a factor of its structure, as for instance in realism). The proof of this statement could be given rather extensively; let us, however, limit ourselves to the most important point: the question of truthfulness does not apply in regard to the subject matter of a work of poetry, nor does it even make sense. Even if we posed the question and answered it positively or negatively as the case may be, the question has no bearing on the artistic value of the work; it can only serve to determine the extent to which the work has documentary value. If in some work of poetry there is emphasis on the question of truthfulness (as in [Vladislav] Vančura's [1891–1942, a modern author] short story *Dobrá míra* [The Good Measure]), this emphasis only serves the purpose of giving the subject matter a certain semantic coloration. The status of subject matter is entirely different in case of communicative speech. There, a certain relationship of the subject matter to reality is an important value, a necessary prerequisite. Thus, in the case of a newspaper report the question whether a certain event has occurred or not is obviously of basic significance.

The subject matter of a work of poetry is thus its largest semantic unit. In terms of being meaning, it has certain properties which are not directly based on the linguistic sign, but are linked to it insofar as the latter is a general semiological unit (especially its independence of any specific signs, or sets of signs, so that the same subject matter may without basic changes be rendered by different linguistic devices, or even transposed into a different set of signs altogether, as in the transposition of subject matter from one art form to another), but this difference in properties does not affect the semantic character of the subject matter. It thus holds, even for works and genres of poetry in which the subject matter is the dominant, that the latter is not the "equivalent" of a reality to be expressed by the work as effectively (for instance, as truthfully) as possible, but that it is a part of the structure, is governed by its laws, and is evaluated in terms of its relationship to it. If this is the case, then it holds for the novel as well as for the lyrical poem that to deny a work of poetry the right to violate the norm of the standard is equivalent to the negation of poetry. It cannot be said of the novel that here the linguistic elements are the esthetically indifferent expression of content, not even if they appear to be completely devoid of foregrounding: the structure is the total of all the components, and its dynamics arises precisely from the tension between the foregrounded and unforegrounded components. There are, incidentally, many novels and short stories in which the linguistic components are clearly foregrounded. Changes effected in the interest of correct language would thus, even in the case of prose, often interfere with the very essence of the work; this would, for instance, happen if the author or even translator decided, as was asked in *Naše Řeč*, to eliminate "superfluous" relative clauses.

There still remains the problem of *esthetic values* in language outside of the realm of poetry. A recent Czech opinion has it that "esthetic evaluation must be excluded from language, since there is no place where it can be applied. It is useful and necessary for judging style, but not language" (J. Haller, *Problém jazykové správnosti* [The Problem of Correct Language], Výroční

zpráva č. st. ref reál. gymnasia v Ústí nad Labem za r. 1930–
1931, p. 23). I am leaving aside the criticism of the terminologi-
cally inaccurate opposition of style and language; but I do want
to point out, in opposition to Haller's thesis, that esthetic valuation is a very important factor in the formation of the norm
of the standard; on the one hand because the conscious refinement of the language cannot do without it, on the other hand
because it sometimes, in part, determines the development of the
norm of the standard.

Let us start with a general discussion of the field of esthetic
phenomena. It is clear that this field by far exceeds the confines
of the arts. Dessoir says about it: "The striving for beauty need
not be limited in its manifestation to the specific forms of the
arts. The esthetic needs are, on the contrary, so potent that they
affect *almost all* the acts of man." [2] If the area of esthetic phenomena is indeed so broad, it becomes obvious that esthetic
valuation has its place beyond the confines of the arts; we can
cite as examples the esthetic factors in sexual selection, fashion,
the social amenities, the culinary arts, etc. There is, of course,
a difference between esthetic valuation in the arts and outside
of art. In the arts, esthetic valuation necessarily stands highest
in the hierarchy of the values contained in the work, whereas
outside of art its position vacillates and is usually subordinate.
Furthermore, in the arts we evaluate each component in terms
of the structure of the work in question, and the yardstick is in
each individual case determined by the function of the component within the structure. Outside of art, the various components of the phenomenon to be evaluated are not integrated
into an esthetic structure and the yardstick becomes the established norm that applies to the component in question,
wherever the latter occurs. If, then, the area of esthetic valuation
is so broad that it includes "almost all of the acts of man," it is
indeed not very probable that language would be exempt from
esthetic valuation; in other words, that its use would not be
subject to the laws of taste. There is direct proof that esthetic
valuation is one of the basic criteria of purism, and that even
the development of the norm of the standard cannot be imagined
without it. . . .

Esthetic valuation clearly has its indispensable place in the
refinement of language, and those purists who deny its validity

are unconsciously passing judgment on their own practice. Without an esthetic point of view, no other form of the cultivation of good language is possible, even one much more efficient than purism. This does not mean that he who intends to cultivate good language has the right to judge language in line with his personal taste, as is done precisely by the purists. Such an intervention into the development of the standard language is efficient and purposeful only in periods when the conscious esthetic valuation of phenomena has become a social fact—as was the case in France in the seventeenth century. In other periods, including the present, the esthetic point of view has more of a regulatory function in the cultivation of good language: he who is active in the cultivation of good language must take care not to force upon the standard language, in the name of correct language, modes of expression that violate the esthetic canon (set of norms) given in the language implicitly, but objectively; intervention without heed to the esthetic norms hampers, rather than advances, the development of the language. The esthetic canon, which differs not only from language to language, but also for different developmental periods of the same language (not counting in this context other functional formations of which each has its own esthetic canon), must therefore be ascertained by scientific investigation and be described as accurately as possible. This is the reason for the considerable significance of the question of the manner in which esthetic valuation influences the development of the norm of the standard. Let us first consider the manner in which the lexicon of the standard language is increased and renewed. Words originating in slang, dialects, or foreign languages are, as we know from our own experience, often taken over because of their novelty and uncommonness, that is, for purposes of foregrounding in which esthetic valuation always plays a significant part. Words of the poetic language, poetic neologisms, can also enter the standard by this route, although in cases we can also be dealing with acceptance for reasons of communication (need for a new shade of meaning). The influence of poetic language on the standard is, however, not limited to the vocabulary: intonational and syntactic patterns (clichés) can, for instance, also be taken over—the latter only for esthetic reasons since there is hardly any communicative necessity for a change of the sentence and intonation structure current until then. Very interesting in this respect is the observation by the poet J. Cocteau in his book *Le secret professionnel* (Paris, 1922, p. 36) that "Stéphane Mallarmé even now influences the style of the daily press without the journalists' being aware of it." By way of explanation it must be pointed out that Mallarmé has very violently distorted French syntax and word order which is incomparably more bound in French than in Czech, being a grammatical factor. In spite of this intensive distortion, or perhaps because of it, Mallarmé influenced the development of the structure of the sentence in the standard language.

The effect of esthetic valuation on the development of the norm of the standard is undeniable; this is why the problem deserves the attention of the theorists. So far, we have, for instance, hardly even any lexical studies of the acceptance of poetic neologisms in Czech and of the reasons for this acceptance; [Antonín] Frinta's article *Rukopisné podvrhy a naše spisovná řeč* [The Fake Manuscripts (Václav Hanka's forgeries of purportedly Old Czech poetry, 1813, 1817) and our Standard Language] (Naše Řeč, vol. II) has remained an isolated attempt. It is also necessary to investigate the nature and range of esthetic valuation in the standard language. Esthetic valuation is based here, as always when it is not based on an artistic structure, on certain generally valid norms. In art, including poetry, each component is evaluated in relation to the structure. The problem in evaluating is to determine how and to what extent a given component fulfills the function proper to it in the total structure; the yardstick is given by the context of a given structure and does not apply to any other context. The proof lies in the fact that a certain component may by itself be perceived as a negative value in terms of the pertinent esthetic norm, if its distortional character is very prominent, but may be evaluated positively in terms of a particular structure and as its essential component precisely because of this distortional character. There is no esthetic structure outside of poetry, none in the standard language (nor in language in general). There is, however, a certain set of esthetic norms, each of which applies independently to a certain component of language. This set, or canon, is constant only for a certain period and for a certain linguistic milieu;

thus, the esthetic canon of the standard is different from that of slang. We therefore need a description and characterization of the esthetic canon of the standard language of today and of the development of this canon in the past. It is, of course, clear to begin with that this development is not independent of the changing structures in the art of poetry. The discovery and investigation of the esthetic canon accepted for a certain standard language would not only have theoretical significance as a part of its history, but also, as has already been said, be of practical importance in its cultivation.

Let us now return to the main topic of our study and attempt to draw some conclusions from what was said above of the relationship between the standard and poetic language.

Poetic language is a different form of language with a different function from that of the standard. It is therefore equally unjustified to call all poets, without exception, creators of the standard language as it is to make them responsible for its present state. This is not to deny the possibility of utilizing poetry as data for the scientific description of the norm of the standard (cf. pp. 42–43), nor the fact that the development of the norm of the standard does not occur uninfluenced by poetry. The distortion of the norm of the standard is, however, of the very essence of poetry, and it is therefore improper to ask poetic language to abide by this norm. This was clearly formulated as early as 1913 by Ferdinand Brunot ("L'autorité en matière de langage," *Die neueren Sprachen,* vol. XX): "Modern art, individualistic in essence, cannot always and everywhere be satisfied with the standard language alone. The laws governing the usual communication of thought must not, lest it be unbearable tyranny, be categorically imposed upon the poet who, beyond the bounds of the accepted forms of language, may find personalized forms of intuitive expression. It is up to him to use them in accord with his creative intuition and without other limits than those imposed by his own inspiration. Public opinion will give the final verdict." It is interesting to compare Brunot's statement to one of Haller's of 1931 (*Problém jazykové správnosti,* op. cit., p. 3): "Our writers and poets in their creative effort attempt to replace the thorough knowledge of the material of the language by some sort of imaginary ability of which they themselves are not too sincerely convinced. They lay claim to a right which can but be an unjust privilege. Such an ability, instinct, inspiration, or what have you, cannot exist in and of itself; just as the famous feel for the language, it can only be the final result of previous cognition, and without consciously leaning on the finished material of the language, it is no more certain than any other arbitrary act." If we compare Brunot's statement to Haller's, the basic difference is clear without further comment. Let us also mention Jungmann's critique of Polák's *Vznešenost přírody* [The Sublimity of Nature] cited elsewhere in this study (see above); Jungmann has there quite accurately pointed out as a characteristic feature of poetic language its "uncommonness," that is, its distortedness.—In spite of all that has been said here, the condition of the norm of the standard language is not without its significance to poetry, since the norm of the standard is precisely the background against which the structure of the work of poetry is projected, and in regard to which it is perceived as a distortion; the structure of a work of poetry can change completely from its origin if it is, after a certain time, projected against the background of a norm of the standard which has since changed.

In addition to the relationship of the norm of the standard to poetry, there is also the opposite relationship, that of poetry to the norm of the standard. We have already spoken of the influence of poetic language on the development of the standard; some remarks remain to be added. First of all, it is worth mentioning that the poetic foregrounding of linguistic phenomena, since it is its own purpose, cannot have the purpose of creating new means of communication (as Vossler and his school think). If anything passes from poetic language into the standard, it becomes a loan in the same way as anything taken over by the standard from any other linguistic milieu; even the motivation of the borrowing may be the same: a loan from poetic language may likewise be taken over for extraesthetic, that is, communicative reasons, and conversely the motivation for borrowings from other functional dialects, such as slang, may be esthetic. Borrowings from poetic language are beyond the scope of the poet's intent. Thus, poetic neologisms arise as intentionally esthetic new formations, and their basic features are unexpectedness, unusualness, and uniqueness. Neologisms created for communicative purposes, on the other hand, tend towards common derivation patterns and easy classifiability in a certain lexical category; these are the properties allowing for their general usability. If, however, *poetic* neologisms were formed in view of their general usability, their esthetic function would be endangered thereby; they are, therefore, formed in an unusual manner, with considerable violence to the language, as regards both form and meaning. . . .

The relationship between poetic language and the standard, their mutual approximation or increasing distance, changes from period to period. But even within the same period, and with the same norm of the standard, this relationship need not be the same for all poets. There are, generally speaking, three possibilities: the writer, say a novelist, may either not distort the linguistic components of his work at all (but this nondistortion is, as was shown above, in itself a fact of the total structure of his work); or he may distort it, but subordinate the linguistic distortion to the subject matter by giving substandard color to his lexicon in order to characterize personages and situations, for instance; or finally, he may distort the linguistic components in and of themselves by either subordinating the subject matter to the linguistic deformation, or emphasizing the contrast between the subject matter and its linguistic expression. An example of the first possibility might be [Jakub] Arbes [1840–1914, an early naturalist], of the second, some realistic novelists such as T. Nováková [1853–1912] or Z. Winter [1846–1912], of the third, [Vladislav] Vančura. It is obvious that as one goes from the first possibility to the third, the divergence between poetic language and the standard increases. This classification has of course been highly schematized for purposes of simplicity; the real situation is much more complex.

The problem of the relationship between the standard and poetic language does not, however, exhaust the significance of poetry as the art form which uses language as its material, for the standard language, or for the language of a nation in general. The very existence of poetry in a certain language has fundamental importance for this language. . . . By the very fact of foregrounding, poetry increases and refines the ability to handle language in general; it gives the language the ability to adjust more flexibly to new requirements and it gives it a richer differentiation of its means of expression. Foregrounding brings to the surface and before the eyes of the observer even such linguistic phenomena as remain quite covert in communicative speech, although they are important factors in language. Thus, for instance, Czech symbolism, especially O. Březina's [1868–1929] poetry, has brought to the fore of linguistic consciousness the essence of sentence meaning and the dynamic nature of sentence construction. From the standpoint of communicative speech, the meaning of a sentence appears as the total of the gradually accumulated meanings of the individual words, that is, without having independent existence. The real nature of the phenomenon is covered up by the automatization of the semantic design of the sentence. Words and sentences appear to follow each other with obvious necessity, as determined only by the nature of the message. Then there appears a work of poetry in which the relationship between the meanings of the individual words and the subject matter of the sentence has been foregrounded. The words here do not succeed each other naturally and inconspicuously, but within the sentence there occur semantic jumps, breaks, which are not conditioned by the requirements of communication, but given in the language itself. The device for achieving these sudden breaks is the constant intersection of the plane of basic meaning with the plane of figurative and metaphorical meaning; some words are for a certain part of the context to be understood in their figurative meaning, in other parts in their basic meaning, and such words, carrying a dual meaning, are precisely the points at which there are semantic breaks. There is also foregrounding of the relationship between the subject matter of the sentence and the words as well as of the semantic interrelationships of the words in the sentence. The subject matter of the sentence then appears as the center of attraction given from the beginning of the sentence, the effect of the subject matter on the words and of the words on the subject matter is revealed, and the determining force can be felt with which every word affects every other. The sentence comes alive before the eyes of the speech community: the structure is revealed as a concert of forces. (What was here formulated discursively, must of course be imagined as an unformulated intuitive cognition stored away for the future in the consciousness of the speech community.) Examples can be multiplied at will, but we shall cite no more. We wanted to give evidence for the statement that the main importance of poetry for language lies in the fact that it is an art. . . .

NOTES

1. It is important to note that Polák himself in lexical notes to his poem clearly distinguishes little known works (including obvious neologisms and new loans) from those which he used "for better poetic expression," that is, as is shown by the evidence, from poetic neologisms.

2. M. Dessoir, *Ästhetik und allgemeine Kunstwissenschaft* (Stuttgart, 1906), p. 112.

4. DESCRIPTIVE LINGUISTICS IN LITERARY STUDIES

M. A. K. Halliday

In this essay, M. A. K. Halliday shows the uses of linguistic theory in explaining different characteristics in the language of two kinds of texts: a Yeats poem and three passages of modern prose fiction. In Yeats's "Leda and the Swan," Professor Halliday demonstrates three different functions of deictic *the,* showing how the patterns in which *the* occurs in the poem differ from those in which it occurs in ordinary language. In considering the verb patterns in "Leda and the Swan," this essay argues that "verbal items are considerably deverbalized": that is, the lexically most powerful verbs do not function grammatically as verbs, but are functionally shifted to become other parts of speech. Professor Halliday's analysis of the prose passages concentrates on nominal group patterns, lexical sets, and cohesion. M. A. K. Halliday is professor of general linguistics and director of the Communication Research Centre at University College London.

In any discussion of the application of linguistic theory and method to the study of literary texts, one of the difficulties that arise is that there is so much background to be filled in before one actually reaches the text. I am not referring to the linguistic theory itself, the exposition of which is clearly outside the necessary scope of such a discussion, although it may be useful to specify what areas of linguistic science are relevant. But while it can be taken for granted that there are within linguistics theories and methods for describing the language of any text,

Reprinted from G. I. Duthie, editor, *English Studies Today* (Edinburgh: Edinburgh University Press, 1964); copyright © 1964 by Edinburgh University Press.

many other things cannot be taken for granted: the place of linguistic statements in literary analysis, the relation between literary and non-literary texts, and the question whether literary texts require special linguistic methods, to name only a few.

So much that is of underlying importance still needs to be said on all these subjects that a speaker runs the risk of devoting all his time to the discussion of principles. I propose to avoid that danger by reversing the more usual order of procedure and starting with some texts, leaving theoretical points to the second part of my talk. Although this may make it less clear what is being illustrated, it will at least ensure that the illustrations are not left out.

Immediately another problem arises: all illustrations in linguistics are misleading. Language does not operate except in the context of other events; even where these are, as with written texts, other language events, any one point made about a piece of text which is under focus raises many further points extending way beyond it into the context. This does not mean that no linguistic statements can be self-sufficient, but that the only ultimately valid unit for textual analysis is the whole text. It takes many hours of talking to describe exhaustively even the language of one sonnet.

However, if students can be asked to comment on the language of literary texts within the time limits of an examination, it should be possible to give selective illustrations of what would be regarded as a good answer to a question on the language of particular short texts. I propose here to refer to W. B. Yeats's poem "Leda and the Swan," and to three short passages of modern English prose, by John Braine, Dylan Thomas, and Angus Wilson.

LEDA AND THE SWAN*

A sudden blow: the great wings beating still
Above the staggering girl, her thighs caressed
By the dark webs, her nape caught in his bill,
He holds her helpless breast upon his breast.

* Reprinted with permission of The Macmillan Company from *Collected Poems* by William Butler Yeats. Copyright 1928 by The Macmillan Company renewed 1956 by Georgie Yeats. Also by permission of M. B. Yeats and A. P. Watt & Son.

How can those terrified vague fingers push
The feathered glory from her loosening thighs?
And how can body, laid in that white rush,
But feel the strange heart beating where it lies?

A shudder in the loins engenders there
The broken wall, the burning roof and tower
And Agamemnon dead.

                 Being so caught up,
So mastered by the brute blood of the air,
Did she put on his knowledge with his power
Before the indifferent beak could let her drop?

W. B. Yeats

The first example will be the use of "the" in "Leda and the Swan." The relevant grammatical background can be summarized as follows. The primary (least delicate) structure of the English nominal group is (M)H(Q): a head, which may or may not be preceded by a modifier and followed by a qualifier. Nearly everything occurring in the qualifier is rankshifted: that is, is of a rank (in fact always clause or group) above or equal to the unit in whose structure it is operating (here the group). In the modifier, on the other hand, only compound "Saxon genitives" and some modifiers of measurement are rankshifted; in general the modifier is an ordered sequence of words (the word being the unit immediately below the group in rank), proceeding from the most grammatical to the most lexical. The first place in the structure of the modifier is occupied by the word class known as "deictics," consisting more delicately of three subclasses of which one contains the items "the," "a," "this," "that," the personal deictics "his," "her," etc., and certain other words. The contextual function of the deictics is to identify, and among them "the" is unmarked and specific: that is, its function is to identify a *specific* subset but to do so by reference to something other than itself; unlike "his" or "that," "the" carries no power of identification but indicates that something else present does. This "something else" may be either (1) in the M/Q elements of the nominal group, (2) in the context, linguistic or situational, or (3) in the head of the nominal group itself. There are thus three distinct relations into which "the" as deictic enters, respectively "cataphoric," "anaphoric," and "homophoric." These can be illustrated from the following passage:

> Accordingly, after a peace-offering of tobacco, in return for a draught of foaming milk, I took leave, and turned to the ascent of the peak.
> The climb is perfectly easy, though I contrived to complicate matters by going the wrong way. The absence of guides generally enables one to enjoy a little excitement, the more agreeable because not contemplated beforehand. Indeed, to confess the truth, a former attempt upon the mountain had failed altogether by reason of my ingeniously attacking it by the only impracticable route. It was with all the more satisfaction that I found myself on the present occasion rapidly approaching the summit, and circumventing the petty obstacles which tried to oppose my progress.
>
> Leslie Stephen

For example—

Cataphoric:
  The absence *of guides*
  the only impracticable route
Anaphoric:
  turned to the *ascent* of the peak. *The* climb
Homophoric:
  the truth

In two instances, "the more agreeable" and "all the more satisfaction," "the" is not a deictic at all but a distinct formal item which operates as submodifier in the nominal group.

The complete statement of the formal properties of these relations, such that they can be recognized as distinct structures, is complex and involves lexis as well as grammar—though in spoken English, since tonicity (the placing of the tonic in the tone group) can be observed, it is possible to make a purely grammatical statement that accounts for most occurrences. In written English the general picture is as follows: there is a high probability that

(*a*) if there is a modifier (other than "the") or qualifier in the nominal group, "the" is cataphoric,

(b) if there is no modifier or qualifier, then
  (i) if in the preceding context there has occurred a lexical item which is either the same item as, or from the same lexical set as, the head of the nominal group, "the" is anaphoric,
  (ii) if not, "the" is homophoric.

Table I * shows all the nominal groups, other than those consisting only of pronoun or personal name, in "Leda and the Swan." Out of a total of 25, no less than 15 have *both* a specific deictic (10 "the," 5 others) *and* a modifier (other than the deictic) or qualifier or both. This contrasts, for example, with Yeats's poem "His Phoenix," which contains 81 nominal groups of which only 17 are of this type. In nominal groups with modifier or qualifier, if "the," or other specific deictic, is present it is usually cataphoric; moreover, samples of modern English prose writing show that the most frequent use of "the" is in fact cataphoric reference to modifier or qualifier, not anaphoric reference ("second mention") as often supposed. In "Leda," however, out of ten nominal groups having "the" and a modifier or qualifier, only one, "the brute blood of the air," had "the" in cataphoric use. The remainder, although they have both (a) items whose place in structure (at M or Q) makes them potentially defining, and (b) the item "the" whose function is usually to show that such potentially defining items are in fact defining, yet have non-cataphoric "the." That is to say, in spite of the "the," "the dark webs" are not identified by their being dark—like "the loins," they are to be identified anaphorically, in fact by anaphoric reference to the title of the poem. The only other type of writing I can call to mind in which this feature is found at such a high density is in tourist guides and, sometimes, exhibition catalogues. (I hope I need not add that this is in no sense intended as an adverse criticism of the poem.)

The second example is the distribution of verbal items in "Leda and the Swan." Most of this poem, especially the first ten and a half lines, is organized in nominal groups; they account for 69 of the 83 words in this first part. There are 14 verbal groups in the poem, and in addition four words of the class "verb" operating directly in the structure of (as opposed to being

---

* The tables are printed at the end of the article, pp. 71 and 72.—Ed.

rankshifted into) nominal groups ("staggering," "loosening," "burning," "broken"). The distribution of verbal groups, finite and non-finite, into the primary clause classes of "free," "bound" and "rankshifted," is shown in Table II.

The table represents a short of scale of "verbness" in the use of verbal items—the "cline of verbality," to give it a jargonistic label. On the extreme left, most "verbish" of all, is the finite verbal group in free clause; the further over to the right, the more the status of "verb" is attenuated, until finally it is subordinated altogether to the nominal element without even the formality of a rankshift. In "Leda," with its preponderance of nominal groups, the verbal items are considerably deverbalized: contrast again "His Phoenix," and also the sixteen lines from Tennyson's "Morte d'Arthur" beginning "Then quickly rose Sir Bedivere, and ran" (columns as in Table II):

	1	2	3	4	5	6
"Leda"	5	2	3		4	4
"His Phoenix"	30	12	2	6	2	2
"Morte d'Arthur" (extract from)	17		3		2	

Of various short passages examined for comparative purposes, the only one showing a distribution at all comparable to that of "Leda" was a passage of prose from the *New Scientist* concerning the peaceful uses of plutonium.

I am not of course saying that the language of "Leda" is like that of the *New Scientist.* The two passages are alike *in this respect:* that is all. Again, no evaluation is implied: even if one criticized the highly nominal style of much scientific writing this is quite irrelevant to "Leda," since (1) the two are quite different registers, and what is effective in one register may not be effective in another, and (2) this feature cannot be isolated from other features in which the two are quite different—for example the lexical items concerned.

It is worth examining the lexical items in more detail. In the *New Scientist* passage, and also in "His Phoenix" (where however the *grammatical* use of verbs is, as we have seen, highly "verbal"), the *lexical items* operating as verbs are in general weak: that is, they are items like "be" and "have" which are collocationally neutral. In "His Phoenix," for example, out of 48 finite verbal groups, 40 are accounted for by the following items: "be" (13), "have" (12), "know" (4), "do," "go," "say," "find," "hear," "live," "walk and talk," "pick and choose," and "please." By contrast many of those in the Tennyson passage are powerful items: that is, items with restricted ranges of collocation, like "plunge," "brandish," "wheel," and "flash." In "Leda," the few verbal items are varied in power, though medium rather than extreme. But they get lexically more powerful as they get grammatically less "verbal": in finite verbal group in free clause we have "hold," "push," "put on," "feel"; while at the other end of the scale, not operating in verbal group at all, are "stagger," "loosen," and "caress."

Lexical power is the measure of the restriction on high probability collocations: the fewer the items with which a given item is likely to collocate (put another way, the more strongly the given item tends to be associated with certain other items), the more "powerful" it is said to be. This, of course, has no evaluative connotations, nor has it anything to do with a denotation of violence or movement. But in fact in "Leda" the more powerful of the verbal lexical items are items of violence; and it is precisely these that perform nominal rather than verbal roles. Thus, while the Tennyson passage, a straightforward narrative, is characterized by a succession of fairly powerful lexical items denoting movement, each constituting by itself a (generally monosyllabic) finite verbal group in free clause, in "Leda," where there are lexical items of movement which are likewise fairly powerful, these either are not verbs at all or are themselves verbs but subordinated to the nominal elements in clause structure.

The third example is a comparison of one or two features in three short passages of prose, which have in common the fact that each is the description of a room. The passages, which are reproduced below, are taken from *Room at the Top* by John Braine, *Adventures in the Skin Trade* by Dylan Thomas, and *The Middle Age of Mrs. Eliot* by Angus Wilson; they are referred to by the abbreviations JB, DT, and AW.

> I looked at it with incredulous delight: wallpaper vertically striped in beige and silver, a bay window extending for almost the whole length of the room with fitted cushions along it, a

divan bed that looked like a divan and not like a bed with its depressing daylight intimations of sleep and sickness, two armchairs, and a dressing-table, wardrobe and writing-table all in the same pale satiny wood. On the cream-painted book-case was a bowl of anemones and there was a fire burning in the grate, leaving an aromatic smell, faintly acrid and faintly flower-like, which I knew but couldn't quite place. . . . There were three small pictures hanging on the far wall: *The Harbour at Arles,* a Breughel skating scene, and Manet's *Olympe.*

John Braine

Every inch of the room was covered with furniture. Chairs stood on couches that lay on tables; mirrors nearly the height of the door were propped, back to back, against the walls, reflecting and making endless the hills of desks and chairs with their legs in the air, sideboards, dressing-tables, chests-of-drawers, more mirrors, empty bookcases, wash-basins, clothes cupboards. There was a double bed, carefully made with the ends of the sheets turned back; lying on top of a dining table on top of another table there were electric lamps and lamp-shades, trays and vases, lavatory bowls and basins, heaped in the armchairs that stood on cupboards and tables and beds, touching the ceiling. The one window, looking out on the road, could just be seen through the curved legs of side-boards on their backs. The walls behind the standing mirrors were thick with pictures and picture frames.

Dylan Thomas

Her little bedroom at the hotel was ugly—the more hideous for having been recently redecorated with a standard "con-temporary" wallpaper. All over the walls floated gay little blue and pink café tables, around them a few Vermouth and Pernod bottles and the word "Montmartre" in pretty childish script. The design was no doubt carefully chosen to enchant cross-Channel travellers; it had no message for Meg. In the first weeks she had sought every excuse to be away from the room; but now suddenly the wallpaper, the pink, bevel-edged, modernistic mirror, and the furniture of shaded pink and silver began to give her a sense of anonymity. They were so remote from anything she knew or cared for that she felt free, safe, and hidden.

Angus Wilson

(*a*) Nominal groups. In DT, all 49 nominal groups have lexical item as head: there are no pronouns or other grammatical heads.

Of these only 11 have any lexical modification or qualification, and of a total of 5 lexical modifiers only "empty" has the value "epithet" in the group structure. By contrast in JB, which has 36 nominal groups of which 4 have grammatical heads, of the remaining 32 with lexical heads 16 have modifier or qualifier (or both) and 22 have deictics. Likewise in AW, with 37 nominal groups of which 9 have grammatical heads, 12 of the 28 with lexical heads are lexically modified or qualified and 15 have deictics. The DT passage is a heap of mainly simple nominal groups (that is, ones consisting of a noun only), with also some heaping of clauses; in AW and JB we have the compound nominal group as the center of attention. All this is obvious; but the fact that it is obvious does not excuse us from stating it accurately. Nor is it useful to count items or patterns without a linguistic analysis to identify what is to be counted.

The following table shows the number of nominal groups with lexical heads, and with lexical and grammatical modifiers and qualifiers, in the three prose passages. The last part of the table shows the distribution of "head" items in the principal lexical sets (see next paragraph).

	JB	DT	AW
Nominal groups	36	49	37
Nominal groups with lexical head	32	49	28
with M/Q (lexical)	16	11	12
with D	22	19	15
Head from "room" set	19	40	9
"furniture and décor"	14	34	5
"constructional"	5	6	4

(b) Lexical sets. Of the 49 lexical items as head of the nominal groups in DT, 40 are assignable to a lexical set under the heading "room": 34 of these to a set (subset of "room") "furniture and décor." Of the 32 lexical heads in JB, only 14 are furniture; and of AW's 28, only 5. Constructional items, however, such as "wall," are distributed fairly evenly among the three passages. In AW especially the furniture is of little interest: even of the 5 non-constructional items, two are occurrences of "wallpaper" and one, "tables," refers to the design of the wallpaper—the tables "float"; the other two items are "furniture" and "mirror." It is interesting to note the different parts played by lexical items from the sets associated with the "room" theme in the three passages.

(c) Cohesion. The principal types of cohesion are shown in Table III. The passages are too short to allow much to be said about their relative degrees, and use of different types, of cohesion; but some differences do emerge. In DT there is no grammatical cohesion at all across sentences or across orthographic sub-sentences (and only one instance even within a sentence: presupposition of "bondage" beginning at "reflecting"). Cohesion is entirely lexical, by constant repetition of items or occurrence of items from within one set. JB is likewise not cohesive grammatically, except for some "linkage" between clauses and the anaphoric "it" in the first sentence (and cohesion by structural parallelism, an important type of grammatical cohesion about which too little is yet known to permit accurate assessment); nor however is there much lexical cohesion in the passage. AW on the other hand is more grammatically cohesive; apart from clause linkage, there are the anaphoric pronouns "it," "she," "they," and the anaphoric "the" in "the walls" and "the design"; at the same time there is, as often in Angus Wilson, lexical cohesion by occurrence of items within a set, for example "ugly . . . hideous."

Other points of interest include: the distribution of lexical items in nominal groups as subject in clause structure; the use of original and of familiar collocations—compare JB: "picture/ hang" with DT: "picture/thick"; the use of items from the lexical sets of color and smell; the distribution of verbal groups and words in the "cline of verbality" and the choice of lexical items, weak and powerful, operating in the verbal groups. But enough has been said to illustrate textual analysis, and by now perhaps the pass mark has been awarded. That the linguist can suggest how to describe a text is perhaps, from the point of view of the literary analyst, the main justification for his existence.

At the very beginning of this paper I used the term "application" to refer to the study of literary texts by the theories and methods of linguistics, and I would stress that it is in fact an application of linguistics that is under discussion. We can be more specific than this. One branch of linguistics is descriptive linguistics, the study of how language works; this contrasts both with historical linguistics, the study of how language persists in time, and with institutional linguistics, the study of the varieties and uses of, and the attitudes to, language. Within descriptive linguistics, one kind of description is textual: the linguist describes a text, written or spoken; this contrasts with exemplificatory description, which presents the categories of the language and illustrates them, or if formalized, generates a set of described sentences and derives others from them. The linguistic study of literature is textual description, and it is no different from any other textual description; it is not a new branch or a new level or a new kind of linguistics but the application of existing theories and methods. What the linguist does when faced with a literary text is the same as what he does when faced with any text that he is going to describe.

But all description involves institutional considerations, and literary description is no exception. When we describe language we have to find out and specify the range of validity of the description; this means taking into account the variety represented, both dialect (variety according to user) and register (variety according to use). Register and dialect differences are of course variable in delicacy: we may talk of the register of literature, subdivided into the registers of prose and verse, each subdivided further into the various genres. At any particular point on the scale of delicacy the total set of registers may form a continuum, and there will certainly be a great deal that is common, linguistically, to all; but there are also linguistic differences between them—otherwise they would not be recognized as different registers. And just as in dialect we eventually, when we get delicate enough, reach the individual: every speaker his own idiolect, or bundle of available individual dialects—so also in register we come finally to the individual: every speaker, and writer, his own bundle of individual registers. Again, it does not need a new branch of linguistics to recognize and account for individual styles: all language is individual activity in a given variety, and thus there is an institutional basis, in the technical sense of institutional linguistics, in all description, literary or otherwise.

This does not mean, however, that for each text or individual writer we start again with a totally new description, with a new set of categories unrelated to what has gone before. Indeed, if many of the things written about the language of particular works of literature are much less useful than they might have been, this is more often than not because the writer, having neither made a description of the language himself nor used one made by someone else (other than the misty image of English that is still so often given in our schools), has invented a set of *ad hoc* categories for each text he has examined. What is said has therefore no relation to what was said about any other text, still less to any description of the language as a whole. If the linguistic analysis of literature is to be of any value or significance at all it must be done against the background of a general description of the language, using the same theories, methods and categories. A literary text has meaning against the background of the language as a whole, in all its uses; how can its language be understood except as the selection by the individual writer from the total resources at his disposal? Yet all too often the observations about the language of a work of literature bear no relation to any descriptive account of those resources.

The same point applies to the comparison of texts: it is impossible to compare one text with another unless both have been described in the same way. All literary analysis, if one is at all interested in the special properties of the language of literary texts or of a particular genre, is essentially comparative. This makes it all the more essential to be consistent, accurate and explicit: to base the analysis firmly on a sound, existing description of the language. While this means restraining oneself from inventing new categories, a temptation to which the literary analyst must be especially exposed, it does not of course preclude new alignments of established categories, such as Professor McIntosh's use of "involvement" in studying Shakespearean dialogue.* These may be required in any linguistic study, but they are perhaps especially fruitful in comparative literary studies. Another example is the relation of cohesion referred to above, which is very valuable in comparing long texts. The concept of cohesion has been developed especially for literary textual analysis; but every category brought together under this heading

---

* See Angus McIntosh, " 'As You Like It': a Grammatical Clue to Character," *A Review of English Literature,* IV (1963), 68–81. —Ed.

is drawn from the total description of English and has exactly the same range of application whatever the text to which it is applied.

Of course no amount of faithful adherence to the same description will be of any use if the description is not a good one in the first place. We are still plagued with steam grammars, with their ragged categories, their jumbled criteria and their fictions; descriptions of English which give little insight into the way the language works or indeed the way any language works, except perhaps the Latin they were originally modeled on. This kind of pre-linguistic linguistics is no use for literary studies. It is no paradox that it is modern scientific, including statistical, linguistics that proves really illuminating when applied to the study of literature—no paradox at least to anyone who studies language seriously, since the study of language perhaps more than anything else shows up the artificial nature of the dichotomy between arts and sciences. Not only do we need to be able to state accurately the role of a particular pattern or item in the language, what it contrasts with, what it may and may not combine with and so on; we may want to know its probability of occurrence under various definable conditions. It is of no interest to show that nine-tenths of all clauses in a certain poem are, say, of the class "interrogative" unless we know how this relates to the probabilities of occurrence of this and the other terms in the mood system. The originality of a person's use of his language consists in his selecting a feature not where it is impossible (has not been previously selected) but where another would be more probable—and even more in his balanced combination of the improbable with the probable, as in the lexis of "Leda and the Swan," which is an interesting blend of old and new collocations.

I have stressed grammar, but this is of course only one of the levels involved, and the usefulness of linguistic theory in application to literary studies depends on its ability both to comprehend and to integrate all the levels of language. That is another reason for insisting on the need for up-to-date linguistics: not only must the literary analyst have access to theories for the description of all levels of linguistic patterning—grammar, lexis, phonology and phonetics, and their graphic parallels—but he must be able to see them in interaction as they must always interact in any language event. He may want to analyze, for example, "her loosening thighs" as a grammatical item, with a certain structure —is it the same as "the staggering girl," or not?; as a collocation in lexis—is "loosen" the same lexical item as "loose"?; as a piece of English phonology—how does it exploit the patterns of English rhythm and intonation?; and in terms of its phonetic properties. He may feel he needs to do all this so that he can see what it is doing in the poem. I have not, for lack of time, given illustrations of phonological and phonetic analysis; but this is a good place to point out that when we speak of "linguistics" in literary studies, this is really a shorthand for "the linguistic sciences," and is to be taken to include them both—linguistics and phonetics.

If it is considered that the meaning of a piece of literature lies between rather than within the lines, it seems likely that linguistics has no message. This is not to say that the literary allusion is outside the scope of linguistic analysis; on the contrary, all use of language is allusion, and textual allusion is only one endpoint on a scale the other end of which is the context of our whole previous experience of the use of an item of pattern: hence the insistence that a work of literature, like any other piece of language activity, is meaningful only in the perspective of the whole range of uses of the language. Similarly it is not to say that literary "figures of speech" cannot be analyzed; it is true, however, that they do need rigorous linguistic definition. Again there is no sharp line to be drawn between metaphor and non-metaphor; but if linguistics cannot describe certain parts of language it is likely to be of little use for any application. Linguistics is not and will never be the whole of literary analysis, and only the literary analyst—not the linguist—can determine the place of linguistics in literary studies. But if a text is to be described at all, then it should be described properly; and this means by the theories and methods developed in linguistics, the subject whose task is precisely to show how language works. The literary analyst is not content with amateur psychology, armchair philosophy, or fictitious social history; yet the linguistics that is applied in some accounts of literature, and the statements about language that are used as evidence, are no less amateur, armchair and fictitious. It is encouraging that literary scholars are coming more and more to reject such statements, and to demand a standard of objective linguistic scholarship that is no less rigorous than the standard of literary scholarship which they expect, and exact, from themselves.

TABLE I

Deixis in Nominal Groups in "Leda and the Swan"

+/−D ＼ +/− M/Q	+M/Q			+M/Q
	M	Q	MQ	
+D specific	the staggering girl the dark webs the feathered glory the broken wall the burning roof and tower the indifferent beak those terrified vague fingers that white rush her helpless breast her loosening thighs	her thighs caressed by the dark webs her nape caught in his bill	the great wings beating above the staggering girl the strange heart beating the brute blood of the air	the loins the air his bill his breast her nape his knowledge his power
+D non-specific	a sudden blow	a shudder in the loins		
−D				body

TABLE II

Verbal Items in "Leda and the Swan"

	1	Items in verbal group (i.e., operating at "predicator" in clause structure) 2	3	4	5	Items in nominal group (i.e., not operating at predicator) 6
(a)	Free	Bound		Rankshifted		(irrelevant)
(b)	Finite	Finite	Nonfinite	Finite	Nonfinite	
	hold push feel engender put on	lie let	drop catch up master		beat caress catch lay	stagger loosen burn break

(*a*) Clause class system: status
(*b*) Group class system: finiteness

TABLE III

Cohesion

  A. Grammatical: 1. Structural (clauses in sentence structure)
         (*a*) Dependence ("bondage")
         (*b*) Co-ordination ("linkage")
      2. Nonstructural
         (*a*) Anaphora
           (i) deictics and submodifiers
           (ii) pronouns
         (*b*) Substitution
           (i) verbal
           (ii) nominal
  B. Lexical: 1. Repetition of item
       2. Occurrence of item from same lexical set

5. AN APPROACH TO THE STUDY OF STYLE

John Spencer and Michael J. Gregory

In this selection from "An Approach to the Study of Style," John Spencer and Michael Gregory set out the theoretical foundations for a method of studying literary style. The linguistics upon which they base their study is in the tradition of John Rupert Firth and his successors, chiefly M. A. K. Halliday. Professors Spencer and Gregory urge a distinction among lexical, grammatical, and contextual meanings and attention to phonic as well as graphic substance in literary texts. In particular, they propose that stylistics concentrate more upon lexis than it has up until now. Questions of usage also are important; here the authors propose the "placing" of a literary text according to the categories of field of discourse (subject matter), mode of discourse (medium), and tenor of discourse (relation between speaker/writer and hearer/reader). Finally, Professors Spencer and Gregory argue that literary language, like ordinary language, must be considered in terms of what Firth, following the anthropologist Bronislaw Malinowski, called the "context of situation." "An Approach to the Study of Style" is essential not only for the student of style, but for the student of modern British linguistics as well. John Spencer is professor of English at the University of Leeds; Michael J. Gregory is professor of English at York University, Toronto.

It is . . . necessary to ask in what specific respects a linguistic to be used for stylistic study should be comprehensive and explicit: what, in other words, does the student of style require

John Spencer and Michael J. Gregory: "An Approach to the Study of Style," from *Linguistics and Style*, published by Oxford University Press, 1964. Reprinted with the permission of the Oxford University Press and the authors.

of a linguistic description. What follows . . . cannot, of course, present a full account in all its details of any one linguistic—let alone deal adequately with the different contributions to stylistics made by various linguistic theories. Those readers acquainted with the field of language study will recognize that the point of view presented here derives very largely from the work in linguistics accomplished in Great Britain during the past two decades.[1] Our intention is, however, not so much to offer an account of a particular model, as to suggest what might be demanded of a linguistic model in stylistic study.

Language is transmitted either by audible sound-waves or by visible marks on a surface: that is, language substance is either phonic or graphic. A linguistic satisfactory for stylistic study needs, in the first place, to take account of this substantial aspect of language; and it needs also to possess the means of enabling us to recognize and deal adequately with the relationship between written and spoken language. Since graphic substance is related to, and in part derives from, phonic substance, all written language has some phonic potential. This leads, in turn, to the recognition, important, as we shall see, in stylistics, that much written language, particularly drama and poetry, is written with its phonic potential, the speaking of it, strongly in mind.

The formal aspect of language, that it exhibits patterns which are meaningful, has also to be acknowledged and dealt with adequately. The need for adequacy entails that the linguist be not only prepared to account formally for the grammar of a language—the type of contrastive word-order pattern which distinguishes in English "dog bites man" from "man bites dog"—but also with its phonology, which distinguishes, for example, "she's a pretty girl" as statement from "she's a pretty girl" as question, with its graphology, which distinguishes "She's a pretty girl." from "She's a pretty girl?", and with its lexical form, which distinguishes "she's an attractive girl" from "she's a beautiful girl." To suggest that these latter utterances differ because the meaning of "attractive" is different from the meaning of "beautiful" is linguistically and descriptively to beg part of the question.[2] We know that the meaning differs, but the linguist will want to ask how far this difference can be accounted for in purely formal terms, without recourse to meaning in the explanation of meaning.

The linguistic must also help to give us an intelligent realization of the consequences of seeing language as part of human social behavior. Language events do not take place in isolation from other events; rather they operate within a wide framework of human activity. Any piece of language is therefore part of a situation, and so has a context, a relationship with that situation. Indeed, it is this relationship between the substance and form of a piece of language on the one hand and the extra-linguistic circumstances in which it occurs on the other, which gives what is normally called "meaning" to utterances.[3] At some stage or other, any linguistic description, if it is to be complete, must take this relationship into consideration.

Stylistic studies are primarily concerned with the examination of written language. It might be thought therefore that phonology has little to contribute. However, as has been already suggested, certain kinds of literature have strong phonic potential. Drama and much verse are written with the spoken word in mind, and particular linguistic features which they consequently exhibit cannot be fully accounted for without a reasonably sophisticated phonology. This phonology should be able to help throw light on such features as alliteration, assonance, rhyme, pararhyme, onomatopoeia, rhythm, and meter. Classical prosody as traditionally applied to English verse could well be modified in the light of phonological studies of this nature.[4]

Thus, for example, the phonemic recurrences characteristic of Hopkins' alliteration cannot be fully understood or described simply in terms of the repetition of initial sounds, which is the definition of this device commonly provided by works on prosody and poetics. The complexity of Hopkins' alliteration, and indeed that of many other poets, requires a recognition of the manner in which vowel contrasts and transitions, consonantal groupings according to the place and manner of their articulation, consonant clusters and positional shifts of the same phonemic units in the structure of succeeding syllables, are all counterpointed, so to speak, to provide a total effect. These are often linked to stress patterns, which are themselves part of larger patternings, of which the metrical line is one.

This suggests that a satisfactory phonology would postulate units to cope with a whole range of contrasts of differing status carried by stretches of sound of different lengths: contrasts in the structure of syllables, contrasts of stress, and of intonation pattern. Any or all of this range of contrasts may be of particular significance in any text, spoken or written, and we need categories to describe them. Also required, for purposes of descriptive consistency and power, is that the various units be viewed in hierarchical relation to each other.[5]

But the fact remains that when studying style we are usually faced with written texts, graphic substance. It is also evident that a precise statement of the relationships between the patterns of phonic substance and those of graphic substance is not easy, particularly in a language such as English. There is certainly no one-to-one correspondence. Nevertheless, it is clear that the graphic substance of English does exhibit patterns: English spelling is not random—for one thing, not all possible combinations of letters can occur. Like English phonology it is polysystemic, even if its systems, in part the result of long historical processes, are notably complicated. Writing has its own means, however inadequate they may be, of indicating some of the patterned contrasts discernible in spoken language. One might instance written language's use of the alphabet, and of combinations of some of its letters, to represent certain, but not all, of the sounds of the language user; its use of punctuation, italicization, capitalization, and so on, to deal, in some measure, with features such as stress and intonation. Written language may also have systems for indicating contrasts which are unconnected with the phonological contrasts of the spoken medium, but as yet there is no clear and satisfactory statement of them. Graphology, the patterned systems of the graphic substance of language and their study, presents a field of investigation in which much is yet to be done, work which might prove to be of relevance to the stylistic study of written texts. Our linguistic must be open to such developments.

Phonological, and in a different way, graphological patterns may be seen as the framework of regularity and contrast which link language substance with language form. Certain aspects of the phonology of a language are given, as it were; the individual speaker of English cannot start, of his own accord, successfully making an aspirated "p" sound contrast meaningfully with an unaspirated "p." Phonology is therefore often thought of as that which relates the substance of a language to its form, as an "interlevel." [6] Because it derives its patterns from phonology, graphology is thought of as relating graphic substance to form by way of phonology. It must still, however, be recognized that certain aspects of phonology provide the user of a language with the means of making a meaningful choice, the sort of choice normally accounted for by grammar. In spoken language the choice of a certain intonation pattern rather than another makes an utterance which is, in other respects, grammatically a statement into a question, as does the graphological choice of the query mark rather than the period mark in written language. In other words phonology and graphology not only connect substance to form, they are themselves aspects of form, patterns which on occasions directly make substance meaningful in a situation.

The study of linguistic form is the examination of the way languages carry contrast in meaning through their internal structure. The linguistic description of the form of any particular language is, then, the description of the meaningful internal patterns of that language, the isolation of those places in the language where there are possibilities of choice which contribute to meaning. What is to be asked of a linguistic in this respect, is whether it helps the analyst in recognizing and accounting for all the places in the language where there is a possibility of such choices, and whether it helps him with the task of stating the range of possible choices at each such place. In this respect the value of a sound and sufficiently complex phonology and graphology has already been indicated. It is, however, grammar (morphology and syntax) which has dominated the description of form, which has in recent years been most refined in linguistics,[7] and which promises most for the analysis of style. Nevertheless, the observable fact that the extent of the range of possible choices varies at different places in a language, that at some only a few choices are open, and at others many, is what led us to suggest earlier that a linguistic capable of providing the sort of formal description most useful for stylistic study does well to draw a distinction within form such as that made by certain linguists in Britain between grammar and lexis. Grammar deals with all those places where there is a choice that has to be made between a small and limited number of possibilities. In other words, grammar can deal descriptively where the choice is between, say, a passive or active verbal group, between a positive or negative verbal group, between a singular or plural nominal group, between a declarative or interrogative clause, and so on.[8] So grammar can indicate where and why "sit" differs from "be seated," "to be" from "not to be," "man of Harlech" from "men of Harlech," "It was done." from "Was it done?". A really useful grammar can also distinguish formally "the book which is lying on the table is mine" from "the book lying on the table is mine," and both of these from "the book on the table is mine," at the same time as it shows the measure of their structural similarity. But grammar cannot indicate why "he had a fear" differs from "he had a hope." A very delicate grammar can volunteer the information that "fear" and "hope" belong to the same subclass of nouns, but it cannot distinguish "fear" from "hope"; at least no grammar has yet done so. Indeed it has often been thought that such a distinction is outside the scope of formal description, and that semantics takes over where grammar ends. But there is no necessity for formal description to end with grammar.

Theoretical categories are required for the formal description of lexis, and two fundamental ones, *collocation* and *set,* have been proposed.[9] Collocation is set up to account for the tendency of certain items in a language to occur close to each other, a tendency not completely explained by grammar. For example, the item "economy" is likely to occur in the same linguistic environment as items such as "affairs," "policy," "plan," "program," "disaster"—most of us could compile quite a long list. These items are termed the *collocates* of "economy" which, because it is the item under examination, is itself termed the *nodal item.*[10] A list of collocates of the nodal item constitutes its collocational range. In formal lexical study, of course, the establishment of the collocational range of an item would be the result of a statistical investigation covering a wide range of texts. If "finance" were taken as the nodal item, and a collocational range established for it, it would probably emerge that there was a considerable overlap with the range of "economy," that these two items share a significant number of collocates. So too, perhaps, if one took "industry" as the nodal item. These three items could then be grouped together into a *set,* the second theoretical category of lexis, which accounts for the tendency of items to share part of their collocational range, to have a collocational overlap.

It will be clear that what constitutes a set in any description

depends upon both the nature and the amount of data being examined, and upon the delicacy of the description; that is, its
degree of detail and specificity. The linguist may group together
as a set items having only a small mutual collocational range. On
the other hand he may demand that they have a good deal of
their collocational range in common before he so groups them.
He may even demand that they share collocations at a number of
removes from themselves, at a distance of one, two or three or
more lexical items. The more mutual collocational range demanded as the criterion for a set, the smaller the sets and the
more delicate the description. Lexical sets, then, are "open" as
compared with the "closed" nature of grammatical systems.

It may be asked what are the advantages of this formal handling of lexis. Items such as "economy," "finance," and "industry"
could, after all, be grouped together on purely semantic grounds.
However, when compared to the referential criterion of meaning,
the formal criterion of collocation has this in its favor: it is more
observational and objective. Its disadvantage for the analyst of
style is that it demands large-scale frequency counts, the extensive statistical examination of many texts. Such work is only just
beginning, and so in the study of style semantically rather than
collocationally determined sets have often to be established.
Nevertheless an awareness of current work by linguists on the
theory of lexis is already valuable in that it throws light on certain aspects of "chain" (one thing *after* another) and "choice"
(one thing *rather* than another) relationships in language not
revealed either by grammar or traditional lexicography.

Collocation is an important concept to have in mind when
studying the language of literature. This is because the creative
writer often achieves some of his effects through the interaction
between usual and unusual collocations, and through the creation
of new, and therefore stylistically significant, collocations. This is
particularly noticeable in poetry. In Dylan Thomas's "In the
room/So loud to my own," one's response to these lines is the
result of an awareness of the usual set of items which would be
likely to occur between "the room so . . ." and ". . . to my
own," a set producing collocations such as "so *close* to my own"
and "so *near* to my own." We contrast these with the normal
collocations of "loud" and realize that it has been led as it were,
to share here two ranges of collocation. This is important in an

examination of how we respond to the use of language in this poem, "Vision and Prayer," where we also encounter such collocational shifts as "the *heart*print of man" and "the inmost marrow of my *heart* bone." And indeed, Dylan Thomas's verse abounds in collocations of this kind: "a *grief* ago," "once *below* a time," "happy as the *heart* was long," "all the *sun* long," "it was Adam and *maiden*." The concepts of collocation and set are therefore indispensable in the study of metaphor.

All this not to minimize the value, in the study of style, of such great works of lexicographic scholarship as the *Oxford English Dictionary* and *Webster's Third International Dictionary*. They make available a great range of organized linguistic information: orthographic, phonetic, grammatical, historical and comparative, and contextual (provided by the definitions). The formal description of lexis to be found in them is, however, limited. It is provided by the citations, examples of a particular word in use with other words. This gives an indication of its collocations, a glimpse of the lexical company it keeps and no more. A thesaurus, in which the sets are collocationally determined, is needed as a complement to the dictionary. It would also be a complement, in formal description, to the grammars of the language. "Fear" and "hope," "beautiful" and "attractive," these pairs may be beyond grammatical distinction, but they may well be distinguished lexically according to their different collocational ranges and their membership of different sets.

The formal relationships observable in language require above all, however, a sophisticated grammar. Fortunately, over the last few decades, as was noted, linguistic science has shifted its attention from phonemic and morphemic analysis to grammar, and very interesting work has been and is being done in America, by linguists both of the structuralist and transformative-generative schools, such as A. A. Hill and S. R. Levin, on the application of different types of grammatical analysis to stylistic study.[11] In Britain development in the field of grammar has led particularly to the realization that it is necessary in grammar, as in linguistic description generally, to distinguish between, and have an articulated idea of, the relationship between theoretical and descriptive categories. It has been realized that in the "linguistic study of language," as in other scientific activities, the more complex and explicit the theory, the simpler and more coherent the description. It is thought necessary, therefore, that a general theory of grammar should lie behind the grammatical description of any particular language, and that the categories which are set up for the purpose of such description should derive from theoretical categories. . . .

More emphasis has been placed, in recent years, on the linguistic description of contemporary language than on historical linguistics. The student of style cannot afford, however, to neglect the historical study of language, particularly as many of his texts will lie outside the modern period. Questions about differences in phonology (did the final "-ed" have syllabic quantity at this time?), in graphology (was the punctuation of this time or this author meant to be "logical," "grammatical," or "rhetorical"?), in grammar (was there a "you/thee *or* thou" system operating at this time?) or in lexis (were the collocations of "wanton" significantly different then from now?), must often be in the stylistic analyst's mind when he is examining a non-contemporary text. And modern linguistics could help him if more attention was given to the problem of describing languages comprehensively and systematically at different stages in their history.

Linguistic science has a history stretching over many centuries. It has had its dark ages and its renaissances, and it has still much to do; but it does now offer a body of scholarship concerning language which the student of literature can ill afford to ignore.

A recognition of the dual and complementary value of intuitive judgment of language use on the one hand, and the more objective techniques of description of language phenomena which modern linguistics makes available on the other, is necessary and indeed fundamental to this view of stylistic study. Our suggestion is that these two approaches to language, the one characteristic of literary criticism and the other of linguistic analysis—and both involving sensitivity to language if the literary critic is to be more than a hack and the linguist more than a technician—can be brought together for stylistic investigation into a relationship which goes beyond the merely complementary.

This type of investigation, the close study of a text for the purposes of examining its style, involves . . . the development of a considered response to the use of language in it; implying, in

Jakobson's terms, a concentration upon the " 'set' towards the message." [12] If impressionistic reactions to the language of the text are to be more than complemented, if they are rather to be developed and modified by the application to them of the categories of linguistics, and if the final developed response is to be made explicit, the stages in this dialectical process need to be clear. This is not to suggest that procedures must be allowed to dominate the process. Procedural rigidity can too easily destroy initiative and intuitive power, with a consequent loss of sensitivity and flexibility. But consciousness of a "procedural model" should be present in the mind of the student of style, whatever short cuts or adaptations he may need to use in any particular investigation.

If a mature literary-linguistic intuition provides clues, indicating certain linguistic features as likely to be of prime importance in establishing a text's particular style, the function of linguistic description is not simply that of making the precise nature of these features explicit, or of producing statistical tables to support the intuitive judgment. Such a procedure involves the danger of fixing the significant stylistic features in advance of careful analysis, thereby closing the door against the possibility of modifying and developing the original "hypothesis." It can also result in too ready a reliance upon impressionistically conceived and generalized norms of style, with a consequent failure to observe the essential distinction between shared and unique features in the language of a text; to a conflation, that is, of features characteristic of a period or a group with the idiosyncratic features of the individual writer, or of either of these with the specific use of language in a particular text. It may well be, as Kroeber suggests, that "judgment and recognition of style are primary, analysis and statistics secondary." [13] But it is necessary to emphasize that a rigorous checking, by means of a description of the total complex of features possessed by the text, of features intuitively judged to be stylistically significant, is likely to uncover other, previously unobserved, significant features; or to demonstrate the inter-relationship of a series of features in such a way as to offer new, or at least modified, responses to the text as a whole. In this way our responses to the style of a text are open to progressive development. Only if we refuse to recognize the validity of responses which result from careful textual study, only if we believe that the immediate, spontaneous response to a work of literature is the sole criterion for critical statements, can such development be regarded with suspicion.

But before impressions are tested and developed in this way it is necessary to interpose a step of considerable importance, which may be termed the *placing of the text*. Failure to undertake some procedure of this sort has often led to error or distorted judgment. Placing the text may be seen as an attempt to objectivize the position of the language of the text in relation to the total available range of language, by reference to *institutional* categories, or dimensions, of usage.

It will be clear that one essential dimension required for placing a text must be historical. The language range of any period can be seen as one of the factors which both restrains the writer's linguistic choices and offers him certain creative opportunities. Linguistic restraints and opportunities, grammatical, lexical, phonological, and even graphological, are never precisely the same in one period as in another. The possibilities for grammatical innovation which the English of Shakespeare's time offered to the creative writer were not the same as those offered by the English of the Augustan period, for example. If all language is perpetually in a state of slow change, which continuously affects it at every level, it must follow that the writer's opportunities of choice, both conventional and creative (the possibilities, in transformationalist terms, for rule-governed and rule-forming creativity), must also change over time.

In relation to the language of the past the literary artist is in a special position. The language of poetry, in particular, has rarely been confined as strictly as other literary forms within the usage range of the language of its period. Poetry, and to a more restricted degree other literary genres, is able to draw upon some of the linguistic patterns of past periods. In placing a text historically, therefore, the student of style needs to be conscious of this historical range in the language available to the writer.

The second dimension to be applied in the placing of texts is that which defines their dialectal range. In any period the linguistic opportunities open to a writer will be determined by his chosen dialect. The advent of a standard form of the language for writing has, of course, affected this situation, to the extent of reducing the degree of difference in this respect we are likely to encounter among texts of the same period. Apart from synthetic poetic dialects like Lallans, therefore, we are unlikely to be faced in contemporary literature with dialectal differences as great as those, for example, which mark off the language of Chaucer from that of his contemporary the Gawain poet. Nevertheless, even today, it would be unwise to overlook the linguistic differences which arise from dialectal variation between the novels, for example, of Sillitoe and Salinger. And within a single work of literature, especially in the case of a play or a novel, dialectal shifts may be used for a variety of purposes.

Three additional inter-related dimensions which provide a valuable means of defining distinctions of linguistic usage not accounted for by reference to historical or dialectal differences, are those for which the present authors use the terms *field* of discourse, *mode* of discourse and *tenor* of discourse.[14]

The field of discourse of a text relates to its subject-matter, and the linguistic features which may be associated with it. It is obvious that in non-literary texts of certain kinds the field of discourse will exercise marked influences upon the grammar and, in particular, upon the lexis, especially if the field is of a technical or specialized nature. Since the literary artist is free to draw upon all possible fields of discourse, and in certain instances may wish to utilize the linguistic resources of certain specialized fields for dramatic, poetic, or evocative purposes, this dimension may need to be applied in examining the language of literature. In long texts there may be shifts in the field of discourse, and these will have linguistic consequences.

The mode of discourse is the dimension which accounts for the linguistic differences which result from the distinction between spoken and written discourse. All written language may be spoken, but it is noticeable that spoken language as such displays many features not present in written language, differences which cannot be accounted for simply by the differences between graphic and phonic substance, but which are also grammatical and lexical. These may be said to result from the differences between the situations in which written and spoken language tend to operate and the conventions associated with them. The literary artist may wish what he writes to be read as if it is spoken, in order to give the illusion of speech; or to be read as if it is overheard, to give the impression of a spoken monologue. Or, if he is a dramatist, he will write in the expectation, or at least the hope, that what he writes will be presented orally. And the poet too will be very conscious of certain features of the spoken mode.

This is not to suggest that in any of these cases the language presented will have precisely the features which mark spontaneous spoken language. It will usually be sufficiently marked to provide an illusion of speech; or, in the case of poetry, certain effects possible in spoken language, particularly phonological effects, are likely to determine, in part, the organization of the language.

Characters in plays and novels never talk quite like people do in life; were they to do so they would be intolerable. But it is important to discover which linguistic markers of mode the writer is using to provide his illusion. In novels he can, if he wishes, simply use graphological means, such as the use of quotation marks and occasional contracted forms, to mark the dialogue off from the narrative. On the other hand he may choose to use a wide range of features, graphological, lexical, and grammatical, for this purpose. The degree to which there are such shifts of mode within one work will depend on the writer's purposes and aims. One may compare in this respect the dialogue in Ivy Compton-Burnett's novels with that in Henry Green's; or the speeches of Ben Jonson's characters with those of Beaumont and Fletcher's; or, in poetry, and within one work, the shifts of mode which T. S. Eliot uses with such advantage in *The Waste Land*. Understanding the ranges of language associated with differing modes offers the opportunity of relating the language of a text to the author's purposes and the effects he is aiming at.

The tenor of discourse is concerned with the degree of formality in the situation which the language mirrors, which can be said generally to depend upon the relationship between the speaker (or writer) and hearer (or reader). This dimension must be seen as a continuum, with no points between the two poles of extreme formality and extreme informality capable of being defined with any precision. Yet, as every native user of a language is aware, different places on this scale are marked by linguistic differences. Shifts of tenor may be used in literature, and not only in dialogue, to produce certain effects.

A poet or a novelist having chosen to use a particular tenor, for the purpose of defining his intended relationship with his reader, certain linguistic consequences will follow; or, more accurately, the tenor of the discourse will be determined for the reader by certain features in the language the writer uses. First-person narrative in the novel often tends to incline the language further along the scale towards the informal than does third person narrative. A number of contemporary novelists, such as Kerouac, Salinger, Barstow, and Sillitoe, are experimenting with forms of narrative, usually in the first person, which are much more informal in tenor than those which would have been used by their predecessors. This informality of tenor is the product of their language.

Shifts of tenor in dialogue are, of course, often used to reflect shifts in relationships between characters in the drama and the novel; since tenor of discourse is situation-tied, the linguistic markers characteristic of particular points on the tenor scale can be used to evoke situations and define relationships.

The dimensions of field, mode and tenor of discourse are, as has been suggested, inter-related and inter-acting. Certain fields of discourse are associated more with one mode than another; a shift of mode is often accompanied by a shift in tenor, and vice versa. Provided this inter-relationship is borne in mind, however, these dimensions of differentiation can usefully be applied, wherever appropriate, together with the historical and dialectal dimensions, in the task of placing the text, or parts of it, and of checking impressionistic judgments of language norms against describable linguistic features. This is a safeguard against overlooking certain effects which derive from the language of the text, or of misinterpreting them even where we are conscious of them. If the writer's range is potentially the whole of the language, we shall by this means see more clearly from which "areas" of the language he is electing to make his choices in any particular instance.

The procedure of placing the text by reference to informed impressionistic norms defined in relation to period, dialect field, mode and tenor of discourse, and their checking in terms of specific linguistic markers, where necessary comparing the text with other texts recognized to be of a similar type, provides a means of bringing shared and unique features into contrastive relief. Consequently, the danger of overemphasizing the idiosyncratic element in the use of language is reduced, and, in addition, a corrective is provided against overpersonalized interpretations of stylistic features. This procedure also permits the contrasts between shared and unique features to become part of the total dialectical process of arriving at a considered and explicit response to the style of a text.

By the time that a careful scrutiny of the text in such terms has been undertaken it is likely not only that the original response will be developing, but also that certain patterns of features will have suggested themselves as being worth investigating for the light which a description of them can throw upon certain intrinsic characteristics of the style. The focus is therefore now shifted from setting features in the text against norms of usage to viewing the patterns of choice within the text from the standpoint of their uniqueness. A selective description must therefore follow of those features chosen for investigation in these terms. It must be borne in mind that these features will form a complex, that examination of them in detail may well lead to the need to investigate other related features, and that lexis, grammar, phonology, and graphology must all come into play to a greater or lesser degree.

For while stylistic diagnosis or identification can rely upon one or two features selected from the language of texts as being sufficient evidence of stylistic uniqueness, a full and explicit statement of style will require a more complex presentation of interrelated features. It may be sufficient, if evidence of authorship is all that is required, to use a computer to determine quantitatively the density in a given text of one or two specific linguistic features; but this is diagnosis, not description. And the features chosen for this purpose may not, indeed probably will not, be features which are stylistically significant in terms of literary response and artistic effect. Or we may identify the style of a writer by referring simply to his preference for certain words, or his predilection for a particular clause structure; and this would certainly bring us nearer to the heart of the matter. But it seems probable that the secret of individual style can never lie in one dominant feature alone; rather, an explicit statement will need to take account of the inter-relation of many parts which make up the whole. Only by careful descriptive studies can these be brought to the surface and weighed one against the other in terms of our developing responses.

In such descriptive studies it needs to be remembered that any item in the text may be significant in relation to more than one system, or to more than one aspect of form; and the nature of the linguistic features thought to be significant will determine with which system or aspect the detailed descriptive work begins. Nor need any requirement be laid down in advance regarding the degree of delicacy to which any part of the description should be pursued; this must depend upon judgment, as the description proceeds, of the significance or otherwise of a particular feature.

. . . Any linguistic feature may of course possess stylistic significance, but it can be no part of a brief presentation such as this to attempt to list them in detail. To do so would, in fact, produce a catalogue of almost every formal and contextual feature in the language. By way of exemplifying the range, and inter-relatedness, of features which may, in different texts, be stylistically significant, therefore, a summary of a few of these will now be made. They have been chosen partly for the illumination they offer of certain stylistic effects and devices often observed but rarely described in detail, and partly also in order to suggest a few lines of inquiry which might bear fruit if pursued in detail in a variety of literary texts.

In the first place, the contribution of grammatical features to stylistic effect has not been much considered or analyzed, apart from the generalized, and again often metaphorical, references to the "rolling" periods or the "involved" syntax of a writer's language. Concepts of syntactical complexity and simplicity often underlie statements of this kind. Linguistic complexity is difficult to measure objectively; but it is possible to describe it in grammatical (and lexical) terms without necessarily quantifying the differences thus exposed. There are, however, not only many degrees of complexity, but many different kinds of complexity; and similarly, a great variety of types of simplicity.

Long sentences do not, of course, necessarily produce a sense of complexity, or what may be termed density of texture. If the clausal relations are paratactic, as they often are in Malory or William Morris, for example, the structure of the prose, being merely additive, is unlikely to give the impression of complexity, other aspects of the text being, so to speak, equal. On the other hand, syntactical hypotaxis is likely to produce the effect of dense, involuted texture, as in much of Henry James' later prose; the rank-shifting which hypotaxis necessarily involves will probably provide, at least in part, a clue to the nature and degree of this complexity. It is clear that the syntactical "texture" of language may be analyzed and tested by grammatical description, provided the grammatical categories and scales which we use enable us to locate different types and degrees of complexity at different places and different "depths," in terms of the structural patterning which units of differing ranks display.

If, for example, as even a casual reading of many of Sir Thomas Browne's paragraphs suggests, there is carefully contrived syntactical "balance," it is only by means of a sophisticated grammar that the nature of this balance can be properly discovered and described. In most cases such "balance," and in Browne even "palindromic" structure—though he never, it seems, managed a perfect syntactical quincunx in a sentence or paragraph—can be located at one rank, with structural asymmetry at other ranks providing the necessary counterpoise and contrast. Alternatively, balance may be evident at primary structure, but varied by asymmetry at secondary structure. The "echo" effect of reiteration in dramatic and rhetorical prose is often of this kind, in that it results from syntactical repetition at one rank, with variation at another. This is also characteristic of much poetry and is highly indicative, for example, of the "set towards the message" in T. S. Eliot's "Ash Wednesday."

Syntactical effects in poetry not only include complexity and recurrence, but also syntactical ambiguity. Lexical ambiguity has long been recognized in the metaphor, the pun, and other types of imagery, but it is important to observe that ambiguity is not restricted to lexis. The syntax of poetry probably deserves more attention than it has hitherto received, particularly since verse, however "free," has a double set of units: those of the line and the stanza, and those of syntax. Often one set is used in counterpoint with the other; in the same way that, at the phonological level, metrical patterns are often counterpointed with the rhythms of speech. It is therefore possible for a poet, by juxtaposing grammatical boundaries with those of the metrical line, to make use of syntactical expectancy, followed by syntactical resolution or surprise. In this way alternative syntactical patterns are able to co-exist, thus contributing to the complexity of the verse.

In the drama and the novel, differentiation between dialogue, monologue, and narrative, or between speakers, is commonly made by grammatical means, though normally with the aid of lexical and graphological features which support and intensify these differences. Interior monologue in James Joyce's *Ulysses*, for example, is usually marked either by syntactical incompleteness or by full syntax without punctuation. Shakespeare and other dramatists often use incomplete or unresolved syntactical patterns, those major characteristics of spontaneous spoken language, to give the impression of a character intellectualizing under strain or in a condition of emotional shock.[15]

A further case which may be instanced where a writer uses grammatical means to produce deliberate effects in his presentation of dialogue is that of Dickens, whose novels richly illuminate the manifold use to which a skillful handling of linguistic differences in speech can be put. An instance of this is his syntactical variation in the presentation of speech in many of his courtroom scenes. A careful examination reveals several different "degrees" of indirect speech; in some cases it is not possible for the reader to determine whether the author is presenting speech directly, or question and answer conflated, or an indirect summary of the speech of the courtroom, so carefully does Dickens withdraw, partially or wholly, at different points, the grammatical markers of indirect speech.

Syntactical investigations of this kind, if they are intended as a contribution to detailed and explicit statements about style, must of course be matched with, and checked against, the results of careful examinations of the lexis and potential phonology of the texts in question. For grammar can only be a partial contributor to most of these effects. The grammar may display complexity of a particular kind; but lexis may also contribute, and phonological patterning may reinforce syntactical or lexical effects. The intricacy with which collocation and set are managed may, even with a comparatively simple syntax, produce similar, though never precisely the same, effects of involved texture and complexity. Dylan Thomas's poem "Fern Hill" has a fairly simple syntax, far simpler than that of some of his poems; what complexity the poem has is largely the result of intricate manipulation of sets and collocations within a relatively complicated metrical form. . . .

———————

Aspects of contextualization have also been the concern of linguists, and modern linguistic theory offers the concept of *context of situation*. In 1950 the late J. R. Firth wrote:[16]

> A key concept in the technique of the London group is the concept of *context of situation*. The phrase "context of situation" was first used widely in England by Malinowski . . . Malinowski's context of situation is a bit of the social process which can be considered apart and in which a speech event is central and makes all the difference, such as the drill sergeant's welcome utterance on the square "Stand at ease." The context of situation for Malinowski is an ordered series of events considered *in rebus*.
> My view was, and still is, that "context of situation" is best used as a suitable schematic construct to apply to language events, and that it is a group of related categories at a different level from grammatical categories, but rather of the same abstract nature. A context of situation for linguistic work brings into relation the following categories:
>
> A. The relevant features of participants: persons, personalities.
>   (i) The verbal action of the participants.
>   (ii) The non-verbal action of the participants.
> B. The relevant objects.
> C. The effect of the verbal action.

It is clear that context of situation was thought of by Malinowski and Firth primarily in relation to spoken language, and it has indeed been used by linguists mainly in the examination of non-literary linguistic events, and particularly those occurring in the spoken mode. Unfortunately, until recently, too little research and too little discrimination has been applied to this concept in contemporary linguistics and so it remains, as yet, largely undeveloped. Suitably modified and extended, however, the concept can be of value both in the understanding of the process of stylistic study and in the process itself. It ensures that any procedures followed in the study of style do not restrict themselves exclusively to an examination of the language of the text.

A literary text may be said to have a context of situation in the sense in which it was understood by Firth. A text may, that is, be regarded as an "utterance" which is part of a complex social process; and therefore the personal, social, linguistic, literary, and ideological circumstances in which it was written need, as literary scholars have always recognized, to be called upon from time to time when any serious examination of a literary text is being made, be it for the purpose of stylistic or indeed any literary study. Recourse to factors such as these may be termed *cultural contextualization*. Although this is often thought of as becoming, for example, a seventeenth-century man in order to appreciate a seventeenth-century text, the process is rather more complex. It requires the ability to glance from one's own cultural position to that of the contemporary reader, and back again, allowing features in the text to appear in relief by means of a kind of stereoscopic vision. Cultural contextualization is also necessary for a modern text, since cultural positions are, in any absolute sense, unique.

Some of the linguistic aspects of this contextualizing process have already been referred to when we indicated the importance of "placing" the language of the text in terms of its diachronic (period), diatopic (dialect), and diatypic (field, mode and tenor) status . . . and the necessity for a linguistic to have an historical dimension . . . even if the study is concerned solely with modern texts, because the creative writer lives in a literary and linguistic tradition, and is often significantly conscious of it. Of considerable importance for our purposes, however, is that context of situation which certain literary genres seem especially to allow the writer to create within the text itself. Genre-consciousness, particularly of the dramatic, first-person narrative and monologue types, may be seen as one of those factors which enables the creative writer to draw our attention away from the "real" context of situation of his work (the addresser-addressee situation and the relevant circumstances of this) and focus it on the "context of situation" the work itself is creating. Part of the willing suspension of disbelief of being an audience or reader of such works is that we allow the former context of situation to recede into the background, and this created one to come into the foreground, of our attention. This must be taken account of in stylistic study—it is part of our data—even if the latter context is, so to speak, embedded in the text with the result that there can be no clear separation, in its case, of text from situation. There is no formal linguistic way of dealing with this. One must contextualize, summarizing the situation the language is creating. In dealing with any portion of a text this contextualization may for certain descriptive purposes be delimited to a specified segment of it. This may be termed the *immediate intratextual context.* Moreover, the reader of a literary work has increasingly available as he proceeds an accumulation of contextual information against which dialogue, monologue, dramatic action, description of situation and mood, internal allusion, etc., may be placed. This may be called the *accumulated intratextual context.* By the end of the text he is thus in possession of the *total intratextual context.*

In the stylistic examination of a literary work use may well be made of all previously mentioned contextualizations, both extratextual and intratextual. This "reading with a sense for continuity, for contextual coherence, for wholeness" [17] must be an essential part of stylistic study; it is a necessary check on the equally necessary discreteness which any aspectual work on a text, linguistic or otherwise, requires.

When examining style, and using linguistics in so doing, the analyst should, we believe, not only take into account linguistic features in isolation, but also consider their relation to other aspects of the text and its contextual setting. Otherwise his final statements will be merely linguistic.

NOTES

1. This work is particularly associated with the names of the late J. R. Firth, and of A. McIntosh and M. A. K. Halliday. The present authors take full responsibility for what appears in this monograph, while at the same time wishing to express their indebtedness not only to the above linguists, but also to David Abercrombie, P. D. Strevens, S. Pit Corder, J. McH. Sinclair, and J. P. Thorne for private discussions on matters linguistic and stylistic.

2. Cf. M. A. K. Halliday, "Categories of the Theory of Grammar," *Word,* XVII (1961), 244–245: "Language has 'formal meaning' and 'contextual meaning' . . . The formal meaning of an item is its operation in the network of formal relations. Contextual meaning, which is an extension of the popular— and traditional linguistic—notion of meaning, is quite distinct from formal meaning. . . ."

3. This relationship for Halliday is the "interlevel" of *context,* and he points out ("Categories," p. 245) that "the contextual meaning of an item is its relation to extra-textual features; but this is not a direct relation to the

item as such, but of the item in its place in linguistic form: contextual meaning is therefore logically dependent on formal meaning." Also "the reason why 'context' is preferred to 'semantics' as the name of this interlevel is that 'semantics' is too closely tied to one particular method of statement, the conceptual method. . . . The latter, by attempting to link language form to unobservables, becomes circular, since concepts are only observable as [exponents of] the forms they are set up to 'explain.' The linguistic statement of context attempts to relate language form to [abstractions from] other [i.e., extratextual] observables." What we regard as an inadequacy in much American linguistics (both transformative-generative and structural) arises from the failure to give due emphasis to this aspect of language study. British linguists have not solved the many problems it raises but these problems are at least recognized as being of concern to the linguist.

4.   David Abercrombie's "Syllable Quantity and Enclitics," *In Honour of Daniel Jones* (London, 1964), and "A Phonetician's View of Verse Structure," *Linguistics,* VI (1964), 5–13, have much to offer here.

5.   See M. A. K. Halliday, "The Tones of English," *Archivum Linguisticum,* XV (1963), 1–28. The units postulated for English are *tone group,* the unit of contrastive intonation contour, *foot,* the unit of contrastive stress, *syllable,* the unit of contrastive syllabic structure, and *phonematic unit,* or *phoneme,* the unit of contrastive articulation. They are thought of as arranged in a hierarchy or "rank scale," descending from the *tone group* to the *phoneme,* each unit consisting of one or more of the units immediately below it in the hierarchy.

6.   See M. A. K. Halliday, "Categories," p. 244, and the discussion of "level" and "interlevel" in Robert M. W. Dixon, *Linguistic Science and Logic* (The Hague, 1963), pp. 21–29.

7.   See, e.g., C. C. Fries, *The Structure of English* (New York, 1952); M. A. K. Halliday, "Grammatical Categories in Modern Chinese," *Transactions of the Philological Society* (1956); N. Chomsky, *Syntactic Structures* (The Hague, 1957); A. A. Hill, *Introduction to Linguistic Structures* (New York, 1958); E. Nida, *Synopsis of English Syntax* (Norman, Okla., 1960); M. A. K. Halliday, "Categories" (1961).

8.   Such choices are choices within a closed system. Closed systems are characteristic of grammar. Choices which do not operate within closed systems, "open" choices, are characteristic of lexis. See M. A. K. Halliday, "Linguistique Genérale et Linguistique Appliquée à l'Enseignement des Langues," *Publications du Centre de Linguistique Appliquée* (Université de Besançon, 1962), pp. 8–9, 20–22; also "Categories," pp. 263–268.

9.   See M. A. K. Halliday, "Categories," pp. 273–277. The many problems, theoretical and procedural, still to be faced in the formal study of lexis are clearly outlined in J. McH. Sinclair, "Beginning the Study of Lexis" [*In Memory of J. R. Firth,* eds. C. E. Bazell, J. C. Catford, M. A. K. Halliday, and R. H. Robins (London, 1966), pp. 410–430].

10.   See J. C. Catford, *A Linguistic Theory of Translation* (London, 1965).

11.   E.g., A. A. Hill, "Towards a Literary Analysis," *English Studies in Honor of James Southall Wilson,* ed. Fredson Bowers (Charlottesville, Va., 1951), pp. 147–165; "An Analysis of the 'Windhover': An Experiment in Structural Method," *PMLA,* LXX (1955), 968–978; "A Program for the Definition of Literature," *University of Texas Studies in English,* XXXVII (1958), 46–52; S. R. Levin, *Linguistic Structures in Poetry* (The Hague, 1962).

12.   Roman Jakobson, "Closing Statement: Linguistics and Poetics," *Style in Language,* ed. Thomas A. Sebeok (Cambridge, Mass., 1960), p. 356.

13.   From *Style and Civilizations* (Ithaca, 1957), quoted by Dell H. Hymes,

"Phonological Aspects of Style: Some English Sonnets," in *Style in Language,* p. 114.

14.   The three categories have been variously defined, and named, by British linguists in the past few years. Sometimes, though in the view of the present authors not very helpfully, they have been subsumed under a major category of *register:* e.g., Angus McIntosh, M. A. K. Halliday, and Peter Strevens, *The Linguistic Sciences and Language Teaching* (London, 1964): "Registers may be distinguished according to field of discourse, mode of discourse, and style of discourse." For obvious reasons we prefer *tenor* to *style* in this context. In J. C. Catford, *A Linguistic Theory of Translation,* the terms *mode* and *style* are used as above, but the term *register* corresponds approximately to that of *field.* Barbara Strang, *Modern English Structure* (London, 1962), uses the term *medium* in place of *mode,* and uses *style* and *register* in slightly different senses from any of the above. Terminology and definition in this area of language study are both clearly in a developing stage; and the part played by *genre* and a consciousness of *genre* in language choices has still to be stated and reconciled with these other dimensions of language variation. *Genre* can certainly be seen from one point of view as the conventional framework which preserves for use by the contemporary writer older forms of the language, forms no longer in extra-literary use.

15.   See, e.g., Shakespeare, *Works,* ed. P. Alexander (London, 1951): *Winter's Tale,* I, ii, 121–127; *Cymbeline,* III, ii, 1–17; *Richard III,* V, iii, 182–193.

16.   J. R. Firth, "Personality and Language in Society," *Papers in Linguistics* (London, 1957).

17.   René Wellek, "Closing Statement from the Viewpoint of Literary Criticism," *Style in Language,* p. 149.

6. POETICS AND LINGUISTICS

Manfred Bierwisch

Translated by Peter H. Salus

Just as linguistic theory must characterize man's ability to produce and comprehend language—that is, linguistic competence—so, Manfred Bierwisch shows in the following essay, must poetics characterize poetic competence: our ability to compose and to understand poetic structures. Dr. Bierwisch argues that many of the central principles of modern generative linguistics bear on a general and abstract theory of poetics.

The poetic "grammar" outlined here is a selectional mechanism, operating on the output of a grammar of ordinary language, that would assign a "scale of poeticality" to a text according to its exploitation of certain poetic devices. Such a mechanism would take account, for example, of the fact that "deviations" from grammaticality in poetic language are understood with reference to the rules of the grammar which the deviant constructions violate: systematic violation of certain kinds of grammatical rules is one logical province for a poetics organized along these lines. Dr. Bierwisch holds that the proper province of poetics is not the formulation of value judgments but a characterization of the linguistic bases of poetic effects. Manfred Bierwisch is associated with the Deutsche Akademie der Wissenschaften zu Berlin, Berlin, German Democratic Republic. The translation is by Peter H. Salus, associate professor of linguistics at the University of Toronto.

1

Anyone who wishes to define exactly and combine systematically impressionistic concepts originating in practical experience

Manfred Bierwisch, "Poetik und Linguistik," originally published in *Mathematik und Dichtung,* ed. Helmut Kreuzer and Rul Gunzenhäuser (Munich: Nymphenburger Verlagshandlung, 1965, 1967), pp. 49–65. Reprinted by permission of the author and publisher. Translation © 1970 by Holt, Rinehart and Winston.

and intuitive reflection so that they become accessible to axio-matization and mathematical treatment must be aware that the explication suggested has to comprehend the crucial phenomena that produced the ideas. He must take care that the apparatus he has introduced still concerns the problem with which he began. Thus, for example, in order to have a "mathematical apparatus" for the explanation of meaning, there grew up more than a decade ago the idea that the term *information* used in the theory of news reporting was an explication of the concept *meaning*. This, however, did not clarify any part of what is understood as the linguistic problem of meaning, and thus it was soon dropped from technical usage. In my opinion, similar dangers exist in many attempts at giving poetics a precisely formulated basis. I shall therefore enunciate some points of view that I feel are necessary for the construction of poetics, if by poetics one understands a theory of the structure of literary texts or verbal works of art and views this as an empirical science that must explicate the given facts. In this discussion, the facts of linguistics will be used in two ways: first, the objects of poetic investigation are verbal phenomena and thus fall within the bounds of linguistics; second, there is a whole series of general methodological problems that run parallel for linguistics and poetics.

In order to set forth more exactly the problems connected with the theoretical side of poetics, I will next characterize briefly two extreme methods of attempting to investigate literary texts scientifically: the Interpretive School, and Textual Statistics. The hermeneutic or [New Critical] method pursues the ideal of ex-amining every artistic work with a minimum of general pre-supposition and assumes that its structure must be determined from itself alone. Each object is thus ultimately absolutely unique, incomparable, and inaccessible to any generalization. This means not only that no researcher can independently say when the analysis of a given text is concluded and how it can and must advance our thinking, but above all that a real theory of the structure of poetic texts is completely impossible. On the other hand, statistical methods subject every text to the same strictly formalized procedures and criteria, in order to ascertain certain individual qualities (for example, textual characteristics such as the number of words per sentence or syllables per word). Through this process, given texts are comparable in specific points of view, the points of view are precisely formulable, completely independent of the researcher, and accessible to general theoretical considerations. Unfortunately they do not come to grips with the specific structures of poetic texts. If we look at a five-line poem like

> Auch die Würmer
> Haben ein Reich: das Erdreich.
> Wer
> Sonst dort leben will, muss
> Tot sein.*

Günter Kunert

we can see that by switching the words around we could arrive at innumerable texts that would exhibit the same statistical characteristics without indicating in the slightest degree the relevant structure that renders the poetic effect—to say nothing of the fact that the statistical values are totally irrelevant in so small a sample. Thus, on the one hand hermeneutics can circumscribe every individual object that (so far as it is concerned) characterizes a quality without ever coming to a theory of these qualities; on the other hand, textual statistics can make general statements without explaining the specific effects. This sketchy description, which nowhere attempts to be just to the methodologies, is merely to show which pitfalls a usable theory of poetics must avoid.

After these considerations we must next set ourselves the seemingly trivial questions of just what poetics must deal with and which facts it must describe and clarify. The simple answer, that the objects of poetics are literary texts, is only valid on first glance. The texts at hand are merely the observable material, the data from which poetics must proceed: the facts are of a completely different nature. The actual objects of poetics are the particular regularities that occur in literary texts and that determine the specific effects of poetry: in the final analysis the human ability to produce poetic structures and understand their effect—that is, something which one might call *poetic compe-*

---

* The German and foreign rights to the works of Günter Kunert belong to Carl Hanser Verlag, Munich.

tence. In order to explain more exactly what must be understood by this, we will here introduce an excursus into the theory of linguistics, so that we can later use concepts from this theory that seem to me to be essential to poetics.

2

Every scientific description of language has as its goal the solution to a basic problem, which may be formulated as follows: How is it possible for a person to master a language and understand, or form and use, any number of new sentences? [1] It is also necessary to explain the amazing fact that every human being has a limited number of learning experiences in the course of which he acquires a finite inventory of basic elements—sounds, words, categories—and certain rules of combination so that he has at his disposal an ever increasing number of sentences, which he masters with all of their syntactic, semantic, and phonological properties. This ability, which is the basis of every act of speech and comprehension, may be described by a mechanism consisting of a system of rules that has as its input the starting symbol SENTENCE and as its output the sentences of the language in question, so that the system *generates* or *enumerates* the sentences in the sense used in mathematics. We might schematically represent such a mechanism as

(1)   SENTENCE $\rightarrow$ $\boxed{\text{G}}$ $\rightarrow S_1 \ S_2 \ S_3 \ \ldots$

where $S_n \ \ldots$ are the individual sentences of the language. This mechanism must be more precisely specified. First it is essential that G not only generate the sequences of words or sounds but also establish the relationships between these elements. G must, for example, determine that the sentence

(2)   Das Leben ist am grössten:
             Es steht nicht mehr bereit.

                                        Brecht

is ambiguous, because *nicht mehr* can be either an object or an adverbial modifier. Taken as a whole, the categories and relationships contained in a sentence are called the structural description (SD), and G must, in addition to concatenations of words, generate SDs: for the sentence (2), two different SDs must be generated. Furthermore, G must consist of several components: syntax, semantics, and phonology. The relationships of these components to one another is such that the semantics specifies the meaning (M) and the phonology the phonetic structure (P) on the basis of the syntactic structure (SS). Our schematic representation (1) can thus be rewritten as:

(3)   SENTENCE → [SYNTAX] → SS ↗ [SEMANTICS] → M
                                    ↘ [PHONOLOGY] → P

P includes all the regular pronunciation variants, M all the syntactic or semantically conditioned variants, of a sentence. It is made clear in (3) that every S_n of (1) is specified by one M and one P, an explication of the notion, stemming from scholasticism, of the dual nature of the linguistic sign. Each of the three components contains several subcomponents corresponding to the general form of rules of which these parts consist. Corresponding to the conditions given earlier, the resulting SD for every sentence thus is made up of various levels in which various structural aspects are represented; for example, the phonetic data by matrices of phonetic features, a part of the syntactic data through trees representing the categorization and relationships of sentential elements.

All of the terms introduced thus far permit of exact definition within various mathematical disciplines. Through mechanism G we thus have the capacity to characterize the theoretically infinite number of sentences of a natural language and all of its structural characteristics by means of a finite descriptive apparatus: the language to be described is precisely that set of sentences generated by G. G is thus a possible and highly plausible explication of the concept "grammar," if we consider this to comprise not only syntax and phonology but also semantics.

On this basis it is necessary for us to describe one more important empirical fact.

(4)   Die nackten Stühle horchen sonderbar

                                                    Lichtenstein

(5)   Das am Telefon wollte der Schuldturn nicht
       sagen

                                                    Johnson

(6)   Dort lint es Böck / dort beint es Hol, / es waldet
       grün und witzt

                                                  Schwitters

(7)   Ein werst übellach fenestraus

                                                      Helms

Sentences (4) through (7) are in different ways and in increasing
degree abnormal for anyone who speaks German; they are deviant
and are so quite independently of their context. We will return
below to the fact that just these deviations constitute some of
their poetic effect. What concerns us here is the empirical ability
to differentiate various degrees and types of deviation from normal sentences. It is clear, for example, that (5) will be understood as an analogy to a sentence like *Das wollte der Mann am
Telefon nicht sagen* and (6) has as its background sentences like
Dort geht es los, dort wird es still, that is, if there were verb-
complexes like *böcklinen* and *Hol beinen* in German. Without
such analogies, the sense of sentences (4) through (7) would be
completely unintelligible, much less their special effect. These
facts find their explication in the grammatical theory outlined
above if we assume that G generates only those sentences (and
associated SDs) which are generally considered normal, whereas
all deviant sentences are generated by a secondary system of relations which connects them with the SDs generated by G. This
means that deviant sentences always have defective SDs, and
that the differences between these and normal SDs (by which
the sentences would normally be understood) make clear the
type and degree of abnormality of the sentences. Expressed differently, this means that deviant sentences come about through
violation of rules in G, and that the violation of various rule-
classes results in various types and degrees of deviance. Just which
sentences are normal must be viewed as an empirically ascertainable datum the securing of which is not, however, without prac-

tical difficulties; of primary importance, though, is the ability to differentiate without doubt between normal and deviant sentences. And it must not be mistakenly assumed that G justifies judgments about normality or deviance; G merely makes explicit which regularities and which qualities cause normality or deviance to come about. For the sake of simplicity we will call the normality or deviance of sentences their *grammaticality* and say that G generates precisely the fully grammatical sentences.

It is important not to confuse the generation of sentences and their SDs with the actual formation of sentences in speech or the step-by-step action of rules in G with the process of sentence formation in the mind. G corresponds to the actual speech act in the same way that traffic laws do to actual vehicular traffic or the rules of counterpoint to the actual composition of a fugue: by means of G, the structure of a normally formed sentence is determined; nothing is said, however, about the factors which determine the choice of deviation from among innumerable possibilities. G is also indifferent to the various processes that transpire within the speaker and the hearer: it describes the ability which both must have at their disposal or which lies at the basis of the acts of forming and comprehending sentences. A description of the actual processes of speech and understanding that does not begin with an abstract symbol SENTENCE and move gradually to phonetic and semantic realization requires an individual theory of the language user that must take into account a plethora of other factors and restrictions, such as the limits of short-term memory and the causes of distractions and defects. Such a description must nonetheless contain G as one of its components as well as a system of relations that relates deviant sentences to G. The abstract schema of the hearer has the form

(8)   Sound sequence → $\boxed{\text{M}}$ → SD

Here M is a mechanism which relates a sequence of sounds to its SD on the basis of G. There is no sense in setting up a corresponding diagram for the speaker, as here entities such as "thought," and "emotion" would have to be inputs, and with our present means these cannot be determined with any precision.

If we designate the assignment of an SD to a phonological sequence as *comprehension,* it is easy to see that this is psychologically no linear system attaching each of the sounds or words sequentially, but a hierarchically differentiated procedure which leads to the formation of simultaneous structures. In a sentence like

> Seine vielen, im Vergleich zu seinem sonstigen Umfang kläglich dünnen Beine flimmerten ihm hilflos vor Augen
>
> Kafka

Seine vielen cannot be ordered and understood until *Beine* is also comprehended. The hearer must reconstruct hierarchically the heard sentence through those rules of G that he has mastered. The lower boundaries of the complexes that arise in this way are determined by the breadth of the linguistic relations—if *Seine vielen* had disappeared from the memory before arriving at *Beine,* no understanding would be possible—and the upper boundaries are delimited by the short-term memory. It is easy to consider just why the formation of sentences cannot be a linear process but demands simultaneous complexes which are ordered sequentially only in the last phase of sentence production, in the articulatory process.

With G, or the schema represented in (1), we have a sufficiently exact determination of what we meant by the ability to speak a given language: competence. With M, or schema (8), we have a representation of our concept of the use of this competence. G must further be distinguished from the ability to acquire a given language, that is, from the general linguistic ability of mankind. The three concepts roughly approximate Saussure's terms *langue, parole,* and *langage.*

For further discussion we will assume that G not only generates sentences but also sequences of sentences, complete discourses. This has been determined on the basis of the linguistic phenomena which act across sentence boundaries.[2]

3

There are analogies to this linguistic apparatus that are applicable to a considerable range of problems of poetics. Jakobson and Lotz begin their *Axiomatik eines Verssystems am mord-winischen Volkslied dargelegt*[3] with the following statement:

> Die Analyse eines metrischen Systems fordert eine genaue
> Bestimmung aller Konstituenten und der unter ihnen beste-
> henden Beziehungen, die einem beliebigen Versmass dieses
> Systems zugrunde liegen; sie soll vollständig und eindeutig
> besagen, welche Metra im System tatsächlich existieren und
> welche nicht vorkommen können. Die ganze Liste der vor-
> handenen metrischen Formen muss also aus den festgestellten
> Grundsätzen vollständig deduziert werden können.

> [The analysis of a metrical system demands an exact speci-
> fication of all constituents and of the relationships holding
> between them which underlie any meter of this system. It
> must completely and unambiguously state which meters can in
> fact exist and which cannot occur in the system. The entire list
> of possible metrical forms must hence be completely deducible
> from established axioms.—Ed.]

A set of verse axioms is an exact parallel to Grammar G
[Schema (1), p. 99—Ed.]; it is a mechanism that generates all
the possible meters and thereby explains the ability to comprehend verse as such and to recognize intentional or accidental
deviations. An essential difference between a grammar and a
metrical system is that a metrical system can only be constructed
on the basis of elements that already occur in the grammar and
that enter into structures set down by the grammar, whereas the
elements of the grammar are autonomous and not composed of
anything made up by an extralinguistic system. Poetic structures
like verse, rhyme, and alliteration are thus parasitic structures
that can only occur on the basis of linguistically primary structures. That this seemingly obvious statement is not trivial, and
that in this grammatical independence optional structural levels
of SD emerging from G come into play, is shown by consideration of further poetic devices—grammatical and lexical parallelism:

(9)   Die Mühen der Gebirge liegen hinter uns
         Vor uns liegen die Mühen der Ebenen.

                                                   Brecht

Both lines of this couplet have the structure

(10)   Die Mühen GENITIVE ATTRIBUTE liegen PREPOSITION uns.

The elements here indicated by grammatical categories are occupied by antonyms. There is no doubt that the poetic effect of these verses is substantially involved in the antithesis. It provides, in fact, the basis for the real point of these two lines— that the noun *Mühen* is not changed to its antonym in the second verse, as one would have supposed. Further, far more complex interdependencies between grammatical and poetic structures are easily adduceable.[4] It is, however, just as clear that an autonomous characterization of poetic structures, possible to a certain extent for simple verse and rhyme systems, is impossible for complex relationships like irregular rhythm, and indeed that poetics does not permit of a general solution to this problem.

We are thus confronted by the problem of just how a description of poetic structures is to be connected to grammar. One possible answer to this question would be to envision a poetic system PS' as a selectional mechanism that takes the SDs generated by G as its input and has as its output two classes SD_1 and SD_2 of which SD_1 contains the structures that correspond to poetic rules. In other words, PS' is seen as a differentiating algorithm which determines whether or not a given sentence is poetic. It would thus be built up like a "recognition grammar," which has the sequence of words as its input and the decision whether or not the sequences were fully grammatical as its output. Just as a recognition grammar would have to contain all the rules of G in order to decide between fully grammatical and deviant sentences, so a system like PS' would have to contain a closed system of rules by which to decide between poetic structures and all others. Such a differentiation obviously makes sense only for certain simple systems such as regular verse.

Before we pursue this empirical aspect, which is directly related to *poetic competence,* I should like to discuss a modification of PS' that provides a more plausible description of the connection between linguistic and poetic structures.

We designate as PS a mechanism that does not divide all SDs into two classes but determines which of two SDs more closely fits certain poetic regularities. PS, in other words, orders certain

SDs in a scale of poeticality. At the same time, grammatically deviant sentences and their SDs must be considered: many grammatical deviations are motivated through rules in PS. We shall return to this in section 5. The construction of PS is to be thought of as taking as input an SD which it marks for certain general but nonetheless strictly formal rules and to which it assigns a certain value according to these markings. In the case of a simple, closed rule-system, like that of regular verse, the function of PS falls together with that of PS'. Here a violation of the rules is also uniquely ascertainable empirically. In the case of more complex poetic structures, however, a dichotomy need not necessarily result. Instead, PS would mark the parallelism and antonyms noted in (9) and would assign a higher value to this couplet than to

(11)   Die Mühen der Gebirge liegen hinter uns
          Vor uns liegen andere Mühen.

Concerning the rule-complex that makes up PS we might set up an exact explication along the general hypothesis formulated by Jakobson: "The poetic function projects the principle of equivalence from the axis of selection into the axis of combination," [5] which—based on our previous assumptions—says the following: in a given sequence in SD there are entities that can be characterized through the same syntactic, semantic, or phonetic features. These entities are marked and form the basis for the assignment of a specific value in the scale of poeticality. We can make this even more precise: C and C' are complexes specified by G which contain m entities, of which n are the same, where $n \leq m$. For $n = m$, C and C' are identical complexes. Just how large n must be when compared to m so that C and C' form a poetic relation must be empirically established. Let SD(C,C') be an SD which contains C and C'. This relationship can be stated definitively. The rules which explicate Jakobson's hypothesis must appear in PS in a form such as

(12)   SD(C,C') → SD(R(C,C'))

where R(C,C') is the relation between the two complexes and (12) assigns to SD(C,C') the marking of this relation.

It must be pointed out that the parallelism thus formulated

is doubtless insufficient to produce poetic effect in all cases. If (9) were completely parallel in structure, without transposition of the adverb of place, the poetic effect would be decidedly less:

(13) Die Mühen der Gebirge liegen hinter uns.
Die Mühen der Ebenen liegen vor uns.

Empirically important constraints must therefore be found and formulated.

In a similar manner there can go into PS the marking of verse structures that sets into corresponding relations certain phonological features in accordance with a verse system contained in PS.

These considerations may suffice to establish the following statements: PS operates on the basis of the SDs generated by G or brought into play by G and marks in them the poetic structures that determine their position in a scale of poeticality. The rules of which PS is composed operate on linguistic structures but are themselves extralinguistic, a formulation which determines quite plausibly the frequently argued relationship between poetics and linguistics. PS renders in an explicit and automatic fashion that which (at least for an appreciable part) hermeneutic interpretation attempts to do intuitively and without general principles, and thereby explicitly explains in which regularities the basis of the poetic effect of the reading or hearing of a given text may be found. It is clear that PS must be specifically formulated for every input language and for specific poetic effects. At the same time, however, the questions of general, independent qualities come up—qualities not anchored to specific languages or specific poetic (verse) systems. The components of PS, the relationships of those components to one another, and the form of the rules of PS are still to be investigated. In other words, the various aspects of PS can be investigated in a general way on the basis of systematic studies of individual problems in specific poetic systems, in exactly the same way as the general form of G is studied in linguistic theory. Finally, the question of just which general features of PS correspond to those of nonlinguistic esthetic systems (music, for example) can be posed exactly. Precisely because of the great complexity of every concrete system PS, the insight gained from such general qualities is of great scientific value.

4

In the general description of P, we have taken for granted a scale of poeticality, and with it an empirically ascertainable facility of the hearer to distinguish grades of poeticality, without which the assumption of such a scale would be meaningless. The problems of this assumption must now be examined more closely, since they form a central point in the methodology of empirical poetics.

We referred above to the fact that difficulties are present in the linguistically basic decision of the individual speaker concerning the grammaticality of a sentence in his language. One can, however, rightly assume that this is ascertainable in large degree through the means of test procedures. Despite all complexities, a natural language is a sufficiently closed system so that a speaker can have unequivocal judgments about just what is normal in his language and what is deviant in varying degree. Similar decisions in the realm of poetics can be made only in comparatively simple form systems, such as highly traditional folk art, or for particular aspects, such as the meter of a specific text. When we look at the totality of the complex structure of a literary work, our assumption seems highly dubious. The incredibly varying judgments that have been made about contemporary texts in every age makes this drastically clear. We will refrain from giving individual examples here. Even when we abstain from viewing ideologically conditioned misjudgments, our assumption of an empirical scale of poeticality seems on first glance to be untenable. Here, however, a possible misunderstanding must be countered. If one considers poetics as an empirical science, then it does not have to make judgments about literary quality or set up norms for literary production; rather, it must explain just which structural qualities form the bases for definite effects. It can and must explicate those consciously or unconsciously followed regularities that lead to the understanding of poetic structure and to a judgment of poeticality. And it can do so only to the degree that these judgments can be based upon the immanent qualities of the text. Poetics cannot refute erroneous judgments or support correct ones; it must accept effects as given and determine the rules upon which they are founded. The situation is exactly analogous to that of descriptive grammar, which cannot prescribe anything about language usage but merely describes it. The difference that leads to the apparent untenability of our assumption is that every speaker is in possession of a complete grammar and as a result can invariably decide questions of grammaticality if they are correctly posed (if this were not so he could not participate completely in the process of communication), but poetic competence is without doubt differently expressed. This is true at least for all stratified societies. Insofar as poetic texts contain linguistic structures, every speaker of the language can understand them; insofar as they are poetic structures, they will be understood only in proportion to the degree of acquisition of system PS. A meaningful investigation that attempts to describe this system PS must thus grow out of the effects and judgments that come about through the maximally adequate understanding of a poetic text. This statement, although apparently obvious, seems to me to be necessary for the clarification of the task of poetics. It does not lie within the scope of poetics to determine which judgment rests upon a suitable understanding of literature, but only to explicate how competent judgments come about. It must assume such suitable understanding if it wishes to achieve significant results. In practice—as in every branch of knowledge —this will have reciprocal effect: absurd judgments will lead to unusable statements about poetic structure, and necessary poetic insights will influence the formation of decisions in questionable cases. Primarily, however, the development of judgments in case of doubt is the field of literary criticism, which has the task of describing the effect of a text on a hearer or reader who is well acquainted with the regularities manifested in the text.

Motivation factors doubtless come into play to which the actual structure does not correspond, just as the unbiased speaker often bases his grammatical judgments upon arguments that, without invalidating the judgments, do not correspond to the grammar. Grammatical as well as poetic rules are to a great extent elements of an intuitive competence. In differentiated sociological circumstances and a literature corresponding to them, poetics would have to set up, for systematically ensuring its empirical basis, a typology of poetic understanding analogous to the "types of musical hearing" sketched by Adorno.[6] The proper task of poetics is the reconstruction of the competence of maximal understanding—in Miller's words, "the cognitive concepts that are the necessary armamentarium of a poet and that enable the critic to recognize a poem when he sees one." [7] That this posing of the assignment has in principle a stable basis is shown by our considerations of examples (9), (10), (11), and (13).

5

The examples we used to make the structure of PS plausible concerned the secondary use of linguistic structural qualities. So long as we view PS in this way, it will specify only those regularities in a literary text that occur in addition to grammatical regularities. It is now frequently maintained that poetic effects arise through intentional deviations from the grammatical rules: through syntactic irregularity, semantically abnormal metaphors, and so forth.[8] It seems to me that the assertion cannot be maintained in this unrestricted form. It must be apparent that not every ungrammaticality generates poetic effect.

(14) Es war an eines Sonntagsvormittags in schönster
        Frühjar.

The two grammatical deviations in (14) do not give rise to poetic effect. Examples (4) through (7), however, show that where a specific effect is desired, mere ungrammaticality is not sufficient: as isolated sentences the examples are merely deviant. They achieve poetic effect only when the deviation has a specific regularity as its basis, when they stop being merely violations of the grammatical rules. This means that poetically effective deviations must be explainable in terms of rules of deviation which themselves specify the conditions and form of the deviations. Thus, for a text like Johnson's *Eine Reise wegwohin 1960* from which (5) is taken, one might formulate a set of rules that in special circumstances produces otherwise abnormal word order and gives this a value in the scale of poeticality. The circumstances and forms of regular deviation must occur in PS just as the previously enunciated rules do. And they assign a degree of poeticality just as those rules do.

We can immediately apply these considerations to such deviations from poetic structure as violated meter. Brecht[9] made clear that the assumptions of a metrical scheme and its simultaneous violation can be a special poetic medium. But here too the violation must be regular; it cannot rest upon mere whim. It seems to me that this principle of secondary deviation has far-reaching importance, for example, for the explanation of modern poetic forms: the trivialization of innumerable poetic regularities continually leads to the establishment of new rules of deviation. This means that such texts are only comprehensible in the light of the rule-system from which they deviate. The analysis of polished systems such as those presented in advertisements of trivial novels is a presupposition for the description of the deviation-regularities that occur in avant-garde literature. To both rule-systems, the trivial and the one composed of the trivial and deviations from it, correspond different types of poetic competence.

It must be apparent that rule-systems of this last type are far less general than primary poetic structures like parallelism or meter and even less general than grammatical rules. Often enough it must be taken into account that a certain rule-system originates in the work in which it is found and did not exist as a prescribed code. With this we have a plausible explanation of the frequently observed fact that the author at first is completely free to select his means but in the course of the work is subject to an increasing pressure which grows out of the text itself. In our concepts this means that optional new rules are taken up by PS and then determine the subsequent text. For the reader or hearer it means that he acquires the understanding of the text according to just how far he has proceeded in the understanding of the new rule-system. He finds himself, as the news media would say, in the situation of the cryptanalyst who does not decode but must break the code. There can be no doubt that in modern literature, for example, in Faulkner and Joyce, this compulsion to break the code yields a consciously instituted poetic fascination. This situation is diametrically opposed to that of the simple speech act and perhaps yields partial explanation of the so-called creative style.

For theoretical analysis, such a wide-ranging variability of PS would seem to indicate that we are still on the level of hermeneutic interpretation: If every literary work is determined (at least potentially) by a special rule system, then it can only be described as something unique. There are two arguments against this. First, every modified or expanded system presupposes a general system without which the modifications and expansions would be impossible. Second, the modifications are not arbitrary but are subject to definite regularities which are doubtless accessible to study and reducible to general principles.

On the other hand, it is apparent that a considerable number of poetic effects escape every general description. Without the reference to *Wanderers Nachtlied* (by Goethe) the following quatrain would not be completely comprehensible:

(15)   Darauf schwiegen die Vöglein im Walde
        Über allen Wipfeln ist Ruh
        In allen Gipfeln spürest du
        Kaum einen Hauch.

Brecht

The deviation here is not founded in a poetic system, but upon a single text. The sole general statement that can be made here is that parody refers to a parodied text. A different feature is shown in example (4), where besides the grammatical deviation (in the sense discussed above) the knowledge of the art–history relationships between *Basel* (the name of Schwitter's poem) and Böcklin, Holbein, Konrad Witz, and Grünewald are used. Facts of this kind can never be expressed in an exhaustive linguistic semantics and they thus mark, together with parody, the boundaries of a complete theory of poetic effect and style.

6

All of the structural qualities about which we have spoken lie in the recording area of the short-term memory: the presupposition for this is that during the process of understanding they can be reconstructed. We might call this the textual microstructure. What we might call the macrostructure lies on quite another level: the construction of fables, the interlacing of episodes, and so forth. It is obvious that there is an essential mediation between the macrostructure and microstructure which results in the total effect, and that a rational literary theory must encompass both realms. Our present knowledge does not enable us to say anything meaningful about the type of relationship. In a process about whose bases and individual steps only vague guesses are possible, the complexes processed by the short-term memory are reduced to unities that stand at the disposal of the long-term memory, and it is certain that they are also transformed structurally. Just what roles microstructure and macrostructure play in these transformations is the central problem of the total effect.

Beyond this unexplained relationship the macrostructure doubtless takes on relative autonomy. The following considerations make this clear. In the translation of a text into another language it is frequently impossible to retain its microstructure; it must be replaced by a newly constructed one which is as similar as possible. But the macrostructure is effortlessly carried from one language to another and with certain limitations even to media other than that of everyday language—for example, film. It is known that the translation of poems, in which the microstructure plays a crucial role, is much more problematic than that of novels, in which the macrostructure plays an essential role. This leads us to the statement that a systematic theory of literature must test the possibility of formulating a general and relatively independent rule-system for macrostructure.

I have frequently indicated the boundaries limiting the explanation of poetic effect by a structural theory of poetics. These boundaries begin in the realm of linguistics: no semantic description can ever encompass all the connotations of a word. They concern, further, various aspects of poetic microstructure and perhaps, to an increased degree, macrostructure. Thus only a sub-part of the complex problem of literary effect, which is determined by historical and sociological facts, can be clarified through poetics. It seems to me, however, to be a decisive part, which can serve as a presupposition for the explanation of other, wider relationships.

Let us sum up our most provisional considerations concerning the conclusions to be drawn from experiences and concepts that have shown themselves to be significant in linguistics. A general theory of poetics must contain at least the following elements:

(16) a) An exact characterization of the types of poetic
           rules and the relationships between them, that is,
           the possible construction of PS;

b) An explication of the necessary types of poetic structural description (PS/SD);
c) An algorithm that uniquely assigns to the generated texts (given PS the corresponding PS/SD).

Empirical examinations on as large a scale of phenomena as possible must indicate which conditions must be fulfilled by (16b). What is required is an exactly formulated representation of the various types of poetic structural characteristics, which is prerequisite to every form of general statement within the realm of poetics. Only through a precisely specified representation of poetic structures will different analyses become comparable. Element (16a) yields the precise formulation of the rules which underlie such structural qualities. We have discussed bases for the fact that (16a) and (16b) presuppose the SD produced by G. Element (16c) makes explicit finally to what extent and in just what form poetic analysis—the assignment of a PSD to a given text under the assumptions of a system PS—is an automatic process. With a theoretical apparatus of this type, the actual object of poetics, poetic competence, can be described, or at least a significant aspect of this competence can be described. Such an apparatus could also be investigated in terms of its mathematical properties.

Only on the basis of such a structural explanation does it make sense to use statistical methods. These, however, do not characterize the poetical system PS, nor the structure of individual texts produced by the PSD, but only the process of application of PS during the construction or comprehension of corresponding texts.

It seems to me that a systematic study of poetic phenomena along the lines sketched here—along with the use of innumerable insights already achieved, including those of hermeneutics—is of considerable significance for an appropriate theory of poetry. The progress of a science does not depend merely upon the amassing of individual insights, but above all upon the formulation of new relationships and the posing of new questions.

NOTES

1. The theory of language here sketched is that definitively developed in the works of Noam Chomsky. A summary presentation can be found in

Chomsky, *Aspects of the Theory of Syntax* (Cambridge, Mass., 1965). A less technical survey is given in Bierwisch, *Modern Linguistics: Its Development, Methods, and Problems* (The Hague, 1969).

2. The first systematic steps toward investigation of structures larger than the sentence were taken by Zellig Harris, and have now been collected in *Discourse Analysis* (The Hague, 1963). For some critical discussion see Bierwisch, "Review of Discourse Analysis," *Linguistics*, XIII (1965), 61–73.

3. Roman Jakobson and John Lotz, *Axiomatik eines Verssystems am mordwinischen Volkslied dargelegt* (Stockholm, 1941), p. 1.

4. Cf., e.g., Jakobson, "Der grammatische Bau des Gedichts von B. Brecht 'Wir sind sie,'" in *Festschrift Wolfgang Steinitz* (Berlin, 1965) and Baumgärtner, "Interpretation und Analyse," *Sinn und Form* (1960), pp. 395–415.

5. Jakobson, "Linguistics and Poetics," in *Style in Language*, ed. Thomas A. Sebeok (Cambridge, Mass., 1960), p. 358.

6. Adorno, *Einleitung in die Musiksoziologie* (Frankfurt, 1962), pp. 13–31.

7. George A. Miller, "From the Viewpoint of Psychology," in *Style in Language*, p. 392.

8. See, for example, Sol Saporta, "The Application of Linguistics to the Study of Poetic Language," in *Style in Language*, pp. 82–93, and the subsequent discussion.

9. Berthold Brecht, "Über reimlose Lyrik mit unregelmässigen Rhythmen," *Versuche*, XII (Berlin, 1953), 141–148.

LINGUISTIC STYLISTICS: METHOD

III

7.   "THIS BREAD I BREAK"— LANGUAGE AND INTERPRETATION

Geoffrey Leech

Geoffrey Leech seeks to differentiate sharply in this essay between linguistic description and critical interpretation. They are, he asserts, "distinct and complementary" ways of explaining a literary text. His analysis of Dylan Thomas's "This Bread I Break" emphasizes "cohesion"—the lexical and grammatical means which the poet draws from standard language to unify the poem. Leech's discussion of cohesion leads him to consideration of how different cohesive patterns are related to foregrounded elements in the poem (see "Standard Language and Poetic Language," Selection 3). Elements that are foregrounded in cohesive patterns lead finally to consideration of context and interpretation of the entire poem. Geoffrey Leech is lecturer in the department of English and assistant secretary of the Communication Research Centre, University College London.

> *This bread I break was once the oat,*
> *This wine upon a foreign tree*
> *Plunged in its fruit;*
> *Man in the day or wind at night*
> *Laid the crops low, broke the grape's joy.*
>
> *Once in this wine the summer blood*
> *Knocked in the flesh that decked the vine,*
> *Once in this bread*
> *The oat was merry in the wind;*
> *Man broke the sun, pulled the wind down.*

Geoffrey Leech, " 'This Bread I Break'—Language and Interpretation," *A Review of English Literature*, **VI** (1965), 66–75. Reprinted by permission of the author.

> *This flesh you break, this blood you let*
> *Make desolation in the vein,*
> *Were oat and grape*
> *Born of the sensual root and sap;*
> *My wine you drink, my bread you snap.**

Dylan Thomas

Linguistic description and critical interpretation are, to my mind, distinct and complementary ways of "explaining" a literary text. By reference to Dylan Thomas's poem quoted above, I shall attempt to show how they are related, and indirectly, what the former can contribute to the latter.

According to a widely held view, the linguist's aim is to make "statements of meaning." [1] "Meaning" here is interpreted in a broader sense than usual, sometimes including every aspect of linguistic choice, whether in the field of semantics, vocabulary, grammar, or phonology. One advantage of this extended use of the word "meaning" is that it liberates us from the habit of thinking that the only type of meaning that matters is "cognitive" or "referential" meaning: a view that literary critics have long found unsatisfactory.[2] On the other hand, a work of literature contains dimensions of meaning additional to those operating in other types of discourse. The apparatus of linguistic description is an insensitive tool for literary analysis unless it is adapted to handle these extra complexities.

1. *Cohesion* is a dimension of linguistic description which is particularly important in the study of literary texts.[3] By this is meant the way in which independent choices in different points of a text correspond with or presuppose one another, forming a network of sequential relations. In Dylan Thomas's poem, the selection of present tense in lines 1, 11 and 15, and of the past tense in lines 1, 3, 5, 7, 9, 10 and 13 are of little interest as isolated facts. What is of interest is the way these choices pattern together: from a starting point in the present, the poet makes an excursion into the past, returning to the present at the beginning and end of the final stanza. Notice, too, how the present

tense patterns with the 1st and 2nd person pronouns "I" (1), "my" (15 twice), and "you" (11 twice, 15 twice), whereas the past tense patterns with "man" (4, 10), the only personal noun in the text (3rd person), and the adverb "once" (1, 6, 8). These distributions accord with the semantic opposition between immediacy ("thisness") and non-immediacy ("thatness") of temporal and spatial reference. The word "this" (1, 2, 6, 8, 11 twice) is, in fact, a bridge between the two distributional patterns: it occurs with both present and past tenses.

Lexical cohesion in this poem is even more marked than grammatical cohesion. The most obvious kind of lexical cohesion consists in the repetition of the same item of vocabulary: "bread" (1, 8, 15), "break" (1, 5, 10, 11), "oat" (1, 9, 13), and many other items occur more than once. But apart from this, choice of vocabulary is largely restricted to items which have a clear semantic connection with other items in the text. One path of semantic connections links "bread," "oats," "crops"; others can be traced through "wine," "tree," "fruit," "grape," "vine," "drink"; "day," "night," "summer," "sun"; "blood," "flesh," "vein"; "joy," "merry," "desolation"; "break," "snap."

In studying cohesion, we pick out the patterns of meaning running through the text, and arrive at some sort of linguistic account of what the poem is "about." In this case, we also notice how tightly organized the relationships are: it might almost be said that the poet makes it too easy to follow his meaning. But this is a very superficial kind of "meaning," yielded by an analysis which could be equally well applied to any text in English—say a Home Office memorandum or a recipe for apricot soufflé. It is superficial, because we have only considered how selections are made from the range of possibilities generally available to users of the language. But poetry is above all the variety of discourse which exploits linguistic unorthodoxy. To bring to light what is of most significance in the language of a poem, we have to deal with choices which would not be expected or tolerated in a normal language situation.[4] This is another dimension of analysis.

2. *Foregrounding*, or motivated deviation from linguistic or other socially accepted norms, has been claimed to be a basic principle of aesthetic communication.[5] Whether or not the concept is applicable to any great extent to other art forms, it is

certainly valuable, if not essential, for the study of poetic language. The norms of the language are in this dimension of analysis regarded as a "background," against which features which are prominent because of their abnormality are placed in focus. In making choices which are not permissible in terms of the accepted code, the poet extends, or transcends, the normal communicative resources of his tongue. The obvious illustration of foregrounding comes from the semantic opposition of literal and figurative meaning: a literary metaphor is a semantic oddity which demands that a linguistic form should be given something other than its normal (literal) interpretation.

A metaphor frequently manifests itself in a highly unpredictable collocation, or sequence of lexical items. In "Broke the grape's joy" (5) there is a collocative clash between "broke" and "joy," and between "grape's" and "joy": to make the sequence "sensible" we would have to substitute a concrete noun like "skin" for "joy," or else replace "grape" by an animate noun and "broke" by a verb such as "spoiled." Of the many foregrounded groupings of lexical items in the poem, two kinds are prominent: those which yoke together inanimate nouns and items denoting psychological states ("grape's joy" (5), "the oat was merry" (9), "desolation in the vein" (12), "sensual root" (14)); and those which consist in the use of verbs of violent action in an "inappropriate" context ("plunged in its fruit" (3), "broke the . . . joy" (5), "knocked in the flesh" (7), "broke the sun" (10), "pulled the wind down" (10), "this flesh you break" (11), "my bread you snap" (15)). The deviation consists in the selection of an item which lies outside the normal range of choices at a particular place in structure. If we set up the frame "pulled the . . . down," it is easy to make a list of nouns (mostly concrete and inanimate) which could predictably fill the empty space. But the noun "wind" is not available for selection in this position: the poet has disregarded the normal conditions of choice.

Less obviously, "foregrounding" can apply to the opposite circumstance, in which a writer temporarily renounces his permitted freedom of choice, introducing uniformity where there would normally be diversity.[6] An example is the grammatical parallelism in line 4: one noun phrase of the structure noun + prepositional phrase ("Man in the day") is followed by another noun phrase of like structure ("wind at night"). Although the language tolerates a great variety of noun phrase structures (deictic + noun, adjective + noun + prepositional phrase, noun + relative clause, etc.) the poet successively restricts himself to the same pattern, thereby setting up a special relationship of equivalence between the two grammatical units. A more striking parallelism is found in the last line of the poem, which divides grammatically into two sections, each having the structure "my" + noun + "you" + verb. I shall refer to such foregrounded patterns, whether in grammar or phonology, as "schemes."

3. *Cohesion of Foregrounding* constitutes a separate dimension of descriptive statement, whereby the foregrounded features identified in isolation are related to one another and to the text in its entirety. A certain pattern of similarities has already been observed in the poem's deviant lexical collocations. There is also cohesion of schemes: for example, other parallelisms in the poem reinforce the initial correspondence of "This bread . . . This wine . . . ," by setting up semantically analogous equivalences: "Laid the crops low," "broke the grape's joy" (5); "My wine you drink, my bread you snap" (15); etc. If a single scheme extends over the whole text, it can itself be regarded as a form of cohesion. Since it is unlikely that absolute uniformity will be preserved in any sequential aspect of a poem, this type of scheme is to be distinguished from cohesion as discussed earlier only by the *degree* of regularity of a certain pattern running through the text. It is ultimately a matter of subjective judgment whether we choose to regard such a pattern as an example of schematic foregrounding—that is, whether the regularity seems remarkable enough to constitute a definite departure from the normal functions of language. The verse structure of a poem is a special case of an extended scheme. Space forbids an analysis of this interesting and complex aspect of the poem. I will only observe that the half-line is an important prosodic unit, and that the final line of each stanza is distinguished from the others by a special metrical pattern.

Further extended foregrounding is observed in the phonology of words: the phonemic congruity of "wind," "wine," "vine," "veins"; and the striking predominance of monosyllabic words in the text as a whole. Of the hundred words in the poem, only five have more than one syllable. This is largely owing to the poet's almost exclusive choice of monosyllabic nouns and verbs. In such words the "closed syllable" structure (consonant cluster + vowel + consonant cluster) is prevalent, whereas in polysyllables the "open syllable" structure (with only one consonant or consonant cluster) is the more usual. A high frequency of monosyllables therefore tends to go with a high density of consonants—another noted characteristic of this text. We can compare in this respect the syllabic structure of line 3 (/plʌndʒd ɪn ɪts frut/: CCVCCC VC VCC CCVC) with that of the word /dɛsəleɾʃ(ə)n/ (13) (CVCVCVC[V]C). Both have four syllables; the one has 11 consonants, the other only 5. The difference between them, in terms of ease and speed of articulation, is considerable; and it is intuitively noted in the quickening of rhythm at the point where the polysyllable occurs. After the vowel, in most monosyllabic nouns and verbs, there is a voiceless plosive consonant (/p/, /t/ or /k/) or a voiced plosive /d/ ("bread," "wind," "pulled"). This foregrounding of particular consonants, together with the overall consonantal foregrounding, builds a characteristic phonological "texture" which strikes the ear as austere and unresonant.

The different types of schematic pattern in the poem are frequently coincident. Formal parallelisms in every case coincide in extent with prosodic units. In several instances, the operative prosodic unit is the hemistich: the second hemistich repeats both the phonological and the grammatical pattern contained in the first. Further, none of the parallelisms have more than two phases or elements. This is by no means a necessary restriction, but it matches other paired features in the poem: the division of the verse line into hemistiches, and the coupling by coordination of *oat* and *grape* (13), and *root* and *sap* (14): structures which while scarcely meriting the name "parallelism" contribute to the general foregrounding of duality. In fact, both phonologically and grammatically, the poem is almost entirely divisible into binary segments.

I have dealt with what I consider to be the principal dimensions on which a linguistic analysis of this poem (or any poem) might proceed, and have exemplified some of the features of each dimension. Such features are, in the linguistic sense, part of the "meaning" of the poem: they are matters of linguistic choice, and can be described in terms of the categories of the language. But in a broader sense, "meaning" is "whatever is communicated to this or that reader": it includes the factor of interpretation. If the task of linguistic exegesis is to describe the text, that of critical exegesis is, from one point of view, to explore and evaluate possible interpretations of the text.

The distinction I make between the text and its interpretation certainly has nothing to do with the familiar dichotomy between "form" and "meaning"; indeed, it has already been made clear that the former includes all that would be traditionally accounted "meaning" in a non-literary text. Instead, the line is drawn between that which the reader is given, and that which he supplies in order to make what he is given fully meaningful. For the purpose of ordinary linguistic communication, it is justifiable to define "intelligibility" as conformity to the linguistic code. A foregrounded feature, as an infringement of the code, is by this standard "unintelligible"—indeed, it can be a positive disruption of the normal communicative process. From the linguistic point of view, literary interpretation can be seen as a negative process: a coming to terms with what would otherwise have to be dismissed as an unmotivated aberration—a linguistic "mistake." Again the simplest illustration is metaphor. An invented metaphor (as distinct from a "dead" metaphor which has become accepted in the language) is unintelligible in the above sense, and communicates only to those who perceive some kind of compensatory connection outside language. To say that the connection is outside language is not to exclude the importance of linguistic context—that is, relations of cohesion—in providing interpretative clues. For example, "the summer blood Knocked in the flesh that decked the vine" (6–7) scarcely admits of any interpretation in isolation. But the words "flesh" and "vine" here look back to "wine," "tree" and "fruit" in stanza 1, and forward to "flesh" and "blood" in stanza 3. What of the interpretation of schematic figures? The parallelism "Man in the day or wind at night" (4) sets up implications of equivalence between "man" and "wind" on the one hand and "day" and "night" on the other. The latter two words have an obvious referential connection; the former apparently have none. Interpretation here consists in finding some plausible sense in which "man" and "wind" are equivalent. We are thus invited to think of the foregrounded aspects of a poem as so many question marks, to which the reader, as interpreter, consciously or unconsciously attempts to find answers. The interpretation of the whole poem is built up from a consistency in the interpretation of individual features.

But there is another aspect of a poem which requires interpretation: its implication of context. Normal discourse operates within a describable communicative situation, from which an important part of its linguistic meaning derives. In literature, it is usually true to say that such contextual information is largely irrelevant. Instead, we have to construct a context by inference from the text itself, by asking such questions as "Who are the 'I' and the 'you' of the poem, and in what circumstances are they communicating?" Obviously these questions relate to the distinction between fiction and actuality. But it is not suggested that the reader is obliged to supply a fictional context: the option of fiction and non-fiction is left open. The reader may decide to interpret "I" and "you" as author and reader respectively, as other "real" people, or as fictional creations.

This choice is indeed open in the present poem: according to one interpretation, it is an allegory of poetic creation, and "I" and "you" are actually "I who am writing this poem" (Dylan Thomas himself) and "you who are reading it." But this in turn presupposes another interpretation, in which "I" stands for Christ and "you" for those who partake in the Lord's Supper. This transferred situation is suggested at the very beginning, in the collocation of "bread" and "wine." Taking it as a starting point, I shall follow its implications through the text, pointing out how it may be used to explain some of the foregrounded features. The Last Supper carries with it a mystical or symbolic identification of "bread" with "flesh" and "wine" with "blood." This association, which is upheld by grammatical parallelism throughout, has a twofold implication: (a) that vegetable growth is invested with the characteristic of animal life (and, in the context of Christ's sacrifice of his own flesh and blood, of humanity): thus the "vine" is "decked" with "flesh" (7); the "grape" is capable of "joy" (5); the "oat" is "merry" (9); (b) that the human animal takes on inanimate characteristics: "man" is represented as an impersonal, destructive force on a par with "wind" (4). The basic argument seems to run as follows: "Christ (the speaker) offers bread and wine, which are the result of the destruction of life in nature (1–5). In this destruction, man collaborates with natural forces (the wind, 4); but whereas natural forces (sun and wind) both

destroy (4,5) and sustain life (5–9), man alone is wholly destructive; he even, in a manner of speaking, destroys the sun and wind
(10), by interfering with the normal course of nature." The last
stanza draws on a further element of symbolism. Christ, in the
Last Supper, makes a sacrifice of Himself; it is His flesh and
blood that provides the meal. The "you" of line 11 might
initially be taken merely as table-companions: those sharing in
the meal. But in line 15, it is clear that they are not so much
feeding *with* the Speaker, as feeding *on* Him.

This account illustrates the cumulative nature of the interpretative process. One enigmatic feature provides the clue to a
succeeding one, which in turn strengthens the preceding interpretation. In the final line, this total interpretation is resolved on
what could without apology be termed its "logical conclusion":
"Man destroys life; so man destroys life in man." The compression
of signification in this last line is achieved partly by intensity of
foregrounding: by the rhyme of "snap" with "sap"; by the collocation of "bread" with "snap" (in contrast with "break" in line 1);
and by the deviant order of clause elements, object + subject +
verb. By such detailed observations as these it is possible to see
a basis in linguistic observables for those most elusive of critical
concepts: climax, resolution, artistic unity.

I have presented only one possible level of interpretation, and
a very partial one at that. The whole notion of "interpretation" is
bound to that of ambiguity and indeterminacy of meaning.
When ambiguity arises in poetry, in contrast to other kinds of
discourse, we generally give the writer the benefit of the doubt,
and take it to be intentional. Intentional ambiguity can only be
understood in one way: by supposing that the poet intends a
peaceful coexistence of alternative meanings. There are at least
two examples in this text of the type of grammatical ambiguity
that is liable to occur in non-literary language: "plunged" (3;
finite verb or past participle?) and "you let" (11; a complete
clause, or part of a clause running into the next line?). But in this
discussion I have touched on much more important sources of indeterminacy of meaning: foregrounding, and implication of context—both of which can only be rendered "intelligible" by an act
of the imagination. Further, foregrounding is a relative concept:
there are degrees of deviation, and in most cases there are no
absolute grounds for regarding feature A as normal and feature B

as foregrounded. So there is room for disagreement on what aspects of a poem *require* interpretation.

Finally, some foregrounded features may not be readily interpretable. For example, why "plunged" in line 3; why "knocked" in line 7? We have the option of being content to regard them as unintelligible; of explaining them in a non-constructive way (e.g., by saying that this sort of collocative clash is a worthless stylistic trick of Thomas's earlier poetry); or of attempting to "stretch" our interpretation of the poem to give them communicative value. Only the last course satisfies Tindall,[7] who in his commentary explains "plunged" and "knocked" as sexual references. Whether or not this is regarded as taking interpretation too far, it illustrates another variable entering into critical explication: the choice of whether to entertain a dubious interpretation, or to let obscurities remain obscurities.

NOTES

1. See J. R. Firth, *Papers in Linguistics 1934–51* (London, 1957), especially pp. 32–33 and 190–215.

2. Notably I. A. Richards and "new critics" influenced by him. Cf. C. K. Ogden and I. A. Richards, *The Meaning of Meaning* (London, 1923), pp. 149–150, 158–159.

3. See M. A. K. Halliday, "The Linguistic Study of Literary Texts," *Proceedings of the IXth International Congress of Linguists,* ed. Horace G. Lunt (The Hague, 1964), pp. 303–305.

4. The stylistic importance of deviation is discussed by C. F. Voegelin in *Style in Language,* ed. Thomas A. Sebeok (Cambridge, Mass., 1960), p. 58. In "Linguistics and the Figures of Rhetoric," in *Essays on Style and Language,* ed. Roger Fowler (London, 1966), I suggest how "deviant" and "normal" can be given an exact linguistic significance.

5. I refer to the theory of aesthetics and language expounded in *A Prague School Reader on Esthetics, Literary Structure and Style,* trans. Paul L. Garvin (Washington, 1964). For the concept of "foregrounding," see esp. J. Mukařovský, "Standard Language and Poetic Language," p. 23 [reprinted in this volume].

6. For varying treatments of this special aspect of poetic language, see Roman Jakobson, "Linguistics and Poetics," in *Style in Language,* pp. 350–377, especially pp. 358–359; and Samuel R. Levin, *Linguistic Structures in Poetry* (The Hague, 1962), pp. 30 ff.

7. William York Tindall, *A Reader's Guide to Dylan Thomas* (London, 1962), p. 97.

8. TAKING A POEM
TO PIECES[1]

J. McH. Sinclair

In "Taking a Poem to Pieces," J. McH. Sinclair shows how
linguistic theory—in this case, the neo-Firthian linguistics of
the "London School"—can contribute new facts and new ways
of examining facts to the explication of poems. His essay thus
is an exercise in the uses of linguistics for literary *study* rather
than for literary *criticism*. Professor Sinclair bases his analysis
of Philip Larkin's "First Sight" upon the distinction between
free (grammatically independent) and bound (grammatically
dependent) clauses. He uses the term *arrest* to describe a sentence
of poetic language in which an expected free clause (or comple-
tion of a free clause) is delayed by one or more bound clauses.
This distinction lays the groundwork for analysis of different
levels of *linguistic* structure (clause and word-group) in the poem's
language and their relation to levels of *poetic* structure (lines
and stanzas) in the poem itself. J. McH. Sinclair is professor of
English language at the University of Birmingham in England.

In recent years a number of linguists[2] have attempted to
describe linguistic features as they occur in literary texts, hoping
that their descriptions might help a reader to understand and
appreciate the text. I have chosen a short, recent, lyric poem.
It contains no magnetic peculiarities of language; in fact most
critics, I imagine, would ignore the language altogether. My
hypothesis is that the grammatical and other patterns are giving
meaning in a more complex and tightly packed way than we
expect from our familiarity with traditional methods of describing language. Modern methods of linguistic analysis, based on

J. McH. Sinclair, "Taking a Poem to Pieces," reprinted from *Essays on
Style and Language,* ed. Roger Fowler, pp. 68–81. New York: Humanities
Press Inc., 1966; London: Routledge and Kegan Paul, 1966.

more comprehensive and detailed theories of language, can at least tackle the problem of describing literature. In this paper the accent will be on grammar; there is little to say about the vocabulary of such a short text when we have no proper description of English vocabulary patterns to use as a basis; the phonology and orthography (the study of the sound- and letter-sequences and combinations) are also largely ignored—with reluctance—for reasons of space and simplicity.

FIRST SIGHT

Lambs that learn to walk in snow
When their bleating clouds the air
Meet a vast unwelcome, know
Nothing but a sunless glare.
5   Newly stumbling to and fro
All they find, outside the fold,
Is a wretched width of cold.

As they wait beside the ewe,
Her fleeces wetly caked, there lies
10 Hidden round them, waiting too,
Earth's immeasurable surprise.
They could not grasp it if they knew,
What so soon will wake and grow
Utterly unlike the snow.*

Philip Larkin

The only phonological units which we shall need are the stanza and the line, and the first question is how congruent are the grammatical and metrical units here? This question splits down into two: what are the relative sizes of the units, and how do they fit together? Sentences are on average three and a half lines, half a stanza long. (Each line has seven syllables except line 9 and 12, and each stanza has seven lines.) Sentences are all about the same length, either three or four lines long. There is complete congruence, then, between line, sentence and stanza, since each sentence-stop ends a line, each stanza-end ends a sentence, and sentences are as nearly uniform in length as is possible. So we are given a framework of grammar and meter where there is an exceptionally good fit; there are no tag ends of sentences at the ends of stanzas, and there is no great discrepancy in the length of sentences.

Moving on to the structure of the sentences, we recognize two elements, in the primary analysis; what we call a *free* clause and what we call a *bound* clause.[3] *They could not grasp it* is a typical free clause, and *when their bleating clouds the air* or *newly stumbling to and fro* are bound clauses. No distinction is made at this depth of detail between clauses containing a finite or a non-finite verb, since their operation in the structure of sentences is almost identical. Using just this one distinction, we can plot the occurrence of these clauses relative to each other and relative to the lines in the poem. (See Table 1, p. 132.)

It will be seen that no account has been taken of two clauses in the poem; in the first line, *that learn to walk in snow* and in the sixth, *they find.* These clauses are not operating in sentence structure at all; instead they are forming part of the structure of what we are going to call *nominal groups.* If they operated directly in sentence structure then *all, outside the fold, is a wretched width of cold* would be isolated as a complete clause. There is nothing in the shape of this word-sequence to prohibit it standing as a clause, but it is not the one in the poem. Clauses which do not form discrete elements of the structure of sentences are called *rank-shifted* clauses.

In everyday English, in the mass of sentences which contain α [free] and β [bound] the sequence $\alpha\beta$ is most common. Discontinuity, i.e. $\alpha[\beta]$ is rarer, and so is the sequence $\beta\alpha$. The last sentence in the poem is a good example of the $\alpha\beta$ type.

It is the only one. The other three have discontinuous α, $\beta\alpha$ sequence, and both, in that order. But we can refine the idea of discontinuity a little with reference to a particular text like this one. As we read along the lines, we can say at certain points that we confidently expect something else to finish off a structure. If at the bottom of a page one reads *He put* one expects on the next page to read about not only something to put but somewhere to put it. If one reads *He played* one is a lot less certain what will follow; in fact, if it was not contrary to normal printers' practice we would not be surprised if the next page started with a period.

TABLE I

Sentence Structure

a and β are elements of sentence structure expounded by free and bound clauses respectively. To account for interruptions, the symbols $a-$ and $\beta-$ in column 3 indicate that a clause is interrupted by a line-ending or another clause, and $(-a)$ and $(-\beta)$ indicate the conclusion of an interrupted clause. In column 4 is given the structure of the four sentences, with square brackets surrounding the symbol for a clause which occurs inside the one whose symbol precedes the bracket.

Exponents of "a"	Line No.	Sentence structure/ line	Exponents of "β"	Sentence structure
Lambs that learn to walk in snow	1	$a-$		
	2	β	When their bleating clouds the air	$a[\beta]a$
Meet a vast unwel- come, know	3	$(-a)a-$		
Nothing but a sunless glare.	4	$(-a)$		
	5	β	Newly stumbling to and fro	
All they find, outside the fold,	6	$a-$		βa
Is a wretched width of cold.	7	$(-a)$		
	8	β	As they wait beside the ewe,	
there lies	9	$\beta a-$	Her fleeces wetly caked,	
	10	$\beta\beta$	Hidden round them, waiting too,	$\beta a[\beta\beta]$
Earth's immeasurable surprise.	11	$(-a)$		
They could not grasp it	12	$a\beta$	if they knew,	
	13	$\beta-$	What so soon will wake and grow	$a\beta\beta$
	14	$(-\beta)$	Utterly unlike the snow.	

Now the effect which we can presume an intruding element to have will depend in any instance on the strength of the current expectations. It is clear that strong expectations have been set up in both the cases of discontinuous clauses here: *lambs that learn to walk in snow* . . . and *there lies*. . . . It is interesting, too, that both occurrences of the item *wait* are in bound clauses which either precede or interrupt free ones. Here there is a serious difficulty in terminology. A term is needed to indicate a sentence in which the onset of a predictable α is delayed or in which its progress is interrupted. Unfortunately, whatever term is coined is liable to be construed as a contextually meaningful label. I want to use the term *arrest* for this type of structure, without wishing to suggest that *any* occurrence of this structure produces an "effect" of arrestment. Pseudo-linguistic literature is already too full of naive correlations between a noise or a structure and explicit meanings. I wish my terms to carry only as much contextual meaning as terms like *finite, predicate*. With this in mind, let us say that the first three sentences in the poem are *arrested,* whereas the last one is not.

In sentence 1, then (structure $\alpha[\beta]\alpha$), the progress of the first α is interrupted by the β. Sentence 2 ($\beta\alpha$) by beginning with β, delays the onset of the α. Both these exponents of arrest appear in sentence 3 ($\beta\alpha[\beta\beta]$) where the solitary α has its onset delayed and its progress interrupted.

Next we must consider the structure of the clauses in this poem. We recognize four primary elements of clause structure, the subject (S), predicator (P), complement (C) and adjunct (A). Every part of every clause must be ascribed to one or other of these four elements (the exceptions are irrelevant to our present purpose). The subject and complement(s) are usually nominal groups, the predicator a verbal group, and adjuncts are adverbial groups. Let us plot the structure of clauses in much the same way as we did the structure of sentences. In this diagram the slanting line (/) denotes the place where an intruding clause appears and the vertical line (|) denotes where a line boundary occurs. The rankshifted clauses in both cases are part of the subject of another clause. The reader is referred to Table II, p. 134.

As with the sentences, let us see how well the clauses fit the lines. Here there is a clear difference between free and bound clauses. Though simple in structure, all the free clauses except the last have a line boundary in the middle, and in the last bound one there is a line boundary.

What is the meaning of a line boundary? [4] Clearly its meaning depends upon its relation to the surrounding grammar. If it

TABLE II

Clause Structure

Exponent	Free	Bound	Rank-shifted
Lambs that learn to walk in snow /| meet a vast unwelcome	S/|PC		
that learn to walk in snow			SPA
When their bleating clouds the air		ASPC	
know | Nothing but a sunless glare.	P|C		
Newly stumbling to and fro		APA	
All they find outside the fold | Is a wretched width of cold.	SA|PC		
they find			SP
As they wait beside the ewe		ASPA	
Her fleeces wetly caked		SAP	
There lies /| Earth's immeasurable surprise.	SP/|C		
Hidden round them,		PA	
waiting too		PA	
They could not grasp it	SPC		
if they knew,		ASP	
What so soon will wake and grow | Utterly unlike the snow.		SAP|A	

occurs between sentences (as at the end of lines 4 and 11) it is *congruent* with the grammar, and its meaning is of reinforcement, or the like. If it occurs between clauses or at any lower rank, then its meaning is dependent on the nature of the predictions that have been set up. Thus a line boundary occurring between α and β in most cases simply reinforces, emphasizes the structural boundary. It adds, perhaps, a slight element of surprise to the occurrence of the β. On the other hand a line boundary occurring between β and α will reinforce the prediction of the β, will reinforce the *arrest* that was mentioned above.

A line boundary within a clause will follow the same pattern, according to the amount of prediction that precedes it. Table III shows the line boundaries in this poem classified by

(*a*) Grammatical rank: sentence, clause and group;

(*b*) Type: i.e., *arresting* (when predictions have been set up),
            releasing (where there are no remaining *grammatical* predictions).

·

TABLE III

Line Boundaries (including stanza boundary)

Line ref.	Rank	Between Structures	Arrest/Release
4	Sentence	Sentence/sentence	
7	Sentence	Sentence/sentence	
11	Sentence	Sentence/sentence	
2	Clause	β/α	Arrest
5	Clause	β/α	Arrest
8	Clause	β/α	Arrest
10	Clause	β/α	Arrest
12	Clause	β/β	Release
1	Group	S/P	Arrest
3	Group	P/C	Arrest
6	Group	A/P	Arrest
9	Group	P/C	Arrest
13	Group	P/A	Release

It is clear from Tables II and III that in the first three sentences the free clauses are all arrested, whereas in the last sentence the free clause is neutral and a bound one is released. The only reason we have to expect the last line in the poem is a metrical one. Again the last sentence is quite different from the others.

One common feature of English grammar is not represented in the clause or sentence structure of this poem. This is *linkage,* words like *and, but, however, in fact* which occur so often in conversation and writing. In this poem, each sentence, and each free or bound clause, stands rather separate. The only examples of such words, the *but* of line 4 and *and* of line 13, link items inside clauses, and do not affect the isolation of clauses and sentences.

All the free clauses are affirmative. No interrogatives, exclamations, imperatives. Also, all free clauses are transitive, and only one bound clause is (line 2). So transitivity is here carried almost entirely by the free clauses. Fennellosa may cry ecstatically[5] but this fact in grammar is no more crucial of itself than any other. The sequence of the elements of clause structure is pretty much what would be expected in everyday English. Unusual sequences of elements of clause structure form a familiar set of devices in the language of poetry, but in this poem it must be noted that the adjuncts scarcely ever occur in other than the commonest position for them. *Newly* (line 5) and *outside the fold* (6) are slightly unusual and are discussed further below; *so soon* (line 13) is perhaps slightly in advance of its commonest position.

Two points must be made, in greater detail, in regard to the punctuation of adjuncts.

(*a*) Line 6, *outside the fold*. Note the comma preceding this adjunct. Without it one would naturally tend to regard *outside the fold* as part of the rankshifted clause and analyze as follows:

$$S \qquad\qquad P \qquad\qquad C$$
all   they   find   outside   the   fold/is/a   wretched
width of cold.

The element *S* would be uttered with one intonation contour with its most prominent point on the last syllable, *fold*. But because of the comma, we analyze

$$S \qquad\qquad A \qquad P \qquad\qquad C$$
all they find/outside the fold/is/a wretched width
of cold

and there are now two separate intonation contours, a falling one, most prominent on *find,* and a slightly rising one, most prominent on *fold*.

The difference in meaning is slight, here, between presence or absence of the comma. A point is made about the lambs actually going outside the fold. Compare the difference using the verb *see*.

> all they see outside the fold, is a wretched width
> of cold.
> all they see, outside the fold, is a wretched width
> of cold.

Since the adjunct, in part of the surrounding non-rankshifted clause, is out of position, the total contrast is similar to the contrast between

> John, outside the office, found it nice.

and

> John found it nice outside the office.

(b) Line 13. There is no comma after *grow,* but there is a line boundary, which has something of a parallel effect, of separating one piece of language from another. Here the difference in meaning is considerable. Compare

> I want him to grow like me (i.e. assuming he will grow, specifying direction)
> I want him to grow, like me (i.e. specifying growth and drawing a parallel)

Because the text has an ambiguous structure at this point, the adjunct "utterly unlike the snow" is, in my interpretation, made to do double duty. A rough paraphrase might run thus:

> The snow will not grow but something else will, and when it does it will grow to look utterly unlike the snow.

These are, of course, not the only points of punctuation. For example, some readers may disagree with the analysis of lines 9–10, on the grounds that *lies hidden* is a unit which cannot be divided by a clause boundary; again the absence of a comma supports this, whereas the occurrence of a line-end suggests the division. The poet has the advantage here also of a combination of the alternative meanings.

We may now consider structure at the next rank below clause, the *group,* the unit out of which clauses are made. It may consist of one or more words, and groups have a direct relation to elements of clause structure. There are three kinds of group, as we have already noted, *nominal, verbal* and *adverbial* (see Table IV). Verbal groups are the simplest kind in this text, since nearly all the verbal groups are single-word, present-tense items. This is only remarkable when one thinks of the enormous variety of choices available, e.g., *might have come, could have been coming, wasn't going to come, came sailing, came to talk, oughtn't to have been going to be avoiding coming to see.* With such a restricted selection, the variations are liable to be quite striking, and as one might expect they distinguish sentence 4 from the others. None of the verbs in this sentence are "simple present" items. Two contain *modal verbs,* i.e. *could* and *will;* one of these is negative and the other "double-headed"—*wake and grow.* The third is a "simple past" item in a bound clause. The only other complication in verbal groups is the *learn to walk* in line 1.

TABLE IV

Groups

Nominal	Verbal	Adverbial
Lambs that learn to walk in snow	learn to walk	in snow
that snow	---	When
their bleating the air	clouds	
a vast unwelcome	Meet know	
Nothing but a sunless glare.		
	stumbling	Newly to and fro
All they find the fold	find	outside the fold
they	---	
a wretched width of cold	Is	
cold		
they the ewe	wait	As beside the ewe
Her fleeces there	caked lies	wetly
them	Hidden waiting	round them too
Earth's immeasurable surprise.		
They it they	could not grasp knew	if
What	will wake and grow	so soon
the snow		Utterly unlike the snow

The adverbial groups are not very prominent. The three main kinds of adverbial group are the grammatical binding groups like *when, if,* the adverbs like *newly* and *so soon,* and the prepositional groups like *in snow.* In this poem the main point again is their simplicity. Of the second and third types, there is no distinction made in the poem that is not covered by facts already adduced and not worth repeating. It is useful, though, to note that free clauses are almost devoid of adjuncts. *Outside the fold,* which has already been discussed, is the only one. In contrast, and excluding *when, as* and *if,* there are eight adjuncts in bound clauses. So the free clauses have complements but not adjuncts, and the bound ones adjuncts but not complements.

The selection of *newly* deserves a note. Although an adverb, *newly* is not one that is commonly found as an exponent of A in clause structure. Its commonest place is as a verbal modifier when that verb is itself a nominal modifier; as in *a newly advertised product, a newly made dress.* I suppose that the average reader notes that there is something a little odd about the line, but has no difficulty, of course, in understanding it.

Before passing on to the nominal group, which has the most variety at this rank, let us note a pattern in the relation between group and line. The first line is one element of clause structure (though containing a rankshifted clause), the fourth is also, and the seventh, apart from the unstressed initial syllable. Line 11 is one group, and so is line 14. So the last line in each sentence contains but one element of clause structure: although the average length of an element is a third of a line.

Although the nominal groups are interesting, they are not nearly as complex as we are accustomed to meeting with quite frequently in normal conversation. Here is a table of them:

TABLE V

Nominal Group Structure

In subject		In complement		Rankshifted	
hq	(lambs that learn to walk in snow)	dh	(the air)	h	(snow)
h	(that)	deh	(a vast unwelcome)		
dh	(their bleating)	h + deh	(nothing but a sunless glare)	dh	(the fold)
hq	(all they find)	dehq	(a wretched width of cold)	h	(cold)
h	(they)	deh	(earth's immeasurable surprise)	dh	(the ewe)
h	(they)				
dh	(her fleeces)	h	(it)	h	(earth)
				dh	(the snow)
h	(they)				
h	(they)				
h	(what)				

h = headword, around which the rest pivots

d = deictic, a word like *the*, *a*, *which*, coming at the beginning of the group

e = an adjective

q = anything which comes after the headword (in this poem the only exponents of q are rankshifted clauses—see "subject" column—and a prepositional group—see "complement" column)

There are no numerals, and no nouns occurring pre-head (like *stone* in *stone wall*). There is never more than one adjective, and not many of those, and only in complements. Subjects are simplest; six out of the ten of them are single pronouns, and the others are the two *hq* structures and two *dh*, the exponent of *d* being a possessive deictic. Those two *dh* groups are subjects in bound clauses.

Rankshifted nominal groups are those which occur as elements in the structure of other nominal groups, or as the "objects" of prepositions. In this poem they are again simple in structure, and regularly consist of a single lexical item, with or without a non-possessive deictic.

The complements are most complex. The single *dh* structure is complement to the only transitive bound clause, and the single *h* structure is, as one might expect, in the last sentence. This leaves us with the four complements involving adjectives, and is an interesting place to pause for a moment because these four complements also contain most of the unusual vocabulary juxta-positions to be found in the poem. *Vast unwelcome* is very un-usual, so also *a wretched width of cold, width* being the odd man out. *Sunless glare* is less striking, perhaps because *sun* and *glare* are common enough together; *immeasurable surprise* is unusual particularly with *Earth's* in front. Any two of the three words might pass unnoticed, but these three in this particular grammati-cal arrangement look very odd indeed.

The paucity of lexical comment reflects the fact that objective description of vocabulary patterns is still impossible. It happens that our present text does not contain many strong lexical pat-terns; apart from those mentioned above, perhaps *bleating clouds* in line 2 is the only one that invites attention.

Parallel to the note on *newly,* above, should be a note on *unwelcome.* This word is commonly an adjective, and one of the features of an adjective is that it is incapable of being headword in a group modified by *a, an.* Here an unusual effect is created by the occurrence of just such a nominal group, forcing us to accept *unwelcome* as a noun.[6] The prefix perhaps regains some of the meaning it could have in Old English.

The structure of the words in this poem brings out a pattern which is worthy of tentative consideration. If we study the *affixes,* it is fairly easy to divide the *inflectional* (e.g., lamb*s*, stumbl*ing*, cloud*s*, lie*s*, fleece*s*) from the others. Of the others, there are a few that mark a different word-class from the same item without the affix, e.g., *wetly, newly, utterly, width.* Lastly there is a small group where the affix drastically affects the meaning of the word: *un*welcome, sun*less*, *im*measurable, *un*like. There is a similarity about these four, so that they may be labeled *reversing affixes,* though here the classification is less rigorous than before. One way or another, these affixes reverse the meaning of the rest of the word of which they form a part. What can we say about the contribution of such word structure in poetry, and in this poem? In poetry it is possible both to have one's cake and eat it, rather more so than in other varieties of a language. But when, for example, a trade union official said recently: "We are not yet talking about strike action," he contrived to be ominous. The paradox of a sentence like "I will never mention the name of John Smith" has a meaning which can be used in poetry. We could describe it as bipartite: in the present case

(a) A statement about the speaker's future intentions. At least one possibility is cut out. By knowing something of what the speaker is *not* going to do, we also know a little about what he *is* going to do. Very little, very vaguely, but by no means negligible.

(b) The accomplishment of the utterance, including the mention of John Smith's name. The physical fact of the utterance can never be ignored in literary writing.

According to the same argument, the last line of this poem contrives to begin to say something about the appearance of whatever is about to wake and grow, and it also manages to mention the snow. The importance of the latter half of the meaning is borne out by the rarity, in love poetry, of lines like:

Her smile was not in the least like the grin of a decomposing vam-
    pire

however notionally accurate they may be.

Three out of the four complex nominal groups in this poem, then, show a reversing affix. On both grammatical and lexical grounds we have shown that these places are important. The fourth,

a wretched width of cold [7]

contents itself with a word-class affix and unusual lexis and grammar.

The last line in the poem also shows this feature of reversal, and the structure of the line above it shows another device, common enough in poetry, which gives the reader only a vague meaning. It is the traditional "brush-off" structure. "Something I'd prefer not to talk about" "Nothing you won't know all about in time" "What doesn't concern you . . ."

The grammar has led us briefly into lexical and contextual matters, but only sporadically. There is still a great deal unsaid about the structure of this little poem, and even what has been said suffers by being in the nature of commentary. Grammar deals with contrasts, multiple choices from a great many systems simultaneously, and the meaning of a grammatical statement can only be fully elicited with reference to the total grammatical description. Nevertheless, the exercise shows how some aspects of the meaning of the poem can be described quite independently of evaluation.

NOTES

1. This selection is a revised version of a paper delivered to the Nottingham University Linguistics Society in January 1964.

2. For example, M. A. K. Halliday, "The Linguistic Analysis of Literary Texts," *Proceedings of the IXth International Congress of Linguists* (The Hague, 1964); A. A. Hill, "An Analysis of *The Windhover*: An Experiment in Structural Method," *PMLA*, LXX (1955); S. R. Levin, *Linguistic Structures in Poetry* (The Hague, 1962).

3. This article is not a suitable place for an exposition of the grammar which I am using. I hope the terms, supported by the examples, will be self-explanatory. M. A. K. Halliday of University College London originated the grammatical categories which are used here. For more detailed information the reader is referred to his "Categories of the Theory of Grammar," *Word*, XVII (1961), 241–292.

4. Some phonological aspects of arrest and release are treated in detail in Roger Fowler's " 'Prose Rhythm' and Metre" [Selection 20].

5. See Davie, *Articulate Energy* (London, 1955), p. 35.

6. Compare *unfamiliar* in Larkin's poem "Next Please."

7. *Width* is usually uncountable; the only occurrence of it with a number marker that comes to mind is *a width of cloth, this material comes in three widths, madam.*

9.   STYLES AND STATISTICS

A Model T Style Machine

Walker Gibson

Walker Gibson's *Tough, Sweet, and Stuffy* uses some modern linguistics and rhetorical theory to isolate three typical American stylistic voices: the restrained he-man, the cute huckster, and the bureaucrat. In this selection he explains, tests, and operates a "style machine": a set of criteria based upon textural characteristics of English prose that will isolate these three voices. Both Professor Gibson's facts and his method commend themselves to the student interested in typologies of prose style. Walker Gibson is professor of English and director of freshman composition at the University of Massachusetts.

> *A recognition of the dual and complementary value of intuitive judgment of language use on the one hand, and the more objective techniques of description of language phenomena which modern linguistics makes available on the other, is necessary and indeed fundamental to this view of stylistic study.*

John Spencer and Michael Gregory
LINGUISTICS AND STYLE

Out of the various observations we have made about our three styles, is it possible—is it even proper—to construct a systematic grammar and rhetoric for each? No, possibly not. Nevertheless what follows is an effort to make a beginning in that direction. I offer here a kind of Style Machine, of a pre-Model T order, designed to measure the tone of a prose passage. It considers only a tiny fraction of the possibilities, it will

Walker Gibson, *Tough, Sweet, and Stuffy* (Indiana University Press, 1966), pp. 113–136.

not discriminate between good and bad writing, it is full of bugs. Much of its terminology is hopelessly square, derived from traditional grammar at least as much as from modern linguistics. But it will serve at least to summarize some of the distinctions setting Tough Talk apart from Sweet Talk and from Stuffy Talk, and it may furthermore suggest to somebody else a way of improving on this primitive beginning.

Let us first see where we have been. We have at hand about three thousand words of prose, approximately equally divided among the three styles. (We have also read several passages—Eliot, Howells, the *Times* and *Tribune,* Dickens—that we did not classify in any such category.) For Tough Talk, we have, once again, the following six items [analyzed in detail in earlier chapters of *Tough, Sweet, and Stuffy*]:

"Private World"—an introduction to a *Saturday Review* article on the teaching of reading. (Chapter 2)

"Frederic Henry"—the opening of *A Farewell to Arms.* (Chapter 3)

"Time"—the opening of a report on Birmingham from *Time.* (Chapter 4)

"Augie March"—the opening of *The Adventures of Augie March.* (Chapter 5)

"Jack Burden"—the opening of *All the King's Men.* (Chapter 5)

"Earl Horter"—the opening of *Love Among the Cannibals.* (Chapter 5)

For Sweet Talk, we have nine items:

"Unrequired Reading"—introduction to another *Saturday Review* article on the teaching of reading. (Chapter 2)

About a hundred words each from eight miscellaneous advertisements in current magazines. (Chapter 6)

Our collection of Stuffy Talk includes:

"Teaching Literature"—still another passage on the teaching of reading, from an educator's textbook. (Chapter 2)

"Smoking"—two passages from the 1964 Surgeon General's report on smoking and cancer. (Chapter 7)

"Revenue"—a passage from a ruling by the Internal Revenue Service. (Chapter 7)

"Admissions"—a passage from a college catalogue. (Chapter 7)

The classification of these passages into the three categories was made, in the first place, impressionistically. That is, it was a question simply as to whether our reading experience brought us into contact with a speaker or voice of the indicated type. The types of individuals we were looking for, to repeat, were defined briefly like this: (1) a hard fellow who has been around in a violent world and who pays us very little mind; (2) an affable fellow who is explicitly familiar with us and who knows just who we are; (3) a bloodless fellow who often speaks for an organization and not for himself, and who keeps his distance from us.

How are these impressions of personalities to be explained in terms of grammar and rhetoric—if they are?

Out of dozens of possibilities, I propose sixteen grammatical–rhetorical qualities as ways of isolating styles, of accounting for distinctions that we feel in the voices addressing us. Several of them we have already considered at some length. I put them in the form of questions.

A. QUESTIONS ABOUT WORD-SIZE

1. What is the proportion of monosyllables in the passage?
2. What is the proportion of words of more than two syllables?

B. QUESTIONS ABOUT SUBSTANTIVES

3. How many first- and second-person pronouns does the passage contain? How many imperatives are there ("*you* understood")?
4. Are the subjects of the finite verbs mostly neuter nouns, or do they refer to people?

C. QUESTIONS ABOUT VERBS

5. What is the proportion of finite verbs to total words?
6. What proportion of these finite verbs are forms of *to be*?
7. What proportion of these verbs are in the passive voice?

D. MODIFIERS

8. What proportion of the total words are true adjectives?
9. How many of these adjectives are themselves modified by adverbs?
10. What proportion of the total words are noun adjuncts?

E. SUBORDINATION

11. What is the average length of the subordinate ("included") clauses?
12. What proportion of the total passage is inside such clauses?
13. How frequently are subject and main verb separated by intervening subordinate structures? How long are these interruptions?

F. OTHER EFFECTS OF TONE

14. How frequent is the determiner *the*?
15. Are there any sentences without subjects, or without verbs, or both? Are there any contractions?
16. How many occurrences are there of these marks of punctuation: parentheses, italics, dashes, question marks, exclamation points?

I now consider each of these questions in detail, with some statistics from my samples.

A. QUESTIONS ABOUT WORD-SIZE

Answers to the questions in this section involve nothing fancier than a simple counting of syllables. Does the word contain one syllable only, or is it composed of three or more? This kind of distinction is commonplace in popular and commercial handbooks of style, to determine the "difficulty" of prose passages: Very Difficult, Easy and so on. . . . It is a useful statistic so far as it goes, but it does not go very far, for obviously a tone is not produced by word-size alone.

To decide what a syllable is, I have innocently trusted my own ear, while conceding that a strict count of morphemes would probably be more satisfactory. I doubt that the relative results would be very different, however.

It may be wondered why, since I am comparing word-size, I do not compare sentence-size as well. Surely we might expect the Tough Talker to use short sentences, the Sweet Talker even shorter sentences, the Stuffy Talker longer ones. To a degree all that is true, but I have nevertheless discarded the length of sentences as a crucial factor. The differences between the styles are surprisingly small, actually. As we have seen [in an earlier chapter], it is evidently possible to sound Stuffy in short sentences, just as one can sound Tough in longer sentences. Jack Burden, for instance, utters the longest sentence in the whole collection.

1. What is the proportion of monosyllables in the passage?

As we have indicated several times, and as common sense would suggest, the Tough Talker uses a high proportion of monosyllables, the Stuffy Talker uses a low proportion of them. For our samples, the facts are 78 percent for Tough Talk and 58 percent for Stuffy Talk. The extremes in each direction are Jack Burden at 86 percent and the official voice of "Admissions" at 50 percent. The adwriter's Sweet Talk . . . is *not* drastically simple, at least in this respect, the proportion of monosyllables falling exactly in between the two others, at 68 percent. For extreme intimacy of tone, in other words, you do not choose a ruthlessly spartan diction, but a more flexible vocabulary that permits a wide range.

2. What is the proportion of words of more than two syllables?

Here of course we have just the opposite gradation, with Tough Talk at 5 percent, Sweet Talk at 12 percent, Stuffy Talk at 26 percent. Extremes are Frederic Henry at 1 percent and the voice of the Revenue Service at 29 percent. These two people are only just speaking the same language!

Without exception all six of our Tough Talkers in the samples fall well under 10 percent in their use of words of more than two syllables; all four Stuffy Talkers are over 20 percent in this category. Most of the Sweet Talkers fall into a 10–19 percent bracket. . . .

B. QUESTIONS ABOUT SUBSTANTIVES

I consider here only the incidence of certain personal pronouns, and a single distinction with respect to the subjects of verbs. Obviously this is a vast area for further investigation. The abstract-concrete issue might be raised, though . . . the distinction is not simple. The question of derivation (Anglo-Saxon vs. Latin), which I have not faced at all, might be relevant here.

The relative frequency of all substantives in my samples seems to be about the same for all three styles, though of course other samples might prove otherwise. Tough and Sweet Talk, however, are far more generous with pronouns than Stuffy Talk is. The Stuffy Talker tends to repeat his nouns, in a legalistic way, rather than relying on pronouns, as if he didn't trust his reader to make the proper reference. The Stuffy Talker purports to be unquestionably clear at all times, at the expense of variety and grace. But the whole measurement of repetition must wait for someone with more arithmetical patience than I have.

3. How many first- and second-person pronouns does the passage contain? How many imperatives ("you understood")?

The Tough Talker, we argued, is a character who, for all his implied intimacy with the assumed reader, often reveals himself to be more concerned with his own attitudes and feelings. The Sweet Talker, on the other hand, makes explicit gestures to the reader, calling him by name (*you*). The Stuffy Talker mentions neither himself nor his reader. Putting it too baldly . . . Tough Talk tends to be I-Talk, Sweet Talk tends to be You-Talk, Stuffy Talk tends to be It-Talk. My figures don't quite justify that statement, but let it stand. Of the 30 first-person pronouns in our samples, 16 are in Tough Talk, 12 in Sweet Talk, 2 in Stuffy Talk. There are 63 instances of the word *you:* 21 in Tough Talk, 42 in Sweet Talk, none at all in Stuffy Talk. In addition there are 8 instances of imperative verbs in Sweet Talk, with the subject *you* "understood." [1]

The word *I* excludes the reader, the word *you* includes him. The word *we* can work either way: it may mean "those people and I, but not you, reader," or it may mean "everybody, including you and me," or it may mean, *à deux*, "you and I, dear reader." I take it that the last meaning ought to be characteristic of Sweet Talk, even though I find no examples in my collection. In fact the only use of the first-person-plural pronoun to include the reader at all occurs in Earl Horter.

4. Are the subjects of the finite verbs mostly neuter nouns, or are they nouns referring to people?

The distinctions here depend to some extent, of course, on what the speaker is talking about: it is predictable that a first-person-singular narrator in a novel should talk about people while the Internal Revenue Service should be concerned with facts and figures. But style matters too, as we can appreciate by returning once more to those first three passages of Chapter 2.* There we encountered three voices, each talking more or less about the same "thing," but each using a different style. (I ignore, for a moment, the fourth passage, Mr. Eliot's.) In those three passages two-thirds of the grammatical subjects in "Teaching Literature" (Stuffy) were neuter, two-thirds of the subjects in "Unrequired Reading" (Sweet) were human beings, and "Private World" (Tough) divided its subjects exactly evenly between neuter nouns and people. It simply makes a difference how you say what you say—for example, how you state a conclusion. You can say "I believe . . . ," or you can say "You will understand . . . ," or you can say "The facts demonstrate. . . ." By such choices you create your voice.

The totals in all my samples are as follows: Tough Talk, 52 neuter subjects of finite verbs, 72 people; Sweet Talk, 45 neuters and 70 people; Stuffy Talk, 52 neuters and only 12 people. Two Tough Talkers and two ads (Henry, Earl Horter, Ads 7 and 8) are exceptional in using more neuter subjects than human beings. All Stuffy Talkers use at least two-thirds neuter nouns as their subjects. This concentration on the nonhuman in Stuffy Talk, as the doer of the action, contributes largely to [a] general air of no-personal-responsibility. . . .

C. QUESTIONS ABOUT VERBS

Under this heading I am considering finite verbs only—no participles, no gerunds, no infinitives. All these deserve atten-

* Reprinted at the end of this selection—Ed.

tion to see how Stuffy Talk compensates for its paucity of finite verbs. There is also work to be done, as indicated below, with auxiliaries and base verbs.

5. What is the proportion of finitive verbs to total words?

The distinction here is remarkably consistent through my samples. The Stuffy Talker uses far fewer finite verbs (6 percent of total words) than do the Sweet and the Tough Talker (both 11 percent). This is part of the general distinction that pervades these figures, between formal-written language and informal-conversational language. We mentioned [earlier] the classic Tough Talker's unwillingness to subordinate, an unwillingness that makes for simple sentence structures and a high proportion of finite verbs. The Stuffy Talker, on the other hand, qualifies his remarks with much subordination and modification, so that in officialese we find the verb followed by a whole series of constructions added to prevent misunderstanding. "Advice *has been requested* concerning the deductibility for Federal income tax purposes of research expenses, including traveling expenses, incurred by college and university professors in their capacity as educators." (One verb in a 29-word sentence.)

My figures are too tiny, but a word can be said in passing about base verbs—that is, uninflected verb forms used without any auxiliary. These are far more common in Sweet Talk than in either of the other two styles, partly because of Sweet Talk's fondness for the second person, including imperatives. "Wait till you taste these new dinners." Two base verbs in a 7-word sentence.

A note may also be added about the modal auxiliaries—may, might, can, could, would, should, must, and ought. These words express some kind of attitude (it has been called "emotional") toward the action that the verb names. Again Sweet Talk is well in the lead, though the figures are minute. In Tough Talk the characteristic verb form seems to be a simple inflection: this happened and that happened. Stuffy Talk, fond of elaborate qualification, takes more advantage of the subtleties offered by auxiliaries. But all this is guesswork needing to be tested.

6. What proportion of the finitive verbs are forms of to be?

Here I am not considering *to be* as an auxiliary. The Tough Talker in my samples is fonder of this verb than the others are; the figures are 36 percent against 25 percent for Sweet Talk and 17 percent for Stuffy Talk. I submit that this is part of the urge for naming mentioned [earlier], a liking for a particular sentence pattern of the "this-is-that" construction.[2] In some of its appearances, it can come close to omniscience, as in *Time*'s "The scenes in Birmingham were unforgettable." The six Tough Talkers are not very consistent about this, but I include the point for what it may be worth.

7. *What proportion of the finitive verbs are in the passive voice?*

There is no problem here. Stuffy Talkers use the passive voice, others do not. It is a sure-fire technique for avoiding personal responsibility for one's statements, and when the Revenue Service winds up for a decision, it does not say "we conclude . . ." but "it is held that. . . ." By whom?

Slightly over one-quarter (26 percent) of the finite verbs in my samples of Stuffy Talk are in the passive. The figure for Tough Talk is 4 percent and for Sweet Talk 2 percent. In all Stuffy Talkers except the marginal "Teaching Literature" the writers use a passive at least once in every six verbs.

D. QUESTIONS ABOUT MODIFICATION

This is another area I am unashamedly skimming. Phrases and clauses used as modifiers of various kinds are unmentioned. What, for instance, is the effect of a series of piled-up prepositional phrases? Are they always Stuffy? How does frequency of adverbs contribute to tone? Etc.

8. *What proportion of the total words are true adjectives?*

. . . One way to distinguish a "true" adjective is to ask whether it can be rendered in the comparative degree, either by inflection or the use of a function word. (*Fine, finer; interesting, more interesting.*) Or whether it can be translated into a sentence with this construction: The interesting story is very interesting. In these ways an adjective can be differentiated from a noun adjunct construction (like *income tax*). One cannot say (and call it English) "The income tax is very income," nor can one say "the tax is more income," "the tax is incomer."

Modification . . . is the bread-and-butter of the adman, and we find accordingly 11 percent of the total wordage in Sweet Talk composed of adjectives as defined above. The Stuffy Talkers are not far behind, at 8 percent. Adjectives in Tough Talk come to 6 percent. All six Tough Talkers are sparing with adjectives, less than one word out of ten in each passage being an adjective as here defined. Almost all the Sweet Talkers use adjectives at least once out of every ten words, and some of them plaster their nouns liberally with this kind of modification. "All brand-new in a pleasing new size . . . wide-open spaces . . . refreshing new styling . . . a huge 27-foot trunk . . ." and so on.

In comparisons and superlatives of adjectives, we may note in passing that Sweet Talk is again far in the lead, though the figures are small. There are only 2 in Tough Talk, 6 in Stuffy Talk, 19 in Sweet Talk. Things being sold are better, newest, finest. In all styles the inflected comparisons are in excess of those adjectives that require function words (as in Smoking's *less extensive*). This is curious in the light of Fries' observation, a quarter century ago, that the ratio of inflected and noninflected comparisons in Standard English was about half and half.[3]

9. How many adjectives are themselves modified by intensifiers or other adverbs?

Here we are looking for a particular example of modification that might be called excessive—that is, when the adjective modifying a noun is itself modified by an adverb. Often this adverb serves only to pad up the force of the adjective (*just right, perfectly adequate*), and can be called an "intensifier." . . . I do not include *more* used strictly as a comparative (but I do count it in the expression *one of the more maddening insolences of criticism*, where it seems to act simply as an intensifier). I do not count *so* in a *so . . . that* construction (*the pressure was so high that . . .*), but do count it when used as an intensifier only (*so many people do not know how to read*).

The figures are tiny but interesting. There are 4 such expressions in Tough Talk, 3 in Stuffy Talk, 12 in Sweet Talk. *More maddening* and *perturbingly moving* occur in "Unrequired Reading," while the ads offer the following: *otherwise well ordered, perfectly adequate, specially and deliciously dif-*

ferent (a double entry), *just right, deliciously smooth, unusually good, homemade good, so much better, all brand-new.*

I surmise that the presence of this construction about once every hundred words is a characteristic of Sweet Talk, but not of the others.

10. *What proportion of the total words are noun adjuncts?*

The particular inventiveness which characterizes many noun adjuncts in advertising was discussed [earlier]. Made-up phrases like *Foodarama living* and *stretch-out interior room* are characteristic of Sweet Talk. Every example in our Sweet Talk collection (except Ad #3) contains at least two noun adjunct constructions, and many of them are of the nonce sort I have illustrated. But the frequency (not the inventiveness) of noun adjuncts in Stuffy Talk is even higher—there are 55 such constructions, over 5 percent of the total words. The Revenue passage is illustrative: *income tax purposes, research expenses, traveling expenses, college and university professors.* The Tough Talkers, on the other hand, employ only ten noun adjuncts throughout, three of them in *Time*'s journalism. The others are conventional expressions like *fruit trees, dirt shoulder, world brotherhood.*

The explanation here is complex. In Sweet Talk, I have argued, the passion for noun adjuncts is part of the passion for naming, and a substitute for Tough Talk's abundance of *to be* and the "this-is-that" sentence pattern. In Stuffy Talk, the multiple names have already been coined, and they roll off the stuffy tongue in great official bundles, like *the College Entrance Examination Board's Scholastic Aptitude and Achievement Test* ("Admissions").[4] But Tough Talk, often, aspires to speech patterns like those of Fries' Vulgar English samples in his famous study. More than once Fries has occasion to point out the relative conservatism, linguistically, of his Vulgar writers; they cling to old forms when others have given them up. Similarly they fail to leap on to current linguistic bandwagons, notably the noun-adjunct bandwagon. Fries found noun adjuncts in his so-called Standard writers four times as frequent as in his Vulgar.[5] This is almost exactly the relation between my Sweet and Stuffy Talkers as against my Tough Talkers.

One would at first surmise that the adman's language aspires to Vulgarity too, but this is only partly true. Unlike Vulgar English and unlike the conversation of most people, Sweet Talk can be daring and resourceful in inventing new forms of expression. This daring is most conspicuous, I think, in the use of the noun adjunct.

Associated with noun adjuncts is the question of the inflected genitive, though my figures are too tiny for more than speculation. The substitution of the inflected genitive for the phrase with *of* is another of *Time*'s contributions to modern journalistic style, exemplified in our materials by the expression *Birmingham's Negroes* in place of the more orthodox *the Negroes of Birmingham*. But that is the only example of an inflected genitive in all of Tough Talk, while the only one in Stuffy Talk is *the College Board's . . . Tests* ("Admissions"). In Sweet Talk, with its desire to give things names, perhaps also to add that crisp authority conveyed by the mannerisms of Timestyle, there are nine instances of the inflected genitive. *Chase Manhattan's dish of tea. The World's best-selling scotch. Foodarama's supermarket selection.* (Inflected genitive and noun adjunct all in one phrase.) All examples are not from adwriters, either; there are three in "Unrequired Reading," though they lack the commercial touch of the ones I mentioned.

E. QUESTIONS ABOUT SUBORDINATION

In this section I consider mostly the sheer bulk of the clauses in my three styles, but there are several other matters with respect to clauses that are too tentative, in the present state of my samples, to put forward as more than faintly suggestive. For one thing there appear to be, in Tough Talk, somewhat more adverbial clauses modifying whole sentences than in the other two. Part of Tough Talk's reluctance to modify nouns specifically? Part of Tough Talk's reluctance to assume a role of omniscience, preferring to modify or qualify an entire statement? This last possibility is encouraged by the discovery of 6 *if* clauses in Tough Talk, only 2 in Sweet Talk and 1 in Stuffy Talk.

Sweet Talk seems slightly partial to the adjective clause, as we might expect. There is furthermore a particular form of noun-modifying clause in which the function word, or "includer" (usually *that*), can be omitted. Examples are *the dust they raised* (Frederic Henry) and *the way you like it* (Ad #6). Jespersen calls this a contact clause, and indicates it has a long and distinguished history.[6] Fries found its use more frequent in Vulgar English than in Standard. Associated as it therefore is with informal discourse, we find two examples in Tough Talk, three in Sweet Talk, none in Stuffy Talk.

11. What is the average length of the included clauses?

An included clause is the modern linguist's term, or one of his terms, for what we used to call a subordinate or dependent clause. One immediately startling fact about my samples is that the sheer number of such clauses is higher in Tough and Sweet Talk than in Stuffy Talk. There are 32 clauses each in the first two, only 17 in Stuffy Talk. The length of the characteristic clauses in the styles is, however, very different: an average of 8 words each in Tough Talk, 7 words each in Sweet Talk, 18 in Stuffy Talk. Of the Tough Talkers, only Jack Burden's windiness exceeds an average 10 words per included clause. All Stuffy Talkers average above this figure, and one ("Revenue") averages 25 words per clause.

12. What proportion of the total passage is inside such clauses?

It follows from the above that Stuffy Talk, in spite of having fewer clauses by a good deal, nevertheless displays a larger proportion of its total text inside included clauses. The figures are 24 percent for Tough Talk, 23 percent for Sweet Talk, 32 percent for Stuffy Talk. Among the last-named, the extreme is "Teaching Literature," half of whose total text appears inside clauses. But this is apparently not always a critical matter, for both "Smoking" and "Admissions" are fairly low in total wordage of clauses.

Insofar as clauses relate to tone, it is clear that frequency of subordination is not much help. Tough and Sweet Talkers use the included clause generously. They do, however, use shorter clauses, and at least in most cases they place a smaller fraction of their discourse within clauses than the Stuffy Talkers do.

13. How frequently are subject and main verb separated by intervening subordinate structures? How long are these interruptions?

Much depends not only on the *number* and the *length* of subordinate structures, but also on their *placing* in the sentence. One can place one's included clause, for example, ahead of one's subject-verb, in what is called a left-branching construction, or behind one's subject-verb, in a right-branching construction. Consider examples from [Charles Dickens and Saul Bellow]. "Whether I shall turn out to be the hero of my own life . . . these pages must show," says David Copperfield, and we sense, as we dive into that complicated clause at the *beginning* of the book, that here is a stylist who already knows how his sentence (maybe his book too?) is going to end. If he is already foisting off on us dependent structures, then he must know what they're going to be dependent *on*. A well-ordered mind. Not so Augie [March], of course: "My parents were not much to me, though I cared for my mother." As an afterthought, a qualification, the clause appears behind the subject-verb and supports the casual voice we [have] observed. . . .

No doubt an analysis of left-branching and right-branching subordination would turn up something with respect to my styles, but I intend to confine myself here to still a third *placing* of subordinate structures—*between* subject and main verb. I am counting, simply enough, all the words that intervene in our passages between a subject and its verb, with the suspicion that what is called "self-embedding" constructions may be a symptom of the Stuffy Talker.[7]

The figures are heartening—and if they were not, I need scarcely say, you would not be hearing about them. The Tough Talkers interrupt their subjects and verbs very little, Jack Burden and Augie March not at all. Out of a total of 102 subject-verb combinations, there are only 24 interrupting words. Sweet Talk is almost as sparing in its separations of subject and verb, 96 combinations and 36 intervening words. (A third of them occurs in the professorial "Unrequired Reading.") In Stuffy Talk we have just the contrary picture: in 57 subject-verb combinations, there are 182 words in "self-embedding" positions. One of the flashier examples occurs in "Smoking": "The *risk* of developing cancer of the lung for the combined group of pipe smokers, cigar smokers, and pipe and cigar smokers *is* . . ."

I conclude that if the total number of "self-embedding" words is less than half the total number of subject-verb structures, the passage is in this respect safely within the Tough-Sweet categories. On the other hand, twice as many interrupting words as there are subject-verb combinations suggests the pontifical voice of the Stuffy Talker.

F. OTHER EFFECTS OF TONE

14. What is the frequency of the determiner the?

The significance of using *the* liberally was discussed at length [earlier], where I argued its function as an *implied* expression of intimacy. If I began a story by saying "The long street down the hill . . . ," I imply that you and I have some relationship already in operation, and that you know me well enough to be aware what street and hill I'm talking about. This intimacy is almost always fictitious, of course, whether in "fiction" or else-where.

There are 97 appearances of *the* in Tough Talk, 39 in Sweet Talk, 65 in Stuffy Talk. In this case it is Stuffy Talk that is in the middle, and 6–7 percent may represent the approximate frequency of *the* in contemporary American prose. (The huge "Standard Corpus" just assembled at Brown University,* how-ever, suggests a frequency as high as 7.8 percent.) At the present state of our findings, the Tough Talker seems to be characteristi-cally above this average figure, and the Sweet Talker below it.

15. Are there any sentences without subjects, or without verbs, or without either? Are there any contractions?

Sweet Talk's directly expressed intimacy of tone can obviously make good use of contractions common to colloquial speech. Of these there are 24 in my samples, appearing in every passage except "Unrequired Reading." Tough Talk, as we know, also echoes speech patterns, in its different way; in my samples there

---

* Now published as *Computational Analysis of Present-Day American English*, by Henry Kučera and W. Nelson Francis (Providence, 1967). —Ed.

are 16 contractions, half of them in Jack Burden. There are no contractions in Stuffy Talk.

Even more telling may be the behavior of the three styles with respect to what are called "sentence fragments." These are groups of words punctuated as sentences, but lacking a subject or a verb or both. Ad #5 is a goldmine of fragments. *Not me, darling. Itchy skin? At any drug or cosmetic counter.* There are 20 of these constructions scattered through 5 of the ads. Example lacking the verb: *Every man his own connoisseur* (Ad #3). Lacking the subject: *Gives my skin precious moisture* (Ad #5). Lacking both: *And a wide range of new decorator colors* (Ad #8).

In Tough Talk there are two verbless sentences, both from Earl Horter, and one subjectless sentence, from Jack Burden. There are no such sentences in Stuffy Talk.

16. How many occurrences are there of these marks of punctuation: italics, parentheses, dashes, question marks exclamation points?

The totals of our three styles in respect to these marks of punctuation are as follows: Tough Talk, 1 question, 2 dashes. Sweet Talk: 7 italics (or boldface or capitals), 4 sets of parentheses, 9 dashes, 8 questions, 5 exclamations. Stuffy Talk: 2 sets of parentheses (both in "Smoking").

Italics. All five devices are used to effect a close relation with the assumed reader (among other functions they may have), and the Sweet Talker accordingly makes generous use of all of them. I first consider italics. As we have seen repeatedly, the Sweet Talker's problem is to simulate as convincingly as he can the voice of intimate conversation. In this effort he is considerably handicapped by the shortcomings of our writing system, which is simply not equipped to express the sounds that a voicebox makes. (The linguist counts in actual speech eight "phonemes" of stress and pitch alone, and these are conspicuously inexpressible by any written symbol, or "grapheme.") It is what the physical voice does *while* it is pronouncing syllables —its undulations of pitch and stress—that the written language particularly disregards. These, the so-called "suprasegmental phonemes," can be graphically expressed only by differences in the appearance of the typeface, differences in the spacing or color

or size or shape. In this essay I am considering only very obvious
cases of conventional suprasegmental emphasis, through italics,
boldface type, or a spelling in capital letters. Of these there
are seven in my Sweet samples. But I emphasize that in the
adwriter's performance there is tremendous pictorial razzle-
dazzle which I am not measuring here, but which contributes
greatly to our comprehension of the speaking voice addressing
us. The artistry that goes into layout, color, and so on is highly
important to the whole effect. To mention one simple example,
variation in line length to bring words and phrases into prominence, as in poetry, is simply not available to the ordinary prose-
writer, whose line endings are controlled by the typographer.
Such a technique may be admired in Ad #5, where I have attempted to reproduce the appearance of the actual ad.

Parentheses. Sets of parentheses, especially when they occur
repeatedly, are a clear call for intimacy. At their most extreme
they are like a whisper, a sotto-voce uttered behind the hand.
You and I share a joke, or a revelation, or a secret, and nobody
else can hear. Sets of parentheses provide another way, crude
though it is, by which the Sweet Talker can indicate variation
in his tone of voice. (Three examples in Ad #5.) When used
more sparingly, parentheses serve a conventional function in
Tough and Stuffy Talk as well, as the two examples in "Smoking" will illustrate.

Dashes. The liberal use of the dash gives an effect of breath-
lessness—literally a characteristic of an actual speaking voice.
Women who punctuate letters entirely with this mark are
presumably endeavoring to capture the sound of an intense
human voice in action. Furthermore, relations between parts
of a sentence connected by dashes remain logically in the air,
another characteristic of our elliptical and loose syntax in conversation. I take it that, other things being equal, the more
dashes I use, the closer I am to you and the more realistically
I echo the sound of intimate discourse.

Questions. When you ask a question, you expect an answer,
or you pretend you do. More than any other mark of end-punc-
tuation the question mark engages the assumed reader directly.
I'm asking *you*—even though you may know I'm about to provide the answer myself. There are seven questions in Ad #5,
another in #3. A single question, a very rhetorical one, appears

in Tough Talk, at the end of Earl Horter. There are no questions in Stuffy Talk, for the Stuffy Talker hardly knows his
reader exists.

Exclamations. The exclamation mark appeals to the reader
by laying stress on the speaker's own excitement. Now hear
this!!! It is a primitive instrument, when you consider the
enormous variations of which the human voice is capable in an
enthusiastic state. Still, the adwriter does what he can, and we
have 5 instances of the exclamation mark in Sweet Talk, none
in Tough Talk or in Stuffy.

And now the style machine. I summarize below the answers
to my sixteen questions, as they are worked out in averages for
the thousand words of each style. . . .

Facts about the Passages

	Tough	*Sweet*	*Stuffy*
1. What is the proportion of monosyllables in the passage?	78%	68%	56%
2. What is the proportion of words of more than 2 syllables?	5%	12%	24%
3. How many first-person and second-person pronouns does the passage contain?	13 1st 21 2nd	12 1st 42 2nd	2 1st 0 2nd
4. Are the subjects of finite verbs neuter nouns, or nouns referring to people?	52 N 72 P	45 N 70 P	51 N 14 P
5. What is the proportion of finite verbs to total words?	11%	11%	6%
6. What proportion of finite verbs are forms of *to be*?	36%	25%	17%
7. What proportion of verbs are in the passive voice?	4%	2%	26%
8. What proportion of words are true adjectives?	6%	11%	8%
9. How many adjectives are modified by adverbs?	4	13	5
10. What proportion of words are noun adjuncts?	1%	4%	5%
11. What is the average length of included clauses?	8 wds	7 wds	18 wds

12. What proportion of total passage is inside such clauses?   24%   23%   32%

13. How many words separate subject and verb?   24 wds   36 wds   182 wds

14. How frequent is the determiner *the*?   97   39   65

15. How many fragments? How many contractions?   2 fr   20 fr   0 fr
    16 cn   24 cn   0 cn

16. How many parentheses, italics, dashes, question marks, exclamation points?
    0 P   4 P   2 P
    0 I   7 I   0 I
    2 D   9 D   0 D
    1 Q   8 Q   0 Q
    0 E   5 E   0 E

The Style Machine

Criteria for Measuring Style

	Tough	*Sweet*	*Stuffy*
1. Monosyllables	over 70%	61–70%	60% or less
2. Words of 3 syllables and more	under 10%	10–19%	20% or more
3. 1st and 2nd person pronouns	1 *I* or *we* per 100 words	2 *you* per 100 words	no 1st or 2nd person pronouns
4. Subjects: neuters vs. people	½ or more people	½ or more people	⅔ or more neuters
5. Finite verbs	over 10%	over 10%	under 10%
6. *To be* forms as finite verbs	over ⅓ of verbs	under ¼	under ¼
7. Passives	less than 1 in 20 verbs	none	more than 1 in 5 verbs
8. True adjectives	under 10%	over 10%	over 8%
9. Adjectives modified	fewer than 1 per 100 words	1 or more	fewer than 1
10. Noun adjuncts	under 2%	2% or more	4% or more
11. Average length of clauses	10 words or less	10 words or less	more than 10 words
12. Clauses, proportion of total words	¼ or less	⅓ or less	over 40%
13. "Embedded" words	less than ½ S/V combinations	less than half	more than twice
14. *The*	8% or more	under 6%	6–7%
15. Contractions and fragments	1 or more per 100 words	2 or more	none
16. Parentheses & other punctuation	none	2 or more per 100 words	none

A. "The Private World of a Man with a Book"

The temptation of the educator is to explain and describe, to
organize a body of knowledge for the student, leaving the student with nothing to do. I have never been able to understand
why educators do this so often, especially where books are concerned. Much of this time they force their students to read the
wrong books at the wrong time, and insist that they read them
in the wrong way. That is, they lecture to the students about
what is in the books, reduce the content to a series of points
that can be remembered, and, if there are discussions, arrange
them to deal with the points.

Schools and colleges thus empty books of their true meaning,
and addict their students to habits of thought that often last
for the rest of their lives. Everything must be reduced to a summary, ideas are topic sentences, to read is to prepare for a distant test. This is why so many people do not know how to read.
They have been taught to turn books into abstractions.

Harold Taylor
SATURDAY REVIEW, XLIV (January 7, 1961)

B. "Unrequired Reading"

The title of this essay may strike you as a typographical error.
You may be saying to yourself that the writer really means required reading, and the phrase conjures up for you, I suspect,
lists distributed on the first days of college courses: Volume
One of this distinguished scholar's work on the Byzantine
empire in the fourth century, that brochure on the economic
interpretation of the Constitution, this pundit's principles of
economics, that pedant's source book.

Or, perhaps, still under the apprehension that I mean required reading, you are reminded by what is now one of the
more maddening insolences of criticism, or at any rate of book
reviewing. "This," says Mr. Notability, "is a *must* book." This
in the atomic age is compulsory reading. In a world of anxiety
this uneasy novel is not to be passed by.

I beg of you to forget such obligations and responsibilities.
To this day you have to forget that you *had* to read *Macbeth* in
order to begin to remember how perturbingly moving a play it
is. Hardly anyone would reread Burke's "Speech on Concili-
ation" if he recalled how he had to make an abstract of it in
high school.

Irwin Edman
SATURDAY REVIEW, XXXIII (November 4, 1950)

C. "Teaching Literature"

Rapid and coherent development of programs in modern literature has led to the production of excellent materials for study from the earliest years of secondary education through the last of undergraduate study. The sole danger—if it be one, in the opinion of others—lies in easy acceptance of what is well done. The mechanics of mass production can overpower and drive out native creativeness in reflecting on literature and so stop individual interpretation in teaching. We hear a good deal of the dangers to imaginative experience in youth from excesses of visual exposure, and we know that they therefore read much less, in quantity, from longer works of prose and poetry. It may prove to be true, therefore, that in the study of literature the critical authority of the printed page will seem an easy substitute for individual analysis of original texts, first for the teacher and next inevitably for students who have never learned to read, with conscious effort in thinking, through verbal symbols.

David H. Stevens
THE CHANGING HUMANITIES
(New York, 1953), p. 173. (Title added.)

NOTES

1. In *Enemies of Promise* (1938), Cyril Connolly speaks of "the new relationship with the reader which is to sweep over the twentieth century and dominate journalism and advertising. It may be described as *you*-writing from the fact that there is a constant tendency to harangue the reader in the second person. It is a buttonholing approach." Connolly calls this style "the New Vernacular," and he distinguishes it from the ornate, traditional "Mandarin" style, "characterized by long sentences with many dependent clauses, by the use of the subjunctive and conditional, by exclamations and interjections, quotations, allusions, metaphors, long images, Latin terminology, subtlety, and conceits." I suppose that in this study I have discriminated between two kinds of Vernacular (Tough and Sweet), while my Stuffy Talk is a dreadful parody of the Mandarin grand manner. . . .

For another, and more recent, attempt to classify styles, see Martin Joos, *The Five Clocks* (Bloomington, 1963). Considering oral speech as well as written language, Joos distinguishes five styles. His labels for them are: frozen, formal, consultative, casual, and intimate.

2. I have made some effort in this study to use the pattern approach to sentence structure to which the structural linguists have been introducing us for some years. However, except for the clear difference in the use of the passive voice of the verb . . . , I found not enough difference in sentence pattern among my styles to warrant including the figures. It is evidently possible to sound Tough or Sweet or Stuffy in any sentence pattern, as

"pattern" is defined by the new grammarian. (The transformational approach, on the other hand, seems likely to offer some genuine opportunities for further classification.) As for the passive voice, I consider that important difference in my next question, where I use the traditional vocabulary.

3. C. C. Fries, *American English Grammar* (New York, 1940), p. 98.

4. Educationese seems to be particularly afflicted. The notorious conflict between colleges of liberal arts and colleges of education, like many conflicts, is fought by means of crucial differences in prose style, and the educationist is characteristically more generous with his noun adjuncts. Battle lines are clearly drawn in a recent article by Reuben A. Brower, who is firmly in the camp of the liberal arts. Professor Brower does not use the term "noun adjunct," but the distinction appears in his very title, "Book Reading and the Reading of Books," where *book reading* is condemned and *the reading of books* is defended. Of the prose style of the educationist, Brower says: "We may forgive the flatness in the interest of objectivity, but not the Germanic compounds of which 'book reading' is a mild example. We hear too often: 'language skills,' 'reading skills,' 'recognition skills,' 'content fields,' and 'content analysis'; and too many plurals such as 'language immaturities,' 'these learnings,' and 'these recognitions.' A climactic sentence in one report ends with: 'the desired pupil learning outcomes.' " Roger H. Smith, ed., *The American Reading Public* (New York, 1963), pp. 23–24.

5. Fries, *American English Grammar*, p. 274.

6. Otto Jespersen, *Modern English Grammar*, III (Heidelberg, 1927), 132–153.

7. Richard Ohmann has summarized the distinction clearly in an article in *Word* (December, 1964) [reprinted in this volume]: "It has often been pointed out that constructions may be left-branching ('Once George had left, the host and hostess gossiped briskly'), right-branching ('The host and hostess gossiped briskly, once George had left'), or self embedding ('The host and hostess, once George had left, gossiped briskly'). Neither left- nor right-branching constructions tax the hearer's understanding, even when compounded at some length ('a very few not at all well liked union officials' 'the dog that worried the cat that chased the rat that ate the cheese that lay in the house that Jack built'). But layers of self-embedding quickly put too great a strain on the unaided memory ('the house in which the cheese that the rat that the cat that the dog worried chased ate lay was built by Jack'). Even a relatively small amount of self-embedding in a written passage can slow a reader down considerably."

10. METRICS AND MORPHOPHONEMICS IN THE KALEVALA

Paul Kiparsky

Paul Kiparsky's "Metrics and Morphophonemics in the Kalevala" must be read in the context of current research in generative phonology, particularly Noam Chomsky and Morris Halle's *The Sound Pattern of English*. Professor Kiparsky views metrics as being governed not by syllable- and stress-count, but by rule and schema. Hence in such phenomena as alliteration, he argues, the poet and his reader or hearer think in terms of *schemata* (possible analyses) rather than of the actual phonetic character of the segments in question. Further, certain facts of Finnish diphthongal alliteration suggest that an alliteration schema applies to certain vowels at a level in their phonological derivation *before* the diphthongization rule applies. Many otherwise anomalous alliterative patterns can be explained by this principle. The same concept—that various sorts of metrical rules operate at stages before the application of certain phonological rules—explains a number of metrical inconsistencies in the Kalevala. Hence, more generally, a word's *metrical value* and its surface form may not be identical. This principle has been invoked in a limited way in some analyses of English verse as well. Paul Kiparsky is associate professor of linguistics and a staff member of the Research Laboratory of Electronics at The Massachusetts Institute of Technology.

It is difficult to think that a professional bard should without motive have left his verse with an irregular rhythm, when any European scholar, without serious practice in the

Reprinted by permission of the author and publisher from *Studies Presented to Professor Roman Jakobson by His Students* (Cambridge, Mass.: Slavica Publishers, 1968).

art of versification, can put it into order for him with
hardly a perceptible alteration in the meaning. It is also
difficult to think that professional reciters and their in-
structors could by mere accident have left stanzas in a shape
which must make them a perpetual burden to the memory.
In these "irregularities" there may be meanings not easily
recognized, and for this reason they deserve to be carefully
studied.

E. V. Arnold
VEDIC METRE (1905)

The prosody of Finnish epic folk poetry has been described, with clarity and in detail, in Sadeniemi's *Metrik des Kalevala-Verses*.[1] This material has important implications for a general theory of prosody which have not yet been drawn. To point out some of these is one of the purposes of the following remarks. Another is to demonstrate that what seem to be systematic classes of exceptions to the general metrical rules established by Sadeniemi actually turn out to be fully regular as soon as justice is done to the phonological structure of the Finnish language. Of the three sections of this paper, the first simply summarizes, and in part slightly reformulates, the essential features of the Kalevala line as stated by Sadeniemi. Section 2 is a discussion of alliteration, in which a new solution is given to the paradox of vowel (or zero) alliteration. Section 3 analyzes the specific form of the phonological representations to which the metrical con-straints must apply. Towards the end of the paper I indulge in some speculation about the role of sound change and morpho-phonemics, and their interaction, in the development of metrical systems.

1. THE METRICAL STRUCTURE OF THE LINE

The Kalevala is composed of octosyllabic lines in which the distribution of quantity and stress is subject to certain restrictions. For example, while the following three lines are correctly formed

Luvan antoi suuri Luoja
("The great Creator gave permission")

Selässä meren sinisen
("On the expanse of the blue sea")

Oi Ukko ylijumala
("O Ukko, supreme god")

these two, likewise octosyllabic, violate the metrical rules:

Rakas oli oma emo
("Dear was [my] own mother")

Vanhalla Väinämöisellä
("Old Väinämöinen [adessive]")

To formulate the constraints on quantity and stress it is necessary to assume an underlying trochaic meter for all lines of the Kalevala. The metrical scheme for a line can be represented as | 1 * | 2 * | 3 * | 4 * |, where the downbeats (ictuses, strong positions) are numbered and the upbeats starred. But the realization of this abstract verse pattern in concrete verse instances[2] is very complex. A recitation of the verses would give prominence to the first syllable of each word, in accordance with the rule of Finnish word stress. Only the first of the three acceptable lines just cited would therefore receive an actual trochaic rhythm in reading, while on the other hand, the first of the two unacceptable lines would also receive a perfect trochaic rhythm. The coincidence of downbeat and stress is therefore neither a necessary nor a sufficient condition for the metrical correctness of a line.

The fundamental rule defining the Kalevala meter in terms of the underlying trochaic pattern is this:

(A)   *Stressed syllables must be long on the downbeat and short on the upbeat.*

To this the immediate qualification must be added that the stringency with which the rule applies increases from zero to 100 percent as we progress from the first foot to the fourth. In the first foot the rule is waived completely: the occurrence of quantity is metrically free. In the second foot the rule applies, but is frequently broken. In the third it is considerably tightened, but we still find exceptions. In the fourth foot the rule is implemented without fail. There is not a single case in Sadeniemi's sample which violates (A) in the fourth foot. Such increase of metrical strictness towards the end of the line is an interesting and almost constant feature of numerous widely differing metrical systems of the world.

Metrical rules are formulated with design and not instance in mind: in actual verse we do, for example, get a statistical preponderance of long syllable in the first downbeat. Two thirds of the lines begin with a long syllable. But Sadeniemi shows by statistical argument that this is simply due to the facts that: (1) the great majority of monosyllabic words are long in Finnish and (2) a majority of polysyllabic words also begin with a long syllable.

Non-initial (unstressed) syllables, whether long or short, can come freely on both the upbeat and the downbeat of any foot. Monosyllabic words count as normal stressed syllables.

In addition to the fundamental rule (A) which implements the underlying trochaic pattern through the linguistic features of stress and length, there exist certain metrical tendencies or preferences which impart other regularities, of a statistical and stylistical nature, to the meter of the Kalevala. Two are of especial interest here because of their wide implications and effects on the verse.

The first tendency can be stated as follows:

(B)   *Other things being equal, the words of a line are arranged in order of increasing length.*

Sadeniemi rightly emphasizes, as others have done, the universal character of this tendency, and its validity outside of strict metrics (e.g., *rough and ready, one and only,* but hardly the reverse).

It is at one point in the line that the tendency towards increasing length hardens into a law. As might be expected, this position of especial strictness is the final foot:

(C)   *A monosyllabic word is not permitted at the end of a line.*

Observe that (C) is strongly reinforced by other rules. Long monosyllables are prohibited in final position anyway because of rule (A), and certain classes of short monosyllables (e.g., conjunctions) cannot occur last in the line for purely syntactic reasons. What justifies the inclusion of (C) at all, therefore, is the fact that even when these other conditions do not operate to exclude a final monosyllable, rule (C) holds without exception.

(D)   *A break often occurs between the fourth and fifth syllables.*

There is, in other words, a tendency for a word-boundary to split the line into two quadrisyllabic cola. Sadeniemi adduces

this tendency to explain various facts: the otherwise incompre-
hensible absence of lines containing a four-syllable word flanked
by two dissyllables; the regularly long quantity of the fifth syllable in lines containing a dissyllable followed by a word of six
syllables; the fact that the first and third downbeats are the preferred sites of alliteration.[3] While the break is not mandatory,
lines which neither have a break nor follow rule (B) are rare
indeed.

2. THE ALLITERATION PARADOX

Most lines (but not all) alliterate in one of two possible ways.
The preferred type of alliteration is for words to share the
initial consonant (if any) and the first vowel. We shall term this
C_0V-alliteration, and distinguish a subtype (a), with a consonant,
and a subtype (b), with no consonant.

$$C_0V \quad \text{(a)} \quad \textit{L}\text{appalainen } \textit{l}\text{aiha poika}$$
$$C_0V \quad \text{(b)} \quad \textit{A}\text{stu leski } \textit{a}\text{itastasi}$$

The second type of alliteration, where only the initial consonant
(if any) is shared, is three times less frequent. In this type,
C_0-alliteration, the analogous two subtypes (a) and (b) can be
distinguished.

$$C_0 \quad \text{(a)} \quad \textit{S}\text{elässä meren } \textit{s}\text{inisen}$$
$$C_0 \quad \text{(b)} \quad \text{Oi Ukko ylijumala}$$

Not only in Finnish poetry, but also in the independent traditions of Germanic and Irish poetry, there is an equivalence, in
terms of function and frequency, between the subtypes (a) and
(b) within both C_0V- and C_0-alliteration. No matter whether the
favorite form of alliteration is C_0V, as in Finnish, or C_0, as in
Germanic, the subtypes with and without the consonant are
treated identically. This equivalence is so ubiquitous that it can
hardly be just a prosodic convention, but must be intrinsic to
the nature of alliteration itself.

Yet this equivalence seems quite paradoxical. Why should the
one-segment alliteration $a \ldots a \ldots$ everywhere correspond
not to the one-segment alliteration $t \ldots t \ldots$ but to the two-
segment alliteration $ta \ldots ta \ldots$? And why should $a \ldots i$
$\ldots$ be a case of alliteration at all, just as much as $ta \ldots ti$
$\ldots$ is? What is it that alliterates in $a \ldots i \ldots$? It cannot

be that the vowels alliterate with each other, for alliteration does not disregard any phonological features: t . . . p . . . or t . . . d . . . are not cases of alliteration.

In Germanic metrics this equivalence of subtypes (a) and (b) is usually explained by assuming that ostensibly vowel-initial words actually began with a glottal stop, and that this glottal stop functioned as the alliterating consonant.[4] *All* alliteration is thereby reduced to subtype (a). This explanation has been rightly criticized by Jakobson, who pointed out that the assumption of a glottal stop before vowels word-initially is unsupported for the old Germanic languages.[5] The fact that such glottal stops are not found in Finnish makes this explanation out of the question for Finnish and helps to cast further doubt on its validity in Germanic.

Jakobson instead sought the locus of alliteration in the (b) subtypes on the *phonemic* level. He argued that vowel-initial words actually begin with a zero phoneme $/\#/$, defined as a lax glide corresponding to the tense glide $/h/$. In this zero phoneme he saw the missing alliterating consonant in the (b) subtypes. I doubt, however, whether it is necessary to set up such a zero phoneme on purely linguistic grounds in any of the Germanic languages or in Finnish. It would have no synchronic function at all, and its distribution would be quite unlike $/h/$ or any other phoneme.

The search for an alliterating consonant which would get rid of subtype (b) appears to have failed. The resolution to the alliteration paradox must lie elsewhere.

Let us instead rethink the concept of alliteration itself. The paradox vanishes if the nature of alliteration is clearly defined. The source of the paradox is that alliteration is thought of as necessarily involving repetition of actual phonological segments (phonetic or phonemic) in two or more words of a line. Let us instead consider it as identity of portions of words defined by an *alliteration schema* fixed by poetic convention. Examples of such schemata are:

$\#C_0V$	(Finnish, one type)
$\#C_0$	(Finnish, the second type)
$\#C_0(V)$	(Finnish, general schema)
$\#\left\{\begin{array}{c}[\text{s}][+\text{obstr}]\\ C_0^1\end{array}\right\}$	(Germanic)

These schemata can be framed in the notation developed by Chomsky and Halle for phonological rules.[6] Here C_n^m means "at least n, at most m, consonants," and C_0^1 accordingly means "one or zero consonants."[7] The symbol # denotes a word boundary. We define the *analysis* of a word by schema P as the biggest piece of it which satisfies P. We can now say that *two words in a line alliterate if their analyses are identical.*[8]

For example, the words *tupa* and *tapa* alliterate by the schema #C_0 because the biggest piece which fits that schema is the identical string #t in both words. Similarly, *ukko* and *akka* alliterate by the same schema because the biggest piece which fits it is the identical string # in both words. But *tapa* and *pata* do not alliterate because their analyses are the different strings #t and #p, and *tapa* and *akka* do not alliterate because their analyses are the different strings #t and #.[9]

Vowel alliteration, or, to use Jakobson's more felicitous term, zero alliteration, is thus simply the special case in which C_0 in the schema is interpreted as "zero consonants." The paradox engendered by the false notion of alliteration as repetition of segments has disappeared. The question "What segments alliterate in *ukko* and *akka*?" was unanswerable because it was wrongly put. The correct question is "What schema do they fit?"

3. THE MORPHOPHONEMIC BASIS OF THE METER AND ALLITERATION

The regularities described in sections 1 and 2 above have numerous exceptions if they are regarded as applying to superficial representations of words. Alliteration furnishes a simple example of this. In C_0V-alliteration, according to the schema proposed above, a geminated vowel can act as the alliterating partner of a simple one:

*Ku*lki *ku*usissa hakona

The schema also correctly reflects the fact that vowels alliterate with the initial segments of diphthongs, e.g., *e* with *ei*, *a* with *ai*, and so on. But oddly enough, the long partner of *a* in C_0V-alliteration is a diphthong whose pronunciation is *oa* in some dialects of eastern Finland, *ua* in others, and which corresponds to standard Finnish *aa*. These dipthongs do not C_oV-alliterate with *o* and *u*, as would be expected since their first segment is *o* or *u*. (Of course, the diphthongs *oa, ua* do C_0-alliterate with *o* and *u*, as they do with every other vowel for the reasons discussed in the preceding section. It is C_0V-alliteration which is relevant here.) Similarly, the alliterating partners of *e, o, ö* are *ie, uo, yö:*

> *S*omer *s*oitti, *h*iekka *h*elkki

The explanation for this apparently deviant alliteration pattern is the fact that these diphthongs are morphophonemically *geminated vowels*. Alliteration, then, is defined on morphophonemic representations, or, at any rate, on representations to which the diphthongization rule has not applied. The alliteration schema is applied while *oa* (*ua*) is represented in its underlying form /aa/, and *ie, uo, yö* are represented in their underlying forms /ee/, /oo/, /öö/. Their alliteration then conforms to the general schema given above. Among the reasons for representing these diphthongs as underlying monophthongs is the fact that if *moa, mua* is /maa/, *tie* is /tee/, and so on, then forms such as the plural cases *maissa, maita, teissä, teitä* can be derived by the same general rule which yields *puissa, puita,* from *puu,* or *pyissä, pyitä* from *pyy,* and so on in all stems with geminate vowels at the end.

In meter the role of underlying representations is even greater than in the case of alliteration, and much more complex. Consider the following lines from the poetry of Ingermanland:

> Vapa vaskinen keäjessä
> Otin oinon, toin kottiin

Both of these lines, and hundreds of others like them, are perfectly acceptable and legitimate instances of the Kalevala meter. Yet they appear to violate the rules given in section 1. The first line has a long stressed (i.e. word-initial) syllable *keä-* in the upbeat of the third foot, in a position where rule (A) requires that stressed syllables must be short. The second line has a long syllable *kot-* in the third upbeat, in violation of rule (A); in addition, it is anomalous in containing only seven syllables instead of the required eight.

A consideration of the underlying forms and the rules which relate them to the phonetic shapes will clarify these seeming irregularities. The exact form of the rules does not interest us here, so that a fairly informal notation will do. The order of the rules, however, is essential to the discussion that follows.

(1) Epenthesis

$$[V] \quad \begin{bmatrix} C \\ -\text{grave} \end{bmatrix} \quad [i] \quad \#$$
$$1 \qquad 2 \qquad\qquad 3 \quad 4 \rightarrow 1 \; 3 \; 2 \; 3 \; 4$$

A palatal glide develops before dentals followed by *i* at the end of a word, e.g. *poikani > poikaini*. In some dialects it is simply a matter of palatalization in the dental consonant; in the dialect under consideration, however, a real diphthong develops, which is regarded as a long syllable in rule (5), and as a closed syllable in rule (2), as we shall see.

(2) Consonant gradation

Consonants are weakened in closed syllables, that is, in the environment _____VC$\{^C_\#\}$, where C denotes either a true consonant or a glide such as the second segment of the diphthongs *ai, au, oi,* etc. Word-initial consonants are not subject to gradation. The results of weakening are complex. I shall simply state verbally what happens. *Geminated* consonants are degeminated. Thus, the genitive of *pappi*, "priest," is *papin*; to the genitive *isättömän*, "fatherless," there corresponds the nominative *isätön*. Similarly, *pappittoman* (genitive "priestless") corresponds to *papiton* (nominative). Note that in the latter form, from underlying *pappittom*, the degemination applies in two places simultaneously, so that *tt* is both the environment for the degemination of *pp* and undergoes degemination itself. *Simple* consonants have various treatments under gradation. The consonants *t* and *k* are generally just dropped, e.g. *kätessä > käessä*, "in the hand," *keskellä > kesellä*, "in the middle," *poikaini* (from *poikani* by the preceding rule of epenthesis) *> pojaini*. The consonant *p* turns to *v*, e.g. *apu* (nominative 'help') *> avun* (genitive). The consonant gradation rules of standard Finnish are in many respects quite different from those of the Ingermanland dialects described here.

(3) Gemination of vowels

$$V \quad V$$
$$1 \quad 2 \rightarrow 1 \; 1 \; 2$$

Vowels are lengthened, that is, geminated, before vowels. This rule lengthens *käessä* (from *kätessä* by consonant gradation) to *kääessä*. The loss of *t* and *k* by consonant gradation is therefore accompanied by what looks like a compensatory lengthening of the preceding vowel in these dialects.[10]

(4) Contraction

$$h \rightarrow \phi \quad / \quad V\text{\_\_\_\_\_}V$$

Intervocalic *h* is lost in suffixes. Thus the form *kotihin* (illative "house") becomes *kotiin*.

(5) Gemination of consonants

$$C \rightarrow 1 \quad 1 \quad / \quad \begin{Bmatrix} C \\ \# \end{Bmatrix} \quad V\text{\_\_\_\_\_}VV$$
$$1$$

Consonants are geminated between a short vowel and a long vowel or diphthong. The form *kotiin*, which arose by the previous rule, turns into *kottiin*. The rule affects not only true consonants, but also glides, so that *pojaini* (from rule 2) becomes *pojjaini*, or, as it is conventionally written, *poijaini*.

(6) Apocopation

$$i \rightarrow \phi \quad / \quad C\text{\_\_\_\_\_}\#$$

A final short *i* drops optionally. For example, *poijaini* or *poijain* would both be possible forms.

(7) Diphthongization

The diphthongization rule has already been described in connection with the discussion of alliteration at the beginning of this section. It raises the first mora of long vowels, e.g. *ee, oo, öö > ie, uo, yö,* and *aa, ää > oa, eä.* The former type of diphthongization, which applies to mid vowels, is found in standard Finnish also, but the latter type, which applies to low vowels, is restricted to eastern Finland.

Examination of the metrics reveals that *the operation of rules (3) through (7) is disregarded in the metrics.*[11] Returning again to the line

Vapa vaskinen keäjessä

we note that the long stressed syllable *keä-* arises from the operation of rules (3), gemination of vowels, and (7), diphthongization.

The derivation is /kätessä/ > (2) *käessä* > (3) *kääessä* > (7) *keäessä,* with *keäjessä* the result of an automatic glide insertion. Up to the operation of rule (3) the word is metrically perfectly correct. In the case of the line

Otin oinon, toin kottiin

the underlying form /kotihin/ is again perfectly compatible with the meter. The violation of syllabicity is only the result of the contraction produced by rule (4), and the long initial syllable *kot-* which violates rule (A) comes about by the operation of consonant gemination (rule 5).

It is important to note that the operation of rules (3) through (7) not only *may* be disregarded in the metrics; it *must* be. For example, the secondary geminates produced by rule (3) almost *never* make the preceding syllable metrically long, whereas underlying geminates almost *always* do so (Sadeniemi, page 51).

Rules (3) through (7) are disregarded by the meter, but the same is not true of rules (1) and (2). For example, the operation of consonant gradation is always metrically relevant. The long initial syllable of underlying /keskellä/, "in the middle," becomes short by consonant gradation (rule 2). Such a syllable is virtually without exception metrically short (Sadeniemi, page 52), so that a line like

Istuu voan kesellä mertä

is fully regular according to rule (A) of section 1.

The conclusion to be drawn from these facts, then, is that *the metrical correctness of a line depends on its form at a certain cutoff point in the derivation,* namely, the representation obtained after the application of rule (2) but before the application of rule (3). This is not a trivial fact. One could, after all, imagine a situation in which there would be no such cutoff point, and the metrically disregarded rules would not form a continuous sequence in the ordering.

Some remarkable consequence may be deduced from these facts. Consider forms like *sukkain,* "my sock(s)," *poijain,* "my boy(s)," from underlying forms *sukka + ni, poika + ni.* Their derivation is as follows:

Underlying form	sukka+ni
(1) Epenthesis	sukkaini
(2) Consonant gradation	sukaini
(5) Consonant gemination	sukkaini
(6) Apocopation	sukkain

In such cases epenthesis happens to have the effect of making the second syllable both closed, so that the consonant gradation applies, and long, so that the degeminated consonant is geminated back again by rule (5). Recalling now that the metrical cutoff point is between rules (2) and (3), we are led to the prediction that the metrical value of the word should be *sukaini,* its form after the application of rule (2). That means that the word should be metrically trisyllabic, and, most extraordinarily, that its initial syllable should be metrically short *although it is long both morphophonemically and phonetically.* This is in fact exactly the situation described by Sadeniemi (page 52), who gives a list of lines like

> Peälle sulkkuse sukkain
> Annan ainuvan poijaini

which confirms this prediction. These lines are metrically correct only if scanned *sukaini, pojaini,* with the short initial syllable produced by rule (2).

These two lines also illustrate the optional character of apocopation (rule 6). It has applied in *sukkain* but not in *poijaini.*

A second unexpected consequence is that there are numerous homonymous words which have different metrical values. According to the rules which have been formulated above, words like /pakko + hon/, (illative) "compulsion" and /pako + hon/, (illative) "flight" merge phonetically to *pakkoon.* However, they retain distinct forms at the metrical cutoff point, where the first syllable of one is long and the first syllable of the other is short. In fact, words of the former type almost invariably begin on the downbeat, whereas those of the latter type almost invariably begin on the upbeat, as required by rule (A). . . . These, then, are word pairs which are always homonymous but never metrically equivalent.

It would be natural to look for a historical explanation for these facts instead of the morphophonemic one which has been proposed here. Could not one assume that the verses were all

composed at a time when none of the sound changes corresponding to rules (3) through (7) had yet taken place, and handed
down across the generations until collected in the nineteenth
century. Such a theory would grossly underestimate the creative
aspect of a tradition of oral epic poetry. As Sadeniemi points out,
the singers of the nineteenth century composed many new poems
on known occasions, which were recorded at the time and are
found to observe an abstract metrical form just as did the older
poems. Since most of the rules in the sequence from (3) to (7)
date back at least to medieval times, a coherent defense of this
simplest form of the historical explanation is hard to imagine.

But if we grant that the basis of the meter is a synchronic,
non-phonetic level of representation, it still makes sense to ask
what the role of history may be in the formation of such an abstract metrics. There is no reason at all to deny that the system
itself which we have described might have a historical explanation. A thousand years ago the metrically relevant forms may
well have been phonetic. We can then assume that after the
sound changes corresponding to rules (3) through (7) took place,
the existing body of poetry was reinterpreted by successive generations of singers as metrically based on abstract, non-phonetic
forms of a fixed kind, namely, those reached at our cutoff point,
and new poetry of the same kind continued to be created. The
superficial violations of the trochaic pattern and rule (A) which
the sound changes produced were not viewed as mistakes but as
the norm to be learned and imitated by the apprentice singer.
The singers were able to learn and continue this norm in a
creative way because they knew (unconsciously, of course) the
morphophonemic structure of Finnish, and the sound changes
continued to operate as living morphophonemic processes in the
synchronic sound pattern of the language. They could therefore
learn (again, unconsciously) to disregard these morphophonemic
processes in order to continue as closely as possible the traditional
body of poetry which they had learned by listening to older
singers.

But this is only possible if the sound changes stay in the
grammar as productive morphophonemic processes, as rules (3)
through (7) unquestionably did. If the sound changes result in
restructuring of the lexicon,[12] leaving no synchronic trace behind of their former existence, a different situation results. This

situation is one in which the poets are *unable to understand* the metrical form of much of the traditional poetry, because it is composed in a language which they cannot reach simply by peeling away some of the morphophonemic rules of their unconscious grammar. Illustrations of this other type of situation are numerous. For example, the final -*e*'s which English lost after Chaucer wrote in the fourteenth century were by and large lost not only phonetically, but also from underlying forms, since the synchronic alternations of the language did not provide any reason for retaining them. As a result, Chaucer's poetry was regarded as metrically irregular for many centuries, though written in the perfectly familiar iambic pentameter. One cannot read him now without the kind of philological information that became available only in the last two hundred years. Or, to cite another case, so-called diectasis (or "distension") in Homer is essentially the attempt of later singers to make sense out of vowel contraction in morphophonemically opaque forms, where the right uncontracted form had been irrevocably lost because no morphophonemic alternations gave any clue about its original shape.

Even if the sound changes which bring about the metrical violations are retained as productive morphophonemic rules in the language, and the underlying forms of the earlier period are retained unchanged, one should still expect some disruption of metrical intelligibility if the synchronic order of the rules is significantly different from the relative chronology in which the corresponding sound changes applied. For if such reordering has taken place, a situation could easily arise in which the former system of phonological rules, necessary for scanning the older poetry, cannot be derived from the new system simply by omitting a block of rules from the end. The morphophonemic rules corresponding to the most recent sound changes would form a discontinuous sequence, and some of them would precede morphophonemic rules corresponding to historically older sound changes, which could not be disregarded in scanning.[13] Of the seven Finnish rules discussed here, only one is ordered in historically the "wrong" place. The epenthesis rule (rule 1), a fairly recent change of some eastern dialects, is synchronically ordered before consonant gradation, a much older rule of at least Balto-Finnic date. The gradation of *poikaini* (from underlying /poika + ni/) to *pojaini* (ultimately *poijain[i]*) is therefore analogical, since the closed syllable which causes gradation in this word is of much later origin than the gradation rule itself. The epenthesis rule has shifted into its present early position in the sequence of rules by a secondary reordering.[14] Presumably, then, poems composed before this reordering would have presented certain metrical anomalies after it, since the operation of consonant gradation would have been metrically relevant except in the cases like *poijani* where it had originated only by the recent analogical extension resulting from the reordering of the epenthesis rule. If this situation ever existed, the attested poetry seems to have no trace of it. The new instances of gradation have come to be treated exactly like the old ones, so that *poijaini,* for example, has a short initial syllable as its metrical value.

I would suggest, then, that phonological restructuring sets certain limits on the direct continuity of a poetic tradition. Restructuring is irrevocable change, and to the extent that restructuring has taken place with respect to metrically significant features of the language, the metrical structure of poems composed in the older language will be understood as "faulty" in terms of the new linguistic system. Extreme cases may even be imagined in which the phonological changes are so far-reaching and disruptive that the older poems not only seem faulty but metrically unintelligible. This might suggest implications for the study of change in metrical systems.

But we must also ask about the synchronic significance of such metrical systems. What conclusions, from the viewpoint of synchronic phonology and of poetics, may be drawn from the metrics of the Ingermanland epics?

That the metrical value of a line should be determined by its representation at a certain point in the synchronic derivation lends support for the theory of phonology proposed by Chomsky and Halle. The cutoff point which we found between rules (2) and (3) would of course not exist in a phonology based on unordered realization rules. The metrical system of the Kalevala could not be described in its full generality on the basis of such a phonology. But by the same token, the existence of such a metrical cutoff point poses an interesting problem which generative phonology at present is not in a position to solve. Generative phonology has disclaimed the existence of any linguistically significant representation intervening between the morphophonemic and phonetic levels. Yet here there is an intervening level which plays a systematic role in the metrics. To be sure, it is not the autonomous phonemic level posited by structuralism, but a good deal more abstract than that. Still, it would be of interest to see whether the metrical cutoff point can be characterized in any general terms, and whether the representations reached at that point in Finnish, or the equivalent level defined in the same general terms in other languages, has any systematic status in phonology at all. Even if this should turn out not to be the case, the fact that an intervening level of representations is even accessible, as its function in metrics shows, is psychologically of some importance.

The conclusions reached in this paper demonstrate the abstractness of metrical structure in two different respects. First, they show how necessary it is to draw, with Jakobson, the distinction between the underlying design of verse and its actual instantiation. The extreme complications which would result from attempting to describe the possible lines of the Kalevala without assuming an underlying trochaic pattern, reflected only indirectly in the actual realization, are obvious when the facts discussed in section 1 are kept in mind. Secondly, they show the abstractness of the linguistic representations which metrical rules can operate to constrain. Neither meter nor alliteration can be understood unless the morphophonemic structure of the language is understood.[15]

NOTES

1. M. Sadeniemi, *Die Metrik des Kalevala-Verses,* Folklore Fellows Communications No. 139, Helsinki, 1951.

2. Roman Jakobson, "Linguistics and Poetics," *Style in Language,* ed. Thomas A. Sebeok (Cambridge, Mass.: M.I.T. Press, 1960); Morris Halle and Samuel Jay Keyser, "Chaucer and the Study of Prosody," *College English,* XXVIII (1966), 187–219; Morris Halle, "Linguistic Aspects of Poetic Meter," *Proceedings of the Xth International Congress of Linguists* (forthcoming).

3. Alliteration is confined to word-initial syllables, which, however, need not necessarily be strongly stressed. Sadeniemi has observed several preferential tendencies concerning the locus of alliteration apart from the preference for the beginnings of the cola. Favorite carriers are: (1) adjacent words, (2) relatively long words, (3) downbeats in general.

4. See, for example, E. Sievers, *Altgermanische Metrik* (Halle 1893); A. Heusler, *Deutsche Versgeschichte* I (Berlin and Leipzig, 1925).

5. Roman Jakobson, "On the So-called Vowel Alliteration in Germanic Verse," *Zeitschrift für Phonetik, Sprachwissenschaft und Kommunikationsforschung*, XVI (1963), 85–92.

6. Noam Chomsky and Morris Halle, *The Sound Pattern of English* (New York, 1968). It is not self-evident that this should be the case. One could easily imagine prosodic schemata which could not be stated in the notation which is needed for phonological rules. The comparison between Germanic alliteration and Gothic reduplication strikingly illustrates the detailed analogies which may be found between phonology and prosody.

7. Because Finnish has no initial consonant clusters, I write simply C_0 "any number of consonants" instead of C_0^1 in the schema for Finnish, though the actual number of consonants covered by C_0 is always either one or zero in this language.

8. Actually, identity of analyses by some schema is a generalized definition of the concept of assonance conceived in its broadest sense. The distinction between alliteration and rhyme is given by the formal properties of the schemata. All schemata which begin with the word boundary ♯ are schemata for alliteration; all schemata which end with ♯ are schemata for rhyme, and so on.

9. It will be seen that the Germanic alliteration schema correctly reflects the fact that *st, sp,* and *sk* alliterate only with themselves, whereas other consonant clusters beginning with *s*, such as *sn, sl,* alliterate with any word beginning with *s* other than the three clusters mentioned.

10. The traditional assumption that compensatory lengthening is involved is cogently criticized by M. Rapola, *Suomen kielen äännehistorian luennot* (Helsinki, 1966), pp. 386–389. Rapola notes that it is restricted to certain vowel combinations.

11. For other, less complex examples of the interaction of morphophonemics and metrics, see p. 90 of Jakobson's article cited in note 5, and V. Zeps, "The Meter of the So-called Trochaic Latvian Folksongs," *International Journal of Slavic Linguistics and Poetics*, VII (1963), 123–128.

12. On the concept of restructuring, see e.g., Roman Jakobson, "Principles de phonologie historique," *Selected Writings*, Vol. I (The Hague, 1962); Morris Halle, "Phonology in Generative Grammar," in Jerry A. Fodor and Jerrold J. Katz, eds., *The Structure of Language* (Englewood Cliffs, N.J., 1964); and George Lakoff, "Phonological Restructuring and Grimm's Law," in *Studies Presented to Professor Roman Jakobson by His Students*, ed. Charles E. Gribble (Cambridge, Mass., 1968), pp. 168–179.

13. On reordering of rules as a form of analogical change, see Paul Kiparsky, "Linguistic Universals and Linguistic Change," in Emmon Bach and Robert Harms, eds., *Universals in Linguistic Theory* (New York, 1968).

14. I have proposed in the cited article that reordering proceeds in the direction which maximizes the application of rules. The present case supports this hypothesis, since the rules end up in what is there termed *feeding order*. That is, the epenthesis rule, in its new place, adds new instances which meet the structural analysis of the consonant gradation rule.

15. This work was supported in part by the National Institutes of Health (Grant MH-13390-02).

11. STYLISTICS AND GENERATIVE GRAMMARS

James Peter Thorne

James Peter Thorne's "Stylistics and Generative Grammars" examines the problem of poetic language and its strategic ungrammaticality in terms of modern transformational-generative theory. He rejects the notion that to characterize ungrammatical sequences in poetry we should increase the complexity of the grammar. Rather, he argues, we should consider a poem as a "sample of a different language." Thus students of poetic language should write grammars for the language of specific poems, and these grammars ought to meet the requirements of logical consistency and generality demanded by the general theory of grammars. The grammar of a poem's language, Mr. Thorne argues, should generate poetic sequences beyond the data, otherwise the "grammar" is a mere classification of facts. Hence to read a poem is to learn a language, "to have intuitions about its structure," and discussions of "grammaticality" in poetry must show how certain irregularities are regular in the context of the poem in which they appear. Poetic language, like standard language, makes infinite use of finite means. James Peter Thorne is on the faculty of the University of Edinburgh.

The proposal that a grammar should be considered as a device which generates all and only the well-formed sentences of a language, which has already had a profound effect upon linguistics in general, has begun to exert some influence on the more particular (if less well defined) subject of stylistics. To understand this, it is necessary to consider the way in which one tests such a grammar. This includes checking that for any grammatical

James Peter Thorne, "Stylistics and Generative Grammars," reprinted from *Journal of Linguistics,* I (1965), 49–59. Published by the Cambridge University Press, and also with the permission of the author.

sentence we observe there exists in the grammar a partially ordered sequence of formulae which would generate it. It is an inevitable outcome of any prolonged examination of a theory of this kind that there will arise cases which can be generated but with regard to which a decision as to whether or not they constitute a genuine example of the phenomena the theory is supposed to cover cannot be arrived at merely by reference to existing data.[1] In linguistics this is called the problem of *grammaticalness*.[2]

Obviously no difficulties would be presented by a sequence like *Up of book the running*. A grammar of English which generated a sequence of this kind would clearly be faulty and corrections would have to be made in it. It is with a case like the (now famous) sentence *Sincerity admires John* that problems arise. It is easy to see how a grammar which would generate *John admires sincerity* could also generate this sentence. It is also clear that while the native speaker would have no doubt about the correctness of the second sentence he might well have doubts about the correctness of the first. The doubtful sentence could be easily eliminated; for example, by amending the grammar so that the word *sincerity* is the product of a rule $N_{ABSTRACT} \rightarrow$, and *John* the product of a rule $N_{NON-ABSTRACT} \rightarrow$, and by rewriting the higher level rule that develops the subject of a clause as $NP \rightarrow N_{NON-ABSTRACT}$. But this is not the point at issue. The problem is in deciding whether it is worthwhile complicating the grammar to this extent in order to exclude these sequences from the class of grammatical sentences.

We have said that the problem cannot be solved by an examination of existing data. Even if a diligent search were to reveal that this sentence was recorded among our data this fact alone would not serve to remove our doubts about its grammaticalness. This calls attention to the fact that it is clearly too much to expect a grammar to be capable of generating all the sentences which might form part of our data. Samuel Levin[3] discusses the difficulties involved in "fixing" a grammar so that it would generate the sentence *he danced his did** which occurs in E. E.

---

* This and all following lines from "anyone lived in a pretty how town" are from *Fifty Poems* by E. E. Cummings. Copyright, 1939, 1940 by E. E. Cummings. Copyright renewed, 1968 by Marion M. Cummings. Reprinted by permission of Duell, Sloan & Pearce, affiliate of Meredith Press.

Cummings' poem "anyone lived in a pretty how town." Uncertainty about its grammaticalness causes Levin to regard it as exemplifying a unique syntactic structure. Therefore he assumes that at the same time as the grammar has to be fixed to make it generate *he danced his did* it has also to be fixed to prevent it generating, say, *We thumped their hads,* which (presumably) is neither intuitively grammatical nor actually observed. The increase in complexity which would arise from building restrictions of this kind into an English grammar would be so great as to make it hardly practicable. It seems, therefore, that there is no alternative but to abandon the attempt to amend it in such a way as to enable it to generate *he danced his did,* even though this sentence is recorded. The same applies in the case of *Sincerity admires John.* As long as one is not prepared to tolerate, say, *Insecurity esteems Agatha,* even if the sentence *Sincerity admires John* is actually recorded, then it is obviously preferable to incorporate the small number of rules which would exclude both rather than the large number of rules which would exclude the one but not the other.

These considerations seem to impose a solution on the problem. Since no appeal can be made to the data, use has to be made of formal criteria, in particular some version of the criterion of simplicity. The generative capacity of a grammar will be finally determined by the degree of complexity the linguist is prepared to tolerate in its structure.

It has been suggested[4] that these sentences, observed but unanalyzed,[5] form the subject matter of stylistics. The suggestion is reinforced by the striking and important observation that sentences of this kind are characteristic of certain types of discourse (in particular poetry) long considered the proper subject of a study bearing this name. Unfortunately, the subject matter of stylistics having been thus defined it is by no means clear how it is to be developed.

The reason for the difficulty is obvious. These sentences were originally excluded from the class of sentences the grammar must account for on the grounds that they exemplify unique structures, and that extending the grammar to enable it to assign analyses to them increases its complexity beyond all reasonable limits. As long as these sentences are regarded in this way the condition will continue to hold, and any attempt to reintroduce them will be impossible—except at the cost of exceeding these limits.

Consider again the sentence *he danced his did*. A grammar which would account for all the fully grammatical sentences of English would produce *did* only as a result of rewriting the elements *Verb* or *Modal Verb*. Levin points out that to ensure that a grammar of English would generate this sentence we would have to include in it either the rule $N \rightarrow did$ or the rule $NP \rightarrow T + V$. He remarks that the consequence of incorporating either of these rules would be that "thousands of unwanted sentences would be generated." He continues:

> We could of course reduce the number of unwanted consequences if we introduced into the new rule, instead of the general class V, some subclass of V. It is not clear, however, just how we would go about selecting such a subclass. Subclasses are set up on the basis of restricted co-occurrence privileges in many clear instances of grammatical sentences: such would be the division of the class V into $V_{INTRANSITIVE}$ and $V_{TRANSITIVE}$ for one example. In the case of *He danced his did,* however, we obviously have no clearly grammatical instances on the basis of which we should decide to what subclass of V *did* should be assigned. Nor would it do to use the subclasses to which *do* belongs in the regular grammatical rules, since the clear cases in which *do* is assigned to that subclass have no obvious relation to the sentence under consideration here. For reasons similar to those discussed above there is no obvious way to select a subclass of N if we adopt the alternative procedure of shifting *did* from V to N.[6]

The dilemma facing anyone who regards the task of stylistics as extending the capacity of grammars to cover all the grammatical sentences plus all the observed sentences seems inescapable and intolerable. Either he must accept a grammar capable of generating a vast number of "unwanted" sentences or he must accept a grammar containing statements so complex that they become virtually meaningless.

Partly in view of the obvious difficulties arising from this approach we suggest here a quite different alternative. Given a text, like Cummings' poem, containing sequences which resist inclusion in a grammar of English it might prove more illuminating to regard it as a sample of a different language, or a different dialect, from Standard English. The syntactical preoccupations of stylistics are to be satisfied, not by adjusting a grammar of Standard English so as to enable it to generate all the actual sentences of the poem, but by finding the grammar which most adequately describes the structure of this other language.

Thus if we concentrate our attention on the text in which the sentence *he danced his did* occurs we find in addition the sentences *he sang his didn't, they sowed their isn't, they reaped their same, she laughed his joy, she cried his grief, someones married their everyones/laughed their cryings and did their dance, they/said their nevers, they slept their dream, noone . . . kissed his face, they dream their sleep, and Women and men . . . reaped their sowing and went their came.* To account for these sentences we postulate that in this language *did,* together with *didn't, isn't, came,* etc., is a member of a subclass of nouns which enter into the formulae which develop objects. We call this Class A. Several words which could be taken as nouns, *spring, summer, autumn, winter, sun, moon, stars, rain (spring summer autumn winter/he sang his didn't. . . . they sowed their isn't they reaped their same/sun moon stars rain),* could also be conveniently classified as adverbs. But since it is likely that the occurrence of the phrases *tree by leaf* and *bird by snow (when by now and tree by leaf/she laughed his joy she cried his grief/ bird by snow and stir by still/anyone's any was all to her)* would lead one to propose a rule for the development of adverbial complements as *N Prep N,* it might prove more satisfactory to include another rule which develops adverbial complements simply as *N.* In both these cases there will be problems in deciding which nouns can enter into these rules and whether those that do can also be included in the rules which generate subjects and objects. The easiest solution seems to be to take the first group *(spring, summer,* etc.) as adverbs and the second as a subclass of a second class of nouns (Class B): adding the restriction that only members of this subclass can occur in rules for generating adverbial complements. The other members of Class B include *women, men, children* and *folk.* As opposed to Class A these nouns always occur in the text as subjects, are not always preceded by possessive adjectives and can be modified by other adjectives. *(children guessed . . . that no one loved him more by more . . .*

only the snow can begin to explain/why children are apt to for-
get to remember . . . busy folk buried them side by side)

Another group of words which are most conveniently treated
as nouns includes *no one, anyone, someones* and *everyones*. It
seems unsatisfactory to take them as indefinite pronouns and
introduce them through transformational rules since in no case
in the text do they appear to be substituting for nouns. On the
other hand the pronouns *he, she, they* can be introduced through
optional transformations on strings containing *no one, anyone,*
etc., in exactly the same way as with strings containing nouns
from Class B. Important selectional rules would include the
rewriting of *anyone* as *he (him* in object position) and *anyone*
as *she (anyone lived in a pretty how town/with up so floating*
many bells down/spring summer autumn winter/he sang his
didn't he danced his did. . . . children guessed . . . that noone
loved him more by more/when by now and tree by leaf/she
laughed his joy she cried his grief). An examination of the text
reveals that these nouns, which we call Class C, can be either subjects or objects (*someone married their everyones*) and never
form compound nominal phrases with adjectives.

It would be possible, then, to construct a grammar for this
language based upon the sample the poem provides in which
(among, of course, a great many other possibilities) three subclasses of nouns are distinguished. It will be noticed that this
putative grammar does not incorporate all the restrictions which
an examination of the data might suggest. For example, it would
generate the sequences *Anyone kissed his children, His no one*
loved her anyone, and *She loved the pretty snow.* In the first
sentence the word *children,* which only occurs in the data as a
subject, forms part of the object. Not only does *children* itself not
occur as an object in the text but none of the nouns in the class
to which we have assigned it occur in this position. Nor do any
of them occur in a phrase containing an adjective. The subject of the second sentence includes a Class C noun and an
adjective whereas in the sentences in the data Class C nouns and
adjectives only occur together in nominal phrases in object
position. In the third sentence a Class B noun is preceded by an
adjective in the object while in the text it is only when they form
part of the subject that this happens. On the other hand this

grammar would not generate *Didn't reaped him, He sang didn't* or *Pretty no one kissed him.*

There are two points to be noticed here: First, although attention has been drawn to the distribution of these classes of nouns they have not been explicitly defined in terms of these observable features. The concepts have deliberately been constructed so that their range is greater than all these observable properties taken together. They are theoretical terms, not explicitly defined but implicitly defined in terms of the position they occupy in the complete grammar.[7] This is why the grammar can generate new sentences over and above those contained in the data. On the other hand there are rules in the grammar which distinguish the three subclasses of nouns. Each rule which specifies either one or two of these subclasses but not all three serves further to differentiate them. This means that although new sentences can be generated there are restrictions on the kinds of sentences that will be generated.

An adequate grammar for a natural language, in which, presumably, there is an infinite number of sentences, must contain theoretical terms. A grammar of this kind is imposed upon the data rather than discovered in it. The notion of what a grammar is is logically prior to the formulation of a grammar for any particular language. In any particular case the number of theoretical terms and the kind of statements into which they enter is controlled not only by the need for the grammar adequately to account for the data it is supposed to cover but also by the need for it to be a true interpretation, or model of a general theory of grammar.

On the other hand it may at first sight seem unnecessary to insist that a grammar constructed as part of the stylistic study of a specific text should contain theoretical terms. It might seem that there is no need to refer to an abstract theory of grammar when the body of data is clearly limited and it is possible to construct a complete description of it employing only categories which are empirically defined in terms of observable features: e.g., in the way described at length by Harris.[8] However, failure to meet this condition more or less precludes the possibility of comparative studies on the syntactical level. The main purpose of constructing a grammar which would provide a satisfactory account of a text like "anyone lived in a pretty how town" would be to discover how such a grammar differed from a grammar of English. But such a comparison presupposes that both grammars are of the same kind. For example, there would be no point in comparing a transformational grammar of English with a phrase-structure grammar of the text. On a more general level it can be argued that since any adequate grammar of English must contain theoretical terms it follows that, if it is to be of any interest, any grammar of the text must do the same.[9]

It can be further shown that it is only grammars containing theoretical terms that can be compared in a non-trivial sense. A grammar for a text in which all the terms are explicitly defined by reference to observable features (for example, occurrence in certain environments) is necessarily a description of that particular text alone. A grammar of this kind may be constructed for (discovered in) another text using the same classificatory criteria but a comparison of these two grammars is nothing more than a covert comparison of the two texts. Since no two texts are exactly like each other no two descriptions of them are exactly like each other, but an account of the differences would be trivial. It would amount to saying nothing more than that they are different because they are different.

Since there is no point in constructing a grammar for a text like "anyone lived in a pretty how town" employing only empirically definable terms, and since it is impracticable, if not impossible, to construct a grammar incorporating theoretical terms which would cover both this text and texts written in Standard English (that is, texts containing only fully grammatical sentences), the only alternative seems to be to take the text as a sample of a different language and to construct a grammar for it of the same kind as we would construct for English. The basis for comparison is not texts but languages. The problem is in constructing a grammar for a language based on such a small body of data. In as far as this problem is solvable it is so because grammars are generative. The validity of the analyses assigned to the sentences in the poem, and hence of the rules incorporated in the grammar, is tested by scrutiny of the sentences which the grammar generates over and above those contained in the poem. Only if it is felt that these "belong" to the same language as that in which the poem is written can the grammar be accepted. Any grammar we construct can be manipulated so as to produce sentences over and above those found in the text. But the emphasis that must be laid here upon the generative capacity of grammars underlines an important difference between linguistics and stylistics. The linguist is primarily interested in data only in so far as it tests his theory (his grammar). In stylistics the theory is also important as a means of formulating possible additional data.

This becomes clearer when we consider the reasons against making the grammar a model of a general theory but removing the theoretical character of statements contained in it by incorporating rules which ensure that only the actual sentences of the poem are generated by it. Since the definite article occurs only once in the poem (*and only the snow can begin to explain/why children are apt to forget to remember*) an example of such a rule would be one which states that the noun *snow* must occur in nominal phrases initiated by a definite article and that no other noun can. The example should serve to bring out the pointlessness of such an undertaking. Making the language coterminous with the text removes most of the point of constructing a grammar for it. It means that any syntactical feature in the text has to be regarded as being as important as any other syntactical feature. For example, the fact that there is only one definite article in the poem would inevitably appear as important as the fact that the word *didn't* seems to be used here in an entirely different way from that in which it is normally used in English. In complete opposition to this point of view it could be claimed that a grammar based on a text is interesting only in so far as it incorporates decisions by the grammarian on this kind of point. The problem could be described as the problem of deciding which are features of the language and which are merely features of the sample, when all the data given is the sample.

This approach sets a high premium on intuition. Reading a poem, it is suggested, is often like learning a language. When we learn a language we develop the capacity to have intuitions about its structure. A grammar is a special kind of statement about these intuitions. Difficult as it is to formulate this statement it is still easier to formulate it than it is to comment upon this formulation. (A point which might explain much of the obscurity of literary criticism.) The question, "Why construct a grammar for this language in such a way that it will generate

Anyone kissed his children but not *Pretty no one kissed him?"* invites the tautologous reply "Because the first seems to me to be grammatical and the second does not." Perhaps this is as far as it is safe to go. However, two suggestions can be offered concerning the rationale likely to govern choices made in the course of constructing a grammar for stylistic studies.

First, the emphasis upon comparison makes it likely that there will be a tendency to make the grammar of the literary dialect as nearly isomorphic with the grammar of the language with which it is most natural to compare it (i.e., the language from which it draws its lexis and phonology) as possible. This means not only that it will be assumed that as far as possible all the terms employed in the latter will also be employed in the former but that as far as possible these will be assigned the same implicit definition (i.e., will occupy similar positions) in the total calculus. Thus of Levin's two suggestions that the occurrence of *did* in the sentence *he danced his did* should be explained (a) by a rule N → *did*, (b) by a rule NP → V, the former seems the more acceptable since it involves a difference between this grammar and a grammar of English only in the implicit definition of the term *did;* whereas the second rule involves a difference in the implicit definition of the far more intricately related term *Verb.*

The second point is that although it is exceedingly difficult to analyze the nature of the relationship it seems that there is a relationship between the structure of the grammar which I propose for the poem and my understanding of it. For example, it would be extremely difficult to explain merely by reference to the text why or how I had constructed rules making *she* the pronominal equivalent of *no one* in subject position. It would be even more difficult to account for the rules which govern the occurrence of *his* in this way. But the association of the set *he, him, his* with *anyone* and the set *she, her* with *no one* is an essential part of what is for me the meaning of the poem. I would assume that it had a different meaning for someone who did not relate these items in this way in a grammar of the poem. Similarly with someone who introduced the terms *no one* and *anyone* through transformational rules and who included rules which allowed these terms to form part of nominal phrases in which adjectives also occur. Although to justify my own equally precise rules I can only make vague remarks about *anyone* and *no one* seeming to me to be names of characters but characters who can only be described by their actions, not by epithets. Equally elusive are most of the motives behind my division of the nouns into three subclasses and my rejection of sentences like *They went came* (as opposed to *They went their came*). Again I can only make vague remarks, which in themselves have nothing to do with the syntax of the poem at all, and suggest that it might have something to do with my impression that the self-preoccupation of the inhabitants is one of the most important features of the world described by the poem.

It has been suggested by psychologists that "If we spoke a different language we would perceive a different world." [10] For example, it has been suggested that Russians and Arabs have a different concept of color from ours because they speak languages in which there are verbs of color as well as adjectives of color: "Perceiving a different world" seems a pretty good description of the experience I receive reading a poem like "anyone lived in a pretty how town." To account for this one would have to provide an explication for some such statement as "the meaning of this sentence is not expressible in Standard English." It is by no means clear how one should go about this in the case of a natural language. But the fact that in the cases we are considering we can link difficulty in understanding a sentence with difficulty in incorporating rules which would account for its structure into a grammar of Standard English, might provide a clue. Such an explication would also have to account for the fact that Standard English is obviously an inadequate metalanguage in which to discuss these sentences.[11]

A grammatical analysis of a sentence is not a metalinguistic statement of its meaning. But presumably a difference in the analysis of one sentence and another, or of the same sentence by different people, reflects a difference in meaning. This is why the study of a grammar that someone else has provided for a poem may throw light on possible meanings in it which would have otherwise escaped me. Moreover this could prove to be the case without any reference at all being made to vague, quasi-explanatory glosses of the kind given above. This also explains why it would be pointless to construct a grammar if it were assumed that the sentences in the text represented the sum total of sentences in the language. The more choices, the more subjective impressions of the structure of the language in which the text is written that the grammar incorporates, the greater the chances are that it might prove illuminating to someone else.

Two further points arise out of this discussion. The first is that it is a mistake to think that how good a theory is depends mainly on how "good" are the data upon which it is based. The second is that it can be misleading to insist that the study of deviant or marginal sentences must be postponed until a grammar capable of covering all those sentences which native speakers would agree are fully grammatical is completed, when, even before it is completed, it can be shown that the sentences under discussion will never prove amenable to inclusion in it. The implication is either that it will eventually be possible to extend the grammar so as to include them in the class of sentences which are assigned analyses by it (a proposal which it is impossible to carry out in most cases) or that it will eventually be possible to demonstrate how these so-called deviant sentences actually do deviate; with the added implication that once the grammar of all grammatical sentences is complete this will turn out to be a quite different procedure from the one adopted here in analyzing the sentences from "anyone lived in a pretty how town."

This is, to say the least, unlikely. Consider again the sentence *he danced his did.* Earlier we referred to such a sentence as being observed but unanalyzed. It would have been more accurate to have called it "multiply-ambiguous." Levin suggests two analyses, (1) $NP \rightarrow (Pronoun)$, $VP \rightarrow (V + T\hat{}N)$, $N \rightarrow did$, (2) $NP \rightarrow (Pronoun)$, $VP \rightarrow (V\text{-}|\text{-}T\hat{}V)$. But this far from exhausts the possibilities. There is nothing to prevent one from suggesting: (3) $NP \rightarrow (Pronoun + V)$, $VP \rightarrow (T + V)$, or (4) $NP \rightarrow (Pronoun\hat{}V + T)$, $VP \rightarrow V$, or even (5) $NP \rightarrow (Pronoun\hat{}V\hat{}T\hat{}V)$, $VP \rightarrow \emptyset$, etc., etc. A non-grammatical sentence is one which cannot be generated by a grammar capable of generating all the fully grammatical sentences of a language. To show how such a sentence deviates from full grammaticalness one has to choose one analysis out of many possible analyses to impose upon it. That is, one constructs the rule or rules not included in the standard grammar which would cause the sentence to be generated. Presumably one's choice would be influenced by a desire to account for a deviant sentence by adding the smallest possible number of new rules, thus making its structure accord as closely as possible with a certain type of grammatical sentence.[12]

What has been suggested here is that this account of grammatical deviation should be considered in the light of the observation that in certain kinds of discourse there is a tendency for deviations of the same type to occur regularly throughout the same piece. In these cases merely to list the kinds of deviations displayed is to obscure something which could be explained. In the case of poems it could be argued that it is to ignore the artificiality, the contrived quality of poetic language, also that characteristic often referred to as the unity of a poem. Admittedly part of the excitement I receive in reading a sentence like *he danced his did* comes from the immediate realization that it breaks the rules of Standard English. But its total effect is controlled by the fact that the kind of irregularity it exhibits is regular in the context of the poem. In some poems it even seems that sentences which appear fully grammatical in other kinds of discourse would be ungrammatical there, or that they exemplify structures not in fact represented in the standard grammar. This cannot be explained by adding sentences previously excluded from the class of grammatical sentences to it by adding to the grammar rules which would generate them. Nor can it be explained by suggesting individually the formulae by which sentences of this type could be generated. The only satisfactory explanation seems to involve postulating an independent grammar, which in turn means postulating an independent language. Only in this direction does there seem to be a way out of the dilemma posed by the fact that all stylistic studies are in some sense concerned with texts while those leading to the construction of grammars ultimately are not.

In conclusion, it should be noticed that there is no reason for restricting the construction of new grammars to cases where the text contains sentences which are obviously deviant. In fact it seems that this approach is likely to prove most illuminating in cases where all the sentences in the text reveal a high degree of grammaticalness when taken as sentences of Standard English. For example, all the sentences in Donne's "A Nocturnall upon S. Lucies Day" would be generated by a grammar of Standard English as long as it contained no selectional rules enforcing gender restrictions. But the analyses provided by this grammar would throw little or no light on the poem. A close examination leads me to postulate a gender system much more complicated than, and quite contrary to, that of Standard English. This is based on the opposition *Animate-Inanimate,* and affects not only nouns and pronouns but also verbs. Roughly speaking, whenever there is an animate noun or a first person pronoun singular in the subject there is an inanimate noun in the predicate; while inanimate subjects can take "animate" verbs. E.g., *who (I) am their Epitaph, I am every dead thing, I am the grave of all that's nothing, I am None, . . . all these (referring to the sun, earth, etc.) seem to laugh, yea plants, yea stones detest and love.* A grammar incorporating these rules would reject *I laugh* and *I love* as ungrammatical sentences. It would also reveal the interesting point that in this language the sentence *Were I a man,* which occurs in stanza four of the poem, is equivalent to *Were I a stone* in Standard English. It does not seem entirely fanciful to suggest that these gender rules explain the effects of chaos and strangeness which so many literary critics have associated with the poem.

NOTES

1. Cf. H. Weyl, *Philosophy of Mathematics and Natural Science* (Princeton, 1949), p. 150.
2. Noam Chomsky, *Syntactic Structures* (The Hague, 1957), p. 15.
3. Samuel Levin, "Poetry and Grammaticalness," *Proceedings of the Ninth International Congress of Linguists,* ed. Horace G. Lunt (The Hague, 1964), pp. 308–314.
4. Sol Saporta, "The Application of Linguistics to the Study of Poetic Language," *Style in Language,* ed. Thomas A. Sebeok (Cambridge, Mass., and New York, 1960), p. 82.
5. That we can assign syntactic labels to the words in these sentences does not mean that we have analyzed them. Such a string of symbols can be said to constitute an analysis only when it has been incorporated into a complete grammar [see pp. 193–194 in this article].
6. Levin, "Poetry and Grammaticalness," pp. 205–206.
7. Cf. R. B. Braithwaite, *Scientific Explanation* (New York, 1960), p. 77.
8. Zellig S. Harris, *Methods in Structural Linguistics* (Chicago, 1951).
9. The differences between a grammar containing theoretical terms and one in which all the terms receive an empirical definition are likely to be considerable. In particular, in the second case, since all the terms are "directly" related to data it is usually felt to be unnecessary to supply a component (i.e., a system of rules) for assigning grammatical terms to it, whereas this will

almost certainly be regarded as essential in the first case. Calling two such different systems "grammars" is admittedly very confusing, but in doing so we are only following standard practice.

10.   Leland W. Crafts, Theodore C. Schneirla, Elsa E. Robinson, and Ralph W. Gilbert, *Recent Experiments in Psychology* (New York and London, 1938), p. 343.

11.   It seems that a similar problem occurs in the communication of certain sciences. N. R. Hanson (in *Patterns of Discovery* [Cambridge, England, 1958], p. 33) writes, "That it is yellow is a passive thing to say about the sun, as if its colour were yellow as its shape is round and its distance great. Yellow adheres in the sun, as in a buttercup. 'The sun yellows,' however, describes what the sun does. As its surface burns, so it yellows. Now the grass would green; it would send forth, radiate greenness—like X-ray fluorescence. Crossing a lawn would be wading through a pool of green light. Colleges would no longer be cold, lifeless stone; now they would emit greyness, disperse it into the courts. As a matter of optics this is rather like what does happen; the change of idiom is not utterly fanciful. Grouping 'The sun yellows' with 'The bird flies' and 'The bear climbs' might incline us to view the dawn as a yellow surge over the horizon, a flood of colour enveloping the earth around us. Every student of optics at some time feels this shift in his concepts. This is not a case of say it how you please, it all means the same —This is not merely to speak differently and to think in the same way. Discursive thought and speech have the same logic. How could the two differ?" Whorf (see "Science and Linguistics," in *Language, Thought and Reality: Selected Writings of Benjamin Lee Whorf*, ed. John B. Carroll [New York and London: The M.I.T. Press, 1956]) makes the same point.

12.   Cf. Chomsky, "Some Methodological Remarks on Generative Grammar," *Word*, XVII (1961), 219–239.

12. COUPLING IN A SHAKESPEAREAN SONNET

One of the earliest monograph-length studies of poetic language which made use of the theoretical principles of modern linguistics was Samuel R. Levin's *Linguistic Structures in Poetry*. In this essay, which also pioneered in the use of transformational-generative theory in literary study, Professor Levin proposed the concept of *coupling* as crucial to poetic language. *Coupling* occurs when there are two convergences of semantic elements with positional elements in a passage of poetry. In Sir Walter Ralegh's "The Nymph's Reply to the Shepherd," for example, coupling occurs in the following line:

> In folly ripe, in reason rotten.

The surface syntactic structure of the line is Prep N Adj, Prep N Adj: the nouns and adjectives thus are positionally equivalent. But they pair as well in natural or semantic equivalence (that is, antonymy), and in this paradoxical contrast show the emptiness of the "gowns, shoes, beds of roses, cap, kirtle, and posies" that the line describes. *Coupling*, Professor Levin argues, is the essence of poetic language.

In this selection from *Linguistic Structures in Poetry*, Professor Levin examines couplings in Shakespeare's "Sonnet 30." Samuel R. Levin is professor of English at Hunter College in the City University of New York.

. . . We shall examine a sonnet by Shakespeare and discuss the roles played in this poem by the two types of coupling that we have stated to be important for poetic unity: syntagmatic coupling . . . and conventional coupling. . . . Our primary aim is

Reprinted from *Linguistic Structures in Poetry* (Janua Linguarum, nr. 23), pp. 51–58, by Samuel R. Levin (The Hague: Mouton and Co., 1962), with the permission of the author and publisher.

to discuss these two structures; discussion of other features which may be present in the poem, and which also contribute to whatever effect the poem produces—features like meaning, metaphor, imagery, etc.—are either not mentioned at all or, as in the case of meaning, mentioned only to the extent which is considered necessary for carrying on the analysis in which we are interested. This procedure should not be taken to imply that the aspects of poetry which are thus scanted are regarded as unimportant to the total poetic effect; it is just that such aspects iie beyond the limits of our present concerns. We are interested here in presenting the principle of coupling and showing how it functions in what are probably the two most important matrices, that of syntagm and that of poetic convention. Similarly, the natural equivalences that we have dealt with—the phonic and the semantic—are probably the most important of the equivalences which could be discussed on *that* level. As a matter of fact, the principle of coupling is a general principle and could be elaborated so as to comprehend characteristics beyond those treated in this study. We could, for example, consider the suprasegmental level as a matrix and define additional couplings in which naturally equivalent forms occur in equivalent suprasegmental positions, that is, accompanied by the same stresses and/or pitches, or as occurring in identical positions with respect to terminal junctures. On the other hand, it might be possible to define, say, metaphoric equivalence (in such a way that it would not be the same as semantic equivalence) and then define couplings in which metaphorically equivalent forms occur in equivalent syntagmatic or equivalent genre positions. Questions of this kind, however, are largely left aside in the analysis that follows. Here we shall be concerned primarily with the types of coupling that have been defined [earlier]. The analysis is therefore not an attempt at a full-scale interpretation; it is an attempt to reveal the role that couplings play in the total organization of the poem.

SONNET 30

1 When to the sessions of sweet silent thought
2 I summon up remembrance of things past,
3 I sigh the lack of many a thing I sought,

4   And with old woes new wail my dear time's
     waste.
5   Then can I drown an eye, unused to flow,
6   For precious friends hid in death's dateless
     night,
7   And weep afresh love's long since canceled
     woe,
8   And moan the expense of many a vanished
     sight.
9   Then can I grieve at grievances foregone,
10   And heavily from woe to woe tell o'er
11   The sad account of forebemoanèd moan,
12   Which I new-pay as if not paid before.
13   But if the while I think on thee, dear friend,
14   All losses are restored and sorrows end.

                                    William Shakespeare

Constructionally, the entire sonnet consists of two conditional
sentences, each one comprising a protasis and an apodosis, which
we may call, respectively, the condition and the conclusion. Lines
1–2 constitute the first condition, lines 3–4 (extended through
lines 5–12) constitute the first conclusion; line 13 constitutes the
second condition, line 14 the second conclusion. A statement like
the one above is an implicit description of couplings. If we had
spoken, instead, of two *if-then* sentences, the statement would
almost amount to an explicit description of couplings. Ordinarily,
couplings do not permit of such characterization, inasmuch as
the semantically equivalent forms do not have such narrowly
grammatical functions as do *if* and *then*. We do not call a sentence like *The boy went out and the girl stayed home* a *boy-girl*
sentence, for example. It is therefore not trivial to say that we
have couplings in these two sentences. These are parallel couplings which unify the poem in the first instance. The couplings
may be described as follows: *when* of line 1 and *if* of line 13 are
semantically equivalent and occur in equivalent syntagmatic
positions; *then,* in its zero form, at the beginning of line 3 is
semantically equivalent to and occurs in the same position as
then, again in its zero form, at the beginning of line 14.[1]
    In the clauses introduced by the respective *if-then*'s there are
also a number of couplings. Before these may be described, how-

ever, some modification must be made of the sentences in which they occur—as follows:

1 When to the sessions of sweet silent thought
2 I summon up remembrance of things past,
3 *Then* I sigh the lack of many a thing I sought
4 And with old woes *I* new wail my dear time's waste.

. . . .

13 But if the while I think on thee, dear friend,
14 *Then you restore all losses* and *you end sorrows*.[2]

The constructions underlying the lines in question may be represented in the following manner:[3]

When − *to* − NP_1 *(the sessions)* − *of* − NP_2 *(sweet silent thought)*
NP_3 *(I)* − VP_1 *(summon up)* − NP_4 *(remembrance of things past)*,
Then − NP_5 *(I)* − VP_2 *(sigh)* − NP_6 *(the lack of many a thing I sought)*.
C − *with* − NP_7 *(old woes)* − NP_8 *(I)* − VP_3 *(new wail)* − NP_9 *(my dear time's waste)*.

. . . .

C − *if* − *the while* − NP_{10} *(I)* − VP_4 *(think)* − *on* − NP_{11} *(thee, dear friend)*,
Then − NP_{12} *(you)* − VP_5 *(restore)* − NP_{13} *(all losses)* −
C − NP_{14} *(you)* − VP_6 *(end)* − NP_{15} *(sorrows)*.

Following are the couplings in these constructions; the natural equivalence is semantic, based either on similarity or antinomy; in the two *if*-clauses: $NP_3 \sim NP_{10}$, $VP_1 \sim VP_4$, $NP_4 \sim NP_{11}$; in the two *then*-clauses: $NP_5 \sim NP_{12}$, $VP_2 \sim VP_5$, $NP_6 \sim NP_{13}$ and, after the conjunctions, $NP_8 \sim NP_{14}$, $VP_3 \sim VP_6$, $NP_9 \sim NP_{15}$.

It ought not to be objected that in the preceding analysis the statements are based on a normalization of the poem and not on the poem itself. We bring to bear a number of things in the reading of a poem, one of these things being a knowledge of that part of the language code which the poet and we have in common. Many of the relations we find in a poem are relations subsisting between linguistic elements actually present in the text; many others, however, subsist between elements some of which are in the text and some of which are in the common language code. It is thus legitimate to introduce into an analysis of a poem whatever we may know about a construction and its history of transformational derivation.[4]

Lines 5–12 amplify the first *then*-clause and likewise comprise a number of couplings:

> 5   Then can I drown an eye, unused to flow,
> 6   For precious friends hid in death's dateless night,
> 7   And weep afresh love's long since canceled woe,
> 8   And moan the expense of many a vanished sight.
> 9   Then can I grieve at grievances foregone,
> 10   And *heavily tell o'er from woe to woe*
> 11   The sad account of forebemoanèd moan,
> 12   *Account* I new-pay as if not paid before.

The beginnings of lines 5 and 9, as being identical (*Then can I*), represent couplings. In the remainders of the two sentences represented by these lines we also find a number of couplings. We may indicate the structure of these sentences, with the modifications, as follows:

> *Then – can – I – VP₇ (drown) – NP₁₆ (an eye), unused to flow,*
> *For – NP₁₇ (precious friends hid in death's dateless night),*
> *C – VP₈ (weep afresh) – NP₁₈ (love's long since canceled woe),*
> *C – VP₉ (moan) – NP₁₉ (the expense of many a vanished sight).*
> *Then – can – I – VP₁₀ (grieve) – at – NP₂₀ (grievances foregone),*
> *C – VP₁₁ (heavily tell o'er) – from – NP₂₁ (woe) – to – NP₂₂ (woe)*
> *NP₂₃ (The sad account of forebemoanèd moan),*
> *NP₂₄ (Account I new-pay as if not paid before).*[5]

Following are the major couplings in these two sentences; the natural equivalence is semantic, or semantic and phonic: VP_7 plus NP_{16} (*drown an eye*) $\sim VP_{10}$ (*grieve*); $NP_{17} \sim NP_{20}$ (*hid in death's dateless night*) is syntagmatically and semantically equivalent to *foregone,* and this fact causes *precious friends* and *grievances,* which occupy equivalent positions in their constructions, to be interpreted as semantic equivalents, hence coupled; $VP_8 \sim VP_{11}$; $NP_{18} \sim NP_{23}$.

The rhyme scheme of the poem is *abab, cdcd, efef, gg.* As we have seen, rhymes constitute couplings. The alternate rhymes of the first four lines occur with the first *if-then* sentence, and alternate rhymes occur with the amplification of this sentence through lines 5–12. The second *if-then* sentence (ll. 13–14) is accompanied by the immediate rhyme, *gg.* There is thus reinforcement of the syntagmatic structure by the rhyme structure. The fact that the sonnet employs the two types of rhyme and that the two immediate syntagmatic constituents correlate with these two types is largely responsible (along with the use of adversative conjunction *but* of line 13) for the sense of juncture at the concluding couplet of the sonnet, and the sense of unity at its close.

In the first amplifying *then* clause (beginning with line 3), we find the following verbs, all semantically equivalent monosyllables, predicated of the subject *I: sigh, wail, drown (an eye), weep, moan,* and *grieve.* Inasmuch as these verbs are all predicated of the same subject, they occur in equivalent syntagmatic positions, in a comparable construction, and thus constitute a series of couplings. The fact that they all occur under the metrical stress renders them couplings on the conventional axis also. As objects of *sigh, wail,* and *moan,* we find *lack, waste,* and *expense,* the latter likewise constituting a series of couplings.

The use of the principle of couplings in the analysis of a poem can be of assistance in determining, or at least in suggesting a way to determine, other features in a poem's structure. Consider the phrase *sweet silent thought* in line 1. As the phrase stands, there is no way to decide whether its immediate constituents are *sweet silent* and *thought* or *sweet* and *silent thought,* that is, whether *sweet silent* is a compound or two separate adjectives modifying *thought.* (Without going into a discussion of the question, it can be said that no reliable inference can be made from punctuation or its absence—especially in a case like the present one.) *Sweet* and *silent,* since they alliterate and both fall under metrical stress, constitute a coupling. In line 6 we have a com-

parable phrase in *death's dateless night,* where *death's* and *dateless* constitute a coupling for reasons similar to those discussed
above. There are other structural similarities between the two
phrases: in both, two words modify a head-word, and these head-
words, *thought* and *night,* end in the same consonant. The immediate constituents of *death's dateless night* are unambiguous:
death's and *dateless night.* This fact gives us a structural reason
for analyzing *sweet silent thought* into *sweet* and *silent thought,*
that is, making *sweet* and *silent* separate modifiers and not a compound. In line with this same analysis, we may wish to consider
the phrase *love's long since canceled woe* in line 7. Here, even
though *love's* and *long* alliterate, it could not properly be claimed
that they constitute a coupling, since they do not occur in equivalent metrical (or syntagmatic) positions. Constructionally, however, the phrase corresponds to *death's dateless night.* This suggests that it should be construed as consisting of *love's* and *long
since canceled woe;* that is, *long since canceled* is a single constituent, modifying *woe.*[6]

Falling under metrical stresses is a whole class of semantically
equivalent words that have to do with a court or legal bar. Beginning with *sessions* in line 1, we come successively upon *summon,
canceled, expense, grievances,* and *account*—all technical terms
associated with action at law. These words thus constitute a series
of couplings. Moreover, the word *thing,* in lines 2 and 3, which
from the synchronic point of view is a quite neutral word, even
flat, assumes a much more significant function in the poem when
it is remembered that it was used in Old English documents to
translate Latin *rēs* in the latter's meaning of case or action at law.
Other meanings cluster around *thing,* which may be inferred from
the meaning of the Old English verb *ðingian,* namely: "to beg,
pray, intercede for, come to terms with, covenant, conciliate, compound with, settle." The older meaning of *tell,* namely "to count,"
and of *pay* "to appease" are also exploited in the poem. If these
historical meanings are summoned up so as to cluster around the
present meanings of these words, then *thing, tell,* and *pay* also
enter into the series of couplings constituted by the courtroom
terms.[7]

In the matrix of meter, there are a number of couplings constituted also by phonically equivalent forms. In lines 1, 4, 5, 6, 7,
8, and 9, to mention only the more striking instances, there is

alliteration of *s*'s, *w*'s, *n*'s, *d*'s, *l*'s, *n*'s, and *g*'s respectively. In lines 9–12, again in the matrix of meter, there are couplings constituted by the repetition of words or word-bases: thus, *grieve*~*grievances; woe*~*woe; forebemoanèd*~*moan;* and *pay*~*paid.* These may be regarded as cases of assonance or internal rhyme.

Other couplings could be described for this sonnet, but perhaps enough has already been done to indicate the integral and thoroughgoing role that these structures play in the poem's organization. Their major function is to unify the poem, this unity being due to the various and interlocking kinds of equivalence which lie behind couplings. But another result of the coupling principle as it is used in poetry is to make the poem memorable. It is frequently maintained, for instance, that rhyme is a mnemonic aid. Obviously, rhyme is such an aid because, having thought of one line in a rhymed piece, the possibilities at the end of the succeeding lines are restricted quite severely by the rhyme requirement. But couplings, by definition, impose similar restrictions at equivalent metrical and syntagmatic positions also. In a poem there are thus numerous points—syntagmatic, metrical, or rhyme—at which the mind is prompted to selection from among the stringently restricted subgroups of forms that are semantically and/or phonically equivalent to the form occurring in the preceding equivalent position. The unity and memorability of poetry are thus related, and find their common basis in coupling.

NOTES

1. The use of zeros makes the analysis simpler; it is not essential. Cf. the following note.

2. The modifications are indicated by italics and consist essentially of introducing morphemes where the text has zero pro-morphemes. For a discussion of zeros and pro-morphemes in transformational analysis, see Zellig S. Harris, "Co-occurrence and Transformation in Linguistic Structure," *Language,* XXXIII (1957), 301 ff. The construction *you restore losses* in line 14 is the kernel sentence (ignoring *all*) which underlies the passive transformation that appears in the poem. The transformation *you end sorrows* from *sorrows end* is one that is possible with a subclass of verbs including, in addition to *end,* such verbs as *boil, burn, tear, turn.*

3. The symbol *NP* (noun phrase) represents essentially nouns and expansions of nouns; i.e., constructions with nouns as their heads. Similarly for *VP* (verb phrase). *C* stands for conjunction.

4. Cf. Robert B. Lees, "A Multiply Ambiguous Adjectival Construction in English," *Language*, XXXVI (1960), 209.

5. The transformation in line 10 is a case of simple word order change. The substitution of *which* by *account* in line 12 is made to facilitate labeling line 12 a *NP*.

6. Cf. the analysis of *dapple-dawn-drawn Falcon* in Archibald A. Hill, "An Analysis of *The Windhover:* An Experiment in Structural Method," *PMLA*, LXX (1955), 970–971.

7. The introduction of the diachronic dimension into our analysis has obviously important implications. We shall not go into them, except to say that the analogy to the diachronic dimension of ordinary language analysis is not in the sense of change or process as these take place in a language's development, but to whatever of a linguistic form's background is still viable on the synchronic level. For a discussion of diachronic meanings in stylistic analysis, see Michael Riffaterre, "Criteria for Style Analysis," *Word*, XV (1959), 165 ff.

APPROACHES TO PROSE STYLE

IV

13.   MODES OF ORDER

Richard Ohmann

Richard Ohmann's *Shaw: The Style and the Man* is the first book-length study of a major writer's prose style to make substantial use of the principles and findings of modern linguistics. In this work Professor Ohmann carries forward his earlier definition (in "Prolegomena to the Analysis of Prose Style") of style as "epistemic choice." "Stylistic preferences," he argues, "reflect cognitive preference"; a writer's ordering of prose reflects his ordering of experience.

In this selection Professor Ohmann demonstrates how certain characteristics of Shaw's prose style—the varied ways in which he seeks similarities—commit him to a search for a certain kind of order and to a view of the world which can be characterized as "leveling," in which similarities are exaggerated and differences minimized.

At many points in this study Professor Ohmann makes use of the insights of modern cognitive psychology; in this use he anticipated a position being taken by an increasing number of scholars in linguistic theory: that there should be a greater integration of linguistics and psychology. Richard Ohmann is professor of English at Wesleyan University.

> *Science could stand a cruel and unjust god; for nature was full of suffering and injustice. But a disorderly god was impossible.**

George Bernard Shaw
PREFACE TO "BACK TO METHUSELAH"

A theory of the linguist Roman Jakobson offers a convenient approach to the ordering force of Shaw's style. According to Jakobson[1] the fashioning of speech requires two modes of ar-

---

* This and all following quotations from Shaw are published with the permission of The Society of Authors, as Agent for the George Bernard Shaw Estate.

rangement: combination and selection.[2] The speaker *combines* phonemes into words, words into sentences, sentences into discourses. At the same time he *selects* the elements to be combined from groups of possible alternatives that are in part equivalent (words from the same grammatical category, for instance) and partly different. Normally the two processes get roughly equal emphasis, but with the pull of personality or culture a speaker usually gravitates, albeit slightly, either to combination or to selection. The aphasic often presents an extreme example of such imbalance; he may rely compulsively on one process and fail grossly to cope with the other. That is to say, aphasia is linguistically of two types, "similarity disorder" and "contiguity disorder." The speaker with a similarity disorder can produce words when the context rather strongly dictates them. He can finish common ritualistic expressions or clichés, given the impetus of syntax, or continue a sentence that someone else has begun for him. He can maintain a flow of words once he is caught up in it. What he cannot easily do is initiate discourse, produce the main subject that will lead into a sequence. Neither can he speak of semantic relationships between words, such as synonymy; he has difficulty saying that A and B are the same thing, or even talking of likenesses between the two. The aphasic with a contiguity disorder, on the other hand, can articulate equivalences—a bachelor is an unmarried man—but is unable to build syntactical structures, conduct ordered discourses, or move from one idea to another that is in some way adjacent. All he can do is deal with similarities.

I mention such extreme disorders, not to hint darkly that Shaw is a pathological case, but merely to suggest that a classification of writers is possible according to which kind of verbal and semantic order they favor. The intellectual bent of the similarity-seeker is quite different from that of the continuity-seeker—compare the sort of mind that finds peace in pigeon-holing with the sort that delights in syllogistic or in narrative. Both methods of dealing with experience are essential to sanity, but it will not be surprising to discover perfectly sane men who stress one or the other, and it will not be surprising to find a writer's preference etched in his style as well as in his thought.

To offer this generalization is not to prove it; it must be

filled out and supported in the course of this [selection]. . . .
But I propose to begin, not by deduction from it, but by looking
at some specific facts about Shaw's style.

1. COLLECTIONS OF THINGS

Within the Shavian repertoire there is no more typical connective than "in short." This brusque, let's-get-on-with-it transition caters to Shaw's penchant for rapid movement.[3] It also signals the presence of an equivalence relationship, since its import
is that the verbal expression which follows is a brief version of
the one or ones that have gone before. Occasionally, to be sure,
Shaw pairs up in this way two expressions that are equivalent
only in a very loose sense: for example he closes a long paragraph on the evolution of religion with a sentence beginning "In
short, there is no question of a new religion, but rather of re-
distilling the eternal spirit of religion . . ." (Back, lxxiv).[4] This
sentence makes explicit a conclusion that has been implicit in
the preceding ones; it takes the argument from evidence to inference. But more often "in short" serves as a bridge between
mutually substitutable expressions: "George Bernard (Sonny):
in short, myself" (SSS, 1). In this apposition all three ways of
referring to the same object—Shaw—are so exactly interchange-
able that the result is coyness, for "in short" promises the reader
an increment of new information, or at least a new formulation,
and here that promise is reneged.

The more common and less quaint use of "in short" is to introduce a summative expression that caps a series:

> such indulgences as tempers, tantrums, bullyings, sneerings,
> swearings, kickings: in short, the commoner violences and
> intemperances of authority.
>
> ST J, 173

> raging and cursing, crying and laughing, asserting his au-
> thority with thrasonic ferocity and the next moment blubber-
> ing like a child in his wife's lap or snarling like a savage dog
> at a dauntless and defiant tradesman: in short, behaving him-
> self like an unrestrained human being in a very trying situa-
> tion . . .
>
> SIMP, 85

by dunderheads, do-nothings, incapable hereditary monarchs, ambitious conquerors, popular speakers and broadcasters, financial and commercial gangs, successful revolutionists who are no rulers or stick-in-the-mud rulers who are no revolutionists: in short, by amateur actors of all sorts clever enough to make themselves the idols of the mob . . .

EPWW, 125

In each case the final phrase defines the class that has just been partly enumerated; it gives the intension, as it were, of a class whose extension has been exampled. This duplication of class specifications clearly sets up a similarity relationship, with "in short" standing as an equal sign between two verbal expressions. Of course more goes on here than synonymic word play or pleonasm, for the second label somehow yields new understanding of Shaw's subject—to name helps to know. But it is important to see that naming a thing twice means establishing a semantic near-equivalence between the two names, and thus counts as an instance of linguistic similarity-hunting. Notice, by the way, that the first of the three examples above is actually a *triple* equivalence; in it Shaw begins with a general term, "such indulgences as," follows this with a list of the several indulgences, then gives them a second general name. Such triple overlaps are not at all rare; another one (without "in short") starts with "grounds for divorce such as," continues with an extensive list of them, and concludes with a descriptive parenthesis: "(all these are examples from some code actually in force at present)" (Dilemma, 258).

The transitional "in short" invariably acts as a marker of equivalence, and occurs so often in Shaw's prose as to be virtually his signature. Of course the trick of following a series with a covering generality can be turned without the favorite transition, and Shaw does so in various ways. Most commonly the last member of the series subsumes the others, as a general catchall:

they can squeal their complaints, agitate for their pet remedies, move resolutions and votes of confidence or the reverse, draft private bills and call on the Government to adopt and enact them, and criticize the Government to their utmost . . .

EPWW, 52

incurably hyperpituitary or hyperadrenal or hysteroid or epileptoid or anything but asteroid.

ST J, 16

monogamy, chastity, temperance, respectability, morality, Christianity, anti-socialism, and a dozen other things that have no necessary connection with marriage.

DILEMMA, 185

a political imbecile, a pompous snob, a vulgar ranter, a conceited self-seeker, or anything else that you dislike . . .

IWG, 391

Syntax does not indicate the equivalence relationship, since the "ands" and "ors" that introduce the last members suggest parallelism rather than inclusion. But meaning does the job, for each last member is more general than its fellows. The phrase "anything else that you dislike" clearly subsumes and extends the four epithets that precede it.

In other catalogues Shaw saves the covering generality for a new sentence:

trusted and mistrusted, free in respect of religion, sex and color, and limited by age and nationality, place and length of residence. Altogether a queer jumble of precautions against tyranny . . .

EPWW, 35

You may. . . . You may. . . . You may. . . . These are . . . things that have been done again and again. They are much worse crimes than . . .

IWG, 113–114

Or the series may be incorporated in a larger equation, usually one built around the verb "to be":

the whole range of Shakespeare's foibles: the snobbishness, the naughtiness, the contempt for tradesmen. . . : all these are the characteristics of Eton and Harrow . . .

MIS, 216

> Langland and Latimer and Sir Thomas More, John Bunyan
> and George Fox, Goldsmith and Crabbe and Shelley, Carlyle
> and Ruskin and Morris, with many brave and faithful
> preachers, in the Churches and out of them . . . were our
> English prophets.
>
> IWG, 5

More often than not Shaw allows himself a semantic overlap, in one of these forms, at the end or beginning of a catalogue.

Now the catalogues themselves, as well as the summative devices, are characteristically Shavian.[5] Their amplitude (I have cut several of my examples drastically) and their exuberance suit his penchant for overwhelming the reader with a cascade of evidence or argument or hypothetical example. And though they are often quite effective, Shaw sometimes protracts these catalogues beyond any rhetorical necessity, as if he delights in the form for its own sake. The torrential series is both a persuasive gimmick and a congenial framework for Shaw's high dudgeon. Moreover, at his best he exploits its force without losing any forward momentum. The following sentence is a good example. Through two separate series and one subseries it runs to ground Paley's famous argument:

> And here was a far more wonderful thing than a watch, a man
> with all his organs ingeniously contrived, cords and levers,
> girders and kingposts, circulating systems of pipes and valves,
> dialysing membranes, chemical retorts, carburettors, ventila-
> tors, inlets and outlets, telephone transmitters in his ears, light
> recorders and lenses in his eyes: was it conceivable that this
> was the work of chance? that no artificer had wrought here,
> that there was no purpose in this, no design, no guiding in-
> telligence?
>
> BACK, xxxviii

This sentence has enough structural intricacy, enough irony, enough buffoonery, and enough dialectical substance to justify the dilation of its catalogues. But examples are not at all rare in which Shaw presses the device beyond the point of marginal utility:

> The lion may lie down with the lamb, or at least cease eating
> it; but when will the royalist lie down with the republican,

the Quaker with the Ritualist, the Deist with the Atheist, the
Roman Catholic with the Anglo-Catholic or either of them
with the Protestant, the Bergsonian with the Darwinian, the
Communist with the Anarchist, the Empire-builder with the
Commonwealth idealist, the Jain with the Brahmin, the
Moslem with the Hindu, the Shintoist with the Buddhist, the
Nudist with the Prudist, etc., etc., etc., etc.?

EPWW, 61–62

This is late Shaw (1944); the knack of compactness and richness
has begun to elude him and he is not above proliferating easy
parallelisms for an easy effect. But the slackness of this sentence
comes simply from the relaxation of a structure that he favors
both early and late. For that reason, and because it fits the
pattern of similarity order I have been describing, the Shavian
catalogue is worth considering somewhat more analytically.

Even failing the presence of a summary phrase or an "in short,"
the very construction of a series implies an equivalence relationship among its members. This is most evidently true when the
series ends with "and so forth," "and the like," or "etc." (or for
that matter, with several boisterous "et ceteras," as above). A
continuant of this sort invites the reader to extrapolate the class
in the direction pointed by the given portion of the extension,
and in order to make his do-it-yourself projection he must first
have understood, consciously or not, the *in*tension of the class.
He must, that is, have grasped the rubric under which the members are *alike*. By far the greater part of Shaw's catalogues (and
that means very many indeed) are open-ended, whether or not
they conclude with a label or a continuant: such a series, that is
to say, does not exhaust the class it defines, does not list all the
days of the week, but stops with Wednesday. In so doing it demands that the reader infer similarity, just as he naturally does
when Shaw gives him only the bare title of a class—ploughman,
poet, philosopher, saint (Imm, xvii)—whose members are sup-
posedly alike.

In fact similarity is invoked merely by the juxtaposition of
several terms in a list. A kind of axiom for interpreting human
artifacts might go, "Things are not placed together without
reason," or "Proximity implies similarity." In prose catalogues
the suggestion of likeness gains a good deal of strength from

the fact that the members share some obvious syntactical characteristics. If they are single words they normally belong to the same grammatical class, and the syntactic interchangeability of, say, "hypochondria, melancholia, cowardice, stupidity, cruelty, muckraking . . ." (StJ, 16) hints at semantic equivalence. It bears mention here that although nouns are notoriously *not* the names of just persons, places, things, and concepts, there is enough truth in the old lie to have kept it alive in the face of linguists' righteous indignation, enough truth to make us feel the semantic pull of formal types. Of course the six nouns above have more in common than grammatical class. They are all abstract, they all refer to human activities or mental conditions, they all have unfavorable connotations. Similarities in meaning such as these probably offer the main clues to the notion that cements a series together. But formal equivalence, I would conjecture, is what orients a reader toward similarity in the first place and sets him looking for likenesses. Furthermore, when the members of the series are not so obviously similar in meaning—when, for instance, Shaw includes the concrete "old-fashioned parents" in a series of abstractions (IWG, 195–196)—sameness of grammatical class encourages the reader to dwell on sameness of meaning.

If the units of a series are phrases or clauses, syntax does the same job that word class does for single words:

> Roman Catholic Protestants or Christian Jewesses, or undersized giantesses, or brunette blondes, or married maids . . .
>
> IWG, 498

> tall or short, fair or dark, quick or slow, young or getting on in years, teetotallers or beer drinkers . . .
>
> IWG, 76

> the number of irreligious people who go to church, of unmusical people who go to concerts and operas, and of undramatic people who go to the theatre . . .
>
> ST J, 54

bored by their amusements, humbugged by their doctors, pillaged by their tradesmen . . .

IWG, 51

Such tight parallelism, through the juxtaposition of identical linguistic frames (grammatical forms) whose slots are filled with different words, clearly signals a collation of meanings. Shaw quite commonly employs this device in his catalogues, even to the point of whole parallel sentences. But still more characteristic of his prose is a looser, more haphazard parallelism, in which only the fact that all the members are introduced by the same connective and contain key words of the same grammatical class underlies their similarity. Generally Shaw is too impatient of artificial stylistic niceties and too concerned with content to make a fetish of euphuistic balance.

His more roughhewn brand of parallelism points up similarity, all the same. Consider this sentence, as an example of parallelism in the Shavian series:

> The result is that powers of destruction that could hardly without uneasiness be entrusted to infinite wisdom and infinite benevolence are placed in the hands of romantic schoolboy patriots who, however generous by nature, are by education ignoramuses, dupes, snobs, and sportsmen to whom fighting is a religion and killing an accomplishment; whilst political power, useless under such circumstances except to militarist imperialists in chronic terror of invasion and subjugation, pompous tufthunting fools, commercial adventurers to whom the organization by the nation of its own industrial services would mean checkmate, financial parasites on the money market, and stupid people who cling to the *status quo* merely because they are used to it, is obtained by heredity, by simple purchase, by keeping newspapers and pretending that they are organs of public opinion, by the wiles of seductive women, and by prostituting ambitious talent to the service of the profiteers, who call the tune because, having secured all the spare plunder, they alone can afford to pay the piper.

BACK, xvi

The five-part series beginning with "militarist imperialists" is bound by the faintest sort of parallelism. Each member has as its focus a plural noun (referring to people) preceded by one or more adjectives, but beyond that little matching up of syntactic slots is possible—two of the members even include subordinate clauses. Yet all five are quite clearly linked by their dependence on "except to." At the end of each phrase syntactic movement halts and reverses itself like a typewriter carriage, as the succeeding phrase seeks its grammatical antecedent back in "except to." Thus the members of the series, however unlike in internal composition, are rendered equivalent by their relationship to an inclusive structure. Likewise the other major series in the sentence, but with a difference. There each of the four members begins with the same word, "by," and the reiterated grammatical peg (it need not have been reiterated) strengthens the sense of syntactic likeness, although the members range in complexity from one word to a complicated system of four clauses. Even in such amorphous parallelism as this, formal similarity pleads the cause of semantic similarity, and witnesses a preference for discourse ordered through equivalence.

The writer who builds a serial structure chooses each successive member with an eye trained on likenesses; he emphasizes the process of selection (to use Jakobson's term) by reiterating linguistic elements that are formally identical and close to each other in meaning. It hardly seems too much to conjecture that these parallelisms take form under an impulse toward similarity.[6]

2. LIKENESSES

In the preface to "Major Barbara" (JBOI, 188), Shaw speaks of "the dramatist, whose business it is to shew the connection between things that seem apart and unrelated in the haphazard order of events in real life." Be that as it may, the laying bare of unexpected connections is crucial to much of this dramatist's non-dramatic writing. The volume *What I Really Wrote About the War* is full of essays such as "Patriotic Indignation" that aim to annihilate the differences between Germany and England and show the two countries' motives to be identical in the large context of capitalistic expansionism, however disparate they seem in the minuscule context of national feeling. Again, Shaw's antipathy toward doctors rises highest when he considers their claim to being *unlike* other men, to being exempt from ordinary human fallibility. His socialism is animated by a sense of the degree to which capitalism soils all things alike: Trench's bread and Sartorius' come out of the *same* mouths, Mrs. Warren's motives are the *same* as those of ostensibly respectable businessmen, and Undershaft combats the *same* forces as does the Salvation Army. Shaw's Marxism is the more exuberant for a pleased discovery that all social malproportion can be reduced to one set of principles. In all these matters he looks for simplicity of theory, a single explanation rather than many parallel ones.

Shaw's knack for effective example belongs to the same pattern: his ability to see the homely economics of housewifery as similar to the grand economics of industry provides *The Intelligent Woman's Guide* with a plenitude of instructive examples. In a poet, this highly tuned awareness of similarity in dissimilars might have found expression in a penchant for metaphysical trope; in Shaw's prose its outlets are the more dilated forms of comparison, and a dialectic that is always reaching into unexpected corners.

Take, for instance, his unscholarly treatment of history. Eric Bentley points out that Shaw wrote his history plays *before* reading the history books, trusting his knowledge of human nature to generate historically accurate plots.[7] The familiar result is drama that coheres psychologically but pays little tribute to conventional history, drama in which the characters talk and act like good twentieth-century Shavians. To quote Bentley, "Shaw was not interested in the peculiar character of each period . . . but in indicating what has not changed. . . . The audience learns that no progress has been made during historical time." [8] The idea that our age has shed the foibles of earlier ones is an illusion, Shaw says:

> Go back to the first syllable of recorded time and there you will find your Christian and your Pagan, your yokel and your poet, helot and hero, Don Quixote and Sancho, Tamino and Papageno, Newton and bushman unable to count eleven, all alive and contemporaneous . . . just as you have them to-day . . .

3PP, 206

In a letter to Hesketh Pearson, Shaw subscribes to the old belief that "human nature remains largely the same." [9] This refusal to worry about psychological anachronism is important because it betokens a faith in constant laws of motivation and allows a telescoping of time that makes Caesar, Warwick, Napoleon, Burgoyne, and King Charles such admirable moderns.[10] And on rhetoric, temporal compression has the effect of making all events and people equally available for comparison, as if past and present coexist in Shaw's godlike field of vision.

The preface to "Saint Joan" is particularly rich in trans-temporal juxtapositions. In the first five pages alone Shaw likens the Maid to Queen Christina of Sweden and the Chevalier D'Eon in her taste for men's dress, to Caesar in pretensions, to Queen Elizabeth in length of life, to Socrates in being mis-understood, to Napoleon, Christ, Herod, Pilate, Annas, and Caiaphas in possessing that superiority which inspires fear, to Mahomet in being both saint and conqueror, and to other dig-nitaries not specifically named. The whole preface is dotted with comparative locutions like these:

Our credulity is grosser than that of the Middle Ages . . .

39

[Joan's death] would have no more significance than the Tokyo earthquake, which burnt a great many maidens.

51

compulsion to take the doctor's prescription . . . is carried to an extent that would have horrified the Inquisition and staggered Archbishop Laud.

39

The difference between Joan's case and Shakespeare's is . . .

10

did not apply to her any more than to George Washington.

8–9

Socrates, Luther, Swedenborg, Blake saw visions and heard voices just as Saint Francis and Saint Joan did.

11

The proportion of marvel to immediately credible statement in the latest edition of the Encyclopaedia Britannica is enormously greater than in the Bible.

48

Joan, like Mrs. Eddy . . .

31

She was much more like Mark Twain than like Peter Cauchon.

30

A few of these historical leaps seek a difference rather than a likeness, but in either case Shaw's appeal is to the comparative faculty, for contrast is merely a sub-species of comparison. The burden of the whole preface is an attempt to rub some of the patina of romance and ignorance off Joan's image and restore its original brightness through analogy with figures less remote.

Historical cross-reference and other patterns of Shavian comparison are sharply etched in his style. My collection of quotations from "Saint Joan" is not united by a single grammatical common denominator, but it includes several related forms that are favorites of Shaw's. Some of them are worth a closer look.

First, and most obviously, there are the simple "like," "as," and "as if" of simile and analogy, which would scarcely need exampling except for his rather special use of them to compare things[11] that are in many ways quite disparate (italics mine, here and throughout this section):

producing bread until it will fetch nothing, *like* the sunlight, or until it becomes a nuisance, *like* the rain in the summer of 1888.

ESSAYS, 18–19

To expect him to enjoy another hundred thousand pounds because men like money, *is exactly as if* you were to expect a

confectioner's shopboy to enjoy two hours more work a day
because boys are fond of sweets.

ESSAYS, 108

Joan was burnt *just as* dozens of less interesting heretics were
burnt in her time.

ST J, 34

These are the forms that most openly set one thing alongside
another to exhibit similarity. Note that the syntax on either side
of the comparative fulcrum often supports the sense of congruence:

Joan was burnt
heretics were burnt;
expect him to enjoy . . . because men like money
expect a shopboy to enjoy . . . because boys are fond of sweets.

Other locutions of comparison insist less on exact equivalence,
but indicate similarity just the same. There is, for instance, the
"as" of equal degree, coupled with an adjective:

quite *as characteristic of* our own age *as of* the Middle Ages.

ST J, 40

great popes are *as rare and accidental as* great kings.

ST J, 37

it would be about *as easy* to persuade a bishop's wife to appear in church nude.

DILEMMA, 417

The reader is asked to compare and find similar not two things
but the extent to which two things share a certain quality. Shaw
frequently suggests the same kind of equivalence by using nega-
tives such as "no more _____ than _____," the blank being filled
by a variety of forms:

the ordinary private surgery . . . could *no more produce* a
complete modern diagnosis *than* a tinker's budget can produce
a ten inch gun . . .

DELUSIONS, 12

statesmen are manifestly *no more "captains* of industry" or
scientific politicians *than* our bookmakers are mathematicians.

MIS, 102

A vegetarian is *not* a person who lives on vegetables, *any more
than* a Catholic is a person who lives on cats.

DELUSIONS, 159

The second term in each comparison is more obviously absurd
than the first, and therefore carries the first down to its level of
plausibility. Actually, the comparisons sink both terms to equality at zero: for "no more than," read "not at all."

These forms point directly to equivalence relationships, but
it is also possible to play on the similarity dimension indirectly,
by pointing to an *in*equality, and Shaw's superlative and comparative forms belong to the same stylistic cluster as the locutions
of equality. To say that x is more blue than y (or less blue than
y, or more blue than green) or that x is the most blue of all is
to focus attention on the tests for congruence, just as much as
to say that x is *as* blue as y. To say that x is the bluest K is
likewise to stress comparison, this time of x with the other K's.
Any of these forms, in other words, throws similarity into relief,
whether by raising it or by depressing it. Shaw's use of the comparative and superlative degrees hardly needs documentation,
but a few examples will suggest the variety of possibilities:

[pure alcohol] proved poisonous, maddening, and destructive
beyond anything that the *worst* modern bootlegger has ever
sold in the *cheapest* speakeasy.

IWG, Stan. Ed., iv

could not manage a baked potato stand honestly and capably,
much less a coal mine.

IWG, 122

It is hard to conceive of anything *more* infuriating . . .

ST J, 44

[without Archer] Ibsen would be *less* known in England than Swedenborg.

QI, 158

All the locutions I have been discussing—"like," "as," "as _____ as _____," "more," "most," etc.—abound in Shaw's prose.[12] Their profusion, as well as their often idiosyncratic functioning, is most simply understood in terms of a preference for similarity order.

The evocation of similarity takes still other shapes that are both less classifiable according to form and less clearly associated with comparison. Of Pavlov's experimental procedures Shaw says, "Give me that much latitude and I can prove, by spectrum analysis, that the moon is made of green cheese" (EPWW, 208). Aside from "that much" there are no words here that directly suggest comparison, and yet the sentence proposes an analogy between Shaw and Pavlov, between spectrum analysis and Pavlov's methods, and between Pavlov's results and proof of the moon's cheese content, as well as equating Shaw's hypothetical carelessness in making inferences with Pavlov's supposed laxity. Again, Shaw speaks of "Americans who have made divorce a public institution . . . refusing to stay in the same hotel with a Russian man of genius who has changed wives without the sanction of South Dakota . . ." (JBOI, 234). In this ironic juxtaposition of two conflicting attitudes Shaw compares without any formal signal whatsoever. So, too, his detailing of incongruities: the English object to seeing religion on the stage, but not to having it invoked amidst the carnage of the battlefield or the horror of the gallows (Theatres, II, 22–23). Exposing this absurdity involves comparison, although no "like" or "as" makes it explicit. Such methods are well entrenched in the Shavian stylistic repertory . . . , but they defy accurate cataloguing.

There does remain at least one classifiable grammatical form that is linked with the comparative mode, though rather loosely: the conditional "would" or "should." That "would" is an ally of "like" and "more" may seem odd, but I think it can be argued,

Take this clause: "Under the strain of invasion the French Government in 1792 struck off 4000 heads, mostly on grounds that would not in time of settled peace have provoked any Government to chloroform a dog . . ." (StJ, 41). The meaning will fail of completeness unless the reader understands that the French Government's idea of grounds for murder in 1792 is being contrasted with the hypothetical stand of a peacetime government on the same issue. The comparison here is moderately overt, but even if a conditional sentence mentions only one term of the comparison it usually makes an implicit juxtaposition of an actual state of affairs with one to be imagined, for how can we know what *would* happen without extrapolating from familiar circumstances? When Shaw says that "to forbid us to read newspapers at all would be to maim us mentally" (Dilemma, 425), he offers no contrast to this supposed state of total censorship, but the reader cannot grasp the import of the supposition unless he sees its relevance to the milder form of censorship against which Shaw is arguing.[13] It is a common thing for him to reach out into the realm of the hypothetical for a comparison, and his prose is more sprinkled with "woulds" than that of most writers.[14]

This characteristic locution, along with the others I have noted, is perhaps enough to show how deeply the habit of comparison is imbedded in Shaw's style. What remains is to give meaning to this stylistic fact by placing it against the background of his intellectual profile.

3. LUCK OR CUNNING

I want, first, to insist on the special appropriateness of the word "order" to the patterns of similarity. To make a synonymic identification of two words ("accidentally" means "inadvertently") is to reduce the complexity of the language one jot by adding that much structure to the lexicon. The same gambit may at the same time reduce the complexity of the extra-linguistic world; that is, knowing that G.B.S. is the same person as Bernard Shaw provides a convenient coupling and adds continuity to experience. The learning of "identity categories,"[15] perceptual or conceptual, is for the child a huge step in the process of mastering his environment; he may simplify his behavior a great deal by discovering the thread of continuity in the set of fleeting visual and tactile impressions that represent his mother and another in those that represent his cradle. Such differentiation and identification is essential to the vital economy of a human being.

Equally essential at a later stage of development is the mastery of "equivalence categories," [16] collections of words or things that are not "the same," but of "the same kind." One may not be able to order his actions so neatly or confidently around the category *furniture* as around the category *Mother,* but the addition of equivalence to identity unquestionably brings a large increase in the conservation of mental energy. The world is so full of a number of things that we should all be as helpless as amoebas without a filing system of categorization. We *order* experience as we order language, by clustering things (or words) along the axis of similarity and difference.

That Shaw's stylistic emphasis on equivalence coincides with a stern, disciplinary attitude toward experience is fairly clear: "The business of a dramatist is to make experience intelligible," not to hold the mirror up to nature, Shaw writes to Pearson.[17] And remember his remark about the dramatist who reveals connections between things that seem separate in the haphazard order of life. One way Shaw reveals connections is through his historical leapfrogging; when he lights on similarities between Joan of Arc and George Washington he reduces, however perversely, the complexity of historical fact. On geographical and anthropological complexity he could also work dazzling condensations. After his world tour in 1932, Pearson asked him if he was impressed by anything he saw: "No. One place is very much like another." "By anybody?" "No. They're all human beings." [18]

And (to turn to style) his frequent use of comparative locutions witnesses a preoccupation with the categorizing of raw data. Saying that one thing is like another, or that it exceeds another in a given attribute, or that it lies at the extreme end of a certain scale, means giving structure to experience by blurring differences and sharpening similarities. Stylistic preferences reflect cognitive preference, so runs my thesis, and if this is so, Shaw's style offers strong evidence of a cognitive system whose crux is similarity and neat, lawful categories. And indeed his stylistic search for order has some recognizable parallels in the most central of his explicit beliefs. His attitudes toward knowledge and discovery, to name the most central, rest on a profound assumption of order.

One use of equivalence categories to a human being is their predictive value; if things are of the same sort they not only look the same, but behave in similar ways, or react in similar ways when acted upon. The category "dangerous intersection" may be useful pragmatically as well as cognitively, for instance. The mind can treat each individual as a member of its type, rather than as a unique specimen, and count on its functioning in already ascertained ways. Within limits, an equivalence category renders the new familiar. Now I have already remarked how Shaw tries to generate accurate history from a few facts, a trick that can be turned only by relying heavily on the premise that like people behave alike, whatever their dates. Likewise he claims always to start a play "from a single fact or incident which strikes me as significant. But one is enough. I never collect authorities nor investigate conditions. I just deduce what happened and why it happened from my flair for human nature." [19] This unscientific disdain for evidence explains his preference for Leonardo over Galileo, Butler over Darwin, inventive theorizers in general over fact-gatherers (PP&R, 73). Thus he admires Frank Harris' extravagantly irresponsible biography of Oscar Wilde because it traps the flavor of its subject, and he advises his own biographer, Henderson, to "consult no documents. Go on your old reading and your knowledge of human nature. . . . What I invent always turns out to be true. What I copy in paraphrases from 'authorities' is invariably wrong." [20]

In pushing toward understanding of things Shaw's fault is more often over-generalization than the opposite—from the failure of his smallpox inoculation to the corruption of medicine, from the success of his own unorthodox upbringing to the inadequacy of all traditional education, and from the *Gemütlichkeit* of his Russian expedition to the superiority of the Russian form of government. He is quick to form categories, and industrious in making experience fit them.

The impulse toward order forms his ideas in more specific ways, too. His social thought, for one thing, plays many variations on the theme of lawfulness. People and institutions are predictable according to their circumstances, Shaw would say, and there is thus a kind of natural law at work in society—or *against* society, rather, since it is a harsh and coercive law, which aids the students of history in their explanations but imposes strict limits on the makers of history. Given its head, history is an enslaver rather than a freer of men; "there is no natural liberty, but only natural law remorselessly enforced" (Essays, 97). The essay from which the quotation comes is called "The Impossibilities of Anarchism": a completely free society would founder, according to Shaw, because it would dissolve man's alliance against inhospitable nature. Similarly, his reservations about democracy stem partly from a conviction that no good can come of such a loose confederation against natural forces. Shaw's natural law is a social version of the second law of thermodynamics. Society tends to run down unless men wind it up, for nature's order is antithetical to human order.

The antidote to this ruthless external law is the counterforce of human institution, human planning. Nature requires that men impose social order or die. She permits communities no freedom "to choose whether they will labor and govern themselves. It is either that or starvation and chaos" (Essays, 97). Mind over chaos—a common Shavian plea. Men must work collectively against chance, which is just another name for natural law. And given the necessity of combatting chance with social organization, a large measure of order is better than a small amount. A partial abdication of social responsibility in favor of chance explains the relative failure of capitalism: its "inconsistencies and contradictions are the accidents of an imperfectly organized society. . . . As social organization progresses and develops . . . conditions now undreamt-of will be attached to our personal activities and liberties" (EPWW, 32). Never one to put individual liberty (that is, license) above a sane disposition of resources, Shaw damns Chesterton for the freedom he would allow people:

> They may idle: they may waste; when they have to work they may make fortunes as sweaters by the degradation, starvation, demoralization, criminalization, and tuberculization of their fellow-citizens, or as financial rogues and vagabonds by swindling widows out of their portions, orphans out of their inheritances, and unsuspecting honest men out of their savings. . . . They may contaminate one another with hideous

diseases; they may kill us with poisons advertized as elixirs; they may corrupt children by teaching them bloodthirsty idolatries; they may goad nations to war by false witness; they may do a hundred things a thousand times worse than the prisoners in our gaols have done; and yet Mr. Chesterton blames me because I do not want more liberty for them.

PP&R, 108

In this view the fatal optimism of nineteenth-century capitalism and nineteenth-century liberalism lay in the belief that "a right and just social order was not an artificial and painfully maintained legal edifice, but a spontaneous outcome of the free play of the forces of Nature" (Essays, 37). Artificial law against natural law: much of Shaw's socialism can be understood in terms of this struggle, for he is always on the side of intelligence against the power of blind chance.[21] The twin corollaries of the capitalist faith in chance are, on one side, "the gambling spirit" (Essays, 4), which encourages each man to dwell on his chances of striking it rich, and on the other, the fatalistic belief that "the source of our social misery is [an] eternal well-spring of confusion and evil" (Essays, 28). Nothing could be more antipathetic to Shaw's temper of mind than these two tenets.

If his social thought turns on an axis whose poles are chance and order, so *a fortiori* does his metaphysic of creative evolution. This rather heroic world view, so bizarre as a scientific hypothesis, is reasonable enough as an attitude, a posture, toward the intractable forces of the natural world, and as such is entirely consistent with Shaw's socialism. For here again the arch-enemy is chance, as his crusade against Darwinism strikingly shows. The soundest reason for regarding Shaw's rejection of natural selection as at least one part emotion to one part science is the kind of language he uses in attacking the role that Darwinists assign to chance. He speaks of natural selection's "hideous fatalism . . . a ghastly and damnable reduction of beauty and intelligence, of strength and purpose, of honor and aspiration, to such casually picturesque changes as an avalanche may make in landscape"; at the thought of this system "your heart sinks into a heap of sand within you" (Back, xlii). Darwinian fatalism is an "unbreathable atmosphere," a "blight" (Back, lxiii). Indicative of the curious collaboration of mind and emotion in this position are passages in which Shaw asks for a "credible and healthy religion" to replace Darwinism (Back, lxxii)—embracing reason with "credible" and the moral sense with "healthy"—or in which he frankly speaks of "my intellectual contempt for Neo-Darwinism's blind coarseness and shallow logic, or my natural abhorrence of its sickening inhumanity" (Back, liv)—acknowledging openly the alliance of emotion and intellect in his stand. Throughout the preface to "Back to Methuselah" his argument allots almost equal weight to empirical and esthetic considerations, giving one to think that the wish is for Shaw at least stepfather to the thought.

Certainly nothing could grate upon Shaw's spirit more than post-Darwinian fatalism, or the mechanistic concept of nature from which it sprung. Mechanism meant mindless, directionless, irresponsible motion: disorder, in short.[22] To be sure, it is the appalling caprice of conventional theology, the "superstition of a continual capricious disorder in nature, of a lawgiver who was also a lawbreaker" (Back, xl), that leads to atheism in the first place. But the pendulum swings too far:

> where there had been a god, a cause, a faith that the universe was ordered however inexplicable by us its order might be, and therefore a sense of moral responsibility as part of that order, there was now an utter void. Chaos had come again.

BACK, lxv

The name *natural* selection is ill-chosen, Shaw says, "a blasphemy, possible to many for whom Nature is nothing but a casual aggregation of inert and dead matter, but eternally impossible to the spirits and souls of the righteous" (Back, xlii). Darwin's hypothesis might better be called "Unnatural Selection, since nothing is more unnatural than an accident" (Back, lvi). Shaw's malaise in the presence of either entrenched deity—the disorderly Noboddady of Christianity or the well-oiled robot of science—leads him to the precarious anthropomorphic compromise of the Life Force, a kind of disembodied Supershaw, hampered neither by the inconsistency of Jehovah nor by the impersonality of materialism.

To see a passion for order as the core of Shaw's epistemology, his socialism, and his creative evolutionism is to oversimplify, for his thinking in these matters turns on a conjunction of major Shavian motifs. . . . But the abhorrence of accident, the drive toward rationality (carried sometimes to the point of irrationality, in the case of the Life Force), and the exalting of organization are too evident to ignore. These quests for order and control constitute a distinct stress in the rhythm of his thought, and one with which the ordering force of his style is altogether consonant.

4. SIMILARITY AND EXAGGERATION

Theorists of perception and cognition, in addition to analyzing the methods by which all perceivers reduce the intricacy of their environment, have paid a good deal of attention to individual variations in perceiving and conceptualizing. The tendency to construct new identity and equivalence categories varies in strength, as does adherence to those already formed. George S. Klein refers to the two incompatible extremes in style of perceiving by the convenient names of *leveling* and *sharpening*.[23] The leveler is more anxious to categorize sensations and less willing to give up a category once he has established it. Red is red, and there's an end on't. He levels (suppresses) differences and emphasizes similarities in the interest of perceptual stability. For him the unique, unclassifiable sensation is particularly offensive, while the sharpener at least tolerates such anomalies, and may actually seek out ambiguity and variability of classification. In the laboratory the leveler is much slower to notice changes in the size of squares that are shown him one at a time, or to recognize figures set against a background designed to obscure them. The sharpener sees color differences that escape the leveler, and more willingly abandons obsolete classifications of pictures whose outlines gradually shade into new forms.

A psychological term for the sharpener's attitude is *concrete*;[24] he stresses the unique and immediate experience, as the abstractor favors the familiar and general. As Klein puts it, for some perceivers reality must remain stable, as they *know* it to be, whereas others conceive it as more variable. The levelers resist distortion, unfamiliar forms, change, disorder—like Shaw they treat reality as constant, orderly, predictable.

Today perception is no longer regarded as a phenomenon to

be studied in isolation from other doings of the organism. We hunger for certain types of perceptual experience just as we hunger for certain foods or emotions. Klein has it that an individual "puts perception to use" in the struggle for "equilibrium between two sources of tension, its inner strivings and the demands of reality." [25] The selectivities of our perceptual apparatus "are the means we have for fending off, choosing and admitting stimulation from the welter of the outside world, which, with free entrance, would traumatize and overwhelm us." [26] This formulation is in harmony with the idea that perceptual and conceptual categories work toward the conservation of mental energy.

From the contention that perception serves each organism's particular purposes it is only a short leap to a theory that integrates perception, cognition, and personality, a theory that has won increasing favor under Bruner's leadership. If perception is geared to the perceiver's vital economy, why shouldn't his own pattern of perceptual idiosyncracies be traceable in his personality as well? In support of this hypothesis Else Frenkel-Brunswik finds that prejudiced children tend to be levelers.[27] Their perceptual conservatism is matched by their too-ready categorization of people according to supposed racial characteristics, and a concomitant unwillingness to risk ambiguity or complexity of judgment. They seek an easy conceptual simplicity; many subscribe to statements such as "People can be divided into two distinct classes; the weak and the strong," and "There is only one right way to do anything." In general, they jump to conclusions, are impatient of conflict, and cling stubbornly to preformed systems and categories. When asked to repeat a once-heard story, they distort its unique details in the direction of these favorite categories. Given this cluster of conceptual tendencies, it seems a reasonable conjecture that the leveler's linguistic behavior will also fall in line. One would expect him to stress similarity patterns in syntax, as in thinking. In this connection it is interesting to note that Frenkel-Brunswik calls the devices of rigidity and flexibility "formal style elements," [28] as opposed to the content of the personality.

The part of Shaw's thought and style that I have discussed so far does assign him the character of a leveler, a similarity-seeker, an order-finder. Only one piece of evidence even remotely suggests the dominance of contiguity order, or as Jakobson puts it, metonymy: Shaw's catalogues. According to Victor Erlich, the writer who works by contiguity (the realist) offers his reader a stage "cluttered with *realia*," [29] and the Shavian series sometimes looks like such a clutter. But the resemblance is superficial, for the constituents of these catalogues are explicitly assembled under headings of similarity, whatever links of contiguity may be present. Shaw brings together the members of a series precisely because they are alike. Let him, therefore, be classed with the levelers. What predictive value does this label have? That is, what stylistic and conceptual habits might Shaw be expected to have in addition to those already mentioned? The rest of this chapter is a consideration of one rather decisive answer.

According to Frenkel-Brunswik, the stylistic complex that includes leveling, polarization, rigidity, and so forth, has as another component exaggeration. This is no great surprise; common sense tells us that to place emphasis on polar, all-or-nothing categories is to invite overstatement in many particular instances, since it is not the nature of most things, when they are classified along a given dimension, to lie huddled in groups at the two extremities without any ambiguous cases in no man's land. A person who is "conservative" in the sense outlined above—who insists on conceptual stability and order—may thus seem quite radical in his mode of articulation. Such is the case of the rigid children who think that "there is only one right way to do anything." And such, I think, is Shaw's case.

It needs no stylistic analysis, of course, to prove that he is much more a partisan of hyperbole than of meiosis. He himself calls attention to his habit of exaggeration, treating it as a matter of strategy: "It is always necessary to overstate a case startlingly to make people sit up and listen to it, and to frighten them into acting on it. I do this myself habitually and deliberately" (EPWW, 49). (An overstatement about overstatement! Note the word "always.") But Shavian exaggeration cannot be dismissed as conscious artifice, and hence not a valid epistemic choice. For one thing, an epistemic choice is hardly the less significant because it is deliberate. Furthermore, even if we agree to accept overstatement as a mask, we are left with the question of why Shaw chose that particular mask rather than another. Not, certainly, because it is the only one to "make people sit up and listen," and to "frighten them" into action, for in point of fact Shaw's rhetoric has probably been least persuasive when it has been most hyperbolic—the fantastic rantings of the court jester win laughs but not votes. Shaw is certainly right in saying that he overstates "habitually," and that habit is not to be explained away by adding "deliberately."

In dealing with the locutions of comparison, I have already listed one that can be considered under the heading of exaggeration: the superlative form of adjectives is a clear instance of extreme statement. To be sure, the statement that x is most a of all K's need not be *untrue*, for there really does exist one building that is taller than all the rest, one man that is oldest, and so on. The point is that Shaw's superlatives often *are* overstatements in the sense of being untrue, and are always overstatements in the sense of being especially strong, or extreme, or radical forms of expression. Even if every Shavian statement in the superlative mode were literally true, the presence in his prose of so many superlatives, and the gusto with which he uses them, would indicate a preference for exaggeration. A man who likes to say that Elgar is "the greatest master of instruments in the world," [30] that Webb is "the ablest man in England," [31] and that "the New Witness is easily the wickedest paper in the world" (PP&R, 40), is clearly no lover of understatement.

Less obviously, adjectives in the comparative degree generally serve the cause of extreme statement and polarization. The point of using "more," "less," or an "-er" form is to establish a familiar point beyond which lies the thing in question, and the comparison can be of little use in communication unless the familiar point stands toward one end of the scale. That is, one gives information by saying that George is bigger than David, but much more by calling him bigger than Goliath, and the latter sort of comparison occurs much more often. Shaw says that except for Archer "Ibsen would be less known in England than Swedenborg," not less known than Kant; that Falstaff is "coarser than any of the men in our loosest plays" (3PP, xiii), not coarser than Peter Pan. In using the comparative degree a writer usually seeks extremes.

Much the same thing is true of forms like "as _____ as _____." One need go no further than our stock of trite comparisons to clinch the point: as dead as a doornail, as quiet as a mouse, as pure as the driven snow, and so forth. Lifeless though these phrases are, they hold a firm place in casual speech because they offer quick verbal access to the supposed extremes of deadness, purity, quietness, etc.[32] Shaw's more original comparisons point just as surely to extremes:

> A life spent in prayer and almsgiving is really as insane as a life spent in cursing and picking pockets . . .
>
> DILEMMA, 199

> The notion that any harm could come of so splendid an enlightenment seemed as silly as the notion that atheists would steal all our spoons.
>
> BACK, lxiv

But these points of reference are arbitrarily chosen for emphasis alone; Shaw more often makes a comparison count as both rhetoric *and* argument, by enclosing within it a miniature *reductio ad absurdum*. Thus when he says that voters "have no more experience of capital than a sheep has of a woolen mill" (IWG, 353), the comparison builds on a logical relationship: voters are to capital as sheep are to woolen mills. Similarly: "an army of light is no more to be gathered from the human product of nineteenth-century civilization than grapes are to be gathered from thistles" (Essays, 63). Many of Shaw's analogies play at the same game:

> To accept a West End manager as an expert in theatres because he is an actor is much as if we were to accept the organist of St. Paul's Cathedral as an expert on music halls because he is a musician.
>
> DILEMMA, 416

All of these equivalence forms represent a reaching out for extremes—what I have been calling exaggeration. Their profusion in Shaw's prose helps create its peculiar vividness, or, in less happy moments, its peculiar stridency.

In addition to these locutions of comparison, which I have previously used to illustrate Shaw's affection for equivalence categories, there are other important stylistic patterns that jibe with his preference for extremities. One particularly common frame is "so _____ that _____"; on just two pages of *The Intelligent Woman's Guide* (pp. 157–158) these six examples occur:

> It soon became so certain that free Capitalism in drink in England would destroy England, that the Government was forced to interfere.

> Spirits can be distilled so cheaply that it is quite possible to make a woman "drunk for a penny: dead drunk for twopence" . . .

> had to pay the Government so much money that he could make no profit . . .

> this made the drink so dear that . . . the working people could not afford to drink as recklessly . . .

> it was prohibited in so many States that it became possible to make a Federal law . . .

> The benefits . . . were so immediate and so enormous that . . .

It is no coincidence that this locution appeals to Shaw, for it both emphasizes the extremity of some attribute and draws a lawlike connection between the attribute and its consequences. The man who likes his categories tight wants them that way so that he may use just one attribute as a reliable clue to many others. From membership in such a category certain results follow, and the "so _____ that _____" pattern gives prominence to this sequence of attribute and effect, as well as to extremity.

Another formal marker of Shavian overstatement that links it with categorization is the high incidence of a certain type of determiner. Determiners are those words which can replace "the" in a linguistic frame.[33] They include the possessive pronouns, the numbers, and, of special interest here, a group of words touching on the relationship between classes and their members: "a," "an," "every," "no," "all," "each," "some," "any," "few," "more," "most," "many," "much." A few are roughly equivalent to the quantifiers of logic, the symbols that indicate whether an expression applies to all x or to at least one x. Here, as often, ordinary language is much richer in distinctions than is logic, and can specify various degrees of fullness or emptiness in its classes.

Naturally these determiners figure prominently in all speech and writing, but one might expect that a writer who, like Shaw, deals both in exaggeration and in neat categories, would favor the more extreme determiners, those that specify either full or empty classes. And indeed, if we count occurrences of these words both as nouns and as determiners, as well as derivatives such as "nobody" and "everything," the frequency is quite impressive. Two pages of Shaw's prose contain the following examples:

everybody	they all
all that he or she had	Nobody
each took	no business
all known to one another	Everybody
all of them	no street lamp
they all	any healthy person (that is, *every*
Each member	healthy person)
Every house	all paid for
have no right	everybody
each family	all we have
they all	do not pay any
every house	at all

IWG, 13–14

Many of these all-or-nothing words are unobtrusively buried in the flow of syntax, to be sure, and cannot have deep significance; but in mass they certainly reveal a predisposition toward sharp boundaries, rigid categories, and exaggeration.

Exaggeration, finally, is a common function of adverbs, particularly those that modify adjectives or other adverbs. In fact, this group of words can be distinguished grammatically from those that modify verbs. One modern grammarian separates them entirely from the adverbs, and calls the resulting class "degree words." [34] Their semantic weight is normally one of intensification, of insisting doubly on the force of the adjective modified. This is clearly true of such degree words as "very," "extremely," "so," "most," and "only"; and it is also true in a less obvious way of many others. The modification of "perfunctory" by "intolerably" (War, 257) brings an increment of new information about the attitude of the writer, but mainly it underscores the perfunctoriness. Or consider "really dangerous" and "quite understandable." Shaw's prose is dotted with such intensifiers; any given page yields a significant number of them (italics mine):

too often	*most* impossible
really effective	*thoroughly* planned
so complete	*grotesquely* realistic
extraordinarily sanguine	*revoltingly* incongruous
seriously *enough*	*more* seriously
quite seriously	

PPU I, xi

"Grotesquely" and "revoltingly" are the only words in this list whose meanings are not entirely devoted to degree, and even they clearly serve to intensify—realistic to the extent of being grotesque; incongruous to the point of revulsion. The high frequency of degree words, then, is another link in the stylistic chain that unites overstatement, polarization, and equivalence.

When these several locutions of hyperbole are added up, together with some miscellaneous ones, the total is a rather impressive indicator of Shaw's allegiance to exaggeration, and to leveling. At the risk of becoming tedious, I shall include one last gleaning (from thirty lines of Shaw), this time a comprehensive catalogue of words and phrases that clearly suggest degree, extent, limits, extremes, quantity, and the like:

less . . . than	best
rather	every other case
less fuss than	such inconvenience . . . as
either party	ten times over
any two	all laws
most laws	stronger
only people	strongest
no position	avowedly illicit
no career	often

as hard . . . as	as tyrannical
the worst	Even when
all normal people	no such
rather than	negligible
not even	How common
so convincingly	nobody
nothing	various other

DILEMMA, 183–84

Insignificant though some of these words are, the size of the list suggests the extent to which Shaw's prose moves in an *ambiance* of degree, and especially, of extreme degree. Hardly a sentence goes by without some prodding of the reader into an awareness of extent.

Shaw has probably gathered as much notoriety for his peccadilloes against common sense as for his championing of it. Everyone knows how he fought vaccination long after the flow of evidence had clearly turned against him, how he allowed the useless sadism of a few experimenters to persuade him that vivisection should be totally outlawed, how his admiration of strong men shaded into perverse enthusiasm for Mussolini, Stalin, and Hitler. Is it not possible that such lapses of reason have their source in excessively rigid categorizing? Some osteopaths, radiologists, and other practitioners unlicensed in Shaw's England have effected cures, and many registered doctors have killed their patients: therefore, doctors are frauds and cranks are men of science. Shaw never proffers such reasoning explicitly; the flaws in it are too crude. But it seems likely that his refusal to divorce lost causes long abandoned by less imaginative people is cousin to the leveler's unwillingness to tolerate change, to his passion for tight categories, and to the associated habit of exaggeration.

The drive toward similarity order is on the whole a great Shavian virtue; to "show the connection between things that seem apart and unrelated in the haphazard order of events" is an intellectual goal of the highest respectability and utility, especially for a social critic. But the defect of the virtue is Shaw's testy inflexibility and his accompanying excesses of exaggeration. Perhaps one cannot spend a lifetime cultivating conceptual order

—and, importantly, stylistic order—without harvesting, in a bumper crop, at least a few weeds.

NOTES

1. "Two Aspects of Language and Two Types of Aphasic Disturbances," in Roman Jakobson and Morris Halle, *Fundamentals of Language* (The Hague, 1956).

2. This distinction parallels Saussure's famous one between *rapports syntagmatiques* and *rapports associatifs* in: Ferdinand de Saussure, *Cours de Linguistique Générale* (Paris, 1955), pp. 170–175. Saussure, however, restricts associative links by equating them with semantic connections in the mind: roughly, *connotations*. I prefer Jakobson's notion of similarity, since it includes purely grammatical likenesses as well.

3. The pace of Shaw's style has been singled out for praise by Dixon Scott in "The Innocence of George Bernard Shaw," in *Men of Letters* (London, 1916), pp. 19–23.

4. My references to Shaw's works are, wherever possible, to the *Ayot St. Lawrence Edition of The Collected Works of Bernard Shaw* (New York, 1930–1932). Page references apply also to *The Works of Bernard Shaw* (London, 1930–1932), for which the same type was used. In the following key to my in-text references the volumes belong to The Ayot St. Lawrence edition unless otherwise specified.

And	*Androcles and the Lion, Overruled, Pygmalion*
Back	*Back to Methuselah*
Black Girl	*The Adventures of the Black Girl in Her Search for God* (London, 1932)
Delusions	*Doctor's Delusions, Crude Criminology, Sham Education*
Dilemma	*The Doctor's Dilemma, Getting Married, The Shewing-Up of Blanco Posnet*
EPWW	*Everybody's Political What's What?* (London, 1944)
Essays	*Essays in Fabian Socialism*
HH	*Heartbreak House, Great Catherine, Playlets of the War*
IK	*The Irrational Knot*
Imm	*Immaturity*
IWG	*The Intelligent Woman's Guide to Socialism and Capitalism*
IWG (Stan. Ed.)	*The Intelligent Woman's Guide to Socialism, Capitalism, Sovietism and Fascism,* Standard Edition (London, 1932)
JBOI	*John Bull's Other Island, How He Lied to Her Husband, Major Barbara*
M&S	*Man and Superman*
Mis	*Misalliance, The Dark Lady of the Sonnets, Fanny's First Play*
Music	*Music in London 1890–94* (3 vols.)
PP&R	*Pen Portraits and Reviews*
PPU	*Plays Pleasant and Unpleasant* (2 vols.)

QI	*The Quintessence of Ibsenism, The Perfect Wagnerite, The Sanity of Art*
Simp	*The Simpleton, The Six, and The Millionairess. Being Three More Plays by Bernard Shaw* (London, 1936)
SSS	*Sixteen Self Sketches, Standard Edition* (London, 1949)
StJ	*Saint Joan, The Apple Cart*
Terry	*Ellen Terry and Bernard Shaw: A Correspondence,* ed. Christopher St. John (London, 1931)
Theatres	*Our Theatres in the Nineties* (3 vols.)
3PP	*Three Plays for Puritans; The Devil's Disciple, Caesar and Cleopatra, Captain Brassbound's Conversion*
Too True	*Too True to Be Good, Village Wooing & On the Rocks. Three Plays by Bernard Shaw* (London, 1934)
War	*What I Really Wrote about the War*

5. See [in *Shaw: The Style and the Man*] Appendix I, Table 1 [an analysis of series].

6. I mean this literally as a conjecture about the mental processes of the writer. There is no use pretending that style (or content) is prophylactically insulated from the mind of the writer. Of *course* action, ideas, and style all issue from a mentality, whatever the scruples of critical theory, and I propose to speculate from time to time about Shaw's mentality, though that is not the main purpose of my analysis.

7. Eric Bentley, *Bernard Shaw* (New York, 1957), p. 159.

8. Bentley, *Bernard Shaw,* p. 160.

9. Quoted in Hesketh Pearson, *G.B.S., A Full Length Portrait* (New York, 1942), p. 196.

10. One of the tenets of Creative Evolution is that the experience of the past is condensed in the living, and this notion of a symbiotic mental relationship between man and his ancestors is merely the inverse of Shaw's vision of history, which projects the experience of the living into the lives of the dead.

11. "Things" in the broadest sense, including events, concepts, situations.

12. See Appendix I, Table 2 [an analysis of comparative forms].

13. He is also making a more direct comparison, for the preceding clause runs "I should not object to a law to compel everybody to read two newspapers. . . ." There is no necessity for a conditional clause to be accompanied by such a foil as this, but it is surprising how often such pairs occur in Shaw.

14. See Appendix I, Table 3 [occurrences of "would"].

15. See Jerome Bruner, Jacqueline J. Goodnow, George A. Austin, *A Study of Thinking* (New York, 1956), pp. 2–3.

16. Bruner et al., pp. 3–5.

17. Pearson, *G. B. S.,* p. 143.

18. Pearson, p. 359.

19. *New York Times Book Review,* Nov. 18, 1945. Quoted by Bentley, *Bernard Shaw,* p. xix.

20. Archibald Henderson, *George Bernard Shaw: Man of the Century* (New York, 1956), pp. xxxi–xxxii.

21. In *Bernard Shaw and the Nineteenth-Century Tradition* (Norman, Okla., 1958), Julian B. Kaye traces the opposition of intelligence and *laissez-faire* mechanism to Carlyle (pp. 10–11), who was one of Shaw's spiritual mentors. Kaye's book usefully points to many nineteenth-century antecedents

of Shaw's thought, but I would resist the conclusion that such genealogy goes far toward *explaining* Shaw. The ideas were there for him to build on, well and good. The question still remains what there was in Shaw that made him adopt precisely these ideas out of the infinity that were available to him.

22. Mechanism antagonizes Shaw wherever he encounters it. He finds the humor mechanistic in "The Importance of Being Earnest," and sums up his reservations about the play by calling it a "mechanical rabbit" (quoted by Pearson, p. 147).

23. George S. Klein, "The Personal World Through Perception," in *Perception; an Approach to Personality*, eds. Robert R. Blake and Glenn V. Ramsey (New York, 1951), pp. 328–355.

24. See Else Frenkel-Brunswik, "Intolerance of Ambiguity as an Emotional and Perceptual Personality Variable," in *Perception and Personality: a Symposium*, eds. Jerome S. Bruner and David Krech (Durham, N.C., 1950), p. 133. Frenkel-Brunswik takes the terms from K. Goldstein and M. Scheerer, *Abstract and Concrete Behavior, Psychological Monographs*, 1941, vol. 53, no. 239.

25. In Blake and Ramsey, eds., *Perception*, p. 335.

26. George S. Klein and Herbert Schlesinger, "Where is the Perceiver in Perceptual Theory?" in *Perception and Personality*, pp. 37–38.

27. "Intolerance of Ambiguity," pp. 108–143. Frenkel-Brunswik does not use the terms "leveler" and "sharpener," but her categories are quite similar.

28. "Intolerance of Ambiguity," p. 140. There is little point in classifying Shaw with Frenkel-Brunswik's prejudiced children, but it may be worth noting that as a boy he was a considerable snob. He was so humiliated at having been sent briefly to a school where the other students were Catholics and sons of tradesmen that he kept the fact secret for over eighty years (SSS, 42–43).

29. Victor Erlich, "Gogol and Kafka: A Note on Realism and Surrealism," in *For Roman Jakobson*, ed. Morris Halle (The Hague, 1956), p. 101.

30. *The Star*. Sept. 27, 1930; quoted by Henderson, p. 203.

31. Quoted by Henderson, p. 211.

32. There are a very few such clichés that pick their point of reference from the bottom of the relevant scale ("clear as mud," for instance), but their purpose is ironic.

33. See Fries, *The Structure of English*, p. 89.

34. Fries, pp. 92–94.

14. CONNECTIVES IN SWIFT'S PROSE STYLE

Louis T. Milic

Louis T. Milic's *A Quantitative Approach to the Style of Jonathan Swift* is the first book-length work that uses both modern descriptive linguistics and the assistance of the electronic computer to study the style of a major writer. In this selection Professor Milic analyzes the rhetorical and stylistic functions of Swift's use of connectives: coordinating conjunctions, subordinating conjunctions, and conjunctive adverbs and phrases. These function words, even though most of them are semantically empty, are of great importance in Swift's style; they lead, Professor Milic argues, to rhetorical persuasiveness rather than clarity in Swift's prose. Louis T. Milic is associate professor of English at Teachers College, Columbia University.

"A close reasoner and a good writer in general may be known by his pertinent use of *connectives*." [1] Although Coleridge illustrated this opinion with a reference to the seventeenth-century Whig, Samuel Johnson, it is especially applicable to Swift. His way with conjunctions and related words is a fundamental aspect of his writing.

Curme traces the history of the modern use of subordination and connection (hypotaxis) from a primitive stage of communication, in which related propositions were simply laid side by side, the relationship to be discerned by the reader (parataxis).[2] Proverbs still retain that paratactic feature: "Easy come, easy go." The intermediate stage between parataxis and full hypotaxis is one in which *and* is made to serve all kinds of connective uses,

Reprinted from *A Quantitative Approach to the Style of Jonathan Swift,* by Louis T. Milic (The Hague: Mouton and Co., 1967), pp. 122–136, with the permission of the author and publisher.

as in such dialects as Irish English, for example: "Did you not hear his reverence, and he speaking to you now?"[3] It is possible to see a remnant of this earlier syntax in the still common omission of such relatives as *which* or *that* in modern English prose; and paratactic clauses are not always considered reprehensible even in formal writing. Nonetheless, the avoidance of connectives is the exception in modern English.

Though it may be surmised that the extensive use of connectives has rendered English less direct and perhaps less colorful, there is no gainsaying that the language has increased in clarity and logical power since their emergence. But more than one writer has probably become aware of the suspicion expressed by the eighteenth-century rhetorician George Campbell: "Of all the parts of speech, the conjunctions are the most unfriendly to vivacity."[4] Perhaps as a product of these conflicting trends, there is a wide variation in the use of connectives, in such matters as choice and range of types, positioning, frequency. In this stylistic feature, it may be expected that mature writers will express a consistent preference which may be isolated by careful examination.[5]

The problem of connectives is closely related to the questions of transition and of reference. A writer articulating his thought wishes to indicate the relationship of each segment to the next and to suggest at intervals how far he has gone in the argument, as well as to set at rest any questions that may arise in the mind of the reader. The solution to this problem is in part structural, a matter of organizing the parts of the discourse into a rational and coherent order. But to do so provides only a partial solution, given the complexity of human thought and the unwillingness of many readers. Connective signposts provide the reader with the author's own key to the relation of the materials and throw the entire composition into focus. Good writers must always be concerned about the appropriateness of their connectives, as Locke suggests:

> The words whereby [the mind] signifies what connexion it gives to the several affirmations and negations, that it unites in one continued reasoning or narration, are generally called *particles:* and it is in the right use of these that more particularly consists the clearness and beauty of a good style. To think well, it is not enough that a man has ideas clear and

distinct in his thoughts, nor that he observes the agreement or disagreement of some of them; but he must think in train, and observe the dependence of his thoughts and reasonings upon one another. And to express well such methodical and rational thoughts, he must have words to show what connexion, restriction, distinction, opposition, emphasis, &c., he gives to each respective *part* of his discourse. To mistake in any of these, is to puzzle instead of informing his hearer: and therefore it is, that those words which are not truly by themselves the names of any ideas are of such constant and indispensable use in language, and do much contribute to men's well expressing themselves.[6]

A plausible place to begin the search for connectives is the beginning of a sentence. I had earlier observed that Swift seemed to have a predilection for coordinating conjunctions at the head of his sentences. A rough preliminary count was made of the first word in several hundred sentences from the works of Swift and a selection of authors whose styles had considerable reputations: Addison, Johnson, Gibbon, Macaulay, Butler, and Hemingway.[7] The predominant impressions emerging from an inspection of the results are these: Gibbon begins forty per cent of his sentences with articles, Swift only ten per cent of his, the others falling between, near the low end; conversely, only ten per cent of Gibbon's sentences begin with pronouns, whereas nearly half of Hemingway's do, Swift being second with thirty per cent; as might have been expected, Hemingway uses fewest introductory conjunctions, but the other writers, headed by Johnson and Swift, are quite uniform in this category. Gibbon and Hemingway, it seems, represent polar extremes in introductory habits; Swift and Butler are remarkably similar, except for conjunctions. The most interesting finding, however, is that Swift uses more than twice as many coordinating conjunctions as Gibbon and Johnson, the runners-up. This count, tentative as it is, supports the observation I had made while reading *Gulliver's Travels* that Swift seemed to begin many sentences with coordinating conjunctions. A more precise count was now in order to test the accuracy of the observation with more significant data.

For this tabulation, the authors are limited to Addison, Johnson and Macaulay, in addition to Swift.[8] Only three classes of introductory words are counted: coordinating conjunctions, subordinating conjunctions, and conjunctive adverbs (and phrases).[9]

The results of this test are gratifyingly conclusive.[10] Table I gives the details.

TABLE I*

Percentage of Initial Connectives in 2000-sentence Samples of Addison, Johnson, Macaulay, and Swift

Connective	Addison	Johnson	Macaulay	Swift
C	5.5	5.8	7.4	20.2
S	7.1	6.2	4.1	5.4
SC	3.3	1.4	1.5	8.3
Total	15.9	13.4	13.0	33.9

* C, coordinating conjunctions; S, subordinating conjunctions; SC, sentence-connectors. [Ed.]

Over-all, Swift's use of the connectives in these three classes is more than twice as great as that of any of the three other writers.[11] To the reader of Swift, it would appear that he begins one sentence in five with a coordinating conjunction and one in three with a connective of some sort. The details of the tabulation further reveal that Swift makes unusually heavy use of *and, but* and *for,* half his connectives consisting of these three, the favorite being *but*.[12] This pattern of preference is surely a striking peculiarity of his style.[13] Perhaps this peculiarity is most striking because of the limitation it implies. A writer who begins one-sixth of his sentences in much the same way will seem monotonous and repetitious. Moreover, it might be difficult to imagine how he could readily adapt such a mechanism to the necessity of varying his transitions from point to point, unless he wrote always about the same subject or unless his arguments followed a rigidly similar pattern.

But limitation seems unlikely. A glance at the list of Swift's writings reveals a wide range of interests: politics, religion, economics, manners, language, history, even "Thoughts on Various Subjects," which may be taken as a symbol of his wide-ranging mind. Neither is it true that his method of argument is always the same. Some works are expository and some persuasive; some operate by *reductio ad absurdum*, some by irony, some by paradox, sarcasm (even vilification); some are satirical, some parodic, some homiletic, some narrative. In this storehouse of matters and manners one can readily detect (what no one seems inclined to deny him) a flexible and versatile mind, unlikely to be dully bound to a minute repertory of introductory devices, especially a mere triad of conjunctions.

The three coordinating conjunctions in question (*and, but, for*) may from the "notional" point of view be considered as additive, adversative, and causal. It is true that these three functions seem to represent the major types of links between related propositions. But it is unlikely that they would alone offer adequate subtlety of nuance for an ingenious reasoner like Swift. I speculated that in some manner these conjunctions were varied, were given a different coloring from one use to the next in order to accomplish the variety of tasks that connectives are used for. A possibility that seemed likely, on the basis of an earlier observation I had made, was the linking of the introductory word with some following word in order to produce a suitable range of compounds, such as *and* plus another connective. An examination of a number of Swift's works reveals that a coordinating conjunction is indeed often followed by another word which may be classified as a connective or which has connective quality.[14]

In English it is normal to expect to find the subject (a noun or nominal) near the beginning of a sentence. When the sentence begins with a connective, it is safe to expect that the next word will be a nominal or a determiner. But a surprising number of times[15] the subject is deferred to make way for a connective or transitional word. Such collocations may be found on almost any page of Swift's works.[16] It is possible to infer, after one has gathered a sufficient number of illustrations of this procedure, that Swift does not use his introductory *and, but* or *for* in the customary way, in order to impart the logical aspect of the connection between one sentence and the next. Rather, he seems to use it as a kind of neutral connective, that is, a word which shows only that one sentence is connected with another without reference to the nature of the connection.[17]

Despite Swift's considerable dependence on a limited number of coordinating conjunctions, his use of connectives of all types is less limited than his contemporaries'. This hypothesis was tested by counting the number of connective types that appear in consecutive 1000-word samples of Addison, Johnson, Gibbon, and Swift. The results, which are merely indicative, are given in Table II.

TABLE II

Number of Different Connective Types in Two 1000-word Samples of Addison, Johnson, Gibbon, and Swift

	Addison	Johnson	Gibbon	Swift
Types	20,20	12,21	19,12	22,25

In a thorough study of Swift's vocabulary, we should expect to find a large number of the standard connectives, a number of words used as connectives which are not primarily connectives (*now, then, again*) and a variety of phrases serving as connectives (*'tis true, for these reasons*). This range of variety together with his predilection for introductory connectives and his dependence on a favorite triad of conjunctions implies a pattern of use which is quite consistent, both with itself and with as much of his personality as it may be relevant to refer to.

The classification of connectives into grammatical types on the basis of their function is a well-established practice, both in traditional grammars and in modern works. The logical or "notional" classification has been set aside, however, with much of the terminology of traditional rhetoric.[18] It is perhaps that readers and especially writers realized that such notional concepts as "causal," "concessive," "adversative," "alternative" and the like did not say enough about the types of relationships possible between propositions. Connectives themselves are mere shorthand means to that end. Obviously, complicated relationships require more than a mere *but* or *however* can provide. Such connections must be outlined with all the logical facilities inherent in discursive prose. But for the purpose of moving the reader's attention in the direction of a certain type of expectation or disappointment, these *buts, fors* and their more elaborate brethren have their use. Curiously enough, the most sophisticated writers have sometimes sedulously avoided making use of any more of these than the inevitable *and,* suggesting in this way that their subtlety of thought transcended mechanical means of showing relationships or perhaps that the relation was so inescapable that marking it would be anti-climactic. Conversely, it is possible to use connective words without reference to their notional significance. It is this that Swift does quite frequently with his *ands, buts* and *fors,* as well as with some others.

Normally, when a sentence begins with *for* (in itself rather uncommon), it is expected that the relationship between the previous sentence and the present one will be causal or resultative or the like, "Introducing the ground or reason of something previously said." [19] Swift, however, begins a sentence with *for* which opens a paragraph containing an announced digression from the main line of narrative:

> But all would not suffice, and the Ladies aforesaid continued still inflexible: To clear up which Difficulty, I must with the Reader's good Leave and Patience, have recourse to some Points of Weight, which the Authors of that Age have not sufficiently illustrated.
>   For, about this Time it happened a Sect arose, whose Tenents obtained and spread very far . . .[20]

It is evident that the purpose of this *for* is merely to supply a connection between the matter being dwelt on and the matter now introduced as illustrative of it. The conjunction *for* in that location might very readily be replaced by *thus* or *so* or even the bare indefinite article ("A sect arose . . ."), and in the prose of another writer might well have been, but Swift prefers to suggest a specious causality as a means of directing his reader.

In the same way, Swift uses the conjunction *nor* in the first paragraph of Section IX of *A Tale of a Tub* ("A Digression concerning Madness"): "nor shall it any ways detract from the just Reputation of this famous Sect, that its Rise and Institution are owing to such an Author as I have described Jack to be." [21] The promise made by that initial *nor* is that the writer will continue to give reasons why the Aeolists' ("this famous Sect") reputation should not be attacked. In fact, in the previous section Swift has introduced the Aeolists and ironically proposed to do them justice but has not given any reasons for the depreciation of their reputation. Instances of this sort, where the notional aspect of the connective is either wholly disregarded or distorted or made use of for the purpose of suggesting a relationship which has not been presented, are very frequent. To this might be added those uses of connectives which exaggerate or intensify beyond what seems reasonable the relationship between the current statement and a previous or remote one.

As an illustration, the two paragraphs which follow may be cited:

> Lord Peter was also held the Original Author of Puppets and Raree-Shows; the great Usefulness whereof being so generally known, I shall not enlarge farther upon this Particular.
>
> *But,* another Discovery for which he was much renowned, was his famous Universal Pickle. *For* having remark'd how your Common Pickle in use among Huswives, was of no farther Benefit than to preserve dead Flesh, and certain kinds of Vegetables; Peter, with great Cost as well as Art, had contrived a Pickle proper for Houses, Gardens, Towns, Men, Women, Children, and Cattle; wherein he could preserve them as Sound as Insects in Amber. *Now,* this Pickle to the Taste, the Smell, and the Sight, appeared exactly the same, with what is in common Service for Beef, and Butter, and Herrings (and has been often that way applied with great Success) *but* for its many Sovereign Virtues was a quite different Thing. *For* Peter would put in a certain Quantity of his Powder Pimperlim pimp, after which it never failed of Success.[22]

In this passage, five connectives are italicized, of which four might very easily be spared as guides to the notional relationship between the elements they govern. This is not to say that they might altogether be spared, because they perform a function of a special nature, unlike the interior *but* whose function is precisely adversative, opposing the sovereign virtue of the pickle with its common appearance. However, the initial *but* implies that the discovery of the pickle will be enlarged on, unlike that of Puppets and Raree-shows which will not, but it actually opposes the dismissal of further discussion about the two items with another discovery for which Peter is renowned. Although this appears to be a mere rhetorical error, it is wholly in the spirit of Swift's irregular use of these introductory particles. This is fully shown by the initial *for* which follows the antecedent *but.* Its value seems closest to *thus* or other illustrative connective, fulfilling a function designed to display a stage or point in the argument, like the *now* which follows it, and whose notional value is approximately null. The final *for* possesses a hint of indispensability, as it pretends to connect the unexpected sovereign virtue of the pickle with an explanation of its operation. Nonetheless, its presence is supererogatory, as can be demonstrated by a re-writing of the passage without the four dispensable connectives:

> Lord Peter was also held the Original Author of Puppets and Raree-Shows; the great Usefulness whereof being so generally known, I shall not enlarge farther upon this Particular.
>
> Another Discovery for which he was much renowned, was his famous Universal Pickle. Having remark'd how your Common Pickle in use among Huswives, was of no farther Benefit than to preserve dead Flesh, and certain kinds of Vegetables; Peter, with great Cost as well as Art, had contrived a Pickle proper for Houses, Gardens, Towns, Men, Women, Children and Cattle; wherein he could preserve them as Sound as Insects in Amber. This Pickle to the Taste, the Smell, and the Sight, appeared exactly the same, with what is in common Service for Beef, and Butter, and Herrings, (and has been often that way applied with great Success) but for its many Sovereign Virtues was quite a different Thing. Peter would put in a certain Quantity of his Powder Pimperlim pimp, after which it never failed of Success.

This passage in the revised version can be understood as readily as the original and is perhaps a little more compact. The change that took place points to the unorthodox use of these connectives. The omission of two *fors*, a *but* and a *now* does not so much obscure the relationship of the parts, which is obvious enough, as it removes the emphasis, the continuity, what might be called the entrainment of the passage. Such use of more words than are strictly necessary, however it may resemble pleonasm, because it is directed toward the more accurate reception of the message, is in the spirit of the redundancy valued by communications engineers.[23]

A similar pseudo-pleonastic use of connectives is found where two are used instead of one. Usually these combinations consist of a coordinating conjunction followed by a conjunctive adverb. The most common, one for which eighteenth-century rhetoricians and lexicographers castigated Swift, is *but however*,[24] as in, "But however, such great Frenzies being artificially raised. . . ."[25]

Other adversative combinations present *but* with a phrase, as in "But on the other side, whoever should mistake the Nature of things so far. . . ." [26] Additive pleonasms are common with *and:* "and, indeed, if the former Danger . . ."; [27] "And besides there was already in the Town . . ."; [28] "And likewise because too great an Affectation of Secrecy. . . ." [29] Other combinations may be found of varying rarity: "But still, there is in this Project a greater Mischief . . .";[30] "Or perhaps they scare us. . . ." [31] A cursory examination reveals that of the cited pairs either word alone would suffice. That Swift uses both should lead us to wonder whether he intends the particular effect or whether the mechanism and the resultant effect were beyond the reach of Swift's consciousness.

Another type of connective use may help to elucidate this question. It has been shown that introductory connectives (usually coordinating conjunctions) are used as mere links or joints in the syntactic architecture of Swift's prose. The actual task of specifying a notional relationship is handed over to a pleonastic or redundant pair. More often, however, the introductory group of connectives is made up of two or more from different notional classes. These usually consist of *and, but, for* followed by a conjunctive adverb or a subordinating conjunction, though others appear as well.

The most common combination is the one beginning with *and,* which is found with a very wide variety of companions: *and after all, and although, and as, and if, and therefore, and thus.* Some more elaborate examples may be unearthed: *and indeed if,*[32] *and likewise because,*[33] *and therefore as,*[34] *and therefore when,*[35] and perhaps most interesting, *and therefore if notwithstanding!* [36] There is a large number of *but if, but though, but when, but whether,* and *but while* combinations, not to mention all the derivatives of *for, or, nor, so, neither, yet.*

If it is recalled that these groupings occur at the head of sentences, it may be inferred that Swift is availing himself of two rhetorical opportunities. He is modifying the plain and rather bare character of the unadorned connective, especially the favored triad, and presenting it in such a variety of guises that his prose achieves a highly diversified appearance, far more so than could be guessed by the frequency with which these particular three recur. Moreover, he presents his reader, at the beginning of each sentence headed by this kind of grouping, with a set of guides to the relationships involved in the thought which is often contradictory, for example, *for although* in "For although he were at last undeceived and reconciled to her, yet I lost all Credit with him." [37] The combination of causal with concessive, pretending to adduce a result of some antecedent happening but diluting it with a concession or diminution of the explanation, is confusing if not contradictory. But in the sentence cited it may be seen that both *for* and *yet* do not function except for emphasis. The sentence makes perfect sense without them. They are not confusing because they are here as in the earlier-cited examples merely emphatic or redundant.[38]

A concatenation such as *and therefore if notwithstanding*, which consists of three essential elements, each one promising the later introduction of a relevant clause, would burden the reader's mind with an excess of difficulty before permitting him to proceed with the argument. Actually, the sentence in which that grouping occurs, even out of context and without punctuation is not difficult to understand:

> and therefore if notwithstanding all I have said it shall still be thought necessary to have a bill brought in for repealing Christianity I would humbly offer an amendment that instead of the word Christianity may be put religion in general which I conceive will much better answer all the good ends proposed by the projectors of it.[39]

To say that something is not difficult to understand is not to say that it is especially clear. The clarity with which Swift has always been credited is not helped by this proceeding. It is well known that Swift favored clarity as a characteristic of style, and it seems therefore likely that he would have eschewed what in his writing might be inimical to it. It can hardly be supposed that he would think the multiplication of non-essential connectives at the beginning of sentences a help to clarity. The conclusion cannot be escaped that Swift was not aware of the extensiveness or the idiosyncrasy of his practice in this regard. Even his manuscript corrections and textual variants do not show any curbing of this trait, but rather a juggling of *yets* and *fors*.[40] He revised the surface but could not modify the fundamental structure. One of his recent editors, commenting on the ineffectiveness of Swift's revisions, specifies it accurately: "He was struggling against a tendency to write in just the way he disliked." [41] This observation is supported by the constant gap between Swift's ideals of style and his practice.

A prose which is as extensively connected as Swift's has been shown to be cannot fail to impress the reader. His attention is inevitably called to the connective tissue between sentences, although the effect must be to a great extent below the threshold of consciousness, judging by the lack of comment about this feature of Swift's writing. Nonetheless, the connectives must diffuse an appearance of great logic, convey the picture of a writer whose material is so ready to his mind that he distributes concessions, hypotheses, causes, results with such freedom that he can scarcely fit them all into his sentences. But, in spite of the forbidding aspect of some of these mounds of connectives, the reader has no difficulty in understanding; in fact, he is not at all put off by the complex web of interrelationships. Because he does not realize that his understanding is due to the redundant nature of the connective guides, he reaches the conclusion that the writer is eminently logical, transpicuously clear, and economical with words to the point of terseness.

Clarity of language, it has often been said, results when clarity of thought is adequately translated into words. That this is an inadequate concept scarcely needs documentation. Swift's reader is permitted to glimpse the complexity of a question or event and given a succession of interrelated data providing a semblance of inevitability, in a manner exuding vigor and confidence. Because the randomness of events has been given form, the reader feels enlightened by order and clarity.

But it is persuasiveness, not clarity, which results from Swift's use of connectives.[42] The enchainment of sentences by means of connectives carries the reader along with great mobility and induces him to believe in the clarity and simplicity of what he has read.[43] He has been moved rapidly through Swift's line of argument, has become persuaded by it and has emerged feeling that everything is clear. And Swift's handling of connectives is an important factor in that success.

Redundancy then, in the sense both of copiousness and of control of meaning, is an integral feature of Swift's style and contributes an important share to his achievement. Though it would be absurd to contend that Swift manipulated series and connectives without conscious art, it is not beyond probability to suggest that the great disparity between his expressed ideals and his practice was due to the unconscious factor in composition, a factor to which he was perhaps unusually susceptible. . . .

NOTES

1. Samuel Taylor Coleridge, "Table Talk," May 15, 1833, in *Complete Works,* ed. W. G. T. Shedd (New York, 1884), VI, 467.

2. George O. Curme, *Syntax* (Boston, 1931), p. 170.

3. Curme, p. 172, a quotation from J. M. Synge's *The Well of the Saints.*

4. George Campbell, *The Philosophy of Rhetoric,* p. 395.

5. The study of individual preferences in the choice of particles is one that has had much vogue in classical scholarship. See, for example, J. D. Denniston, *The Greek Particles,* 2d ed. (Oxford, 1954), pp. lxxviii–lxxxii. Cf. Gilbert Highet, *Poets in a Landscape* (Harmondsworth, 1959): "It is possible . . . to learn much about Plato by studying something apparently so insignificant as his use of particles—the little almost-meaningless words of emphasis and qualification like 'of course,' 'certainly,' 'at least,' in which the Greek language is so rich, and which (in written prose) perform the same function as gestures, voice-tones, and facial expressions in conversation" (p. 157). *Particles* is a broader term than *connectives,* but some of the connectives considered here have only ill-defined connective functions.

6. John Locke, *An Essay Concerning Human Understanding,* ed. A. C. Fraser (Oxford, 1894), II, 98–99.

7. The sample of Swift included material from his "signed" and his "anonymous" material and was about 1300 sentences in extent. The material for the other authors included about 400 sentences for each. The grammatical categories are the conventional ones. The evidence is not presented in any detail because no conclusions are drawn from the figures.

8. Samples are 2000 periods long.

9. Examples of coordinating conjunctions (C), *and, but, or*; subordinating conjunctions (S), *after, when, if*; conjunctive adverbs, or sentence-connectors (SC), *however, therefore, in the meantime, in short.*

10. With a standard deviation of 8.8, the results are significant at the five percent level, though there are only four subsamples.

11. It would be interesting to be able to compare these figures with those of some other worker. But the only possible comparison is not very instructive. Robert R. Aurner, "Caxton and the English Sentence," *Wisconsin Studies in Language and Literature,* no. 18 (1923), does not define *connective* and uses samples of 100 sentences. He finds that Addison begins 2 sentences with connectives, Macaulay 16, and Johnson 17 in the *Rambler* and 5 in the *Lives* (p. 50).

12. Of the 2000-sentence sample, Swift begins 678 with a connective and 354 with *and, but* or *for.*

13. It seems to be a practice frowned on by the more puristic rhetoricians. See, for instance, James Harris, *Hermes* (London, 1751): ". . . in the mod-

ern polite Works . . . scarce such a thing as a Particle, or Conjunction is to be found." Even more particular is *The London Universal Letter-Writer* (c. 1800): "I hate particles where they are avoidable; be therefore sparing in your *fors,* your *buts,* and your *ands.*" Both are quoted in *English Examined,* compiled by Susie I. Tucker (London, 1961), pp. 81, 146–147. See also *"And* at Beginning," in Campbell, *Philosophy of Rhetoric,* pp. 441–442.

14. Expressions with such connective quality include, apart from conjunctive adverbs, a number of adverbs, such as *perhaps, then, surely,* and phrases like *of course, to be sure, on the other hand.*

15. On the basis of a rough count without statistical pretensions, I would say between a quarter and a third of the time.

16. In *Works,* III [*The Prose Writings of Jonathan Swift,* ed. Herbert Davis, 14 vols. (Oxford, 1939—in progress). Referred to as *Works*—Ed.] the following examples were found: "But, although" (58), "And first" (58), "But then" (59), "But, at present" (59), "But, by the Way" (60), "And for that Reason" (61), "And indeed" (63), "But as" (63), "And, not to mention more" (65), "But however" (65), "Or else" (66), "But beside" (67), "And so" (69), "But after all" (71), "For where" (75). Doubtless, more varied examples could be found in a wider area of search.

17. It is possible to observe a similar use in the King James version of the Bible and in some other seventeenth-century stylists. Swift was, it must be recalled, thirty-three before the century ended and it is not unreasonable to suppose that he was subject to the same influences as affected the other writers of his time. That is, if he uses introductory conjunctions in the same way as the King James version, it need not be because he imitated the Biblical style, though he was doubtless subject to its influences. It is more probable that he responded to the challenge of connection in the same way as the translators of the Bible did.

18. Both classifications are used in two such different books as George O. Curme, *English Grammar* (New York, 1947), and Harold Whitehall, *Structural Essentials of English* (New York, 1956).

19. *Oxford English Dictionary,* s.v. *For,* conj.

20. *Tale of a Tub, Works,* I, 45–46.

21. *Works,* I, 102.

22. *Tale of a Tub, Works,* I, 67–68, italics supplied.

23. The purpose of safeguarding the message need not be conscious, however.

24. Sterling A. Leonard, *The Doctrine of Correctness in English Usage 1700–1800* (Madison, 1929), p. 280.

25. *Examiner, Works,* III, 65.

26. *Tale of a Tub, Works,* I, 31.

27. *Examiner, Works,* III, 63.

28. *History of the Four Last Years of the Queen, Works,* VII, 142.

29. *Free Thoughts, Works,* VIII, 81.

30. *Argument, Works,* II, 30.

31. *Examiner, Works,* III, 17.

32. *Examiner, Works,* III, 63.

33. *Free Thoughts, Works,* VIII, 81.

34. *Freemen of Dublin, Works,* XIII, 85.

35. *Hatred of Clergy, Works,* XIII, 124.

36. *Argument, Works,* II, 37.

37. *Gulliver, Works,* XI, 50.

38. This closely resembles what Denniston, *Greek Particles,* p. xli, calls

the "corresponsive use of particles" in Greek: "Coherence of thought is adequately secured by the presence of a backward-pointing particle. The reader or listener, when he has reached a certain point, meets a particle which looks back to the road he has traversed, and beckons him on in a certain direction. But greater coherence is attained if in addition a forward-pointing particle warns him in advance what path he will soon have to travel, the connexion being expressed reciprocally, from rear to van and from van to rear."

39. The original, punctuated, version follows: "And therefore, if, notwithstanding all I have said, it shall still be thought necessary to have a Bill brought in for repealing Christianity; I would humbly offer an Amendment, that instead of the Word *Christianity*, may be put Religion in general; which I conceive, will much better answer all the good Ends proposed by the Projectors of it" (*Argument, Works*, II, 37).

40. E.g., the textual notes to *Gulliver's Travels* in *Works*, XI.

41. Jonathan Swift, *An Enquiry into the Behavior of the Queen's Last Ministry*, ed. Irvin Ehrenpreis (Bloomington, 1956), p. xxxi. Ehrenpreis notes a number of amplifications serving to introduce smoothness by means of additional introductory conjunctions.

42. Johnson well says: "it will not be easy to find . . . any inconsequence in his connections, or abruptness in his transitions." *Lives of the Poets*, ed. Hill, III, 52.

43. To discover how successfully, see Johnson's famous comment on Swift's pamphlet, "The Conduct of the Allies," in *Boswell's Life of Johnson*, ed. George Birkbeck Hill and L. F. Powell (Oxford, 1934–1964), II, 65: "He had to count ten, and he has counted it right."

15. GENERATIVE GRAMMARS AND THE CONCEPT OF LITERARY STYLE

Richard Ohmann

Literary style generally has been defined as a writer's typical use of linguistic variables. In any English prose text, for example, most elements in sentence patterns are required by the rules of English grammar. But there are other elements that a writer can vary without changing meaning. In "Generative Grammars and the Concept of Literary Style," Richard Ohmann integrates this concept with modern transformational-generative linguistics. The theory of generative grammar holds that semantic interpretation, meaning, is a function of deep structure—the basic logical relationships holding among elements of a sentence. Transformations—the formal operations by which postulated deep structures become the surface structures we can observe—are meaning-preserving. Hence "John asked me to read the book" means the same as "I was asked by John to read the book." Most transformations are *obligatory:* transformations must operate to change the (simplified) deep structure *John asked me I read the book* (not a grammatical sentence) to *John asked that I read the book.* But some transformations are *optional: That it was raining was obvious* means the same as *It was obvious that it was raining;* the transformation moving *that it was raining* from before to after *was obvious* is not required, for either sentence is grammatical. Professor Ohmann argues that in prose a grammar suitable for stylistic analysis of syntax must generate a writer's alternatives for a given passage as well as the passage itself. (James Peter Thorne makes the same point in discussing

Richard Ohmann, "Generative Grammars and the Concept of Literary Style," reprinted from *Word,* XX (1964), 424–439, by permission of the author and publisher, The Linguistic Circle of New York, Inc.

poetry—see Selection 11.) Both analysis of a writer's typical strategies in utilizing optional transformations and scrutiny of his employment of different kinds of transformational operations are essential in the study of prose style.

A style is a way of writing—that is what the word means. And that is almost as much as one can say with assurance on the subject, which has been remarkably unencumbered by theoretical insights. Yet we know a good deal more than that, in a way: the same way, roughly in which a native speaker "knows" the grammar of English, although no existing grammatical analysis gives a full and adequate account of his linguistic intuition. Readers familiar with literature have what might sensibly be called a *stylistic* intuition, a rather loosely structured, but often reliable, feeling for the quiddity of a writer's linguistic method, a sense of differences between stretches of literary discourse which are not differences in content. In fact many readers can tell, by skimming a batch of unfamiliar passages, not only that the differences are there, but who the authors are. Read the first few paragraphs of a *New Yorker* story and you can often (without a surreptitious glance at the end) identify it as a Cheever, an O'Hara, an Updike, or a Salinger, even if the subject matter is uncharacteristic. Further evidence, if any is needed, of the reliability of stylistic intuitions is the ability of some to write convincing parodies, and of others to recognize them as such. Thus the theorist of style is confronted by a kind of task that is commonplace enough in most fields: the task of explicating and toughening up for rigorous use a notion already familiar to the layman.

But in stylistics the scholar has always had to make do with a theoretical apparatus not far removed from that of the layman. And although many practitioners have plied their craft with great subtlety, a survey of their work leaves one far from certain what that craft *is*. For the attempt to isolate the cues one attends to in identifying styles and in writing stylistic parody has sprawled out into an almost embarrassing profusion of critical methods. And most of these methods, I believe, are interesting in inverse proportion to their emphasis on what we sense as style. The following list will suggest, but not exhaust, the multiplicity of approaches:

(1) What might be called "diachronic stylistics," the study of changes in national literary style from one period to the next. Clearly this approach presupposes a mastery of what might be called

(2) "Synchronic stylistics," or the study of this or that period style. Since the style of a period can only be the sum of linguistic habits shared by most writers of that period, synchronic stylistics presupposes in turn the ability to describe the style of a single writer. But there is little agreement upon how such description is to be managed; many methods compete for critical attention.

(3) Impressionism: the application of metaphorical labels to styles ("masculine," "limber," "staccato," "flowing," "involuted," etc.), and the attempt to evaluate (Swift's style is the best, or the most natural to English). This sort of criticism makes agreeable parlor conversation, records something of the critic's emotional response, and gives intuition its due, but little else can be said in its favor.

(4) The study of sound, especially of rhythm. This approach is capable of some rigor, but the more rigor (that is, the more strictly the critic attends to physical or to phonemic features), the less relevance to what we sense as style. For —let me state this dogmatically—in prose, at least, rhythm as perceived is largely dependent upon syntax, and even upon content, not upon stress, intonation, and juncture alone.

(5) The study of tropes. Attention to metaphor, antithesis, synecdoche, zeugma, and the other figures of classical rhetoric often proceeds from a desire to see the writer's style in terms of what he thought he was doing, and to this extent points away from a descriptive analysis of style, and toward the history or philosophy of rhetorical theory. Even when the studies of figurative language maintain a descriptive focus, they embrace only a small, though important, part of style, and liberally mixed with content, at that.

(6) The study of imagery. The fact that a writer favors images of disease, money, battle, or the like, is frequently of great interest, but imagery divorced from its syntactic embodiment is surely more a matter of content than of style.

(7) The study of what is variously called "tone," "stance," "role," and so on: roughly, the writer's attitude toward what he is saying, toward his reader, and toward himself, as suggested by his language. The critic in this vein infers, from the locutions on the printed page, a hypothetical live situation in which such language would be appropriate, and discusses the social and emotional features of that situation. This approach has unquestionably been fruitful. Its success depends on a highly developed sense of connotative meaning, both of words and of constructions, and this sense is something that many critics possess in abundance. Tone, however, like figurative language, is only a part of style, and the question remains in what measure tone itself is a product of formal linguistic features.

(8) The study of literary structure, which, like the study of tropes and tone, has flourished among the new critics. And to be sure, patterns of organization in a literary work are *related* to style (the way a novel is put together may have an analogue in the way a sentence is put together), but to consider structure a *component* of style, except perhaps in a short poem, stretches the meaning of the term "style" to its limits.

(9) The analysis of particular and local effects—a change of verb tense, or the placement of an interrogative, for instance, in a certain passage. Clearly, individual strategies of this sort fit more comfortably under the heading of *technique* than of style, for style has to do primarily with the habitual, the recurrent.

(10) The study of special idiosyncrasies, such as the omission of causal connectives from contexts where they usually appear. Such quirks are doubtless stylistic elements, and they can richly reward analysis, as a number of studies by Leo Spitzer have shown. But a few idiosyncrasies do not add up to a style, by any method of calculation.

(11) The study of a writer's lexicon, as pursued, for example, by Josephine Miles. Lexical preferences, unless seen in the context of a ramified system of word classes, are like imagery patterns, in that they reveal more about content than about style.

(12) The statistical study of grammatical features—abstract nouns, adjectives, subordinate clauses, questions, and the like. This method is without doubt pertinent, but significant results have been highly elusive. One reason is the crudeness of the categories which traditional grammar has made available to critics, whose knowledge of linguistics generally seems to lag by a few decades. (Linguists, by and large, have not busied themselves with stylistics.) Another reason, equally important, is the overwhelming inefficiency of the procedure, given the very large number of grammatical categories, and the lack of any grammatical system that relates them in meaningful, formally motivated ways. Without such a theory, a collection of counts is simply a collection of counts.

And indeed, the inability of these and other methods, in spite of many partial successes, to yield a full and convincing explication of the notion of style seems in general to follow from the absence of an appropriate underlying linguistic and semantic theory. A style is a characteristic use of language, and it is difficult to see how the *uses* of a system can be understood unless the system itself has been mapped out. It is no surprise, in other words, to find stylistics in a state of disorganization when syntax and semantics, upon which stylistics clearly depends, have themselves been hampered by the lack of a theory that is inclusive, unified, and plausible.

The situation in stylistics is understandably analogous to that in the philosophy of language,[1] though more muddled still. Just as philosophers have tended to concentrate on this or that discrete feature of language—words, or groups of words, or grammatical predication, or the relation of reference, or logical structure—in isolation from the rest, so analysts of style have talked about sound, tropes, images, diction, devices of conjunction, parallel structure, and so on, without any apparent sense of priority or centrality among these concerns. Thus, in a time when linguistic theory and practice have passed through at least one renaissance, the most serviceable studies of style[2] continue to proceed from the critic's naked intuition, fortified against the winds of ignorance only by literary sophistication and the tattered garments of traditional grammar. Especially damaging is the critic's inability, for lack of a theory, to take into account the deeper structural features of language, precisely those which should enter most revealingly into a stylistic description.

It is my contention that recent developments in generative grammar, particularly on the transformational model, promise, first, to clear away a good deal of the mist from stylistic theory, and, second, to make possible a corresponding refinement in the practice of stylistic analysis. In the remainder of this paper I hope to state a case for the first of these claims, and to make a very modest initial thrust toward documenting the second.

That Chomsky's formulation of grammatical theory is potentially useful should become apparent from an examination of the common sense notion of style. In general that notion applies to human action that is partly invariant and partly variable. A style is a *way* of doing *it*. Now this picture leads to few complications if the action is playing the piano or playing tennis. The pianist performing a Mozart concerto must strike certain notes in a certain order, under certain restrictions of tempo, in a certain relation to the orchestra, and so on. These limitations define the part of his behavior that is fixed. Likewise, the tennis player must hit the ball over the net with the racket in a way partly determined by the rules of the game (errors and cheating are not style). But each has a significant amount of freedom, beyond these established regularities: the tennis player, for instance, chooses from a repertory of strokes, shots, and possible placements (analogous, perhaps, to the linguistic resources of the writer or speaker), and he also has freedom of intensity, smoothness, flamboyance, etc. (as the writer or speaker has freedom in the use of paralinguistic resources like loudness and emphatic punctuation). The tennis player's use of these options, in so far as it is habitual or recurrent, constitutes his style. But the relevant division between fixed and variable components in literature is by no means so obvious. What *is* content, and what is form, or style? The attack on a dichotomy of form and content has been persistent in modern criticism; to change so much as a word, the argument runs, is to change the meaning as well. This austere doctrine has a certain theoretical appeal, given the supposed impossibility of finding exact synonyms, and the ontological queerness of disembodied content—propositions, for instance—divorced from any verbal expression. Yet at the same time this doctrine leads to the altogether counterintuitive conclusion that there can be no such thing as style, or that style is simply a part of content.[3]

To put the problem more concretely, the idea of style implies that words on a page might have been different, or differently arranged, without a corresponding difference in substance. Another writer would have said *it* another *way*. For the idea of style to apply, in short, writing must involve choices of verbal formulation. Yet suppose we try to list the alternatives to a given segment of prose: "After dinner, the senator made a speech." A dozen close approximations may suggest themselves ("When dinner was over, the senator made a speech," "The senator made a speech after dinner," "A speech was made by the senator after dinner," etc.), as well as a very large number of more distant renderings ("The senator made a postprandial oration," "The termination of dinner brought a speech from the senator," etc.). Which ones represent stylistic variations on the original, and which ones say different things? We may have intuitions, but to support them is no trivial undertaking. Clearly it would help to have a grammar that provided certain relationships, formally statable, of alternativeness among constructions. One such relationship, for example, might be that which holds between two different constructions that are derived from the same starting point. And, of course, a generative grammar allows the formulation of precisely this sort of relationship.

In the phrase structure component, to begin with, there are alternate ways of proceeding from identically labeled nodes, alternate ways of expanding (or rewriting) a symbol. A verb phrase may be expanded [4] into a transitive verb plus a noun phrase, a copula plus an adjective, a copula plus a noun phrase, or any one of several other combinations.[5] The various possibilities for rewriting at this stage of the grammar account for some of the major sentence types in English, and since the structural meaning of, say, $V_t + NP$ differs considerably from that of $Be + Adj$, a writer's preference for one or another of these forms may be a stylistic choice of some interest.

But notice that the possibility of alternative routings in the phrase structure component does not really solve the problem of style in a satisfactory way. I have been looking for linguistically constant features that may be expressed in different ways. The difficulty with taking a unit like the verb phrase for such a constant is its abstractness, its lack of structure. The symbol VP merely stands for a *position* in a string at one level of description. Two different expansions of VP will both occupy the same position, but will not necessarily retain any structural feature in common. Nor will the sentences that ultimately result from the two derivations necessarily share any morphemes or even morphemes from the same classes. Thus, the rewriting of VP as $V_t + NP$ is part of a derivation that leads eventually to the sentence "Columbus discovered America," among others. But there is no kernel sentence corresponding (semantically) to this one which results from a derivation in which NP is rewritten $Be + Adj$. Sentences like "Columbus was brave," or possibly "Columbus was nautical" are about as close as one can come. And certainly they are not stylistically different expressions of the same thing, in the sense required for stylistics—not in the way that "America was discovered by Columbus" is. The phrase structure part of the grammar does not account for intuitively felt relationships of sameness and difference between sentences, for the possibility of saying one "thing" in two different ways. Perhaps this is one reason why almost no important work in stylistic criticism has evolved from the grammatical analyses of American linguists.

To be of genuine interest for stylistics, a grammar must do more than simply provide for alternate derivations from the same point of origin. There are at least three important characteristics of transformational rules which make them more promising as a source of insight into style than phrase structure rules. In the first place, a large number of transformations are optional, and in quite a different sense from the sense in which it is optional how VP is expanded. VP must *be* expanded by one of the various rules, or of course no sentence will result from the derivation. But an optional transformation need not be applied at all. Given a string or pair of strings so structured that a certain optional transformation can apply, failure to apply it will not keep the derivation from terminating in a sentence.[6] Thus "Dickens wrote *Bleak House*" is a sentence, as well as "*Bleak House* was written by Dickens," which has undergone the passive transformation. Likewise, "Dickens was the writer of *Bleak House*" is a sentence, one that comes from the same kernel string as the other two, via a different optional transformation: agentive nominalization.[7] Technically, transformations apply to underlying strings with certain structures, but for the purposes of this paper they may be thought of as manipulations—reordering, combination, addition, deletion—performed on fully formed sentences, rather than as ways of *getting* to parts of fully formed sentences from incomplete, abstract symbols such as NP. Each application of a different optional transformation to a sentence results in a new sentence, similar in some ways to the original one. Thus a grammar with transformational rules will generate many pairs and limited sets of sentences, like the set of three sentences about Dickens, which belong together in an intimate structural way—not simply by virtue of being sentences. Many such sets of sentences will strike a speaker as saying "the same thing"—as being alternatives, that is, in precisely the sense required for stylistics.

A second and related reason why transformational happenings are relevant to style is the very fact that a transformation applies to one or more *strings,* or elements with structure, not to single symbols like VP, and that it applies to those strings by virtue of their structure. A transformation works changes on structure, but normally leaves *part* of the structure unchanged. And in any case, the new structure bears a precisely specifiable relationship to the old one, a relationship, incidentally, that speakers of the language will intuitively feel. Moreover, the transform retains at least some morphemes from the original string; that is, transformations are specified in such a way that "Columbus discovered America" cannot become, under the passive transformation, *"Bleak House* was written by Dickens," although this sentence has the same structure as the proper transform "America was discovered by Columbus." This property of transformations —their preserving some features from the original string—accounts for the fact that sets of sentences which are transformational alternatives seem to be different renderings of the same proposition.[8] Again, this is the sort of relationship which seems intuitively to underlie the notion of style, and for which only a transformational grammar offers a formal analogue.

The third value of a transformational grammar to the analyst of style is its power to explain how complex sentences are generated, and how they are related to simple sentences. Writers differ noticeably in the amounts and kinds of syntactic complexity they habitually allow themselves, but these matters have been hard to approach through conventional methods of analysis. Since the complexity of a sentence is the product of the generalized transformations it has gone through, a breakdown of the sentence into its component simple sentences and the generalized transformations applied (in the order of application) will be an account of its complexity.[9] And since the same set of simple sentences may usually be combined in different ways, a set of complex sentences may be generated from them, each of which differs from the others only in transformational history, while embodying the same simple "propositions." Such differences should be interestingly approachable through transformational analysis. So should major variations in type of compounding: self-embedding as against left- and right-branching, for example, or the formation of endocentric as against the formation of exocentric constructions. These deep grammatical possibilities in a language may well be exploited differently from writer to writer, and if so, the differences will certainly be of stylistic interest.

Let me summarize. A generative grammar with a transformational component provides apparatus for breaking down a sentence in a stretch of discourse into underlying kernel sentences (or strings, strictly speaking) and for specifying the grammatical operations that have been performed upon them. It also permits the analyst to construct, from the same set of kernel sentences, other non-kernel sentences. These may reasonably be thought of as *alternatives* to the original sentence, in that they are simply different constructs out of the identical elementary grammatical units.[10] Thus the idea of alternative phrasings, which is crucial to the notion of style, has a clear analogue within the framework of a transformational grammar.

But is it the *right* analogue? What I have called "transformational alternatives" are different derivatives from the same kernel sentences. The notion of style calls for different ways of expressing the same content. Kernel sentences are not "content," to be sure. Yet they *have* content, and much of that content is preserved through transformational operations. "Dickens was the writer of *Bleak House* and America was discovered by Columbus" says much the same thing, if not exactly the same thing, as "Dickens wrote *Bleak House*; Columbus discovered America." Of course some transformations import new content, others eliminate features of content, and no transformation leaves content absolutely unaltered. The analogue is not perfect. But it is worth remembering that other kinds of tampering with sentences (e.g., substitution of synonyms) also change content. And, to look at it another way, the most useful sense of "content"—*cognitive* content—may be such that transformations do generally leave it unaltered (and such that synonyms do exist).[11] In any case, transformational alternatives come as close to "different expressions of the same content" as other sorts of alternatives; moreover, they have the practical advantage of being accessible to formal, rather than to impressionistic, analysis. There is at least some reason, then, to hold that a style is in part a characteristic way of deploying the transformational apparatus of a language, and to expect that transformational analysis will be a valuable aid to the description of actual styles.

So much for theory and prophecy. The final proof must come, if it comes at all, from a fairly extensive attempt to study literary styles in the way I am suggesting. For a transformational analysis, however appealing theoretically, will not be worth much unless it can implement better stylistic descriptions than have been achieved by other methods—"better" in that they isolate more fully, economically, and demonstrably the linguistic features to which a perceptive reader responds in sensing one style to be different from another. The space available here will not suffice for a full scale demonstration, nor do I now have at my disposal nearly enough stylistic description to prove my case. Besides, the necessary grammatical machinery is by no means available yet (in fact, it is too early to say with certainty that Chomsky's plan for grammars is the right one—there are many dissenters). I shall use the rest of this paper merely to outline, by example, a simple analytic procedure that draws on the concept of grammatical transformations, and to suggest some virtues of this procedure.

My first specimen passage comes from Faulkner's story, "The Bear." It is part of a sentence nearly two pages long, and its style is complex, highly individual, and difficult—if it is read aloud, most hearers will not grasp it on first hearing. It is also, I believe, quite typically Faulknerian:

the desk and the shelf above it on which rested the ledgers in
which McCaslin recorded the slow outward trickle of food
and supplies and equipment which returned each fall as
cotton made and ginned and sold (two threads frail as truth
and impalpable as equators yet cable-strong to bind for life
them who made the cotton to the land their sweat fell on),
and the older ledgers clumsy and archaic in size and shape, on
the yellowed pages of which were recorded in the faded hand
of his father Theophilus and his uncle Amodeus during the
two decades before the Civil War, the manumission in title
at least of Carothers McCaslin's slaves: . . .[12]

I propose to reduce the complexity of the passage by reversing
the effects of three generalized transformations, plus a few related singular transformations:

(1)   The relative clause transformation (GT19 in Lees' *The
       Grammar of English Nominalizations,* p. 89), along with
       the wh-transformations (Lees, T5 and T6, p. 39), the trans-
       formation which later deletes "which" and "be" to leave
       post-nominal modifiers (Lees, T58, p. 94), and the trans-
       formation which shifts these modifiers to prenominal posi-
       tion (Lees, T64, p. 98).[13]

(2)   The conjunction transformation (Chomsky, *Syntactic
       Structures,* p. 36).

(3)   The comparative transformation, which, along with sev-
       eral reduction transformations and one order change,[14]
       is responsible for sentences like "George is as tall as
       John."[15]

Without this grammatical apparatus, the passage reads as follows:

the desk. The shelf was above it. The ledgers$_1$ rested on the
shelf. The ledgers$_1$ were old. McCaslin recorded the trickle
of food in the ledgers$_1$. McCaslin recorded the trickle of
supplies in the ledgers$_1$. McCaslin recorded the trickle of
equipment in the ledgers$_1$. The trickle was slow. The trickle
was outward. The trickle returned each fall as cotton. The
cotton was made. The cotton was ginned. The cotton was
sold. The trickle was a thread. The cotton was a thread. The
threads were frail. Truth is frail. The threads were impalpable.
Equators are impalpable. The threads were strong to bind
them for life to the land. They made the cotton. Their
sweat fell on the land. Cables are strong. The ledgers$_2$ were

old. The ledgers$_2$ rested on the shelf. The ledgers$_2$ were clumsy in size. The ledgers$_2$ were clumsy in shape. The ledgers$_2$ were archaic in size. The ledgers$_2$ were archaic in shape. On the pages of the ledgers$_2$ were recorded in the hand of his father during the two decades the manumission in title at least of Carothers McCaslin's slaves. On the pages of the ledgers$_2$ were recorded in the hand of his uncle during the two decades the manumission in title at least of Carothers McCaslin's slaves. The pages were yellowed. The hand was faded. The decades were before the Civil War. His father was Theophilus. His uncle was Amodeus.[16]

There is some artificiality in this process, of course. The order of the reduced sentences is in part arbitrary. More important, the transformations I have reversed are not the last ones applied in the generation of the original construction; hence precisely the set of sentences (strings) above would not have occurred at any point in the derivation. Nonetheless, this drastic reduction of the original passage reveals several important things:

(1)   The content of the passage remains roughly the same: aside from the loss of distinctions between "and" and "yet," "as ——— as" and "more ——— than," relative clauses and conjoined sentences, and the like, changes in content are minor. But the style, obviously, has undergone a revolution. In the reduced form of the passage there are virtually no traces of what we recognize as Faulkner's style.

(2)   This denaturing has been accomplished by reversing the effects of only three generalized transformations, as well as a few related singular transformations. The total number of optional transformations involved is negligible as against the total number that apparently exist in the grammar as a whole. In other words, the style of the original passage leans heavily upon a very small amount of grammatical apparatus.

(3)   Most of the sentences in the reduced version of the passage are kernel sentences. Most of the rest are only one transformation away from kernel sentences. Further reduction, by undoing any number of other transformations, would not change the passage or its style nearly so much as has already been done.[17]

(4)   The three major transformations I have deleted have an

important feature in common. Each of them combines two sentences that share at least one morpheme,[18] and in such a way that the transform may contain only one occurrence of that morpheme (or those morphemes), while preserving the unshared parts of the original sentences. That is to say, these transformations are all what might be called "additive." To put the matter semantically, they offer methods of adding information about a single "thing" with a minimum of repetition. Thus the two sentences "The threads were impalpable" and "The threads were frail" might be combined through any one of the three generalized transformations at issue here: "The threads which were impalpable were frail" (relative); "The threads were frail and impalpable" (conjunction); and "The threads were more frail than impalpable" (comparison). The three transforms are somewhat similar, both formally and semantically; and it seems reasonable to suppose that a writer whose style is so largely based on just three semantically related transformations demonstrates in that style a certain conceptual orientation, a preferred way of organizing experience.[19] If that orientation could be specified, it would almost certainly provide insight into other, non-stylistic features of Faulkner's thought and artistry. The possibility of such insight is one of the main justifications for studying style.

The move from formal description of styles to critical and semantic interpretation should be the ultimate goal of stylistics, but in this article I am concerned only with the first step: description. My first example shows that the style of at least one short passage can be rather efficiently and informatively described in terms of a few grammatical operations. It might be objected, however, that the transformations I have concentrated on in destroying the style of the Faulkner passage are of such prominence in the grammar, and in the use of English, that *any* writer must depend heavily upon them. To show that this is not universally the case, it is sufficient to perform the same reductions on a characteristic passage from the work of another writer with a quite different style. Consider, therefore, the conclusion of Hemingway's story, "Soldier's Home":

> So his mother prayed for him and then they stood up and Krebs kissed his mother and went out of the house. He had tried so to keep his life from being complicated. Still, none of it had touched him. He had felt sorry for his mother and she had made him lie. He would go to Kansas City and get a job and she would feel all right about it. There would be one more scene maybe before he got away. He would not go down to his father's office. He would miss that one. He wanted his life to go smoothly. It had just gotten going that way. Well, that was all over now, anyway. He would go over to the schoolyard and watch Helen play indoor baseball.[20]

Reversing the effects of the relative and comparative transformations barely alters the passage: only the prenominal modifier "indoor" is affected. Removing the conjunctions does result in some changes:

> So his mother prayed for him. Then they stood up. Krebs kissed his mother. Krebs went out of the house. He had tried so to keep his life from being complicated. Still, none of it had touched him. He had felt sorry for his mother. She had made him lie. He would go to Kansas City. He would get a job. She would feel all right about it. There would be one more scene maybe before he got away. He would not go down to his father's office. He would miss that one. He wanted his life to go smoothly. It had just gotten going that way. Well, that was all over now, anyway. He would go over to the schoolyard. He would watch Helen play indoor baseball.

Notice that the reduced passage still sounds very much like Hemingway. Nothing has been changed that seems crucial to his style. Note too that although the revised passage is quite simple, none of the sentences is from the kernel. Hemingway is not innocent of transformations: he is relying on pronominalization, on a group of nominalizations, and, most notably, on a sequence of transformations responsible for what critics call the *"style indirect libre."* These transformations work this way:

(1)   GT; quotation, or reported thought:

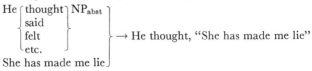

(2)   Indirect discourse (change of pronouns and of verb tense):

He thought, "She has made me lie" → He thought that she had made him lie

(3) Deletion:
He thought that she had made him lie → She had made him lie[21]

The original passage, stripped of the effects of these transformations, reads as follows:

> So his mother prayed for him and they stood up and Krebs kissed his mother and went out of the house. He thought this: I have tried so to keep my life from being complicated. Still, none of it has touched me. I have felt sorry for my mother and she has made me lie. I will go to Kansas City and get a job and she will feel all right about it. There will be one more scene maybe before I get away. I will not go down to my father's office. I will miss that one. I want my life to go smoothly. It has just gotten going that way. Well, that is all over now, anyway. I will go over to the schoolyard and watch Helen play indoor baseball.

The peculiar double vision of the style, the sense of the narrator peering into the character's mind and scrupulously reporting its contents, the possibility of distance and gentle irony—all these are gone with the transformational wind.

To be sure, these transformations do not in themselves distinguish Hemingway's style from the styles of many other writers (Virginia Woolf, Ford Madox Ford, James Joyce, etc.). But it is interesting, and promising, that a stylistic difference so huge as that between the Faulkner and Hemingway passages can be largely explained on the basis of so little grammatical apparatus.

Up to this point, I have been exploring some effects on style of particular transformations and groups of transformations, and arguing that this method of description has, potentially, considerable value for literary critics. But there are at least two other ways in which transformational machinery will aid the analyst of style.

First, it has often been pointed out that constructions may be left-branching ("Once George had left, the host and hostess gossiped briskly"), right-branching ("The host and hostess gossiped briskly, once George had left"), or self-embedding ("The host and hostess, once George had left, gossiped briskly"). Neither left- nor right-branching constructions tax the hearer's understanding, even when compounded at some length ("a very few not at all well liked union officials"; "the dog that worried the cat that chased the rat that ate the cheese that lay in the house that Jack built"). But layers of self-embedding quickly put too great a strain on the unaided memory ("the house in which the cheese that the rat that the cat that the dog worried chased ate lay was built by Jack"). Even a relatively small amount of self-embedding in a written passage can slow a reader down considerably.

With these preliminaries, consider the following sentence, which begins a short story:

> She had practically, he believed, conveyed the intimation, the horrid, brutal, vulgar menace, in the course of their last dreadful conversation, when, for whatever was left him of pluck or confidence—confidence in what he would fain have called a little more aggressively the strength of his position— he had judged best not to take it up.[22]

The style is idiosyncratic in the highest degree, and the writer is, of course, Henry James. His special brand of complexity is impossible to unravel through the method I pursued with Faulkner. A number of *different* transformations are involved. But notice that most of this complexity results from self-embedding. With the embedded elements removed the sentence is still far from simple, but the Jamesian intricacy is gone:

> She had practically conveyed the intimation in the course of their last dreadful conversation, when he had judged best not to take it up.

The following are the deleted sentences, with their full structure restored:

> He believed [it].
> [The intimation was a] horrid, brutal, vulgar menace.
> [Something] was left him of pluck or confidence.
> [It was] confidence in the strength of his position.
> He would fain have called [it that], a little more aggressively.

The embedded elements, in short, significantly outweigh the main sentence itself, and needless to say, the strain on attention and memory required to follow the progress of the main sentence over and around so many obstacles is considerable. The difficulty, as well as the Jamesian flavor, is considerably lessened merely by substituting left- and right-branching constructions for self-embedding, even though all the kernel sentences are retained:

> He believed that in the course of their last dreadful conversation she had practically conveyed the intimation, a horrid, brutal, vulgar menace, which he had then judged best not to take up, for whatever was left him of pluck or confidence—confidence in the strength of his position, as he would fain have called it, a little more aggressively.

It seems likely that much of James's later style can be laid to this syntactic device—a matter of *positioning* various constructions, rather than of favoring a few particular constructions. The relevance of positioning to style is, to be sure, no news. But again, transformational analysis should clarify the subject, both by providing descriptive rigor and by making available a set of alternatives to each complex sentence.

Finally, styles may also contrast in the kinds of transformational operations on which they are built. There are four possibilities: addition, deletion, reordering, and combination. Of these, my final sample depends heavily on deletion. The passage is from D. H. Lawrence's *Studies in Classic American Literature,* a book with an especially brusque, emphatic style, which results partly from Lawrence's affection for kernel sentences. But his main idiosyncrasy is the use of truncated sentences, which have gone through a variety of deletion transformations. Here is the excerpt:

> The renegade hates life itself. He wants the death of life. So these many "reformers" and "idealists" who glorify the savages in America. They are death-birds, life-haters. Renegades.
> We can't go back. And Melville couldn't. Much as he hated the civilized humanity he knew. He couldn't go back to the savages. He wanted to. He tried to. And he couldn't.
> Because in the first place, it made him sick.[23]

With the deleted segments replaced, the passage reads, somewhat absurdly, like this:

> The renegade hates life itself. He wants the death of life. So these many "reformers" and "idealists" who glorify the savages in America [want the death of life]. They are death-birds. [They are] life-haters. [They are] renegades.

> We can't go back. And Melville couldn't [go back]. [Melville couldn't go back, as] much as he hated the civilized humanity he knew. He couldn't go back to the savages. He wanted to [go back to the savages]. He tried to [go back to the savages]. And he couldn't [go back to the savages].
>
> [He couldn't go back to the savages] because, in the first place, it made him sick [to go back to the savages].

One does not need grammatical theory to see that Lawrence is deleting. But the restoration of the full form which is allowed by the grammar does reveal two interesting things. First, there is a large amount of repetition in the original passage, much more than actually shows. Perhaps this fact accounts for the driving insistence one feels in reading it. Second, Lawrentian deletion is a stylistic alternative to *conjunction,* which can also take place whenever there are two sentences partly alike in their constituents. The reasons for Lawrence's preferring deletion to conjunction might well be worth some study.

And in general, study of that sort should be the goal of stylistic analysis. All I have done here is outline, briefly and in part informally, a fruitful method of stylistic *description.* But no *analysis* of a style, in the fuller sense, can get off the ground until there are adequate methods for the humble task of description. Such methods, I think, are provided by transformational grammar. Furthermore, I have argued, such a grammar is especially useful for this purpose in that it alone is powerful enough to set forth, formally and accurately, stylistic *alternatives* to a given passage or a given set of linguistic habits.

Now there is no reason to generalize from four passages to infinity, and in fact full stylistic descriptions of the work of even the four writers I have discussed would need to be far more elaborate than the sketches I have offered here. Moreover, many styles that readers perceive as distinctive are more complex in their syntactic patterns than these four. Finally, though syntax seems to be a central determinant of style, it is admittedly not the whole of style. Imagery, figures of speech, and the rest are often quite important. But to perform on various styles the kind of analysis I have attempted in this paper is to be convinced that transformational patterns constitute a significant part of what the sensitive reader perceives as style. Transformational analysis of literary discourse promises to the critic stylistic descriptions which are at once simpler and deeper than any hitherto available, and therefore more adequate foundations for critical interpretation. Not only that: if, as seems likely to happen, generative grammars with transformational rules help the linguist or critic to explicate convincingly the elusive but persistent notion of style, that achievement will stand as one more piece of evidence in favor of such grammars.

NOTES

1. See Jerrold Katz and Jerry Fodor, "What's Wrong with the Philosophy of Language?" *Inquiry*, V (1962), 197–237.

2. William K. Wimsatt, *The Prose Style of Samuel Johnson* (New Haven, 1941), and Jonas Barish, *Ben Jonson and the Language of Prose Comedy* (Cambridge, Mass., 1960), to name just two of the best.

3. For an earlier attempt by the present author to deal with this problem, see "Prolegomena to the Analysis of Prose Style," in *Style in Prose Fiction; English Institute Essays, 1958,* ed. Harold C. Martin (New York, 1959), pp. 1–24.

4. I do not mean to suggest that a speaker or writer actually performs these operations. But the different possibilities of expansion in the grammar do offer an analogue to the choices open to the writer.

5. Possibly some other order of expansion is preferable, such as the one Lees uses: VP → (Prev) Aux + MV. See Robert B. Lees, *The Grammar of English Nominalizations,* Part II, *International Journal of American Linguistics,* XXVI, no. 3 (1960), 5. If the grammar takes this form, then the choice I am speaking of enters only with the expansion of the main verb. Such questions are immaterial, however, to my point.

6. This is simply to rephrase the definition of an optional transformation; see Noam Chomsky, *Syntactic Structures* (The Hague, 1957), p. 45.

7. Lees, p. 70 (transformation T47).

8. Notice that many such sets, including the three sentences about Dickens, will share the same *truth conditions,* to use the philosopher's term. This fact gives further encouragement to anyone who would treat transformational alternatives as different expressions of the same proposition.

9. Since deletions and additions will probably have taken place in the course of the derivation, the complex sentence will naturally not contain all and only all of the linguistic elements contained in the component sentences. These must be reconstructed and supplied with appropriate hypothetical elements, but there is generally a strong formal motivation for reconstructing the component sentences in one way rather than another.

10. Of course the alternative forms need not be complete sentences, or single sentences. That is, the alternatives to sentence A may include (1) sentence B, (2) part of sentence C, and (3) the group of sentences, D, E, and F. The most interesting alternatives to a given sentence often arrange the kernel material in units of different lengths.

11. I owe this point and several others to correspondence and conversation with Noam Chomsky.

12. William Faulkner, "The Bear," in *Go Down Moses* (New York, 1942), pp. 255–256.

13. For another version of these transformations, see Carlota S. Smith, "A Class of Complex Modifiers in English," *Language,* XXXVII (1961), 347–348, 361–362.

14. Strong as cables → cable-strong.

15. Lees, "Grammatical Analysis of the English Comparative Construction," *Word,* XVII (1961), 182–183. Carlota S. Smith, in "A Class of Complex Modifiers in English," offers a fuller treatment of such constructions, but Lees' simpler analysis is adequate for my present purposes.

16. Subscripts mark differences in referent.

17. Passives and pronouns are also fairly prominent here, but not enough to make them striking as stylistic features.

18. Except that conjunction may also operate on two sentences with no common morphemes.

19. It is apparently common for stylistic features to cluster like this in the work of an author. See my study, *Shaw: The Style and the Man* (Middletown, Conn., 1962) [An excerpt is reprinted in this volume as "Modes of Order," Selection 13—Ed.] for numerous examples, and for an attempt to link style with cognitive orientation.

20. *The Short Stories of Ernest Hemingway* (New York, 1953), pp. 152–153.

21. Morris Halle (Massachusetts Institute of Technology) explained these transformations to me.

22. "The Bench of Desolation," *Ten Short Stories of Henry James,* ed. Michael Swan (London, 1948), p. 284.

23. D. H. Lawrence, *Studies in Classic American Literature* (New York, 1955), p. 149.

16. A STUDY IN PROSE STYLES: EDWARD GIBBON AND ERNEST HEMINGWAY

Curtis W. Hayes

Curtis W. Hayes suggests in this transformationally based study that students of prose style should go beyond intuitive labels and that transformational-generative syntax provides important possibilities for formalizing intuitive stylistic judgments. He holds that the most important characteristic of prose style is sentence complexity.

  In a statistical comparison of one hundred sentences each from the prose of Edward Gibbon and Ernest Hemingway, Professor Hayes reduces each sentence to its "source sentence(s)" and traces its transformational history. He finds that Gibbon's typical employment of generalized transformations produces parallelism and balance. Hemingway, on the other hand, almost never employs embedding and transformational expansion. Professor Hayes concludes that use of a transformationally oriented methodology brings greater precision and a broader range of evidence to the study of prose style. Curtis W. Hayes is assistant professor of English at the University of Nebraska.

I. INTRODUCTION

  This paper is in part an exercise in the analysis of prose style and in part an abstract of a larger study that I made on the prose style of Edward Gibbon.[1] In that study I pointed out that

  Curtis W. Hayes, "A Study in Prose Styles: Edward Gibbon and Ernest Hemingway," *Texas Studies in Literature and Language,* VII (1966), 371–386. Copyright © 1966 by the University of Texas Press. Reprinted by permission of the author and publisher.

sensitive readers of literature have certain stylistic "intuitions" that enable them to identify certain familiar authors. For instance, if two extracts from the authors chosen for this study, Edward Gibbon and Ernest Hemingway, were given to these readers they would have little difficulty in determining their authorship. This intuitive ability may not, I believe, be adequately accounted for by the more familiar approaches to stylistic analysis. By "more familiar" I mean the school of literary criticism that attaches impressionistic labels to prose styles. For example, Hemingway's style in the more familiar stylistic analysis has been described as "simple," "direct," and sometimes "linear." Gibbon's style, which is intuitively more complex than Hemingway's, has been labeled as "grand" and "majestic."

These labels, however, do not describe style, but rather mirror an impression one receives when reading extracts from these two authors. The analysis must go beyond the mere tagging of impressionistic labels to prose styles. It is the analyst's job to account for these subjective impressions. I believe that recent developments in linguistic science, particularly the development of the transformational-generative concept of syntax, is an invaluable aid in formalizing the notion of what one means when he attaches descriptive labels to prose styles.

Generative grammarians have in recent publications stated the inherent advantages of a generative-transformational model for representing syntax.[2] In particular they maintain that a generative grammar following the Chomskian model would have the ability to generate (a better term would be enumerate) all the well-formed sentences of a language and would be able, further, to provide a deep structural description for each. Since in great part the impression that a sensitive reader perceives from a given work rests upon the types of syntactical processes that an author uses, it would seem that the theory and methods of generative grammarians might lend themselves to the explication of literary style. The following study is thus an experiment in the applied use of generative grammar and reflects the thesis, already implicitly stated, that such a grammar is a "powerful" and valuable tool in analyzing literary style.[3]

For the purpose of this paper, style may be defined as a characteristic, habitual, and recurrent use of the transformational apparatus of language. Whatever is "characteristic, habitual, and recurrent" must be, moreover, amenable to statistical measurement. There are certain transformations (statistical attributes) in Gibbon's style, for example, that can be measured and these transformations can be compared to those of another writer. In this sense, the study of style is a study of the complexity of sentences.

The basic unit of description in this paper is the textual sentence. Here defined, a textual sentence corresponds to the "institutionalized" sentence: that is, any body of material occurring between one period or question mark and the following one. Textual sentences are not always simple or kernel sentences, but are often complex sentences, which have been generated from two or more underlying source sentences. It is best to consider the ultimate textual sentence (the one which appears after the final transformation) a composite of two types of source sentences. The matrix (independent) sentence forms the overall pattern, the frame, of the ultimate sentence. Those sentences which are embedded, nested, or added to the matrix sentence are the constituent (dependent) sentences. This view of matrix and constituent sentence, Robert B. Lees says, "makes essential use of the notion that part of the syntactic structure of a sentence is the set of underlying, sometimes very abstract, representatives of the simple sentences from which it may be said to be derived by explicit grammatical rules called transformations." [4]

Textual sentence:	The boy who is wearing the cap is my brother.
Matrix:	The boy is my brother.
Constituent:	The boy is wearing the cap.

The constituent sentence, *the boy is wearing the cap,* is embedded in the matrix sentence by the use of an "explicit grammatical rule," the relative-clause transformation.

II. TRANSFORMATIONS

The following transformational rules (one-string and two-string), though not complete, provide the descriptive framework for describing an author's style. The rules in pure form are complex, but for the purpose of this paper I have simplified them.[5]

A. The passive transformation takes an active sentence and transforms it into the passive voice:

Nom + X-Vtr-Nom'-Y → Nom' + be + En-Vtr-by-Nom
   Nom = Nominal
    Vtr = any transitive verb
    En = past participle inflection
   X, Y = symbols included to cover material which may appear
          after Nom, Nom', such as post-nominal modifiers
       → = "rewrite" (convert the left-hand symbol into the right-
          hand representation of that symbol)

Sentence: Mary called Joy → Joy was called by Mary.

The agent *by Mary* can be optionally deleted:

Sentence: Joy was called by Mary → Joy was called.

B. Certain transformations called *Generalized Transformations* involve the manipulation of two or more strings (sentences). The *Nominalizing Transformation* is just one type of generalized transformation.

Nominalizing transformation T_{to} (Infinitive)
Nominalizing transformation T_{ing} (Gerund)

These rules convert a sentence having the structure *NP + VP* into a noun phrase of the form *to + VP* or *ing + VP*. These "crippled" sentences may then be embedded into the nominal slot of the matrix sentence.

-ing + VP (Gerundive Nominal)
Textual sentence: John enjoys playing the piano.
                  1   2
Matrix: (John enjoys) + (Nominal: it)
                  3   4
Constituent: (John + Tns + Be:) + (-ing + play the piano).
   Transformation: 1 + 2⎱
                        ⎰ → 1 + 4 → John enjoys playing the
                   3 + 4   piano.
to + VP (Infinitival Nominal)
Textual sentence: I asked him to play the piano.

                          1
Matrix: (I asked him)
                   2   3
Constituent: (He + Tns) + (play the piano).
   Transformation: 1   ⎫
                         ⎬ → 1 + to-3 → I asked him to play
           2 + 3 ⎭   the piano.

The final Nominalizing Transformation to be explicated is the *Factive Nominal*. The rules which generate factive nominals will handle the following constructions.

Subject: "that" clause
     1   2
(Nominal: it) + (was evident)
     3
(He did it)
   Transformation: 1 + 2 ⎫
                       ⎬ → that-3 + 2 → *That he did it* was
              3 ⎭   evident.

Subject: "question–word" clause
     1   2
(Nominal) + (was a surprise)
     3   4
(He went) + (there)
   Transformation: 1 + 2 ⎫
                     ⎬ → where-3 + 2 → *where he went* was
           3 + 4 ⎭   a surprise.

"Non-Action" Verb Object
     1
(I know) + (Nominal: it)
     3
(He did it)
   Transformation: 1 + 2 ⎫
                     ⎬ → 1 + that-3 → I know *that he did it.*
              3 ⎭

A sentence (NP + VP) may fill an adverb slot and the process is known as "adverbialization." For example, in the sentence, *he killed the man* + (*Adv*), the *Adv* slot may be filled either by a single lexical item, a phrase, or by a clause (a "crippled" sentence):

He killed the man + (quickly)
He killed the man + (in the dark)
He killed the man + (while the city burned)

The constituent sentence which fills the *Adv* slot in sentence three is embedded through these operations:

$$1 \qquad\qquad 2$$
Matrix: (He killed the man) + (Adv)
Constituent: (the city burned).
Transformation: $1 + 2 \left.\begin{matrix} \\ \\ 3 \end{matrix}\right\} \rightarrow 1 +$ while-3 (right-branching)

The constituent sentence and its slot may be optionally permuted to sentence-initial position (left-branching):

While the city burned, he killed the man.

Or the construction may be self-embedded.

He, *while the city burned,* killed the man.

The *Relative Clause Transformation* is an adjective-transformation. Some linguists believe that prenominal adjectivals are ultimately derived from the reduction of the relative-clause construction. The *red* of *the red house,* they posit, can be derived in the following way:

the house is red → the house which is red → the house red → the red house.

Other linguists, who combine the transformational and tagmemic approaches, would not hold to the notion that a phrase such as *the red house* may be derived from any kind of sentence in which the word *red* appears in predicate position. Archibald A. Hill, for example, points out that the two approaches—tagmemic and transformational—seem to be falling together, in that the transformational grammarians are accepting the notion of slots for modifiers which can occur before the noun. This avoids the necessity of assuming (at least in this paper) that *the red house was burned down* is anything more than a slot with a filler in it, whereas *the house was burned down* has the same slot but has left it empty.[6] In this paper adjectives will not be considered as being derived from the reduction of relative clauses.

The relative-clause transformation involves these processes:

$$\begin{array}{cc} 1 & 2 \end{array}$$

Matrix: (The boy) + (is my brother)

$$\begin{array}{cc} 3 & 4 \end{array}$$

Constituent: (The boy) + (is here)

Transformation: $\left.\begin{array}{c} 1 + 2 \\ 3 + 4 \end{array}\right\} \rightarrow 1 + \text{WH-4} + 2$

$$\begin{array}{ccc} 5 & 6 & 7 \end{array}$$

Result: (The boy) + (who is) + (here is my brother)

Deletion (ellipsis): $5 + 6 + 7 \rightarrow 5 + 7 \rightarrow$ The boy here is my brother.

The additive process (in essence, a transformational expansion) is signaled by a coordinate conjunction. The entire process may be called *addition: expansion of X slot*. There are various types of slot expansions that a speaker or a writer may perform: he may conjoin sentences:

$$\left.\begin{array}{c} S^1 \\ S^2 \end{array}\right\} \rightarrow S^1 + \text{conjunction: and/but/or} + S^2$$

There are other possibilities of slot expansions. For instance, one may do as Gibbon habitually does and employ the following transformational expansions:

$$\left.\begin{array}{c} N \\ N \end{array}\right\} \rightarrow N + \text{conj} + N$$

$$\left.\begin{array}{c} NP \\ NP \end{array}\right\} \rightarrow NP + \text{conj} + NP$$

$$\left.\begin{array}{c} V \\ V \end{array}\right\} \rightarrow V + \text{conj} + V$$

$$\left.\begin{array}{c} VP \\ VP \end{array}\right\} \rightarrow VP + \text{conj} + VP$$

$$\left.\begin{array}{c} \text{Prep Phrase} \\ \text{Prep Phrase} \end{array}\right\} \rightarrow PP + \text{conj} + PP$$

If the expansion includes only two lexical items (e.g., Caesarea was *plundered and burnt* by the licentious barbarians), then the constituents which fill the slot are referred to by the generic name, *doublet.*

III. STATISTICAL METHODS

A linguist when selecting a corpus of linguistic material for analysis takes from that corpus a sample that he hopes will be typical and representative. He does this because a corpus is often too large for individual analysis. Sampling is an economical procedure and it is particularly necessary in this paper, since it would be uneconomical to analyze each sentence in *The Decline and Fall.* Each sample should be tested for reliability. To test for reliability a linguist employs the following statistical formula:[7]

A. *Reliability:*   Standard Error = $\sqrt{PQ/N}$

P equals the proportion (frequency) of one of the items being counted; Q equals the absence of that item. $P + Q = 100\%$. N is the total number of items counted. For example, assume that 70 sentences contain a given stylistic device, while 30 sentences do not. In that event,

$$SE = \sqrt{\frac{.70 \times .30}{100}}$$
$$= \sqrt{.0021}$$
$$= 4.6\%$$

If the SE should exceed 5 percent, more items must be selected to reduce the error.

Earlier I posited that style is in part a habitual and characteristic use of the transformational apparatus of one's language. To determine whether a defined stylistic device (transformation) is characteristic of one author in comparison to another author, a linguist must test for statistical significance. In a randomly chosen sample suppose he finds that in author X 70 sentences out of 100 contain doublets, while in author Y the doublet is found in only 60 sentences. He wants to determine whether these two proportions (frequencies) can be said to belong to the same population (*no* statistical significance) or to belong to different populations (statistical significance). To test for significance, a linguist employs these formulas:

B. *Significance:*

$$P = \frac{N_1P_1 + N_2P_2}{N_1 + N_2}$$

The value *P* is simply the proportion for the two samples combined. That is, 130 of the 200 sentences contain doublets.

$$P = \frac{100 \times .60 + 100 \times .70}{100 + 100}$$
$$= 130/200$$
$$= .65$$

With the above information the sampling variance (the Standard Error of the difference between two proportions) may be calculated:

$$\sigma P_1 - P_2 = \sqrt{\frac{PQ + PQ}{N_1 + N_2}}$$
$$= \sqrt{\frac{.65 \times .35 + .65 \times .35}{100 + 100}}$$
$$= \sqrt{.00455}$$
$$= .0675 \text{ (Standard Error of the Difference between two proportions)}$$

The *actual* difference between the two proportions is .10 (.70 − .60 = .10).

Significance in Standard Errors

$$= \frac{\text{Actual difference}}{\text{SE difference between two proportions}}$$
$$= \frac{.10}{.0675}$$
$$= 1.48 \text{ Standard Errors}$$

Consultation of a probability table shows that deviations of this size (1.48) are expected to occur by chance alone in 13.88% of the samples. The difference between the proportions is, therefore, not significant. A percentage of probability above 5.0% is usually taken by statisticians to denote a *chance* deviation; a factor other than chance is responsible if the percentage of probability is below 5.0%; e.g., if the SE is 1.96 or more, the difference between the proportions is significant at the 5.0% level. Anything less than 1.96 denotes that the Standard Error is nonsignificant.

IV. METHOD OF ANALYSIS

I selected at random one hundred sentences from each author. These textual sentences were first *rewritten* into simple source sentences and the "history" of each (a detailed analysis of the generalized transformations which the textual sentence could be assumed to have undergone) was then shown. Numbers are assigned to the appropriate constituents for the purpose of a structural description. The following sentence from J. B. Bury's edition of *The Decline and Fall* (VI, p. 108, Sentence 7) will demonstrate the method of analysis:

Textual Sentence:

> Their discontents were secretly fomented by Laetus, their praefect, who found, when it was too late, that his new emperor would reward a servant, but would not be ruled by a favourite.

Source Sentences:

1. Their discontents were secretly fomented by Laetus.*

   * This sentence is a passive transform of the active sentence: Laetus secretly fomented their discontents.

   A. Laetus was their praefect.
   (1)   Laetus found + [Nominal] + (Adv)
         a. It was too late + (then)
         b. His new emperor would reward a servant.
         c. His new emperor would not be ruled by a favourite.*

   * This sentence is a passive transform of the active sentence: A favourite would not rule his new emperor.

Generalized Transformations: "History"
1. Addition: expansion of VP slot

1

(His new emperor would reward a servant)

2

(His new emperor would not be ruled by a favourite)

Transformation:
$$\left.\begin{array}{c}1\\2\end{array}\right\} \rightarrow 1 + \text{but} + 2$$

3

Result: (His new emperor would reward a servant but) +

4   5

(his new emperor) + (would not be ruled by a favourite)

Deletion: $3 + 4 + 5 \rightarrow 3 + 5$

2. Factive Nominal: "that" clause

6   7   8

(Their praefect found) + ([Nominal]) + ((Adv))

9

(His new emperor would reward a servant, but would not be ruled by a favourite)

Transformation:
$$\left.\begin{array}{c}6 + 7 + 8\\9\end{array}\right\} \rightarrow 6 + 8 + \text{that-}9$$

3. Self-embedding: adverbial clause

10   11   12

(Their praefect found) + ((Adv)) + (that his new emperor would reward a servant, but would not be ruled by a favourite)

13   14

(It was too late) + (then).

Transformation:
$$\left.\begin{array}{c}10 + 11 + 12\\13 + 14\end{array}\right\} \rightarrow 10 + \text{when-}(14)\text{-}13 + 12.$$

4. Right-branch embedding: relative clause

15

(Laetus was their praefect)

16   17

(Their praefect) + (found, when it was too late, that his new emperor would reward a servant, but would not be ruled by a favourite)

Transformation:
$$\left.\begin{array}{c}15\\16 + 17\end{array}\right\} \rightarrow 15 + \text{WH-}17$$

5. Right-branch embedding: relative clause plus deletion of $WH + V$.

18

(Their discontents were secretly fomented by Laetus)

    19   20

(Laetus) + (was their praefect, who found, when it was too late, that his new emperor would reward a servant, but would not be ruled by a favourite)

Transformation: $\left.\begin{array}{l} 18 \\ \\ 19 + 20 \end{array}\right\} \rightarrow 18 + \text{WH-}20$

21

Result: (Their discontents were secretly fomented by Lae-

        22   23

tus) + (who was) + (their praefect, who found, when it was too late, that his new emperor would reward a servant, but would not be ruled by a favourite).

Deletion: 21 + 22 + 23 → 21 + 23 = *Textual sentence*

The following I found to be typical of the type of sentence that Gibbon and Hemingway employ:

Gibbon:

> A sense of interest attached these more settled barbarians to the alliance of Rome, and a permanent interest very frequently ripens into sincere and useful friendship.
> The whole force of Constantine consisted of ninety thousand foot and eight thousand horse; and, as the defence of the Rhine required an extraordinary attention during the absence of the emperor, it was not in his power to employ above half his troops in the Italian expedition, unless he sacrificed the public safety to his private quarrel.
> Whilst Rome lamented the fate of her sovereign, the savage coldness of his son was extolled by the servile courtiers as the perfect firmness of a hero and a stoic.
> The religion of Zoroaster was abundantly provided with the former, and possessed a sufficient portion of the latter.

Hemingway:

> I gave them money for platform tickets and had them take my baggage.
> We looked at each other in the dark.
> I lowered the vermouth bottle to the other side of the bed when she came in.
> We walked along together through the town and I chewed the coffee. I looked back and saw her standing on the steps.

V. RESULTS OF ANALYSIS AND STATISTICAL COMPARISON

What follows are the result of this analysis and a comparison of the types of transformations that Gibbon and Hemingway employ. This is done in an effort to determine whether statistical significance exists in Gibbon's use of a specific transformation compared to Hemingway's use of the same transformation. The attributes (transformations) are in the left-hand column, the frequency of the transformation is in the center column, and significance is noted in the right-hand column.

TABLE I

Attribute	Gib-bon	Hem-ingway	Standard Errors
Transformations per sentence	4.3	1.3	....
Sentences undergone GT	98%	60%	SE = 6.5
Passive	68%	2%	9.48
Doublet	68%	8%	9.0
Sentences containing only one doublet	40%	8%	....
Sentences containing 2 doublets	18%	0%	....
Sentences containing 3 doublets	7%	0%	....
Sentences containing 4 doublets	1%	0%	....
Sentences containing 5 doublets	2%	0%	....
Total # of doublets	111	8	....
# N doublets	64	4	....
# Adj doublets	33	4	....
# V doublets	13	0	....
# Adv doublets	1	0	....
NP expansions	16%	0%	....
VP expansions	14%	28%	SE = 2.6
PP expansions	7%	2%	1.7
Factive Nominal expansions	2	0	....
% of S which have doublet expansions	79%	36%	SE = 6.0
Triplet	14%	4%	2.5
# N expansions (triplet)	4	2	....
# NP expansions	2	0	....
# V expansions	2	0	....
# VP expansions	3	0	....
# Adj expansions	0	2	....
# PP expansions	2	0	....
# Factive Nominal expansions	1	0	....

TABLE I (*Continued*)

Attribute	Gibbon	Hemingway	Standard Errors
Quadruplet	3	0	....
# N expansions	1	0	....
# NP expansions	1	0	....
# Factive Nominal expansions	1	0	....
Nominalizations	49%	22%	SE = 4.0
Infinitival Nominal	31%	9%	3.9
Total Number	37	10	....
S containing 1 Infinitival	25	8	....
S containing 2 Infinitivals	6	1	....
Gerundive Nominal	16%	4%	.... 2.8
Factive Nominal	19%	13%	1.17
Embedding			
# S which have embedded elements	64%	20%	6.3
Total # of embedded structures	105	24	....
# S containing 1 embedded structure	36	16	....
# S containing 2 embedded structures	18	4	....
# S containing 3 embedded structures	7	0	....
# S containing 4 embedded structures	3	0	....
S having Rel. Cl. structures	51%	8%	7.0
Total # of RC structures	77	10	
S having 1 RC	30	6	
S having 2 RC	16	2	....
S having 3 RC	5	0	....
Types of Branching			
Right Branching	26	4	....
Deleted Right Branching	14	4	....
Self Embedded	19	0	....
Deleted Self Embedded	17	2	....
S having *Adv Clause* structures	23%	12%	2.0
Total # Adv Clauses	28	14	....
S containing 1 AC	19	10	....
S containing 2 AC	3	2	....
S containing 3 AC	1	0	....
Types of branching			
Right Branching	9	8	....
Deleted Right Branching	2	0	....
Left Branching	12	4	....
Deleted Left Branching	1	2	....
Self Embedded	4	2	...
Additive Process: Expansion of S Slot			
% of S which are expansions	68%	32%	5.1
S having 2 conjoined S	41	30	....
S having 3 conjoined S	18	1	....
S having 4 conjoined S	9	0	....

The table indicates what we already knew intuitively, that the styles of Gibbon and Hemingway are different—that the style of Gibbon is "grand," "majestic," "complex," and that the style of Hemingway in comparison is "simple." The importance of the tables, however, is that they offer us an objective measure to "capture" this intuition. In other words, we may use the table as a tool to show the reasons behind our intuition. Instead of basing our analysis on subjective impressions and using opaque terminology to describe these impressions, we may say exactly how two styles differ. Generative grammar is important to the literary analyst for that reason: it offers him a device through which objective statements can be made about style. For instance, he can say that the style of Gibbon is more complex than that of Hemingway, since the number of transformations per sentence is an indication of that complexity. This is further indicated by the number of sentences having embedded structures (relative clauses, adverbial clauses), nested structures (nominalizations), and expanded structures within them. Rarely are there transformational expansions or embedded structures within Hemingway's sentences.

It is traditional to say that Gibbon's style is characteristically balanced. The table shows the degree of this parallelism. Not only can we say that Gibbon uses a high degree of parallel

TABLE II

	Significance in Standard Errors
Passive Transformation	9.48
Doublet	9.0
Infinitival Nominal	8.9
Relative-clause transformation	7.0
S having undergone transformation	6.5
% of S having embedded structures	6.3
% of S having doublet expansions	6.0
S which are additive	5.1
% of S having Nominalizations	4.0
Gerundive Nominal	2.8
VP expansion	2.6
S having 3 conjoined S	2.5
Adverbial Clause	2.0

Transformations which did not show statistical significance (below 1.96)

Prepositional Phrase Expansion	1.7
Factive Nominal	1.17

structures, we can also say something about the kinds of parallel structures. We can say that the number of doublet expansions in Gibbon far exceeds those found in Hemingway; and that there are other types of balanced structures in addition to the two-membered balanced entity (for example, the balanced noun phrases, verb phrases, and prepositional phrases). In sum, the table enables us to make exact descriptions of each author's style.

[Table II] is a statistical summation of the transformations counted. The list is graded from most significant (the passive) to least significant (adverbial clause) to nonsignificant.

VI. CONCLUSION

Explicit in this paper has been the hypothesis that a generative-transformational grammar based upon the Chomskian model is an extremely effective and useful tool in capturing the notion of style; and, further, that the transformations which an author employs to express content is a significant part of what a reader perceives as literary style. This hypothesis stems from the notion that speakers (and thus writers) may employ various and different models (sentence types) to express relatively the same content. That is, an author theoretically has an option at each linguistic situation. Whether an author, for example, generates *John hit the ball* or *the ball was hit by John* is a linguistic choice. To be more specific, whether an author habitually generates sentences in the passive voice, as Gibbon does, or whether he prefers the active voice, as Hemingway does, is an alternative which the language provides. Notice that a choice in this sense is not a lexical choice but a choice of a transformational rule.

In brief, a transformational-generative grammar has the power to differentiate different styles. As transformationalists are fond of saying, their grammar formalizes the notion of how complex sentences are produced and the manner in which complex sentences are related to simple source sentences. The amount of complexity, it follows, is an indication of how an author employs the rules of his language; and by breaking down ("rewriting") sentences into their kernel components and by specifying the types of grammatical transformations used to construct the ultimate textual sentence, one may arrive at the degree of complexity, which, I have maintained, is one indication of an author's style.

Since complexity is only one indication of style, the complexity in Gibbon's sentences may not differ from the complexity in the sentences of similar authors, say Samuel Johnson and David Hume. In that case, if one may hypothesize, the difference, if there is any, may exist on other levels (imagery, metaphor, etc.).

After making these strong claims for the efficacy of a transformational model in literary analysis, it is perhaps self-defeating to point out that this method is not a panacea for correcting the ills of past stylistic analyses. With this in mind, it would be perhaps helpful to state what this study has accomplished and what the limitations of such a study are. First, the study as presented is an attempt toward capturing the elusive notion of literary style. Yet, as pointed out, style exists at all levels, not merely at the syntactical level; and certainly style exists beyond the sentence, say in the realm of imagery. This study, in other words, has not exhausted the possibilities of discovering the inherent differences in Hemingway's and Gibbon's styles. Nothing, for example, has been said about their respective vocabularies. Certainly Gibbon's vocabulary is more latinate than Hemingway's; and this is a distinctive difference. Moreover, a transformational study could be deeper in some respects: for example, in pointing to the position of adjectives. Gibbon's adjectives, which usually occur in attributive position, could be compared to Hemingway's adjectives, which normally occur in predicate position. To conclude, the importance of this type of analysis is that the intuitively felt differences between two differing styles can at least be explained by the types (and frequencies) of transformations that each author employs in constructing his sentences.

NOTES

1. See my study, "A Linguistic Analysis of the Prose Style of Edward Gibbon," unpublished dissertation (University of Texas, 1964).

2. For example, see Paul Postal, "Constituent Structure: A Study of Contemporary Models of Syntactic Description," *International Journal of American Linguistics*, XXX, Part 3 (January, 1964).

3. The motivation for such a study has been clearly stated by Richard Ohmann, "Generative Grammars and the Concept of Literary Style," *Word*, XX (1964), 423–439. See also James Peter Thorne, "Stylistics and Generative Grammars," *Journal of Linguistics*, I (1965), 49–59. [Both reprinted in this volume.]

4. "The Promise of Transformational Grammar," *English Journal*, LII (1963), 330.

5. The reader may wish to examine the formal and more detailed rules of transformational grammar. I suggest that he consult the works of Noam Chomsky, especially *Syntactic Structures* (The Hague, 1957) and *Aspects of the Theory of Syntax* (Cambridge, Mass., 1965); Robert B. Lees, especially his "Grammar of English Nominalizations," *IJAL*, XXVI, Part 2 (1960; revised, March, 1961); and Carlota A. Smith, "A Class of Complex Modifiers in English," *Language*, XXXVII (1961), 342–365 and "Determiners and Relative Clauses in a Generative Grammar of English," *Language*, XL (1964), 37–52.

6. Professor Hill made this suggestion in a paper delivered before the Linguistic Society of America, December, 1964.

7. A complete account of the statistical methods incorporated in this paper can be found in publications by David W. Reed. See his "The History of Inflectional *n* in English Verbs before 1500," *University of California Publications in English*, VII, iv (1950), especially pp. 172–180, and "A Statistical Approach to Quantitative Linguistic Analysis," *Word*, V (1949), 235–247.

17. NOMINAL AND VERBAL STYLE

Rulon Wells

In written English prose, a verbal style ordinarily is preferred over a nominal style. In this essay Rulon Wells discriminates these styles more exactly, and shows that this distinction depends not only on nouns and verbs themselves, but upon other stylistic criteria such as sentence length, the number of clauses in each sentence, and the number of sentence patterns. Choice of a "nominal" or "verbal" style thus entails consequences for a wide range of syntactic characteristics. Professor Wells concludes with a discussion of nominal style in Sanskrit and Greek. Rulon Wells is professor of linguistics at Yale University.

DESCRIPTION AND EVALUATION

Pronouncements about style are of two sorts, descriptive and evaluative. Description is logically prior to evaluation, in that a reasoned description is possible without evaluation whereas a reasoned evaluation is not possible without description. Some who do descriptive stylistics do it in deliberate abstraction from evaluation, that is, without the intention of proceeding to evaluate; others do the description primarily for the sake of the evaluation which they regard as the end to which description is a means.

What should be a mere distinction is widely regarded as an opposition; a division that should only divide subject from subject too often divides man from man. There is a reason for this.

Reprinted from *Style in Language,* edited by Thomas A. Sebeok, by permission of The M.I.T. Press, Cambridge, Massachusetts, copyright © 1960 by The Massachusetts Institute of Technology.

It is not the case, in practice, that the "describers" and the "appraisers" study the same things from different points of view. For the two intents—sheer description, on the one hand, and description conjoined with evaluation—lead to different selections. In principle the appraiser evaluates or appraises all texts, but in practice, in addition to the obvious specialties (texts in French, or English texts of the Elizabethan period, or Latin poetry), he tends to select for study the texts that he will evaluate *favorably*.[1] In particular, he is likely to shy away from spending his efforts on the meaner texts, those that do not even purport to be literature, and to concentrate on belles-lettres, which more vigorously exercise his powers. And equally, the sheer describer, who in principle describes all texts, tends in practice to focus on less pretentious texts precisely because they are less complicated. Experimentalists and statisticians, in particular, are likely to regard belles-lettres as too complicated for fruitful study. The time may come when this limitation is passed beyond, but I am speaking of the present day.

In general, then, appraiser and sheer describer tend to study mutually exclusive phenomena or aspects. But there are exceptions. One of these is the degree to which nouns and verbs are used in various styles. Here is a variable of style at once simple and interesting. Nominal (nominalizing) style, the tendency to use nouns in preference to verbs, and the opposite verbal or verbalizing style, which tends to use verbs rather than nouns, are two features that are fairly easy to describe yet are of great interest to appraisers. Those who appraise at all mostly appraise nominal style as inferior to verbal. And yet it crops up again and again, defended on the ground that it is adapted to its purpose.

NOMINAL AND VERBAL STYLE

In this and the next two sections I shall confine my discussion to English, and to written English. The advice to shun the nominal style is sometimes put this way: "Don't use nouns where you could use verbs; don't shrink from the use of verbs." This way of putting it takes two things for granted: first, that nominality and verbality are matters of continuous degree, and second, that the continuum is characterized by the proportion of nouns to verbs in a given text. These presumptions, in turn, seem to indicate a "quantization" (quantitative measure) of our variable, by defining it as a ratio—the sort of thing that might be dubbed the Noun-Verb Quotient (NVQ). Before this indication can be precise, however, three points need to be settled.

1. What is a noun? (*a*) Shall we count pronouns and adjectives as nouns? They share many of the characteristics that distinguish nouns from verbs. (*b*) Shall a noun phrase count as a single noun? For example, shall "the foot of the mountain" be reckoned as containing one noun or two?

2. What is a verb? (*a*) Do nonfinite forms (infinitives, gerunds, participles) count as verbs, as nouns, as both, or as neither? (*b*) Shall a periphrastic verb like "will do" count as one verb or as two? (*c*) Shall the verb "to be" count the same as other verbs? (The feeling is sometimes expressed that the copula is not a true verb, since it has a purely logical function. On the other hand, it has person, tense, etc., like other verbs. Thus a discrepancy between its form and its meaning is felt. We might recognize this discrepancy by counting occurrences of forms of "to be" one-half, rather than one; or we might take the view that there is no quantitative way of recognizing the peculiar nature of the copula.)

3. The advice might be formulated a little differently. "Keep the proportion of nouns low and of verbs high." An index that would show whether this advice was being followed would have two parts: a Noun-Word Quotient (NWQ) *and* a Verb-Word Quotient (VWQ). For any given text the sum of these two quotients cannot exceed 1.0 and will only equal 1.0 if there are no other parts of speech in the text, but beyond that there is no necessary connection between the two quotients. It would be interesting to determine experimentally whether there is a consistent inverse relation between them.

The problem of quantizing nominality will not be pursued further here. It might well turn out that some of the questions raised are insignificant, for example, that the NVQ of scientific writers differs markedly from that of literary writers, no matter how noun and verb are delimited. But of course these facts could only be determined by experiment, for which reflections such as those of the present paper are a necessary preamble but no substitute.

There is a further consideration of which any treatment, quantitative or otherwise, should take account. Style is understood to be optional, like vocabulary, as contrasted with grammar. So far as the writer of English has a choice, what he writes is *his* diction and *his* style; so far as he has none, it is the *English* language. A treatment that respects this optionality will somehow take account of whether, and in how many ways, a sentence with a certain degree of nominality could be replaced by one with a different degree, for example, a highly nominal by a highly verbal sentence. And of course it is understood that mere variation of style is made not to alter the substance or content of what is expressed but only the way of expressing it; underlying the very notion of style is a postulate of *independence of matter from manner*. If a given matter dictates a particular manner, that manner should not be called a style, at least not in the sense that I have been speaking of. But this postulate does not preclude that a certain matter shall favor or "call for" a certain manner—the so-called fitness of manner to matter, or consonance with it.

CONSEQUENCES OF NOMINALITY

The advice to prefer verbs to nouns makes it sound as though it were a simple substitution, like the choice of familiar words in preference to rare ones, or of short words in preference to long ones. Occasionally this is so, but not in the usual case. In the more nominal phrase "the doctrine of the immortality of the human soul," the particles are different from those in the more verbal phrase "the doctrine that the human soul is immortal"; the one uses prepositions, the other a conjunction. In changing the verb of "He began to study it thoroughly" into the noun of "He began a thorough study of it," we must follow through by a corresponding change of adverb to adjective. The elementary fact of syntax that prepositions and adjectives go with nouns, conjunctions and adverbs with verbs, prevents the contrast of nominality and verbality from being *minimal*.

This fact has two consequences. (1) When nominality is evaluated good or bad, the ground may lie in whole or in part in features entailed by nominality, although distinct from it. (2) And so the nominal-verbal contrast is not a *pure dimension* of style, that is, it is not a variable which can vary without variation in the other basic factors of style.

The aforementioned consequences are necessary ones. Another class must be acknowledged, the probable consequences. From the statistical point of view, necessary consequences appear as those whose probability is 1.0, impossible consequence as those with probability .00, and the less or more probable consequences as those having intermediate probability values.

Even an impressionistic study can estimate some of these probabilities. To facilitate discussion, let us pretend—what is false, but not grossly false—that nominalizing and verbalizing sentences can be paired, so that we can speak of *the* nominal counterpart of such and such a verbal sentence and of the verbal counterpart of a given nominal sentence. The intent of this fiction is to concentrate our discussion on differences as near to minimal as is syntactically possible.

A nominal sentence is likely to be longer, in letters and in syllables, than its verbal counterpart. The greater length in the diction of those writers who favor nominal style results from the fact that the noun corresponding to the verb is likely to be longer than the verb—usually because it is derived from the verb stem by suffixes—and the entailed changes (loss of verb endings, replacement of conjunctions by prepositions, etc.) are not likely to compensate. Compare "when we arrive" with "at the time of our arrival"—fourteen letters (including word spaces) replaced by twenty-six, four syllables by eight.

Another likelihood is that the average number of clauses per sentence tends to decrease (the minimum being 1.0), for nominalization replaces conjunctions by prepositions. The sentence "If he does that, he will be sorry" has two clauses; its nominal counterpart "In the event of his doing that, he will be sorry" has only one.

A third likelihood, entailed by the second and also somewhat likely even in the absence of the second condition, is that the number of distinct sentence patterns will decrease. Compound sentences (both with coordinating and with subordinating conjunctions) tend to disappear, so that only simple (subject-predicate) sentences, more or less swollen by parentheses and modifiers, will be left.

EVALUATION OF NOMINALITY

Nominality is judged bad by some, good by others.

1. Those who judge nominal style bad judge it so for one or more of the following reasons:

a. Nouns are more static, less vivid than verbs. Sometimes this view is defended on deep philosophical grounds. For example, Étienne Gilson[2] sees in Aristotle's remark (*De interpretatione* 3.16b19) that "verbs in and by themselves are substantival" a revealing clue to his philosophy; not Aristotle but Thomas Aquinas is the one who gives to "is," to existence *in actu exercito,* its full due. And to the argument that the traditional, semantical definitions of noun and verb are of no avail because what one language considers an action, another may treat as a state, the rejoinder might be made that this is just the point: the contrast of action and state varies with the point of view, and one that does not reduce all actions to states is to be recommended. Something like this seems to be intended by Peter Hartmann, to whom I shall refer in the next section.

b. Longer sentences are (on the whole) less vivid and less comprehensible than shorter ones.

c. A text whose sentences are all or mostly of one basic pattern will usually be monotonous. Verbal style allows more diversity, and a good style will exploit the genius of its language.

2. Those who judge nominal style good do so implicitly, for the most part; nominal style is practiced more than preached. The implicit reasons in its favor appear to be these:

a. It is easier to write. Thus it is natural for those who are more concerned with what they say than with how they say it to choose this style, or to drift into it.

b. It helps impersonality. In scientific writing ("scientific" in the broadest sense, including philosophy, and as contrasted with artistic and literary writing), expressions of personality are frowned upon. Now personality can be avoided in various ways. One is the use of the passive voice. Where the seventeenth and eighteenth centuries would have been anecdotal—"I collected sea anemones at low tide"—the nineteenth and twentieth centuries would cast the reporting subject into the shadow of implicitness: "Sea anemones were collected at low tide." Another way to avoid personality is to avoid finite verbs altogether, by nominalizing.

c. Nominality offers another advantage to the scientific writer. The finite verb has not only person but also number and (as does the participle) tense. Of these three dimensions tense is widely felt to be the most fundamental; similarly Aristotle distinguishing the Greek verb from the Greek noun does it on the basis of having or lacking tense (*De interpretatione* 2.16a19, 3.16b6). Now to the extent that a writer can avoid finite verbs and participles (including forms of the verb "to be"), he can avoid commitments as to tense. Indeed, it is partly because of this fact that the pairing of nominalizing and verbalizing sentences is a fiction. "At the time of our arrival" has not one verbal counterpart but two, "when we arrived" and "when we arrive."

d. The very fact that nominality is contrary to conversational style has its value. It sets off the writing as esoteric, specialized, technical. Nominal style in English can be used to play the role (although much less conspicuously and effectively) that Latin played until several hundred years ago.

Certain neutral remarks can be made about these judgments. Those who approve nominal style and those who disapprove it are not in utter disagreement. Its advocates do not claim that it is graceful or elegant, and its critics do not deny that it achieves impersonality and the rest. But after the mutual concessions, a residue of disagreement remains. It is admitted by all that verbal style is harder to write than nominal style; is it *worth* the trouble? This would raise the broader question whether good style is being urged for its own sake (i.e., as an end), or as a means to some other end, or on both grounds. Advocates of nominal style usually defend it as a means to an end; its attackers might argue that it does not achieve its end, and that for the very same end verbal style is more effective. In that case, verbal style would be preferable to nominal both as an end and as a means.

NOMINAL STYLE IN SANSKRIT AND IN GREEK

I have spoken only of noun and verb, neglecting the other parts of speech. It has been a feeling of Indo-European speakers through the ages that noun and verb are the major parts of speech; both Plato (*Sophist*) and Aristotle (*De interpretatione*) take this view, and Plutarch[3] explicitly defends Plato against the charge of neglecting the others, on the ground that they are only like the seasoning in a meat dish. It is curious that the Greeks, of all people, should have taken this view, for they had developed a syntactical device, I mean the definite article, that gave their language a conciseness and flexibility exceeding that of any other Indo-European language. But this device will be better appreciated against the background of some other, similar language.

I pick Sanskrit because of the recent book by Peter Hartmann.[4] The underlying ideas in his books seem to be that the fundamental distinction of noun and verb is semantical, not formal; that therefore a language may have formal verbs that are semantically nouns (Japanese is his example); and indeed that possession of a true verb is very nearly a peculiarity of the Indo-European family. Against this background . . . he discusses nominality in Sanskrit. Nominalization is a matter of style on the part of Sanskrit writers, which it could not be in any language which lacks a true verb; we have then the interesting phenomenon of a group of writers deliberately neglecting the feature which is most distinctive of their language family. The case is the more interesting because nominal style reaches a higher degree with them than with any other group of writers in any other Indo-European language.

One reason for this is that the verb "to be" can be omitted altogether. Omission of this verb is familiar in Greek and other languages when it functions as the copula, but the Sanskrit nominal style omits it even when it means "exists." For instance (Hartmann, *Nominale Ausdrucksformen*, p. 48), "tasya ca rūpa-vattvāt karmavattvāt ca dravyatvam [asti]," literally "of-it and from-coloredness from-activeness and materialness [exists]," that is, "And [there exists] materiality of it [sc. darkness] because of coloredness and because of activeness." A still freer and more idiomatic translation that gives the same sense is "And it [darkness] is a material because it has color and because it acts." This same example shows how other verbs are replaced, for example, "acts" by "activeness."

The teleological explanation and historical antecedents of this style are not investigated by Hartmann; but certain facts are obvious. (*a*) This style is very like the "sutra style" in which Panini's grammar, the Vedanta-sutra's of Badarayana, etc., are written, and which therefore (because of Panini's date) goes back as early as about 400 B.C. (*b*) In Panini, it seems to be designed for the sake of brevity. Not only nominality but also many other means are used to this end. Brevity, in turn, seems to have been desired, even at the price of ambiguity and obscurity, in order that the sutras might be memorized entire, and also, later at least, as an elegance. (*c*) The nominal style in question also makes extensive use of compounds. Now a fondness for compounds also marks the literary writers—poets, storytellers, and sometimes dramatists. These compounds are often inherently ambiguous, but the ambiguity is often resolved by the context, and on the other hand it is sometimes deliberately sought as a word play. If the scientific writers do not cultivate ambiguity, at least they do not seem to mind it either.

So the phenomenon of nominal Sanskrit has not yet been explained, but its nature has been made fairly clear. Nominal Sanskrit is possible (*a*) because of the wealth of suffixes by one or another of which an abstract noun can be formed from any part of speech, and (*b*) because "to be," in either meaning, can be elided.

Classical Greek does not form abstract nouns with quite the freedom of Sanskrit, but it has another resource, its definite article. In fact, the singular neuter article differs formally from the Sanskrit suffix -*tva* in hardly more than this, that it precedes rather than follows what it accompanies. There is a more important semantical difference, namely that the Greek device is sometimes ambiguous. *To leukon* may mean either "the white thing" or "the color white." [5] But if an infinitive follows the article, there is not this ambiguity.

That Greek has here an unusual resource was a fact of which the Latin translators were keenly aware. How to translate *to einai* into Latin? Before William of Moerbeke (*ob.* 1285 or 1286), translators had simply complained; but Moerbeke *did* something:

he changed the Latin language. He introduced the Romance article *le* to render *to*, and, once or twice, even introduced the possessive *del* to render the genitive *tou*: *ultra del esse* apparently translates *epekeina tou einai*.[6] His innovation did not stick, but it is an interesting attempt.

That noun and verb will require different definitions in different languages (or more exactly, in those in which the contrast can be found at all) is hardly a controversial proposition nowadays.[7] The contrast of Sanskrit with Greek is meant to illustrate this fact. In Sanskrit it would be proper to count as verbal a style that used infinitives, but in Greek, owing to its versatile definite article, the infinitive when preceded by the article plays much the same role as the Sanskrit (or English) abstract noun. It is still verbal, though, in that it can have an accusative direct object where the corresponding abstract noun would require a modifying genitive. Thus not only noun and verb, but also nominal style and verbal style, would be distinguished differently in different languages.

NOTES

1. At least to the extent of finding them interesting. A critic may pronounce the style of some poem or essay a failure but add that it is a distinguished failure, or a significant experiment, or the like.
2. Étienne Gilson, *Being and Some Philosophers,* 2d ed. (Toronto, 1952), p. 199. On quite different grounds some philosopher mentioned but not named by Aristotle (*Physics* 1.2.185b28) proposed to replace, for example, "The man is white" by "The man whites," coining a verb for the purpose if need be.
3. Moralia 1010C (*Quaestiones platonicae 10*); cited in F. M. Cornford, *Plato's Theory of Knowledge: The Theaetetus and the Sophist of Plato* (London and New York, 1935, 1951), p. 307.
4. Peter Hartmann, *Nominale Ausdrucksformen im Wissenschaftlichen Sanskrit* (Heidelberg, 1955). Part of a series, along with Hartmann's *Einige Grundzüge des Japanischen Sprachbaues* (Heidelberg, 1952); *Probleme der Sprachlichen Form* (Heidelberg, 1957), *Wortart und Aussageform* (Heidelberg, 1956, and *Zur Typologie des Indogermanischen* (Heidelberg, 1956).
5. W. D. Ross, *Aristotle's Metaphysics* [Oxford, 1934, 1953], I, xcii, n. 3.
6. R. Klibansky and C. Labowsky, *Plato Latinus, Volumen III* (London, 1953), 28a23–28b26 and 44.26; see pp. xv–xxv on Moerbeke, and p. xxii, n. 3, on the complaints of predecessors.
7. R. H. Robins, "Noun and Verb in Universal Grammar," *Language,* XXVIII (1952), 289–298.

APPROACHES TO METRICS

V

18.   THE COMPONENTS

OF ENGLISH METER

Seymour Chatman

Seymour Chatman's *A Theory of Meter,* from which the following excerpt is taken, seeks to establish a firm theoretical
foundation for metrical analysis and criticism in the work of
George L. Trager, Henry Lee Smith, and Dwight L. Bolinger on
English stress, pitch, and juncture. His book contains a full
account of the psychological and physiological bases of rhythm
and meter, and concludes with an analysis of eleven different
performances of Shakespeare's "Sonnet 18" using the sound
spectrograph in an attempt to establish criteria for scansional
decisions. In this selection Professor Chatman sets out the
theoretical bases for such fundamental concepts as scansion,
syllable count, foot, and ictus (a metrical term preferred to the
linguistic terms "stress" and "accent"). Ictus is shown to arise
from different combinations of four syllabic weights, which Professor Chatman argues are basic to English meter. Seymour Chatman is professor of speech at the University of California,
Berkeley.

Why do we need metrics at all? [1] The answer seems obvious.
The phenomenon of verse exists. It is in part a product of the
constraining of language by a supervening system we call meter.
The science of metrics has arisen to specify and categorize the
elements of the system. Metrics thus exemplifies the general
human need to categorize, which, psychologists assure us, we
possess for five good reasons: to reduce the complexity of our

Reprinted from *A Theory of Meter* (Janua Linguarum nr. 36), pp. 101–127,
by Seymour Chatman (The Hague: Mouton & Co., 1965), by permission of
the author and publisher.

environment, to identify the objects in the world about us, to reduce the necessity of constantly treating things as if they were new occurrences, to aid in problem-solving, and to discover (or invent) orders and relations among events.[2]

But other, more specifically literary, motivations may be adduced, too. Through metrical analysis, we are able to distinguish the effects of phonetic surface in poems, a matter of some critical consequence. Since meters are complex organizations, they can be handled by poets in idiosyncratic ways, and so are appropriate subjects for stylistic analysis. Furthermore, metrics aids in esthetic evaluation to the extent that meter and meaning are mutually informative or mutually appropriate. Too easy assumptions of "expressive form" need close examination, but if such appropriateness exists or is even merely useful as a metaphor for something less expressible, metrical analysis qualifies as an important preoccupation of literary criticism. In any case, the difference between prose and verse must be accounted for, and meter is obviously central to that distinction.

Success and persuasiveness in metrical analysis depend upon the adequacy of the theory behind it. Too often metrists are arbitrary and unwilling to justify or even disclose their tacit assumptions. Many propose and debate scansions on *ad hoc* grounds, without considering basic premises or even acknowledging the need for their consideration.

One thing is clear: people do learn how to scan poems. The ability cannot be intuitive, but must develop by virtue of their native command of their language and certain simple rhythmic assumptions. Further, it seems clear that scansions can only derive from recitations—whether actually vocalized or "silent," that is, the scanner cannot but proceed by actually reading the words and coming to some decision about their metrical status. A metrist's proper task, then, is to try to discover by observation[3] what people do when they perform metrical analysis. If he were to run experiments by tabulating the responses of skilled metrists to a standard passage, he would discover that metrical judgment varies widely. A simple search through the standard handbooks shows the same thing. Why is there variation? Let us recall the two essential features of meter as a rhythmical phenomenon, the metrical *event* and the metrical *prominence*. We have equated the former with the syllable but were unable to find any single unequivocal linguistic feature to represent the latter. Three reasons for variation in metrical practice suggest themselves:

1. Metrists do not agree upon the number of syllables in a given word or line;
2. Metrists do not agree upon whether a given syllable is prominent or not;
3. Metrists do not agree upon how the syllables are grouped.

Disagreements stemming from the second and third reasons are complex and more profound than those stemming from the first, since the number of syllables in English words is usually easy to agree upon. However, the phenomenon of metrical elision does exist as a historical fact and deserves theoretical consideration.

I propose that the scansion of a recitation is not the same thing as the meter, but merely one version of it.[4] The scansion is not a sheer record, i.e., a full phonetic or phonemic transcription. It is, rather, a conventionalized or formulaic reduction of the phonetic complex of the performance to the simple distinctions implicit in such terms as "ictus" and "non-ictus." My view of the mechanism of this reduction will be described in detail below.

The meter of a poem is not some fixed and unequivocal characteristic, but rather a structure or matrix of possibilities which may emerge in different ways as different vocal renditions. Obviously, these will not be of equal merit; but value judgments should not obscure the range of linguistic possibility even before inquiry begins. It is a mistake in method to confuse the metrical abstraction (in the sense of "derivation of common features") with any of its actualizations. Evaluations which assert that one rendition is more valuable than another ("better," "richer," "more meaningful," "more profound") must ultimately be made. But one can hardly proceed to grasp the meter of a poem in the fullest sense (the history of metrics shows) if he is so committed at the outset to his own rendition that other possibilities are not even conceivable, let alone acceptable. Who has not read with surprise the claim that a certain scansion *is* the meter when it seems so clearly only one way of reading the verse?

It has long been clear that descriptive orientations are more appropriate to metrics than prescriptions. It is hard to express the need more clearly than did Lascelles Abercrombie more than thirty-five years ago:

> The art of Prosody is . . . not a matter of rules and prescriptions, but of the empirical use of certain laws which are themselves no more than general statements of the methods that actually have proved capable of being used for expressive purposes. Any "art of prosody" that professes to explain how prosodic expression is to be obtained, beyond a description of the proved means available to obtain it, is to be profoundly mistrusted.[5]

We shall extend Abercrombie's phrase "general statements" to mean not only that meter is what poets do, not what metrists say to do, but also that the meter of any poem is best described as the matrix of all meaningful scansions.

Two terms need to be distinguished at the outset. By "scanning" I shall mean identifying aspects of recitations as rudimentary rhythmic patterns (according to some convention to be described) in order to show how secondary rhythm is being verbally manifested, by perceived word-stress, phrase-accent, or in other ways.[6] By "metrical analysis," on the other hand, I mean the process of summing the scansions of all intelligible recitations. Thus, the meter of a poem is at once more and less than any feasible scansion; more because it presupposes not only that scansion but others as well, and less by virtue of its very inclusiveness, for at points it must be indeterminate to include the possibility of variation. The meter in this sense is a consensus, not a normative formulation.[7] Implicit in this view is an appreciation of the complexity of meter. It is not like rhythm, which can be defined in the simplest perceptual terms since the experience is easily discoverable, in experiment and real life, in sets of temporal recurrences of only one or two standard events. It is wiser to think of meter as a concept, rather than a percept, even though it is based on the percept of rhythm; it is the mind, not the senses, which performs the task of reducing disparate linguistic phenomena to simple distinctions, learning to measure and to equate things which are very different indeed in their absolute physical nature. Rhythms can be perceived by any human being with ears, but one must know English before he can grasp its metrical pattern.

SYLLABLE COUNT

The numerical aspect of meter—the count of syllables per line —does not vary extensively from recitation to recitation, and metrical indeterminacy is ordinarily the result of other factors. Furthermore, when questions arise, the metrical context usually shows us how many syllables to attribute to a word. For example, it is not difficult to see that *oblivious* is metrically trisyllabic in

And with some sweet oblivious antidote

> Shakespeare
> MACBETH

but *oblivion* is quadrisyllabic in

Wherein he puts alms for oblivion

> Shakespeare
> TROILUS AND CRESSIDA

Saying, in the first example, that *oblivious* is metrically trisyllabic, does not necessarily prescribe elisions to reciters (say, the actual pronunciation /ɨblɪvyɨs/ instead of /ɨblɨvyɨs/). By distinguishing between scansion and metrical analysis, we may conceive of either performance, with or without scansional elision, without denying the *metrical* existence of elision at this point. Devices have been used by poets and editors to make the numerical intention clear: spelling modifications (preterite "-ed" becoming "-t"), apostrophes ("-ed" becoming "-'d" or "-'t"), grave accent marks ("-èd"), etc. In the view of a metrist like Robert Bridges, elisions can often be assumed even where diacritics do not appear in the text.

Phonology can help explain the mechanism by which elisions— adjustments of syllable-count by omission[8]—and their opposites, insertions, may be manifested in speech. Consider the example cited by Bridges:

> In English verse when there is poetic elision of the terminal vowel of one word before the initial vowel of the next word, the sound of it is not lost, the two vowels are glided together, and the conditions may be called synaloepha.

For instance, the first example of terminal synaloepha in
[*Paradise Lost*] is

Above th' Aonian Mount, while it pursues

i.15

where the final vowel of *the* is glided into the *A* of *Aonian,* it
is still heard in the glide, though prosodically asyllabic.[9]

Bridges is implying that there is necessarily a disparity between
the meter of this line and any recitation of it: that this elision is a
paper matter only, prosodic bookkeeping so to speak, since the
elided vowel is still heard, although it doesn't quite "count." (In
another place, he speaks of "the fiction of elision.") But this
accounts for only one recitational style. It is quite possible to say

/ðeːonyɪn/,

in which the whole vowel of "the" is deleted, even though modern
readers would probably prefer

/ðiː + eːonyɪn/.

It is also possible to convert the vowel to the consonant /y/:

/ðyeːonyɪn/,

a pronunciation which Bridges might have liked. The scansional
status of these pronunciations could be described as follows:

Meter	*Recitation*
1) /ðeːonyɪn/elision	elision
2) /ðiː + eːonyɪn/elision	non-elision (recitational exception)
3) /ðyeːonyɪn/elision	"pseudo-elision" (see below)[10]

The point is that regardless of current recitational practice, many
of the elisions indicated in older texts can actually be articulated.
The metrist should understand their phonological nature, even if
he prefers to ignore them in his own recitations. And who is to
say whether we may not turn again to the widespread articulation
of elisions in some future era of formalistic recitation?

The consideration of syllable-adjustment—elision and insertion
—requires a review of some purely linguistic notions. [Earlier,]
distinctions were made between phonetic types—"contoids" (contact sounds) and "vocoids" (unobstructed sounds)—and their

phonemic counterparts, "consonants" and "vowels." The term "syllabic" was also introduced as a name for the centermost part, the "crest" or "peak" of syllables, and it was pointed out that certain contoids, like [n], [m], [l], and [r] may function as syllables.[11]

Their peculiar phonetic character allows these contoids to function syllabically. Contoids occur as two basic types: stops and continuants. Stops are single brief articulatory acts: our lips can explode only one [p] or one [b] at a time. It is obvious, therefore, that a stop cannot be sustained long enough to be a syllabic. Continuants, on the other hand, like vowels, can be sustained for as long as our breath holds out: we can say [mmmmmm] or [ffffff] or [zzzzzz] indefinitely, just as we can say [aaaaa] or [iiiii]. Phoneticians subdivide continuants into fricatives and resonants. Fricatives are formed by forcing air through small apertures in the mouth—between the lips and the teeth ([f] and [v]), between the teeth and the tongue ([θ] and [ð]), and between the tongue and the roof of the mouth ([s] and [z]). The resultant friction makes these sounds "noisy" (in the physicist's sense), that is, anharmonic, or composed of random sound waves. Fricatives can function as syllabic crests but do so very infrequently in English, precisely because they are so unlike harmonically regular vocoids. They usually occur in marginal words like "pst," "tsk," "fft," etc. But the resonants are much more vocoid-like and hence more easily syllabicized. We form the resonants by causing large areas of the vocal canal above the glottis to resonate or vibrate sympathetically with vocal cord vibration, just as they do in the utterance of vowels. Resonants differ from vowels only in that the mouth is partially or totally closed. Unlike fricatives, resonants are not made noisy by being squeezed through small openings, but emerge with comparatively little obstruction ([m]and [n] through the nose, and [l] down the sides of the tongue). [r] in many English dialects is even more vocoid-like since it does not involve closure at all: the tongue is held in approximately the same position as for [ə] but its tip is rolled back ("retroflexed"). Some phoneticians even represent the sound as a vocoid [ɚ], where the "tail" stands for retroflexion. Resonants frequently occur as crests in unstressed syllabels: "help 'em" [helpm̩], "button" [bətn̩], "bottle" [batl̩], "water" [wɔtr̩] (or [watr̩]).

Although, as we have seen, the contoids [m], [n], [l], and [r] do occur as syllabics in English, it is preferable from the phonemic point of view to analyze them as combinations of nonsyllabic consonants with a vowel, thus /ɨm/, /ɨn/, /ɨl/, and /ɨr/. The reduced vowel phoneme /ɨ/ is inserted because the syllabic phones [m̩], [n̩], [l̩], and [r̩] are in complementary distribution with syllables formed by the vowel /ɨ/ before the nonsyllabic phones [m], [n], [l], and [r]. Although there are phonetic differences between these sets of syllables, the differences do not correlate with differences of meaning, and so are linguistically non-significant. It is more economical to treat the syllabic variants [m̩], [n̩], [l̩], and [r̩] as allophones of /ɨm/, /ɨn/, /ɨl/, and /ɨr/ than to set them up as separate phonemes, even though the phonemicizations /bətɨn/, /batɨl/, etc., may seem misleading as representations of the pronunciations [bətn̩], [batl̩], etc.[12]

In the metrical adjustment of syllables we can recognize three basic categories of elision: losses, transformations, and pseudo-elisions. These can additionally be distinguished according to their position: within words (syncope) or between words (apocope).

Either consonants or vowels may be elided. 1) In *simple consonant loss,* consonants may be elided such that the syllables on either side are fused, often by the loss or change to a glide of the second vowel (for example, "by his /baɨ+hɨz/ becomes "by's" /baɪz/, "power" /pauɨr/ becomes "pow'r" /paːr/, "being" /biːɨŋ/ becomes "be'ng" /biːŋ/). 2) In simple vowel loss, vowels are elided without alteration of contiguous consonants ("medicine" /mɛdɨsɨn/ becomes "med'cine" /mɛdsɨn/). 3) In *complex vowel loss,* vowels are elided in such a way that accompanying consonants are shifted into other syllables; for example, a preceding consonant may become initial in a following syllable ("the army" /ðiː + armiː/ becomes "th'army" /ðarmiː/ and "to write" tɨ + raɪt/ becomes "t'write" /traɪt/), or the shifted consonant may have been originally syllable-final ("it is" /ɪt+ɪz/ becomes " 'tis" /tɪz/). The latter is particularly common in apocope where resonant consonants are involved ("amorous" /æmɨrɨs/ becomes "am'-rous" /æmrɨs/, "groveling" /grəvɨlɨŋ/ becomes "grov'ling" /grəvlɨŋ/, "countenance" /kauntɨnɨns/ becomes "count'nance" /kauntnɨns/).

One of the chief elisional transformations is consonantization: the desyllabization of the /iː/ and /uː/ into /y/ and /w/ respectively (for example, "many a" /mɛniːɨ/ becomes "many'a" /mɛnyɨ/ and "shadowy" /šæduːiː/ becomes "shad'wy" /šædwiː/).

Finally, the term "pseudo-elision" may be used to refer to the assumption of elision between two consonants that cannot be clustered, i.e., that cannot really occur in English without an intervening syllabic (for example, the scansion of words like "prism" /prɪzɨm/ or "heaven" /hɛvɨn/ as if they could actually be pronounced as monosyllables –*/prɪzm/ and */hɛvn/); or the postulation of consonant clusters that go against native clustering habits (for example, writing "th'sea" or "th'loss" or "th'grave" even though /ðs-/, /ðl-/, and /ðg-/ are not possible initial clusters in English).

The opposite of elision is insertion; for example, giving full syllabic value to a vowel-letter not currently pronounced; thus "marked" /markt/ becomes "markèd" /markɨd/, etc. Another common sort of insertion is the syllabification of resonant consonants. For example, "evenings" /iːvnɪŋz/ becomes /iːvɨnɪŋz/, "assembly" /ɨsɛmbliː/ becomes /ɨsɛmbɨliː/, and "entrance" /ɛntrɨns/ becomes /ɛntɨrɨns/.[13]

The logical status of elisions and insertions depends upon the extent to which the syllable adjustment has become a part of the language.[14] If the adjusted word has become totally accepted in the language *as* a word, then its occurrence is metrically irrelevant. An example is *'tis;* presumably no one, even in our metrically naturalistic age, would read

> Where ignorance is bliss
> It is folly to be wise.

On the other hand, if the syllable adjustment is not totally incorporated into ordinary usage, its actualization will vary with prevailing recitational habit. In the eighteenth century, indications for syllable adjustments were apparently rigidly adhered to in performance;[15] in later times, the common view was that the sounds are not really lost but "heard in the glide, though prosodically asyllabic." Furthermore, the degree of acceptability of an elision has varied from word to word and from sound to sound. Many elisions occur as variants in everyday speech, and presumably these would be acceptable even to naturalistic reciters. For example, few modern readers would question the propriety of either the bisyllabic or trisyllabic pronunciations of *champion.*

On the other hand, most of us would object to the monosyllabic pronunciation /daɪt/ for *diet*. In the line

> And rapture so oft beheld? those heav'nly shapes

Milton

PARADISE LOST

we might not like a vowel elision like "rapture s'oft," because it is too easily confused with "rapture soft." Even where lexical confusion is not at issue, many indicated elisions seem too extreme for modern taste, for example, where punctuation intervenes or an initial /h/ must be dropped:

> To a fell Adversary, *h*is hate or shame

Milton

PARADISE LOST

Or where a whole syllable is deleted: /yu:/ from the contracted form "pop'lar" for "popular," or from "artic'late," "cred'lous," etc.

Thus, whether a syllable is elided or preserved in pronunciation is a matter of the reciter's taste and the taste of his age, and all arguments pro or con are essentially scansional, not metrical.[16] Elisional marks like the apostrophe resemble musical ornaments in a score—grace notes, turns, and mordents—which may or may not be performed, depending upon our feeling of their appropriateness.

Most decisions about elision are up to the performer, but a few elisions may not be possible to articulate at all, existing merely as orthographic conventions, concessions to metrical norms with no relation to the linguistic facts. This is the category of "pseudo-elision." We cannot admit the recitational reality of forms which are not in fact pronounceable within normal definitions of the English phonological syllable; so that apostrophes appearing in expressions like "th'loss" and "th'sea" must be considered purely conventional, artificial (i.e., nonphonemic) metrical ligatures introduced to maintain numerical decorum. Here we may speak genuinely of "metrical fictions."

Thus, syllable-count qualifies as a genuine metrical abstraction. The poet may select his words in part by considering the numbers of syllables they contain, and ordinarily he can be sure that this feature will be conveyed to his reader. The selective feature of number becomes a part of the poem's mode of existence and is not ordinarily subject to interpretational variation. The feature "decasyllabicity" can be said to exist in a poem and can be abstracted from it by the metrist, since it is not merely a property of the printed line, nor of any single reading, but of all conceivable readings.

Syllable-count or metrical numeration has meaning only by reference to constancies of line-length. Lines are metrically formal units (that is, in the central isosyllabic verse tradition) printed separately to help us understand that they contain standard numbers of syllables; and where exceptions occur, these are of a predictable sort, usually one syllable more or less, although occasionally there are greater deviations. In this respect, syllable-count adds a third dimension to metrical structure. In addition to the components of event (syllable) and prominence (yet to be discussed) by which foot-grouping exists, meter includes the factor of numerical regularity. Syllable-count as a structural feature is a form of "secondary grouping" (to distinguish it from the primary grouping of the foot itself). Meter, then, is an instance of complex secondary rhythm, since it contains not only grouped events, but also groups of grouped events (lines) and even groups of groups of grouped events (stanzas). And it is in metrical numbers that poets can count on the least discrepancy between the meter of the poem and any reader's scansion of it.

The theory presently offered describes the meters of poems in the "isosyllabic" or syllable-counting tradition of English verse— the tradition of Chaucer, Spenser, Shakespeare, Milton, Pope, Wordsworth, Keats, and Tennyson. There exists another tradition —the "isoaccentual" or "isochronic" tradition of Old English poetry, some Middle English poetry, and a variety of modern revivals. In the isochronic tradition, the number of syllables in the line is irrelevant; all that counts is the number of ictuses, their relative distribution, and possibly other unifying features, like alliteration. Some special problems occur in describing isochronic meter, but it is the simpler and less important metrical type in later English poetry, and discussion may be saved for another occasion.

Since syllable-count is the most relatively constant feature of meter, on the principle of simplicity we may give it priority of application in the analysis of isosyllabic verse. That is, the computation of line length should be the first step in scansion and metrical analysis. After counting, the metrist can decide on the basis of simplicity of patterning which sum constitutes the normal line (or lines). Then, having determined the normal line, he may proceed to determine foot divisions.

THE FOOT

. . . Temporal equalities among feet were characterized [earlier] as putative and conventional. These adjectives need elaboration. For generations metrists saw no reason to doubt that the assumption of equality of measure in verse corresponded to reality, that periods that seemed equal were literally and exactly equal. Coventry Patmore, for example, wrote:

> These are two indispensable conditions of metre,—first, that the sequence of vocal utterance, represented by written verse, shall be divided into equal or proportionate spaces; secondly, *that the fact of that division* shall be made *manifest* by an "ictus" or "beat," actual or mental, which, like a post in a chain railing, shall mark the end of one space, and the commencement of another.[17]

For Patmore, temporal equality was an accepted fact, "recognized with more or less distinctness by all critics who have written on the subject to any purpose." [18]

But the evidence from machines has long since demonstrated clearly that feet are not physically equal or even mathematically proportionate. Later metrists like Sonnenschein grasped this fact and explained the foot as a purely psychological concept:

> . . . the durations found in these [kymograph] records do not stand to one another in exact ratios. This, however, can only be understood when the phenomena of verse are regarded from a *psychological* or *æsthetic,* as distinct from a purely physical, point of view. What we are concerned with in all manifestations of rhythm is not so much a physical fact as a psychological fact—i.e., the impression made by the physical fact upon the mind of man through the organs of sense. And here two important points have to be considered, which may

be briefly summed up as follows: (1) The mind of man acting through the organs of sense is not an exact chronometer, and therefore fails to distinguish ratios which differ from one another in only a relatively small degree; (2) ratios which are recognized by the mind as distinctly different may, nevertheless, be unified or identified as representative of or intended for one and the same ratio. . . . Just as the eye may accept a line that is actually far from straight as representing a straight line, or a figure that is far from circular as standing for a circle, so the ear may accept as equal two ratios which actually differ perceptibly from one another. This "acceptance" involves a certain *rapport* between the mind of the observer and the mind of the creator of the rhythm. The observer, knowing the intention of the poet to produce a rhythmical scheme of verse, recognizes that certain syllables or groups of syllables are meant to stand in a certain ratio to other syllables or groups of syllables, and accepts their actual durations as representing these intended durations.[19]

In short, we conceptualize metrical time in terms of rough equalities; we treat syllables of varying durations *as if* they were identical in duration. That we should do so is not remarkable from the psychological point of view; it is simply one more instance of our propensity to categorize experience, to consider things in terms of structural groups rather than fragmentarily, as legions of disparates. The motive is a simple principle of human economy:

Were we to utilize fully our capacity for registering the differences in things and to respond to each event encountered as unique, we would soon be overwhelmed by the complexity of our environment.[20]

Psychologists have a nice distinction between *equivalence* categorization and *identity* categorization:

We speak of an equivalence class when an individual responds to a set of discriminably different things as the *same kind of thing* or as *amounting to the same thing.*[21]

The perception of metrical equality is clearly an equivalence rather than an identity categorization.

Scanning is learned behavior, and precisely what is learned is how to take complexly different entities—syllables of varying phonetic shapes and weights—as instances of the same thing. The scanner who feels that he controls the process in a completely intuitive manner is simply unconscious of how he really learned it. The difficulty in metrics is not a deficiency of scanning ability among modern readers but rather an inability to come to agreement about which metrical categorizations make most sense; behind that lies the question of how one decides such things. It has been tacitly assumed [throughout] that scansion and metrical analysis may be reduced to something like a scientific method. If this is presumptuous, at least unsuccessful attempts may suggest some external criteria by which success may be measured. Let us assume that scansion and that metrical analysis to be best which most simply, economically, and consistently account for all the facts, that describe with least complexity a mechanism by which language may create secondary rhythms. Let us start by considering the metrical foot.

Not the least important justification for metrical feet is that they permit a simpler and more elegant descriptive statement of metrical and scansional facts. It is simpler to assume that the series $\cup - \cup - \cup - \cup - \cup -$ consists of five recurrences of one event, $\cup -$, than that it constitutes some single homogeneous event. For then we would have to concede that the patterns

$$\cup - \cup - - \cup \cup - \cup -,$$
$$\cup - - \cup \cup - \cup - \cup -,$$

and $\qquad - \cup \cup - \cup - \cup - \cup -$

also constitute separate single events. It is simpler and more elegant to interpret the above three sets of events as variations of the first set with the substitution of $- \cup$ for $\cup -$ a different position in each case.

Another reason for recognizing the metrical foot is psychological. From the outset, the present theory has sought its foundation in the general human perception of rhythm. It is an established psychological fact that people tend to "group" rhythmic phenomena, even where there is little or no justification in the actual temporal reality. Since these groups are so clearly a part of general rhythmic activity, they must also exist in each species of rhythmic activity, for example, meter.

Metrical feet are conventions for analyzing the grouping behavior of syllables which in their metrical aspect are not treated as sound complexes but as mere rhythmic counters of one of two values. Feet have nothing else to do with language: they are non-grammatical and non-lexical, and so do not bear any relation to word-integrity, phonological juncture, or any other real linguistic feature. Foot boundaries may split words, and two words separated by even the strongest juncture (say the one represented by a period) may occur within the same foot. Feet, in short, are purely "notional." [22]

Determining the composition of the normal foot logically comes after counting the syllables of the normal line. Its composition is assumed to be the smallest *submultiple* of the normal line. For example, in most sonnets, the normal line, by inspection, has ten syllables. The submultiples of ten are five and two. But a two-syllabled foot is intrinsically simpler to assume than a five-syllabled foot. It allows only four possibilities, namely $|\cup -|$, $|-\cup|$, $|--|$, or $|\cup \cup|$, whereas the five-syllabled foot allows many more possibilities, thirty-two to be exact:

$$|\cup \cup \cup \cup \cup|\ |-\cup \cup \cup \cup|\ |--\cup \cup \cup|\ |---\cup \cup|\ |----\cup|$$

$$|-----|\ |\cup -\cup \cup \cup|\ |\cup --\cup \cup|\ |\cup ---\cup|\ |\cup ----|$$

$$|\cup \cup -\cup \cup|\ |\cup \cup --\cup|\ |\cup \cup ---|\ |\cup \cup \cup -\cup|\ |\cup \cup \cup --|$$

$$|\cup \cup \cup \cup -|\ |-\cup -\cup \cup|\ |-\cup \cup -\cup|\ |-\cup ---\cup|\ |-\cup ---|$$

$$|-\cup \cup \cup -|\ |-\cup -\cup -|\ |\cup \cup -\cup -|\ |---\cup -|\ |--\cup -\cup|$$

$$|--\cup --|\ |--\cup \cup -|\ |-\cup \cup --|\ |\cup --\cup -|\ |\cup -\cup -\cup|$$

$$|\cup -\cup --|\ |\cup -\cup \cup -|$$

Obviously such a formulation is too complex to be acceptable. Most metrists have found it possible to restrict the constituency of the metrical foot in English to two and three syllables. If we allow residues, all lines can be rather simply explained in terms of feet of one of these two lengths.

Consider as a concrete example of the problem of determining foot-composition the relative merits of these analyses:

$$-\cup|\cup -|\cup -|\cup \cup|--$$

vs.

$$\wedge -|\cup \cup -|\cup -|\cup \cup -|\wedge -$$

(or)

$$-\cup \cup|-\cup|-\cup \cup|-\wedge|-\wedge$$

(where $\wedge$ = "metrical pause" equivalent to a syllable). One metrist[23] has written that the first division is "meaningless for met-

rical analysis," that there can be only one kind of metrical variation, namely variation in the *number* of syllables, and that the
metrical inversion (foot-reversal) does not exist. But this denial
entails a sacrifice in economy, for by abandoning inversion the
number of exceptional feet is increased from three to four: the
perfectly normal second foot ∪ — must be re-interpreted as trisyllabic.

To wield Occam's razor metrically is to assume that the best
analysis is the one which most effectively, efficiently, and reasonably accounts for the largest variety of verses with the fewest
units, rules, and exceptions.

Usually what happens in a poem is that one foot-type comes to
dominate over the others because of its recurrence in linguistically
unequivocal settings. Lanier described the process clearly:

> When a poet puts forth his verse in print, he indicates the
> manner of grouping the verse-sounds for secondary rhythm by
> arranging words whose accent is known in such a manner that
> the ordinary pronunciation-accent [i.e., lexical stress] falls
> where the rhythmic accent [ictus] is intended to fall. For
> example if the poet wishes the rhythmic accent to fall upon
> the first sound, and upon every third sound after, so as to
> group the whole series into threes . . . he may indicate such
> a grouping by beginning with a couple of three-syllabled words
> whose pronunciation-accent falls on the first syllable, thus
> initiating the type of the rhythm which the reader is intended
> to carry on through the poem; as, for example
>
> Wístfully | wándering | óver the | wáters, she
> 1   2 3   1   2 3   1 2   3   1 2   3
> Sought for the | land of the | blessed.[24]
> 1   2   3

Of course, the syllable *-ing* in *wandering* may just as easily bear
ictus, if it occurs in a line whose contraint is duple:

> Art thou pale for weariness
> Of climbing heaven, and gazing on the earth,
> Wandĕrīng companionless
> Among the stars that have a different birth

Shelley
"TO THE MOON"

ICTUS

Analyzing ictus[25] is perhaps the most critical problem in English metrical theory. . . . There is no simple linguistic entity—say "stress"—which can be equated with it. The act of assigning ictus actually involves a number of variables which tradition has not always been able to keep clearly apart. Even the best metrists have often been too simplistic:

> . . . it is evident that any notation which professes to give the complete range of accentuation or anything near it will be not only unnecessary but misleading. Unnecessary, because the nature of metre requires no such thing as the reproduction in speech-rhythm of the uniform accentuation supposed in the base; misleading, because it would tend to make the nature of metre rest in speech-sound as actually heard, instead of in speech-sound heard with reference to an ideal constancy; and for the purpose of that reference the mere fact of accent being perceptible is sufficient, without regard to the strength of the accent.[26]

And more recently, as a reaction to linguistic metrics:

> We wish in the main to avoid the cumbersome grammar of the new linguists. For all we know there may be, not four, but five degrees of English stress, or eight. How can one be sure? What one can nearly always be sure of is that a given syllable in a sequence is more or less stressed than the preceding or the following.[27]

Asserting that a notational system should be simple and binary[28] to reflect the simple binary dimensions of rhythm, however correct from the metrical point of view, does not disprove the usefulness of considering the means by which the language fleshes the rhythmical base out. At issue is the difference between applied and theoretical metrics. Applied metrics is content to scan; it does not trouble itself with the nature of the phonetic perceptions underlying its judgments. Theoretical metrics wants to know what it is to scan, that is, how and which elements in and out of the language are interpretable as metrical features.

The expression "in and out of the language" needs some explanation. Let us recall the distinction . . . between stress and accent: stress is a phonemic constituent of full-vowelled monosyllabic words, and of one syllable in each polysyllabic word, which enables us to distinguish the word from other words. It is learned as part of the word, is marked in dictionaries, and specifies the syllable which may be accented in actual utterance. Accent, on the other hand, is not a part of words as words but rather a function of their occurrence in phrases, marking the point of emphasis or attention. The actual sound components of stresses and accents are the same, although their degree varies, accented syllables by definition being more prominent than unaccented.[29]

In metrics proper, we have distinguished two realms: scansion—the reduction of a given recitation to two variables, ictus and syllable count—and metrical analysis in the broader sense—the determination of the consensus or common denominator of all intelligible scansions. Another way of putting it is that meter is an abstract system, each of whose concretions is a scansion, the scansion in turn being an abstraction of two basic elements from the complex phonetic reality of the recitation: the number of syllables and whatever it is that the scanner responds to as ictus. Since some syllables are perceived as ictic which possess neither stress nor accent, we must conclude that extraphonemic features may be used to mark ictus. Consider the famous line:

The mūl | titū | dinous sēas | incār | nadīne

Only three syllables bear ictus by virtue of being lexically stressed: *-tud-, seas,* and *-car-*. How then do we know that *mult-* and *-dine* are also ictic?

If ictus is not totally discoverable in the linguisture structure itself it must partly be the product of some extralinguistic phenomenon, like the metrical "set" (in the psychological sense), the running disposition of ictus and non-ictus established by preceding sequences, particularly where these were linguistically unequivocal. This is not an untraditional view, although it may seem to be expressed in an unfamiliar way.[30]

Insofar as the language does provide the cue to ictus, it is stress which is the most unequivocal indication at the poet's command. Since stress is most clearly highlighted in polysyllabic words, these are particularly useful in establishing the meter. Thus, *beyond* must carry ictus on the second syllable and *fitting* on the first; and this statement is true without any reference to the variety of ways in which stress can be vocally indicated. Even if *be-* or *-ing* happen, by a quirk of recitation to be "actually" more prominent than *-yond* or *fit-* (show pitch-obtrusion, or longer or louder traces on instruments), speakers of the language will not notice it and will continue to assume the normal stress relationship. . . . The lexical stress patterns of polysyllabic words are fixed parts of their phonemic structure and normally cannot be changed by intonational and accentual contingencies.[31] Despite variations in recitational style, the position of stress in these words cannot ordinarily vary from scansion to scansion unless the word itself has alternative pronunciations. Lines composed of bisyllabic words present theoretically the clearest meter; they are totally unequivocal since the fixed positions of stress cannot reasonably be altered in recitation:

Beyond | the fit | ting me | dium of | desire

Byron
CHILDE HAROLD'S PILGRIMAGE

Define | their pet | tish lim | its, and | estrange

Keats
"LAMIA"

Under | yonder | beech-tree | single | on the |
green-sward

Meredith
"LOVE IN THE VALLEY"

The scansion is extremely clear where a single bisyllabic word comprises a foot (*Běyōnd, děsīre, děfīne*) and where the unstressed and stressed syllables occur in different contiguous words (*-tǐng mēd-, -tǐsh līm-*). The unstressed syllable, of course, may itself be full-vowelled: *bēech-trěe, grēen-swǎrd*, etc.

But there are many other possible foot combinations, and it is best to proceed in a systematic manner. Our classificatory purposes are well served by distinguishing between four different sorts of syllables, or more accurately, syllabic *weights:*

  a. full-vowel monosyllabic words
  b. stressed syllables of polysyllabic words
  c. unstressed full-vowel syllables of polysyllabic words
  d. unstressed reduced (degraded) syllables of polysyllabic words

Category *a* consists of monosyllabic words with full stressed vowels. We may distinguish two subclasses of such words: re-ducible and non-reducible. The reducible subclass contains words whose vowels can be degraded so powerfully as actually to lose their distinctive vocalic color, approaching the position of /ɨ/, the unstressed vowel. Examples are *a* /e:/ → /ɨ/, *to* /tu:/ → /tɨ/, *shall* /šæl/ → /šɨl/, *you* /yu:/ → /yɨ/, *it* /it/ → /ɨt/, *can* /kæn/ → /kɨn/, *them* /ðɛm/ → /ðɨm/, etc. This subclass is smaller than the non-reducible subclass which contains the bulk of Eng-lish monosyllabic words—*tea, lit, sped, crash, rock, law, vogue, stool, budge,* etc. Words in the reducible subclass are likely to appear in reduced form when they occupy non-ictic positions and in full form when they serve to show ictus. For example . . . *shall,* the first word of Shakespeare's 18th sonnet, is usually pro-nounced /šɨl/ by those who prefer the scansion

> Shăll Ī compare thee to a summer's day?

and /šæl/ by those who prefer

> Shāll Ĭ compare thee to a summer's day?

The reducible subclass will be referred to as class a^1.

It is usually the consideration of the larger metrical context or set which prompts one to assume ictus upon such words, even though he may not wish to give it full-blown accent in recitation. A good example occurs in the seventeenth stanza of Tennyson's "Maud":

> Go not, happy day
> From the shining fields,
> Go not, happy day,
> Till the maiden yields.
> Rosy is the West,
> Rosy is the South,

> Roses are her cheeks,
> And a rose her mouth.

Lexical stresses on *Rosy* and *Roses* signal ictus on the first syllable of the first foot so unequivocally that the reader finds himself promoting to ictus the metrical values of ordinarily humble monosyllabic words like *from, till,* and *and.* This promotion will probably not amount to more than a slightly clearer and steadier pronunciation of the syllable, although some readers may wish to introduce actual accentual prominences:

$$\text{Till }_{\text{the}}{}^{\text{maid}}{}_{\text{en}}{}^{\text{yi}}\text{el}_{\text{d}_\text{s}}$$

$$\text{And }_{\text{a}}{}^{\text{ro}}\text{se her }{}^{\text{mo}}\text{u}_{\text{th}}$$

Category *b* is the stressed syllable of polysyllabic words. Categories *c* and *d* refer to unstressed syllables in polysyllabic words, *c* being the class of full vowels and *d* the class of reduced vowels. Reduced syllables contain the reduced vowel /ɨ/, either simply or in the diphthongal combinations /ɨɪ/ and /ɨʊ/. For example, the first "i" in *inspiration* is a full vowel /ɪ/ and the second is the reduced vowel /ɨ/. Similarly, /ɨ/ occurs in the last syllables of

crescent
passionate
savage

The italicized vowels in the following are full but unstressed:

constellation /a/ or /ɑ/
cataracts   /æ/
neighborhood /ʊ/
stowaway   /e:/
acme   /i:/
playwright   /aɪ/

Some syllables vary between full and reduced articulations:

digestion   /aɪ/ or /ɨ/
reserved   /i:/ or /ɨ/
microscopic   /o:/ or /ɨ/
visionary   /æ/ or /ɨ/

Syllables with full vowels are likely to be more prominent than those with reduced vowels in length, loudness, and pitch-obtrusion, but the prominence is not significant.

Nonphonemic prominences are available for metrical use, and the tradition shows that ictus is quite commonly signalled by such prominences. This is particularly clear in lines made up of a few long words:

With *in*terchangeable suprema*cy*

Wordsworth
PRELUDE

The *mul*titudinous seas incarna*dine*

Shakespeare
MACBETH

But ictus can only be registered on unstressed syllables when they occur in metrically set positions. For example, it does not appear on syllables adjacent to phonemically stressed syllables in the same foot:

Mǎgnī̄ | ficent, his six days' work, a world

Milton
PARADISE LOST

And prophesying with ac | *cěnts* tēr̄r | ible

Shakespeare
MACBETH

O Ro | *meō,* Rō | meo! Wherefore art thou Romeo?

Shakespeare
ROMEO AND JULIET

Unstressed reduced-vowel syllables may also function ictically. For example, the final syllables in *bottomless, beautiful,* and *difference,* all containing the reduced vowel /ɨ/, carry ictus in the following lines:

To bottomlḗss perdition, there to dwell

> Milton
> PARADISE LOST

I see, not feel, how beautifūl they are!

> Coleridge
> "DEJECTION: AN ODE"

Doubts 'mongst Divines, and diffḗrence of texts

> Spenser
> "MOTHER HUBBARD'S TALE"

It is obvious that these syllables will not carry ictus in most other metrical contexts:

Burnt after them to the bottomlĕss pit

> Milton
> PARADISE LOST

The beautifŭl Annabel Lee

> Poe
> "ANNABEL LEE"

And each the other's diff'rĕnce bears

> Marvell
> "EYES AND TEARS"

We recognize ictus on reduced-vowel syllables under the alternativity principle: three syllables occur between the unequivocal ictuses *bot-* and *-di-*, namely *-om, -less,* and *per-*. None of these three syllables is stressed, nor is there any semantic reason for giving any accentual prominence. But the metrical set, the established pattern of alternativity, endows *-less* with ictus. Position is all. Our instinct to "understand" a beat where one does not literally occur was clearly demonstrated in the experiments referred to [earlier]. This kind of imaginative projection is a sort of metrical "promotion." Heeding the pressure of metrical set, we mentally increase the value of a linguistically unprominent syllable. In recitation, the ictus may be completely covert, or only the slightest increase in actual voice prominence (pitch obtrusion, length, loudness, clarity) may be allowed to seep through.

It is a metrical advantage of the English vocabulary that it possesses many polysyllabic words with full vowels disposed in alternate syllables. Most five-syllabled words, for example, follow a pattern in which full vowels are separated by a single reduced vowel:

> mathematical   zoological   eradication   contiguity
> communication nationality propositional   proliferation

Hence the metrical smoothness of many polysyllabic words:

'twere well

It were done quickly: if the *assassination*

Shakespeare
MACBETH

One cordial in this *melancholy* vale

Burns
"COTTER'S SATURDAY NIGHT"

Where the *nightingale* doth sing

Keats
"BARDS OF PASSION AND OF MIRTH"

A few polysyllabic words have full-vowelled syllables contiguous to the stressed syllable, but since ictus is a matter of relative prominence, these function easily as non-ictus:

> monstrosity backbiters insecticide day-workers

A few English words have full vowels separated by two syllables:

> contradistinction antediluvian multiplication
> extracurricular   peripatetic   supercolossal

These are not very useful for establishing bisyllabic meter but are excellent for the purposes of triple meter.

NOTES

1. "Why do we want to measure verse? For the same reason that we study laws of colour, or laws of musical harmony. In each case we seek to analyze results which have pleased us in the work of poet, painter, or musician. By measuring, by dividing this into its units, we hope to throw light on its architecture. Such knowledge is not necessary to the artist, nor even to his intelligent admirer. It will not make a genius, nor teach us infallibly to detect one; we can but judge of results, not lay down laws for the future." T. S. Omond, *A Study of Metre* (London, 1903), p. 1.

2. J. Bruner, J. Goodnow, and G. Austin, *A Study of Thinking* (New York, 1956), pp. 12–13.

3. The need for inductive, empirical metrics was clearly asserted by Elder Olson, *General Prosody* (Chicago, 1938), p. 98: ". . . prosody is inductive; the prosodic hypothesis is established by particulars, and is finally discarded, if it ever is discarded, because of its inability to analyze particulars. The theorist who cannot or will not illustrate his hypotheses with examples showing that what he asserts as actual or as possible does indeed exist, as possibility or fact, does not deserve serious hearing. The fabrication of a theory which has only logical excellences can be admired by logicians alone."

4. This distinction is implied in L. Abercrombie, *Principles of English Prosody* (London, 1923), p. 79: scansion is "the exhibition of the natural speech-rhythm of verse in its metrical form. Scansion does not establish the verse-rhythm as metre; that is done, if at all, in the hearing of the verse; and scansion has to show *how* it is done. Since what is actually heard in verse is the natural sound of the words, but, since, if there is metre, this is heard with reference to a constant schematic pattern of rhythm, the problem of scansion is to show, precisely and unmistakably, the manner of the reference." ("The constant schematic pattern of rhythm"—what Abercrombie elsewhere calls "the rhythm of the Base"—is defined in this book as the meter itself, as a structure of possibilities.) The point was repeated by Abercrombie on page 116: ". . . the fact that very many lines may be metrically spoken in several ways does not belong to scansion; scansion merely has to exhibit the speech-rhythm natural to the speaker."

5. Abercrombie, pp. 77–78. Cf. John Lotz, "Notes on Structural Analysis in Metrics," *Helicon*, IV (1942), 125–126: "Verse, in contrast with prose, might be described as bound by some restrictions aiming at a greater regularity of construction, and a repetition of some of its parts (rhythm). These restrictions may be formulated in rules. These rules will have the nature of norms, as in all branches of normative social science like linguistics, law, ethics, etc. Of course the validity of norms cannot be compared with that of a natural law; norms describe a given (eventually individual) phenomenon and have only the validity of description, not of control. Thus, on a metrical basis, it can never be decided whether a verse be objectively good or bad in a metric sense, only, how far it conforms to a given norm accepted by the community. These norms need not at all be conscious, the knowledge consciously formulated of them may even be erroneous (as in the case of popular etymology, or, the naive attitude some poets assume towards verse)."

6.   The schoolboy's accentual distortion

The ^{boy} stood ^{on} the ^{burning} deck

Whence ^{all} but ^{he} had $^{fl}e_d$

is a reduction in *recitation* to conform to scansion—accommodating the voice in an elemental fashion to the rhythmic simplicities of finger-tapping. A description of this sort of scansional parsing appeared as early as 1775 in an anonymous elocutionary treatise called *The Art of Delivering Written Language* (see T. S. Omond, *English Metrists* . . . [London, 1907], p. 65).

7.   The problem of what constitutes the meter—whether there is one meter necessarily common to all acceptable performances of a poem—was discussed by W. K. Wimsatt and M. Beardsley in "The Concept of Meter: An Exercise in Abstraction," *PMLA*, LXXIV (1959), 590–591, and by Rulon Wells, *Style in Language*, p. 198. Wells seems to agree that all the different possible interpretations of a line need not have the same meter although they may.

8.   For a discussion of the propriety of the term to cover all cases of omission, see Robert Bridges, *Milton's Prosody* (Oxford, 1921), pp. 9–18.

9.   Bridges, p. 9.

10.   In two sample pronunciations which I measured spectrographically, /ðe:onyɨn/ was 18 centiseconds long and /ði:+e:onyɨn/ was 27 cs. The latter had a double vowel movement in the second and third formant, corresponding to /ði:+e:-/.

11.   Leonard Bloomfield, *Language* (New York, 1933), p. 121. For a discussion of these phones, see James W. Abel, "Syllabic /n, 1/," *Quarterly Journal of Speech*, XLVIII (1962), 151–156.

12.   See W. Nelson Francis, *The Structure of American English* (New York, 1958), pp. 149–150.

13.   See Bridges, p. 28.

14.   I am grateful to Professor Monroe Beardsley for his views on this matter.

15.   See Paul Fussell, *Theory of Prosody in 18th Century England* (Connecticut College Monographs no. 5, 1955), p. 71: "Unpleasant as it may be to recognize the fact, contemporary evidence leads to the conclusion that almost all readers in the early 18th century *both* scanned and pronounced 'am'rous,' 'om'nous,' etc." And George R. Stewart, Jr., *Modern Metrical Technique as Illustrated by Ballad Meter* (1700–1920) (New Yor:, 1922), p. 30, after reading 18th century elocutionists like Mason, Rice, Sheridan, and Beattie, concluded: "There can be little doubt, however, that general practice in the eighteenth century read such lines as commonly printed. One of the best proofs of this is the fact that about the middle of the century a series of rhetoricians began to protest against such a conventionalized reading of verse. If the practice had not been general, such a protest would not have been necessary."

16.   See, for example, arguments discussed by Egerton Smith, *The Principles of English Metre* (London, 1923), pp. 37–38.

17.   Coventry Patmore, "English Metrical Criticism," *North British Review*, XXVII (1857), 136.

18.   Patmore, p. 134.

19.   E. A. Sonnenschein, *What Is Rhythm?* (Oxford, 1925), pp. 35–36.

20.   Bruner et al., *Study of Thinking*, p. 1.

21.   Bruner et al., p. 4.

22. Abercrombie, pp. 103–104: ". . . the foot-division of words, of actual sound, is notional. The boundaries of the feet may fall in the middle of words, where not even the most infinitesimal pause can be supposed; and, on the contrary, strong sense-pauses may occur in the middle of feet, so that the syllables composing the feet, so far from attracting, repel one another. The foot-division of speech-rhythm takes no notice of these things. It conveys no suggestion that the syllables within a foot necessarily cohere more than they adhere to syllables outside of it; it conveys no suggestion that poetry is heard, spoken, or composed in feet." ". . . Feet, that is to say, belong wholly to scansion; they are a formality used in the investigation of metre, and have nothing to do with its composition or with its real nature."

23. Egerton Smith, p. 13, and see pp. 56f., where the concept of reversal is rejected.

24. Sidney Lanier, *The Science of English Verse* (New York, 1880), p. 110.

25. The old-fashioned word "ictus" seems best for the purely metrical phenomenon and avoids confusion with linguistic terms like "stress" and "accent." Martin Halpern, "On the Two Chief Metrical Modes in English," *PMLA*, LXXVII (1962), 180, has coined the terms "major" for ictus and "minor" for non-ictus.

26. Abercrombie, p. 91.

27. Wimsatt and Beardsley, p. 593.

28. The term "binary" is an oversimplification, since there exists a kind of verse with two degrees of ictus, often called "dipodic." See George Stewart, pp. 95–113. An example is:

The winter it is past, and the summer comes at last
And the small birds sing on every tree;
Now everything is glad, while I am very sad,
Since my true love has parted from me.

29. Some metrists, for example Schramm, have concerned themselves with the problem of determining precisely where *within* the syllable ictus falls. This seems a largely fruitless kind of inquiry for two reasons: 1) Two of the most important parameters of stress and accent—length and pitch obtrusion —do not by definition entail any sort of maxima, and 2) the phonemic domain of stress and accent is the entire syllable, not any point in the syllable.

30. But Rulon Wells' germinal remarks in *Style in Language,* pp. 197–200, prepare for a rigorous "logical construction" of meter and offer a set of rules for the conversion of phonemic stresses into ictuses.

31. Except in certain rare "metalinguistic" situations, for example, where someone might repeat a word with an essentially non-English stress pattern to insure clarity of perception in noisy circumstances: "I said fitt*ing* not fitt*ed*." Also excepted, of course, are older stress-patterns: for example, we know that Milton pronounced *exile, product,* and *process* with stress on the second syllable. See Bridges, pp. 81, 117–118, and discussions of "Recession of Accent" in Milton's verse, pp. 67–76, any of the Shakespearean grammars, and Sir George Young's studies of Chaucer's meter in *An English Prosody on Inductive Lines* (London, 1928), chapters 2–6.

19. LINGUISTIC STRUCTURE AND THE POETIC LINE

John Thompson

John Thompson's "Linguistic Structure and the Poetic Line" outlines the theoretical framework of his *The Founding of English Metre,* an essential book for any student of metrics or Elizabethan poetry and poetics. Professor Thompson argues that the essence of English verse consists in the relationships among English phonology, abstract metrical pattern, and the sound pattern of a line of verse. These relationships create a distinctive trait of poetic language: tension between the abstract metrical patterns of a line of poetry and the realization of that line in the sound structure of the English language. John Thompson writes criticism for *The New York Review of Books* and is associate professor of English at the State University of New York at Stony Brook.

This paper presents in summary form a statement of the source, purpose, and function of meter in English verse. The theory developed is applied in an outline of the history of this verse and in an outline of a categorical instrument for the criticism of English verse.

The paper exploits the work of many scholars of prosody from Aristotle to Jakobson, but no specific acknowledgments are made here.

The basis of the skeletal theory here presented is an extensive statistical study of Elizabethan verse, with a less extensive study of earlier and later verse in English. The presentation here,

Reprinted by permission of the author from *Poetics,* ed. Donald Davie (Warsaw: Polish Scientific Publishers, 1961). Also by permission of Routledge & Kegan Paul Ltd.

however, does not include this material and is intended to have only the validity of a model which may be tested by introducing into its machinery any appropriate materials.

The thesis of this study is that the essential element of verse is found in the relations existing between three structures of sound that may be distinguished, for purposes of analysis, in any line of English verse. These three are, first, the structure of sound of the English language, second, the structure of sound of the metrical pattern, and third, the structure of sound of the line of verse. Their relations may be described thus: the metrical pattern imitates the structure of sound of the language; the line of the poem imitates the metrical pattern; and, therefore, the line of the poem imitates the structure of sound of the language. This last statement is a summary presentation of the source, purpose, and function of meter in English poetry.

These three statements and their relations will be considered briefly, and their meaning in the history of English verse and in literary criticism will then be stated.

The metrical pattern imitates the structure of sound of the language.

The common understanding of the various meters of English verse would seem to be quite correct insofar as the metrical patterns themselves are concerned: meter is a pattern of sounds, easily represented in symbolic form, which may be considered quite apart from any particular line of English verse. And in the general understanding, I believe, meter is regarded as the definitive element of verse. We need not be troubled here with definitions of poetry; let the very broadest understanding of that term be assumed. But it might be well at this point to review some of the first, simple, mechanical aspects of verse, a kind of poetry. The word comes to us from the Latin *versus*, a turning round as of the plow at the end of the furrow, and thus it meant also a furrow, a row, a line of writing. In verse the language turns from time to time and forms a new line. It turns at a point determined by the meter; meter is *metrum*, a measure, and in verse it is a measurement of sounds.

The metrical patterns of most English verse are made of the features of sound called stress. The language of this verse is chosen and arranged so that its stronger and weaker stresses fall more or less according to the design of the metrical pattern. Sometimes these stresses occur in exact alternation, as in Milton's line:

> And swims or sinks, or wades, or creeps, or flyes.

Or the stresses may be arranged more freely, as in Coleridge's *Christabel,* where the poet said the pattern consisted only of four strong stresses to each line. There may be as many as eight weakly stressed syllables, or as in the third line below, none at all:

> 'Tis the middle of the night by the castle clock,
> And the owls have awakened the crowing cock;
> Tu—whit!—Tu—whoo!
> And hark, again! the crowing cock,
> How drowsily it crew.

Other features of sound have also been used to form patterns for English verse. In the following lines the metrical pattern is formed only by the number of syllables, without regard for their degree of stress. These two lines have the same metrical pattern, because they both have exactly nine syllables:

> Prince Rupert's drop paper muslin ghost,
> white torch—'with power to say unkind*

> Marianne Moore
> "PEDANTIC LITERALIST"

Subtler features of sound may be abstracted, too, and formed into metrical patterns. In the following line, the pattern is made of "short" and "long" quantities. The poet believed these abstractions corresponded to something he heard in the sounds of vowels; he also believed he was working within a complex set of conventions about "short" and "long" quantities in this meter, a system borrowed from classical verse. The pattern here is that of one of Vergil's hexameters:

---

* Reprinted with the permission of The Macmillan Company from *Collected Poems* by Marianne Moore. Copyright 1935 by Marianne Moore, renewed 1963 by Marianne Moore and T. S. Eliot. Also by permission of Faber and Faber Limited.

Mīdwăy ŏf āll thĭs trăct, wĭth sĕcŭlăr ārms ăn
ĭmmēnse ēlm*

Robert Bridges
IBANT OBSCURI

Thus, even when the features of sound selected for the metrical
pattern may be, as in the last example, little more than misunder-
stood phonetic features of the language, it is obvious that they
are always drawn from the sounds of the language itself. However, the significance of this for the study of prosody in English
has become clear only with the application of structural linguistics to the English language. Only with the recognition that
language is an ordered structure of sound, rather than a system
of logical or "grammatical" categories, could we see that the
features of sound so essential to verse were more than decorative
or aesthetic elements. They are, in fact, the flesh and bones of
the language. The usual metrical pattern in English verse is an
abstraction formed of the phonemic elements of our language,
and its order imitates the order of these elements in our language. The iambic foot consists of the simulacra of two syllables.
The order of the simulacra is fixed; that representing the weaker
stress comes first, with certain exceptions or variations such as the
initial trochee. The stress system of English is represented in
this simplified way. It is a model of the way the words and phrases
of English are made: phonemes into syllables, syllables into words
or word-groups, word-groups into sentences. The primary stress
of a phrase in our language will come as near the end as possible
in speech, with exceptions for special occasions. Every primary
stress is followed by one terminal juncture at some point subsequent to it. Our understanding of the foot as a unit is our understanding of its representation of a phoneme of terminal juncture;
a foot has a beginning and an end. Since terminal juncture is a
function of pitch, the foot has thus provided simulacra of the
four kinds of phonemes essential to English. The line or measure
with its combination of feet and its representation of juncture,
the end of the line, is a model of the larger units of language. The

* From *Ibant Obscuri* by Robert Bridges. Published with permission
of The Clarendon Press, Oxford.

metrical pattern, then, is a structure of sounds that imitates the structure of sounds of the language.

The line of verse imitates the metrical pattern.

A peculiarity of meter, the measurement of verse, is that the units of measure are not discarded and forgotten when the measurement has been made and the line is completed. That is why the measure is more a pattern than a yardstick. As a pattern, as a model or guide to the making of something, the metrical pattern is strange, too. For it is used not only by the poet in making his line, but by the audience in hearing or reading the line. Ordinarily the audience knows the pattern, or the poet makes his pattern known to the audience by repeating it clearly in his language as the poem begins; once the metrical pattern is known, it has in turn some influence on the way the language of the line is heard. For as it is generally recognized today, there is in any line of verse a degree of difference between the pattern of stresses which the words and phrases would have as they might occur in the language of speech, and the pattern of stresses in the meter. The adjustment of these two things to one another in any particular line can never be final; each reader must deal with this tension as best he can, in his own voice; and he will find this strained relation everywhere in verse. It exists in Milton's line:

> And swims or sinks, or wades, or creeps, or flyes.

The iambic metrical pattern of alternating weaker and stronger stresses is plainly the same as that of the speech stresses of the language. But even here there is some degree of difference. We may note (taking the text simply as it exists in the edition of 1667, without necessarily supposing anything about Milton's intention, or the printer's) that there is no comma after *swims;* does this mean that the words *And swims or sinks* form a minimal complete utterance differing from the shorter utterances *or wades, or creeps, or flyes?* Let the commas represent terminal junctures, and there could be only one primary stress for the four syllables *And swims or sinks,* whereas there would be a primary stress for each of the other verbs.

> And swims or sinks, or wades, or creeps, or flyes.

It happens that in Milton's next line the metrical pattern must be satisfied with a tertiary speech stress for a strong metrical stress:

> ˘ ́ ˘ ˎ ˘ ́ ˘
> At length a universal hubbub wilde.

(I have not marked the complete line.) The first syllable of *hubbub* and the word *wilde* have degrees of stress stronger than that of the second syllable of *hubbub,* but now much stronger?

A few lines further on in *Paradise Lost,* it seems that if the requirement of the metrical pattern for five strong metrical stresses is to be met, one of them will have to be satisfied with a weak speech stress, on *of:*

> ˘ ^ˎ ˘ ˘ ^ˎ ˘ ˘ ́
> Or Spirit of the nethermost Abyss.

The metrical pattern may endure even greater divergences:

> With head, hands, wings, or feet pursues his way.

In speech, *head, hands, wings,* and *feet,* each probably requires a primary stress. *Pursues his way* might in the usual matter-of-fact speech be said thus, *pŭrsùes hĭs wáy.* In this line, then, there are six speech stresses of more than weak degree. For most readers it probably seems that it is not the one of these which may be least strong, *pŭrsùes,* that represents the weak degree of metrical stress, but one of the primary speech stresses, *hánds;* and the line would be *scanned* (but surely not read) in this way:

> o s / o s / o s / o s / o s
> With head, hands, wings, or feet pursues his way.

The reading, in whatever voice the reader uses for Milton, would doubtless show some compromise between the metrical pattern and the phrase pattern the ordinary uses of speech would suggest.

The line of the poem imitates the structure of sound of the language.

The line of verse imitates the metrical pattern; the language of verse is ordered in part by patterns which themselves have been made in imitation of the structure of the language.

"Imitation" is here used in the simplest physical sense. The metrical pattern is a copy, a mimicry, a counterfeit without intention to deceive, of the basic elements of our language and of their order. When this metrical pattern and a set of words or phrases are placed in conjunction, a tension exists between them, a strained state of mutual relations; and the language, when we read it as part of a poem, has been strained into something different, into a resemblance to an imitation. It is thus partly imitation itself, and it is this which makes it an art.

Here it is not necessary to pursue "imitation" into metaphysics, nor to try to define or justify art. My assumption, of course, is that Aristotle has made clear the distinction between art and other activities and products of human beings: all art is imitation. Should we seek explanations of that statement, we might find them in Freud. But let us rest with the assumption that there is an art called poetry and that verse is one kind of poetry. We are concerned with the way verse is distinguished from other arts which use the same medium of language; it is distinguished from them by its use of meter, and while meter may incidentally be exploited for some purpose of expression and communication according to the usual intentions of language, it has but one essential and defining purpose: to make the language with which it is joined take on some part of the quality of the metrical pattern, and thus be transformed into the line of verse, an object which is art.

Meter thus does for language what the forms of any art do for their materials. It abstracts certain elements from the experience of the senses and forms them into patterns, as in painting elements are abstracted from what the eye perceives, in dancing from what the body perceives as it moves, in music from what the ear perceives. The elements are ordered in patterns similar to those the senses experience all the time, but art characteristically makes the patterns simpler and clearer, and the artist regards them as having a kind of independent existence they do not have in everyday experience. The forms are used then to order a presentation of the everyday experience of the senses. In the art of verse, meter does these things; if it does other things as well, these are incidental to the function of imitation. Of course in altering the natural speech rhythms of the language in verse, these patterns alter the meaning of the language, and good poets use this fact to the advantage of their meanings; but this use of the metrical pattern does not define all verse. If there is one meaning which the metrical pattern enforces on all language submitted to its influence, it is this: *Whatever else I may be talking about, I am talking also about language itself.*

The history of meter in English verse in the formative years 1557–1580 is largely a matter of the shifting and clarification of the relations between the three structures of sound: metrical pattern, sound-pattern of speech, and the sound-pattern of the line of verse created by the tension between the first two structures. There are three chief possibilities of relation: a loose metrical pattern allows easy accommodation of language and meter; language distorted to minimize the sound-patterns of speech also allows easy accommodation; finally, when the language is colloquial and the metrical pattern strict, the accommodation of the two may be accomplished only with a considerable degree of tension.

The first stage of this history appears in the work of Wyatt and others of his period, for instance in John Dolman's contribution to *The Mirrour for Magistrates.* It seems that the poet had the intention of maintaining in his verse a relation to a metrical pattern that is generally iambic, but his primary interest was in the sound of the spoken language and the values of reality inherent in it; the metrical pattern is often little more than an approximate measure for the line of verse.

> It was no dreme: I lay brode waking.
> It was no dreme; for I lay broade awakyng.

The second stage begins with alterations, such as those above, made in Wyatt's text by the editor of Tottel's *Miscellany.* It culminates in the verse of George Gascoigne and in Gascoigne's exposition of his metrical principles in his *Certayne Notes of Instruction concerning the making of verse or rime in English.* His principle of meter is that the language of the line of verse is absolutely dominated by the metrical pattern.

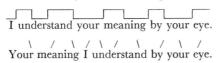

I understand your meaning by your eye.

\ / \ / \ / \ / \ /
Your meaning I understand by your eye.

> In these two verses there seemeth no difference at all, since the one hath the very selfe same woordes that the other hath, and yet the latter verse is neyther true nor pleasant, & the

first verse may passe the musters. The fault of the latter verse
is that this worde *understand* is therein so placed as the grave
accent falleth upon *der,* and thereby maketh *der,* in this word
understand to be elevated: which is contrarie to the naturall or
usuall pronunciation: for we say *ùndèrstánd,* and not *ùndér-
stànd.*

The final phase of the founding of English meter was completed by Philip Sidney. In the *Arcadia* poems, he achieved the
perfection of the system he inherited, a regular correspondence
of metrical pattern and language, in a variety of powerful styles
and with the most exquisite precision.

> Gett hence fowle greeffe, the Cancker of the
>   mynde.

> And thus she did. One day to him she came,
> And (though against his will) on him she leand.

> Shall I that saw Eronaes shining haire
> Torne with her hands, and those same hands of
>   snow.

> His being was in her alone:
> And he not being, she was none.

In *Astrophel and Stella,* Sidney developed fully a new system
of meter, a conventional correspondence of strict metrical pattern
and colloquial language retaining the force of the sounds of
speech.

> Flie, fly, my friends; I have my death wound, fly;
> See there that boy that murthring boy, I say.

> And then would not or could not see my blisse.

This system became the standard for English verse because it
provided a complete set of relations between a meter with precise imitation of the structure of the language and a language
with maximum possibilities of reference to human experience.
Between 1580 and the early years of our own century, meter for
English poets was largely a question of what they could develop
for a personal style out of the possibilities in Sidney and Spenser.

A categorical distinction of the three possibilities of relation between the structures of sound in a line of verse can serve literary
criticism by defining the proper area of concern with metrical

intentions and achievements. This should help avoid confusion between these concerns and other judgments necessary to the interpretation and estimation of verse. The distinctions may be stated in terms of degrees of tension.

This tension, the strained state of mutual relations between metrical pattern and language, can be severe or mild; there are two main ways of reducing it. First, the poet can keep it at a minimum by using a metrical pattern which is loose or free and can easily be accommodated to the pattern of sounds of speech. At an extreme this reduction of tension can cause the metrical pattern to be so closely assimilated to the natural rhythm of the language that the tension is scarcely noticeable. Of course, the language itself may have great virtues of power and reference, and this kind of verse may well be extremely valuable.

> Loaf with me on the grass, loose the stop from
> your throat,
> Not words, not music or rhyme I want, not cus-
> tom or lecture, not even the best,
> Only the lull I like, the hum of your valvèd voice.
>
> Whitman

> It seems, as one becomes older,
> That the past has another pattern, and ceases
> to be a mere sequence—
> Or even development: the latter a partial fallacy,
> Encouraged by superficial notions of evolution,
> Which becomes, in the popular mind, a means of
> disowning the past. *
>
> Eliot

Second, tension may be reduced by using language that does not itself carry any strong suggestion of a pattern of sound from speech. This kind of language can easily be accommodated to an abstract pattern of sound. Perhaps this kind of poetry will be of somewhat less interest than the other kinds, because it must sacrifice so large a part of the resources of speech.

---

* From "The Dry Salvages" in *Collected Poems 1909–1962* by T. S. Eliot. Reprinted by permission of the publishers, Harcourt, Brace & World, Inc. Also by permission of Faber and Faber Limited.

> The woods shall to you answer, and your echo
>   ring.
>
> Spenser

> She only said, "My life is dreary,
>   He cometh not," she said;
> She said, "I am aweary, aweary,
>   I would that I were dead!"
>
> Tennyson

Finally, metrical tension is greatest when the metrical pattern is strict and the language is colloquial, and when the mutual relation is strongly indicated by a readily recognized convention for all the more important individual sound-relations. We must not forget the metrical pattern, and if the poet is successful we cannot forget the sounds demanded by English speech. Here the usual act of piety will be to recall a few lines of John Donne.

> Rebell and Atheist too, why murmure I
>   As though I felt the worst that love could doe?
> Love might make me leave loving, or might trie
>   A deeper plague, to make her love mee too.

It is the third line of these four that is the proper model of English meter.

20. "PROSE RHYTHM" AND METER

Roger Fowler

In " 'Prose Rhythm' and Meter," Roger Fowler investigates the relationship between units of *grammar* (morphemes, words, phrases, clauses, and sentences) and units of *meter* (feet, lines, and stanzas). Comparison of boundaries of larger grammatical units and boundaries of poetic lines leads Mr. Fowler to a discussion of how argument can move against prosody in the poetry of Milton and Shakespeare. When prose rhythm and meter interact at the level of foot, Mr. Fowler argues, syncopation can occur when these units do not cohere. He shows that syncopation is a productive device for stylistic variation in poems, and that it can lead to complication of the linguistically assigned stress pattern of a given line. Roger Fowler is lecturer in English literature at the University of East Anglia, Norwich, England.

1

Wellek and Warren (*Theory of Literature,* 3rd ed., p. 169) distinguish three dimensions of the sound-structure of poetry: performance, metrical pattern, and prose rhythm—a useful scheme as a basis for the study of metrical form as it is perceived, allowing for a statement of the complexity of relationships between levels which critics and readers may feel to exist. *Theory of Literature* hints at the relationship between the levels thus: "The specific performance of a reciter will be irrelevant to an analysis of the prosodic situation, which consists precisely in the

Roger Fowler, " 'Prose Rhythm' and Meter," reprinted from *Essays on Style and Language* (ed. Roger Fowler), pp. 82–99. New York: Humanities Press Inc., 1966; London: Routledge and Kegan Paul, 1966.

tension, the "counterpoint," between the metrical pattern and the prose rhythm." Seymour Chatman, in a discussion of Robert Frost's "Mowing," seems to make a similar point.[1] His analysis assumes "a tension between *two* systems: the abstract metrical pattern as historical product of the English verse tradition, and the ordinary stress-pitch-juncture system of spoken English, determined as it is by requirements of meaning and emphasis." Chatman uses the methods of one form of linguistic description— that championed by Trager and Smith—to analyze the features of stress, intonation, and juncture (transition between juxtaposed linguistic units) found in eight spoken readings of the poem, and diagrammatically compares these features with "the abstract metrical pattern" which the poem is presumed to have because it belongs to one tradition of English verse.[2] The approach of Chatman is open to at least two objections. First, it arrives at the prosody wholly by way of performance: because it does not distinguish performance from prose rhythm, the stresses of the poem are deduced from readers' interpretations, not from the linguistic form of the poem itself. We must, as Wellek and Warren do, discount certain phonological features of an individual recitation: expressive features such as drawling, irrelevant intonation patterns, variations of tempo, dialect pronunciations. This is not an exclusion of everything except the designed metrical scheme. There remains the "prose rhythm": a composite of phonological elements which derive from the grammatical and lexical form of the poem, and which can be readily deduced without having recourse to oral renditions.

The second objection alleges the inadequacy of a purely phonetic approach for making critical statements about poetic form. Because metrical shape is derived from the grammar and diction, as well as from the meter the poet chooses to employ, a critical description of meter should identify it at least partly by reference to the rest of the form of the text. The phonological character of a poem is rarely offered as its main attraction, for we no longer delight in linguistic virtuosity for its own sake. We are disposed to consider how it works with grammar and vocabulary to contribute to "meaning." So metrical patterns (for example, rhymed couplets) are identified by reference to their grammatical and lexical, as well as phonological, exponents, not only because that is the best way of describing them without leaning too heavily on performance—as Chatman does—but because they must be related, in a critical description, to two larger linguistic contexts: the total metrical form (e.g., sonnet form) and the total linguistic form.

What we hear in an iambic pentameter depends on one of the mass of relations within poetic form: that between two competing phonological structures. One is the meter: a skeleton with a few regularly proportioned and articulated parts. It is built up on the basis of one unit, the foot; five feet form a line; lines may be grouped into sets ("couplets," "stanzas," etc.) by rhyme. These three units—foot, line, and stanza—are identified by phonetic characteristics. The foot has a light followed by a heavy stress; within the line, all light and heavy stresses are equated, giving only two grades of stress. The line is marked off, not only by the number of feet, stresses, and syllables it contains, but by certain terminal sound-features: perhaps by a pause, but more probably by a prolongation of its last vowel and/or voiced consonant; often by a change in the pitch of the voice. The stanza is identified by its rhyme-scheme and often by a fall in the pitch of the voice at the end. Some other minor conventions govern the form of the pentameter: for example, the light and heavy stresses of the first foot may be reversed (but not too often); the stresses of the second foot may not.

This metrical skeleton has to be filled out by linguistic elements—grammatical and lexical units—which have their own expectations of phonological form: "prose rhythm," the second of the structures I have referred to. English grammar, like English pentameter meter, has a scale of units of different "sizes": morpheme, word, phrase, clause, sentence, in ascending order of magnitude. These units of grammar have their own stress-patterns which—and this is the whole point of this essay—may or may not correspond with those of the metrical matrix that they are made to occupy. The ends of sentences are inevitably marked by a change in the pitch of the voice; no matter how this is interpreted by different performers, it must occur in some form. Now the sentence is a unit of great variation in length, so the "terminal juncture," as the end-marker is called, may or may not fall in the same places as the natural terminal junctures of the meter: at line- and stanza-ends. The smallest unit in the meter is the metrical point: it is always ' or ×; any two in sequence are likely to be different; the order in which they combine to make up a foot is almost always ×′. The smallest unit in the grammar is the morpheme. It is most often a monosyllable, and may have any one of four stresses: ′, ^, ˋ, or ˘ in descending order of loudness.[3] The selection depends on the adjacent stresses, and these in turn are governed chiefly by the grammatical construction in which the morpheme occurs. *Greenfly* has ˋˋ; *green fly* ^ ′; *apart* ˘′; *-itab-* in *inevitable* ˋ^. So in verse any two consecutive syllables derive their actual stresses from a compromise between two coexistent patterns of prosody: one produced by the meter, one by the requirements of the grammatical construction into which they enter, and the syllable-context in which they occur. Additionally, the boundaries between grammatical units may be adjusted to coincide or not with those between metrical units.

Clearly, we cannot say that there are two coexistent stress-systems: this would be physically impossible. We can, however, talk of two coexistent influences on the stress-pattern of a poem, or of the result on metrical stress of the imposition of the stresses produced by the grammar. How does meter found in convention-determined phonological features work with or against meter inherent in the grammatical and lexical forms chosen to fill metrical positions? I want to sketch out some answers to this question by looking at the metrical-grammatical relationship as it affects units of two sizes: the relation between the line and the larger units of grammar; and between the foot and the smaller grammatical units.

The grammar of a poem may reinforce or subtly resist the division into lines which is implied by other features—number of syllables, end-rhyme, arrangement on the printed page. In the case of reinforcement, the lines do not have to be end-stopped in the sense that they end with the end of a *sentence;* the conditions are that each line in a sequence contains roughly the same grammatical unit and/or ends with a grammatical boundary of about the same weight:

> As, to behold desert a begger born,
> And needy nothing trimmed in jollity,
> And purest faith unhappily forsworn,
> And gilded honour shamefully misplac'd,
> And maiden virtue rudely strumpeted,

And right perfection wrongfully disgrac'd
And strength by limping sway disabled,
And art made tongue-tied by authority,
And folly, doctor-like, attending skill,
And simple truth miscall'd simplicity,
And captive good attending captain ill—

Shakespeare
"SONNET 66," 2–12

Prayer, the Church's banquet, angels' age,
    God's breath in man returning to his birth,
    The soul in paraphrase, heart in pilgrimage,
The Christian plummet, sounding heaven and
        earth;

Engine against the Almighty, sinner's tower,
    Reversèd thunder, Christ-side-piercing spear,
    The six-days'-world transposing in an hour,
A kind of tune, which all things hear and fear;

Herbert
"PRAYER," 1–8

The waker goos; the cukkow ever unkynde;
The popynjay, ful of delicasye;
The drake, stroyere of his owene kynde;
The stork, the wrekere of avouterye;
The hote cormeraunt of glotenye;
The raven wys; the crowe with vois of care;
The throstil old; the frosty feldefare.

Chaucer
"PARLIAMENT OF FOWLS," 358–364

But not:

The sparwe, Venus sone; the nyghtyngale,
That clepeth forth the grene leves newe;
The swalwe, morthere of the foules smale
That maken hony of floures freshe of hewe.

Chaucer
"PARLIAMENT OF FOWLS," 351–354

In each of the first three examples it may be said that the two systems coalesce as far as line-division is concerned: the set of junctures marking the ends of grammatical units cooperates with those produced by the phonological units of line-measurement (stresses, rhymes, and number of syllables) to produce periodicity in the distribution of line-end pauses. Pope makes his couplets self-contained, that is, reinforces them as metrical units by making the strongest grammatical break, that which falls after a sentence, coincide with the strongest metrical break, that which falls after the second word of a rhymed pair. T. S. Eliot, working without rhyme, often has a high degree of correspondence between grammatical units and lines—in fact, the clause or phrase conditions line-length. In "Rhapsody in a Windy Night" we have clause-governed lines:

> The lamp sputtered,
> The lamp muttered in the dark.
> The lamp hummed:
> "Regard the moon,
> La lune ne garde aucune rancune,
> She winks a feeble eye,
> She smiles into corners.
> She smooths the hair of the grass.
> The moon has lost her memory. . . ." *

And phrase-based lines:

> Of sunless dry geraniums
> And dust in crevices,
> Smells of chestnuts in the streets,
> And female smells in shuttered rooms,
> And cigarettes in corridors
> And cocktail smells in bars.*

Wellek and Warren spoke of "counterpoint" as a product of the tension between metrical pattern and prose rhythm. Enjambment, by which a grammatical unit overflows a line-end, produces one sort of counterpoint, although not the sort that Wellek and Warren had in mind. There are degrees of enjambment, degrees

---

* From "Rhapsody in a Windy Night" in *Collected Poems 1909–1962* by T. S. Eliot. Reprinted by permission of the publishers, Harcourt, Brace & World, Inc. Also by permission of Faber and Faber Limited.

of tension between the meter, wanting to make a break, and the grammar, wanting to be continuous. It seems that the smaller the grammatical unit concerned, the greater is its resistance to being stretched over a metrical boundary. Similarly, there are metrical boundaries of different weights, the pause after the second rhyme of a couplet, for example, being more "final" than that after the first line. One might construct a scale for enjambment, ranging from cases where the greatest grammatical break (between sentences) coincides with the firmest metrical rest (end of a set of rhymed lines) to cases where the smallest grammatical juncture (between the components which make up words, morphemes) is forced to coincide with a compelling metrical break (e.g., between stanzas). Pope, who shuns enjambment, consistently makes the major juncture between couplets fit with that between sentences—although we frequently find marks other than full stop at this point. He tolerates smaller grammatical junctures at the end of the first line of a couplet.

Between the clauses of a sentence:

> Some thought it mounted to the Lunar
>   sphere,
> Since all things lost on earth are treasur'd there.
>
> RAPE OF THE LOCK, V, 113–114

Between the phrases of a clause—much less frequent:

> Triumphant Umbriel on a sconce's height
> Clapp'd his glad wings, and sate to view the fight:
>
> RAPE, V, 53–54

This sort of grammatical run-on, with a clause overflowing a line-end, is primarily what we think of as enjambment. We have to go to other poets, more noted for enjambment, to find many examples of this, and of even more powerful forms, where phrases and even words spill over the ends of lines.
Line-end between phrases:

> Here the stone images
> Are raised, here they receive

> The supplication of a dead man's hand
> Under the twinkle of a falling star.*

Eliot

"THE HOLLOW MEN"

Between the words which make up a phrase: very frequent in Milton, as for example at the beginning of Book VI of *Paradise Lost:* "in Gold/Empyreal, had thought/To have reported, the Cause/Of Truth, my Sons/Invincible."

Between the morphemes which make up a word: a very rare kind of enjambment because we (poets and readers) are unwilling to put a rhythmical break[4] at a point where the grammar requires a close transition between elements. Byron (*Don Juan,* XII, 75) demonstrates that, in comic verse, this trick is on a par with the other devices he employs at line-ends—feminine rhymes, rhyming two words with one, lexically ridiculous juxtapositions through rhyme:

> She cannot step as does an Arab barb,
>   Or Andalusian girl from mass returning,
> Nor wear as gracefully as Gauls her garb,
>   Nor in her eye Ausonia's glance is burning;
> Her voice, though sweet, is not so fit to warb-
>   le those *bravuras* . . .

Non-comic examples are Dylan Thomas's "the hay/Fields," "the coal-/Black night"; Hopkins's "king-/dom of daylight's dauphin," "all un-/warned"; Donne's "this blind-/nesse too much light breeds."

Occasional examples of enjambment in a poem which is largely end-stopped create points of tension. So the last example I gave from Pope—for him, a bold enjambment—stands out among the end-stopped couplets which have, at the most, only a clause-boundary after the first rhyme of the pair. At a different point in the scale, Thomas's *hay/Fields* strikes us because it is the most violent enjambment in the poem. This is a matter of degree, as "Fern Hill" has a high proportion of run-on lines with a relatively powerful sort of enjambment—twenty-five out of fifty-four.

---

* From "The Hollow Men" in *Collected Poems 1909–1962* by T. S. Eliot. Reprinted by permission of the publishers, Harcourt, Brace & World, Inc. Also by permission of Faber and Faber Limited.

Where similar degrees of enjambment recur at similar metrical positions, we have the beginnings of a sort of play between grammar and meter. Thomas, with lexical and grammatical similarity to aid him, has

> Time let me hail and climb
> Golden in the heyday of his eyes

and

> Time let me play and be
> Golden in the mercy of his means*

at similar points in the first and second stanzas of "Fern Hill," but he does not sustain the correspondence of grammar at regular points in the other stanzas. We can hardly talk about "counterpoint" unless there is an extensive and *regular* relation between grammatical and metrical patterns. Milton's run-on lines are so numerous that, in many extended passages, we can sense the tension between two systems, the movement of the argument (linguistically identifiable by grammatical and lexical forms) against that of the prosody:

> Th'infernal Serpent; he it was, whose guile
> Stird up with Envy and Revenge, deceiv'd
> The Mother of Mankinde, what time his Pride
> Had cast him out from Heav'n with all his Host
> Of Rebel Angels, by whose aid aspiring
> To set himself in Glory above his Peers,
> He trusted to have equal'd the most High,
> If he oppos'd; and with ambitious aim
> Against the throne and Monarchy of God
> Rais'd impious War in Heav'n and Battel proud
> With vain attempt. Him the Almighty Power
> Hurld headlong flaming from th'Ethereal Skie
> With hideous ruine and combustion down
> To bottomless perdition, there to dwell
> In Adamantine Chains and penal Fire,
> Who durst defie th'Omnipotent to Arms.

PARADISE LOST, I, 34–49

* Dylan Thomas, *Collected Poems.* Copyright 1939, 1946 by New Directions Publishing Corporation. Reprinted by permission of New Directions Publishing Corporation, New York. Also by permission of J. M. Dent & Sons Ltd. and the Trustees for the Copyrights of the late Dylan Thomas.

But there is not the regularity of relation between grammatical and rhythmical boundaries—between grammatical caesura and line-end—which gives rise to counterpoint. We find our best examples of this in the blank verse of Shakespeare's later plays. Kermode[5] speaks of "straddled lines," sentences or clauses which start in the middle of one line and end half-way through the next, forming a pentameter within two pentameters:

> . . . Beyond a common joy! and set it down
> With gold on lasting pillars: in one voyage . . .
>
> THE TEMPEST, V, i. 207–208

Often Shakespeare makes a pattern with a series of caesurae at similar points in alternate lines:

> . . . When he comes back; you demi-puppets that
> By moonshine do the green sour ringlets make,
> Whereof the ewe not bites; and you whose pastime
> Is to make midnight mushrooms, that rejoice
> To hear the solemn curfew; by whose aid . . .
>
> THE TEMPEST, V, i. 36–40

Sometimes a whole series of "metrical" lines is straddled by a series of "grammatical" lines, offering the regularity of relation which I have mentioned:

> . . . Whom now I keep in service. Thou best
>   know'st
> What torment I did find thee in; thy groans
> Did make wolves howl, and penetrate the breasts
> Of ever-angry bears: it was a torment
> To lay upon the damn'd, which Sycorax
> Could not again undo: it was mine Art . . .
>
> THE TEMPEST, I, ii. 286–291

Straddled lines are very frequent in Old English poetry. They are particularly effective, because the obligatory caesura in the center of the line invites the beginning of a clause, and yet the alliteration binding the two half-lines together resists the pull of a clause which starts with one "b" half-line and ends with the

next "a" half-line. In the following example, the straddled lines
are italicized:

> Gegremod wearð se guðrinc: *he mid gare stang*
> *wlancne wicing,*   þe him þa wunde forgeaf.
> Frod wæs se fyrdrinc,   *he let his francan wadan*
> *þurh ðæs hysses hals;*   hand wisode
> þæt he on þam færsceaðan   feorh geræhte.
> Da he oþerne   ofstlice sceat,
> þæt seo byrne tobærst;   *he wæs on breostum wund*
> *þurh ða hringlocan,*   *him æt heortan stod*
> *ætterne ord.*
> "BATTLE OF MALDON," 138–146

The beginning of *The Waste Land* has an interesting example of
this sort of counterpoint: a series of straddled lines starting and
finishing at regular points relative to the basic lines:

> April is the cruellest month, breeding
> Lilacs out of the dead land, mixing
> Memory and desire, stirring
> Dull roots with spring rain.
> Winter kept us warm, covering
> Earth in forgetful snow, feeding
> A little life with dried tubers.*

The counterpoint is reinforced by the repetition of the present
participle at the ends of lines 1–3, 5, and 6: a grammatical pattern
analogous to rhyme, and more powerful than the *-ing* rhyme
which accompanies it. Wimsatt[6] implies that rhymes of the same
part of speech may be flat. This is not such a case. Grammatical
repetition takes the place of rhyme; the phonological parallelism
is incidental.[7]

11

Now my treatment of counterpoint and tension so far may appear to be not at all what Chatman, or Wellek and Warren,
have in mind. Tension, for them, is tension between the stresses

---

* From "The Waste Land" in *Collected Poems 1909–1962* by T. S. Eliot.
Reprinted by permission of the publishers, Harcourt, Brace & World, Inc.
Also by permission of Faber and Faber Limited.

implied by a chosen metrical pattern and the stresses produced by the "prose rhythm" which is the grammatical-lexical exponent of the pattern. They are interested in meter as rhythm, stress-patterns *within* the line. I also have been discussing tension between prose rhythm and meter: between the phonology of grammar and the phonology which is "written-in" by a particular metrical convention. The distinction is largely that we have been concerned with units of different sizes. My basic principle—that there can be coincidence or non-coincidence of metrical units and grammatical units and/or their boundaries—can be extended to take in the relation of the metrical foot to the smaller units of grammar, and so to approach more closely the critics' view of counterpoint.

Gerard Manley Hopkins, who was outstandingly sensitive to the rhythms of English, has much to say on the subject of counterpoint rhythm.[8] He connects it with the "reversed foot," in which the rising rhythm established in the poem is interrupted by a falling foot: "putting the stress where, to judge by the rest of the measure, the slack should be and the slack where the stress" (Pick, p. 122). He continues:

> If however the reversal is repeated in two feet running, especially so as to include the sensitive second foot, it must be due either to great want of ear or else is a calculated effect, the superinducing or *mounting* of a new rhythm upon the old; and since the new or mounted rhythm is actually heard and at the same time the mind naturally supplies the natural or standard foregoing rhythm, for we do not forget what the rhythm is that by rights we should be hearing, two rhythms are in some manner running at once and we have something answerable to counterpoint in music, which is two or more strains of tune going on together, and this is Counterpoint Rhythm.

Chatman ("Comparing Metrical Styles") discusses this phenomenon under the heading of *metrical point displacement*. Among the examples he gives is Pope's *Thus much I've said, I trust, without offence*[9] with a reversed first foot. This is obviously a case of prose rhythm—the phonology required by the meaning—playing against meter, a meter firmly established by Pope's extremely regular couplets. Pope has allowed the prose rhythm to show through the meter at a point—the first foot—where convention permits. In Donne, who, according to Chatman, has a much higher proportion of reversed feet, the tension is less because the metrical pattern is obscured. Hopkins's "counterpoint" is in fact high-frequency reversal; when it is excessively frequent it produces sprung rhythm.

Sprung rhythm (which "consists in scanning by accents or stresses alone, without any account of the number of syllables, so that a foot may be one strong syllable or it may be many light and one strong" [Pick, p. 90]), like reversed feet, approximates to the prose rhythm of English by accommodating the tendency of the language to isochronism—relatively regular spacing of strong stresses, regardless of the number of intervening light stresses—and to the occasional juxtaposition of strong stresses. As Hopkins says, occasional reversed feet set up a counterpoint of the prose rhythm against the meter, but thoroughgoing sprung rhythm is an autonomous rhythm with no counterpoint.

At this point we may recapitulate on the link of theory between the two parts of this chapter, and suggest a shift in terminology. Throughout, I am concerned with the "fit" of grammatical and metrical units, and its consequences for the actual, perceived phonology of a poem. In a sense, the effects described in Part I are a "large-scale" variety of those to be dealt with below: the difference is one of size (e.g., sentence/line as opposed to word/foot). Above, I spoke of "points of tension" created by occasional vigorous enjambment or caesura-placing; periodicity of enjambment and caesura-placing, on the other hand, produces an effect which can justly be called counterpoint. The verse-form is more subtle than one totally reinforced by grammar, and subtle in a way which justifies the musical analogy: two phrases appear to play at the same time without conflict, and as in Bach they have different starting-points along the time-scale. An isolated reversed foot is analogous to a "point of tension"; there can be total reinforcement in "small-scale" grammetrics,[10] and there can be a situation (Hopkins's "counterpoint") where the prose rhythm makes itself felt as something playing against the ostensible meter. But extreme lack of fit of words with feet results in the total assertion of prose rhythm.

Our observations about large- and small-scale grammetrics

tend to be parallel; but the effects we describe are, phonologically, in different categories. Counterpoint and reinforcement as described in Part I of this [paper] are effects produced by the distribution relative to each other of the *terminal junctures* of grammatical and metrical units; Hopkins's "counterpoint," Chatman's "tension," and the processes described in the rest of this [paper] involve juncture only indirectly, the feature of primary importance being *stress-modification*. I want to underline this distinction by utilizing a second musical term, "syncopation." Although "counterpoint"—melodic interplay—suits regular periodic enjambment well, it is less appropriate to the effect Hopkins describes under that name, which is properly a matter of accent. In music, disturbance of an established beat by the imposition of a different, or more usually "unsynchronized" rhythm constitutes syncopation. It is disturbance of the metrical beat by prose rhythm that we shall consider in the remainder of this [paper].

A type of syncopation may be proposed which, unlike that described by Hopkins, involves no displacement of strong stresses, and which can be accounted for as an accentual effect produced by the overrun of metrical boundaries by grammatical units. It is an almost constant feature of superficially regular English pentameters. Compare the following lines:

1 But if for me ye fight, or me will serve
2 Both slow and swift alike do serve my tourne
3 But when he saw her toy, and gibe, and geare
4 Doe love, where loves does give his sweete alarmes

FAERIE QUEENE, II, vi. 34.1; 10.6; 21.7; 34.7

with these:

5 More swift than swallow sheres the liquid skie
6 And all the way the wanton damsell found
7 Tho up he started, stird with shame extreme
8 Accompanyde with Phaedria the faire

II, vi. 5.2; 6.1; 27.7; 28.2

In lines 1–4 Spenser's iambs are filled by grammatical units whose natural stress-patterns correspond closely with those of the meter: rising, two-syllable. A number of English constructions fit the iambic pattern: for example, prepositional phrases (*for me*); monosyllabic subject plus monosyllabic verb (*ye fight*); auxiliary plus verb (*does give*); certain two-syllable words (*alarmes*). Lines which utilize these grammatical patterns exclusively have their iambic metrical patterns reinforced: there is coalescence of the prose rhythm and the meter. They are used either to establish the meter against which the prose rhythm is later to play to produce syncopation (so Spenser often puts them at the beginnings of stanzas) or for special effects: *I burne, I burne, I burne, then loud he cryde.* With this sort of meter, the only variation possible is in the types of grammatical boundary which coincide with the limits of feet. Although in both cases there is coincidence of metrical and grammatical boundaries, there is a difference between *for me/ ye fight* and *ye fight,/ or me* because a clause is split in the first, a sentence in the second.

But verse which is continuously symmetrical in this way is rare. It is difficult to write this sort of verse, for it requires avoidance of polysyllables, and frequent inversions of word-order (as in *loud he cryde,* which gets round the necessity for an unnatural stress on *he*). Moreover, it is dull. Syncopation avoids dullness, and can be managed without displacement of stresses. The beginnings of syncopation can be detected in line 3, where the construction *he saw her* overruns the iamb *hĕ sáw.* If we have *hĕr tóy* after a juncture following *saw,* we misinterpret the grammar,[11] so we make a "pause" after *her*—within an iamb. The perceived pause will be, phonetically, not a moment of silence, but a product of the stress-relations: the metrically weak *her* is "promoted" to a grade higher than the iambic pattern requires, though still lower than *sáw* and *tóy.* Perhaps, *sáw hèr tóy* instead of *sáw hĕr tóy;* cf. line 1, *if fòr mé.* Examples 5–8 exhibit forms of syncopation which are dependent on this adjustment of stress through non-coincidence of grammatical and metrical boundaries. One sort of diagramming which might be used to demonstrate this would use / for grammatical and | for metrical junctures. So in non-syncopated, or "symmetrical" verse / and | would always fall together. But in line 6 we have:

And/all|the way/|the wan|ton dam|sell/found

and in line 8:

Accom|panyde/| with Phaed|ria | the faire.

But this means of indicating syncopation visually would need
to be made more precise: / is of several kinds, and differentiation is necessary to distinguish between the interruption of a
foot by / as in -ed,/ stird, (7), and by / as in -ow/ sheres, (5).

A better way will be to acknowledge the actual phonetic
nature of syncopated rhythm: the iambic foot is modified by the
grammar, not through the displacement of stress, but through
the "promotion" of some light and "reduction" of some heavy
stresses—the two-stress system of symmetrical verse is turned into
a stress-system with more, and more delicate, contrasts. Non-
syncopated rhythms need be described in terms of only two
degrees of stress, heavy and light (or stressed and unstressed);
the description of syncopated rhythm needs finer discrimination
of stress-levels, as that of colloquial English does. The famous
Trager-Smith analysis of English postulates four (relative, not
absolute) levels of stress. There may be more or less in poetry.
In non-syncopated rhythm there are only two. Syncopation has
more than two, and, as the four-stress approach is well docu-
mented, we could adopt this and look for four. Let us apply it
to some of the Spenser examples.

Line 8 is the most interesting. We should have no doubt
about giving the highest degree of stress (4, or ′) to syllables 2,
6, and 10—even syllables, so there is no displacement of stress.
Because English polysyllabic words can have only one ′, the
fourth and eighth syllables are reduced to ˆ (3). The "stresses"
of the line are thus ′ ˆ ′ ˆ ′: this against the background of
′ ′ ′ ′ ′ in the two-grade scheme of the underlying iambic line.
The "unstressed" syllables of the pentameter are variously filled
by the lowest grades, ` (2) and ˘ (1): `′˘ˆ `′˘ˆ `′. We acknowledge the prose rhythm of this sort of line by saying that it has
three (or four, most usually) stresses; we acknowledge the
syncopation by saying that it is *a pentameter with three stresses.*
Line 6 is a different case. None of the main stresses is reduced,
the five even syllables all taking ′. The syncopation, in which
the grammar resists the insertion of the metrical junctures
wan|ton dam|sell, manifests itself in the promotion of the weak
metrical stresses on *-ton* and *-sell,* perhaps to ` . The same hap-

pens to the metrically weak syllables 5 and 9 in line 5. Line 7, where the grammar requires a caesura within the third foot, fulfils this requirement by a greater promotion: the metrically weak fifth syllable is raised to ˆ.

In this promotion and reduction of stresses, a result of running grammatical and metrical units gently against each other, lies the key to Pope's achievement of variety within a strict measure. Even the most orthodox-looking line may have one point which prevents our reading it with the simple two-stress rhythm:

> Say first, of God above, or Man below

ESSAY ON MAN, I, 17

All is "regular" except the first foot. Even this could be transcribed as ˣ′, a conventional iamb: there is not the clear reversal of *Thus much*. But we cannot have the verb *say* so completely overweighted by the adverb *first* which modifies it: the stress-component of ˣ cannot be Trager and Smith's ˘; it must be ′. Once we acknowledge this (and the grammar makes us do this automatically) our view of the whole line is changed: the possibility is opened up of a rhythm more subtle than that of the two-grade, up-and-down iambic. Pope goes on:

> 18 What can we reason, but from what we know?
> 19 Of Man, what see we but his station here,
> 20 From which to reason, or to which refer?
> 21 Thro' worlds unnumber'd tho' the God be known,
> 22 'Tis ours to trace him only in our own.

Line 18 is much more seriously disturbed. It begins with a reversed foot which throws us straight into the second foot, because a strong grammatical juncture is unthinkable between *can* and *we*. At the ostensible end of the second foot there can be no break: réa|sŏn is nonsense, so ˣ must be promoted from ˘ to ′. *But,* coming after a pause and being grammatically of little significance, is reduced to almost ′, and the metrical break between *but* and *from* disappears. In line 19 the clause *what see we* sits uneasily on one and a half iambs: ˣ′|ˣ; *we* is promoted to ′, and *but,* as in line 18, reduced. The second syllable of *station* is promoted, unlike *we* in the corresponding position in line 18.

The middles of lines 20 and 21 are treated as in lines 18 and 19: syllable 5 is promoted, 6 reduced. So there is some repetition of the patterns of syncopation over four lines (18–21): the centers parallel one another in the way grammar overrides meter, while the iambs which open and end the lines are treated in a variety of ways. Line 22, closing this section of the argument, breaks the pattern, offering a milder form of syncopation. The grammar resists the insertion of a metrical boundary between *trace* and *him*, promoting *him* from ^{x} to '; similarly, *ón*|*lý in* becomes *ónlý ín*.

This sort of syncopation, truly a tension between prose rhythm and metrical system, is normal among English poets, and its range of varieties is exploited for metrical excellence. There is, it appears, a fundamental incompatibility between rising-rhythm, syllable-counted meters and the prose rhythms—the phonology of grammar—of English. This, paradoxically, may help to explain why the iambic measure is felt to be suited to English: not because its pattern corresponds to the prose rhythms of the language, for it does not; but because it necessitates a constant syncopation of prose rhythm against its own rhythm, inviting poets to be metrically complex, not to jog along with simple regularity.[12]

NOTES

1. Seymour Chatman, "Robert Frost's 'Mowing': An Inquiry into Prosodic Structure," *Kenyon Review*, XVIII (1956), 422.

2. This method of analysis, with or without reference to the abstract metrical pattern, has come to be one of the chief ways of applying linguistic methods to poetry. It is based on the account of English phonology found in G. L. Trager and H. L. Smith, *Outline of English Structure* (Washington, 1951). The application to metrics was first proposed by Harold Whitehall (*Kenyon Review*, 1951, 1956) and has recently been advocated once more by Terence Hawkes, "The Problems of Prosody," *Review of English Literature*, II, no. 2 (April 1962), 32–48. John Thompson, *The Founding of English Metre* (London, 1961), makes considerable use of the method. A linguistic treatment of metrics from a slightly different angle is Seymour Chatman's "Comparing Metrical Styles," in *Style in Language*, ed. Thomas A. Sebeok (Cambridge, Mass., 1960), pp. 149–172. See also D. Abercrombie, "A Phonetician's View of Verse Structure," *Linguistics*, VI (1964), 5–13.

3. According to Trager and Smith.

4. Except that between feet, on which see section II below.

5. *The Tempest* (Arden ed., London, 1958), p. xvii.

6. "One Relation of Rhyme to Reason," *The Verbal Icon* (Lexington, Ky., 1954), pp. 153–169.

7. Donald Davie (*Articulate Energy* [London, 1955], pp. 90–91) has a nice analysis of the opening of "Ash Wednesday," where grammatical parallelism is again used to link lines together.

8. See John Pick, *A Hopkins Reader* (London, 1953), index under "Versification."

9. Donne's "Satire II" Versified, 125. The comma after *trust,* which occurs in some editions, does not affect the present point.

10. For the term "grammetrics" see P. J. Wexler, "On the Grammetrics of the Classical Alexandrine," *Cahiers de Lexicologie,* IV (1964), 61–72.

11. Making *her toy* a noun phrase.

12. Since writing this [paper] I have read W. K. Wimsatt, Jr., and M. C. Beardsley, "The Concept of Meter: an Exercise in Abstraction," *PMLA* LXXIV (1959), 585–598; the similarity to my own views will be obvious. Recently published is a full study, S. Chatman, *A Theory of Meter* (The Hague, 1965), which I discuss in a review article, "Structural Metrics" [*Linguistics,* no. 27 (1966), 49–64].

21. CHAUCER AND THE STUDY OF PROSODY

Morris Halle and Samuel Jay Keyser

The publication of "Chaucer and the Study of Prosody" spurred reexamination of the basic principles of metrical analysis. In this work Morris Halle and Samuel Jay Keyser bring to the theory of prosody the principles and findings of their research on the history and development of English stress (to be published by The M.I.T. Press as *The Evolution of Stress in English*). Also implicit in their study of Chaucerian meter are some basic tenets of generative phonology.

Professors Halle and Keyser argue that a theory of prosody must do more than establish a norm and state exceptions. It must account in a principled way for most metrical lines of poetry. Chaucer's iambic pentameter line, then, must be viewed as consisting not of five feet, but of four potential stress contrasts, where stress is assigned by the rules of English phonology. Hence, in traditional terms, the first and the last "feet" in an iambic pentameter line are free. This freedom (and others like it), they assert, is not accidental, but a part of the rules of English meter which every poet and reader of poetry in English intuitively understands.

Morris Halle is professor of linguistics and a member of the staff of the Research Laboratory of Electronics at the Massachusetts Institute of Technology. Samuel Jay Keyser is assistant professor of English at Brandeis University.

INTRODUCTION

In this article we propose to characterize the accentual-syllabic meter known as iambic pentameter in the form in which it was first used by Geoffrey Chaucer. We view this

Morris Halle and S. J. Keyser, "Chaucer and the Study of Prosody," *College English*, XXVIII (December 1966), 187–219. Reprinted with the permission of the National Council of Teachers of English, Morris Halle, and S. J. Keyser.

meter as an abstract pattern which the poet has created or adopted, perhaps only in part consciously. The poet uses this pattern as a basis of selection so that he may choose out of the infinite number of sentences of natural language those which qualify for inclusion in the poem. In the verse of interest here the pattern consists in the regulation of two linguistically given properties, the number of syllables in a line and the placement in a line of syllables bearing linguistically given stress greater than that of adjacent syllables. Thus we begin with the assumption that stress placement is a relevant linguistic fact which is utilized by the English poet writing in the iambic pentameter tradition. (It is not, of course, the only linguistic given utilized by the poet.) We shall restrict our attention to stress placement and the number of syllables only insofar as they participate in the construction of a single line of verse. We shall not attempt in any systematic way to go beyond the single verse line to more complex structures.[1]

Let us first turn our attention to the facts of English stress placement. In a word like *celestial,* a speaker of modern English knows that the primary stress is on the second syllable, thus *cel$\overset{1}{e}$stial* and not *c$\overset{1}{e}$lestial.*

There are other facts about English stress which are also relevant for purposes of meter. Thus compound nouns such as *bl$\overset{1}{a}$ckb$\overset{2}{i}$rds* are clearly stressed *bl$\overset{1}{a}$ckb$\overset{2}{i}$rds* and not *bl$\overset{2}{a}$ckb$\overset{1}{i}$rds.* Indeed, the latter stress assignment automatically entails the sequence being understood as the noun phrase *bl$\overset{2}{a}$ck b$\overset{1}{i}$rds* and not the compound noun. Similarly, if a complex noun like *k$\overset{2}{i}$tchen t$\overset{1}{o}$wel r$\overset{3}{a}$ck* is stressed as *k$\overset{2}{i}$tchen t$\overset{1}{o}$wel r$\overset{3}{a}$ck* it is understood as meaning "a towel rack for the kitchen" while if it is stressed as *k$\overset{1}{i}$tchen t$\overset{3}{o}$wel r$\overset{2}{a}$ck* it is understood as meaning "a rack for kitchen towels." And if it is stressed as *k$\overset{1}{i}$tchen t$\overset{2}{o}$wel r$\overset{3}{a}$ck* it is clear that it is un-English.[2]

Still other facts about English are obvious to the native speaker. Thus articles such as *a,* and *the,* as in *a new home, the old man,* prepositions such as *of* or *in* in phrases such as *of the people, in the house,* conjunctions such as *and* and *or,* pronouns such as *him, his,* etc., are without stress, or with very little stress.[3]

Beginning with the observation that a poet (like his audience) has at his disposal certain linguistic givens, we may ask how these linguistic givens are utilized for purposes of prosody. There are, of course, two possibilities. The first is that the poet develops a metrical form which is completely independent of the linguistic givens of stress so that *celéstial* is as acceptable as *célestial*. This hypothesis entails that the poet may radically depart from the linguistic basis of his (and his audience's) language. The second possibility is that the poet does not violate the linguistic givens of his language but rather incorporates them into a metrical pattern which, while extra-linguistic in that the pattern is not a fact of the spoken language, is nonetheless perfectly compatible with the linguistic givens of the spoken language.

An advocate of the first view is Ten Brink[4] who supposed, for example, that while the facts of Chaucer's spoken English demanded a stress pattern of the sort *cóminge,* nonetheless Chaucer violated this linguistic given by actually shifting the stress for metrical purposes to rhyme with words like *springe,* thus *comínge.*[5]

> On this view the present lines which have been
> devised so that a word boundary falls
> after the tenth, twentieth, thirtieth
> etcetera syllable is written
> in perfect iambic pentameter.

Moreover, on this view the meter of a line such as Keats's:

> Silent upon a peak in Darien

which is metrically regular, cannot be distinguished from that of the title of the sonnet

> On First Looking into Chapman's Homer

which is not. Given a principle of stress shift for metrical purposes, both lines must be viewed as regular. But this clearly is not the case. Indeed, it is precisely the difference between these two lines that a successful theory of prosody ought to characterize.

In what follows we shall adopt the second alternative, namely that basically the poet does not violate the linguistic givens of his language but, rather, attempts in general to utilize them in actualizing the metrical pattern.

From this point of view, a line like:

(1)   Celestial, whether among the thrones, or named

from Milton's *Paradise Lost,* Book XI, line 296 (hereafter **PL.** XI. 296) must be viewed as beginning with an unstressed syllable followed by a stressed syllable precisely because it is a linguistic given that *celestial* is stressed as *celéstial.* Similarly, because *région* is so stressed, we suppose that a line such as:

(2)   Regions of sorrow, doleful shades, where peace
                                                          PL.I.65

begins with a stressed syllable followed by an unstressed syllable.

It has been customary to identify these lines as examples of a meter called "iambic pentameter," a poetic meter which has been used by English poets from Geoffrey Chaucer to the present. In what follows we shall adopt this name without prejudice and attempt to characterize in as precise a fashion as possible what we intend by it.

Suppose, then, that by iambic pentameter one meant a metrical form which adhered to the following metrical principles:

Principle 1.
    The iambic pentameter line consists of five feet to which may be appended one or two extra-metrical unstressed syllables.
Principle 2.
    The iambic foot consists of two syllables.
Principle 3.
    Each even syllable is strongly stressed.
Principle 4.
    Each odd syllable is less strongly stressed.

We shall refer to the above principles as the strict interpretation of the iambic pentameter line. Notice that (1) above is a regular line in terms of these principles.

Thus the line may be scanned as follows:

$$\overset{1}{\text{Ce}}\text{lestial, }\overset{1}{\text{wheth}}\text{'r }\overset{1}{\text{among}}\text{ the }\overset{1}{\text{thrones, or }}\overset{1}{\text{named.}}^6$$

But notice that (2) above may now be offered as a counter-example to the iambic pentameter theory, thus:

$$\overset{1}{\text{Re}}\text{gions of }\overset{1}{\text{sorrow, }}\overset{1}{\text{doleful }}\overset{1}{\text{shades, where }}\overset{1}{\text{peace}}$$

This is a counter-example precisely because it is a linguistic given that *regions* is stressed $\overset{1}{\text{regions}}$ and not $\overset{1}{\text{regions}}$. The strict iambic pentameter theory would force us to regard this line as irregular, whereas in fact lines with "inverted first feet" are perfectly regular in iambic verse.

Another counter-example to the strict iambic pentameter theory is the opening couplet of Shakespeare's Sonnet 30:

(3)   When to the sessions of sweet, silent thought
           I summon up remembrance of things past

In the first line of (3) the strict iambic theory requires that the preposition *to* receive greater stress than *when,* and *of* receive greater stress than *sweet* in violation of the linguistic givens of spoken English. Moreover, it requires that in the phrase *sweet, silent thought* the adjective *sweet* receive less stress than *silent.* But since this stress pattern is in direct violation of English, the line must be classed as deviant.

Similarly, the second line of (3) would also be classed as irregular by the strict iambic pentameter theory, for clearly the preposition *of* has less stress than the following noun *things.* Thus the strict iambic theory entails that lines which abound in the writings of the best poets are metrically deviant. Evidently such a theory cannot be considered tenable.

It is obvious on other grounds as well that this interpretation is untenable. Thus the strict interpretation says, in essence, that a poet writing in this meter is writing doggerel. And it requires little poetic sensitivity to know that Chaucer, Milton, Pope, and Lowell do not write doggerel. Indeed, when Ten Brink assumes legitimate shifting of the stress of the spoken language to conform to the meter, it is noteworthy that the meter he is attempting to conform to is strict iambic pentameter, that is, doggerel. This fact in itself renders his principle of the "legitimate stress shift" suspect (see note 4).

Prosodists have, of course, been well aware of these difficulties with the strict iambic pentameter theory. They have tried to shore up the theory by giving a list of allowable deviations. Thus, P. Baum lists in his *Chaucer's Verse* (Durham, N.C., 1961), pp. 13–14, as poetical "liberties and licenses," the following departures from the strict iambic pentameter: "(1) the weak stress, including secondary accent in polysyllables, in different positions in the line; (2) the heavy foot or spondee; (3) the inverted foot or trochaic; (4) the variable use of syllabic *e*; and (5) elision, contraction, and the slurs which may or may not certify the admission or exclusion of tri-syllabic feet."

In very similar terms Wimsatt and Beardsley in their important article on "The Concept of Meter" (*PMLA*, LXXIV, 1959) speak of "the inverted first foot, the dropping of the first slack syllable, the extra slack syllable internal to the line (elided, or not elided in the anapest) . . ." as deviations from the strict iambic pentameter that "occur so often as to assume the character of an accepted complication of the norm."

The introduction of "allowable deviations" constitutes a significant modification of the theory. The modified theory is clearly an improvement over the strict iambic interpretation in the sense that unlike the latter it is not contradicted by a significant fraction of the lines it is supposed to characterize. But even with these modifications the theory does not recommend itself especially, for it fails to provide any explanation for the fact that only certain deviations are tolerated and not others. Since the allowed deviations share only the property of being included in a list, why could not other deviations also be included in such a list? Rather than look upon headless lines, lines with an inverted first foot, etc., as somehow deviant—though perhaps less deviant than some other lines—we propose below a set of principles or rules which by their nature yield a large variety of metrical patterns, in the same way that rules of syntax yield a large variety of syntactic patterns. With respect to these rules, there will be one of two possible judgments. Either a line is metrical by virtue of conformity to the rules, or else a line is unmetrical by virtue of nonconformity to the rules. As we have said, it is precisely this distinction which a theory of prosody of a given poet or poetic tradition must make.[7]

The rules we propose establish an abstract pattern that is satisfied by particular arrangements of linguistic givens. They are not to be equated with precepts for performing a particular type of verse.[8] The meter of a poem determines to a great extent the manner in which the poem is to be performed. It never determines the performance completely, however, any more than a score of a sonata completely determines the way in which the sonata should be performed. The study of prosody is the study of the abstract patterns—the different arrangements of linguistic givens—that underlie all performances of a given poem; it is not the study of the myriad ways—some good, others bad, most indifferent—in which a poem might be recited.

MIDDLE ENGLISH STRESS

It is obvious that a theory of prosody which takes the linguistically determined stresses of a language as part of the elements manipulated by the poet assumes an understanding of what these stresses are. In other words a theory of prosody based, in part at least, upon stress placement necessarily presupposes a theory of stress placement. In modern English such a theory of stress placement may be taken for granted since the prosodist, the poet, and the reader, as speakers of the same language, have all internalized the same system of stress assignment. In discussing Middle English prosody we may not make this assumption. We must, therefore, give a brief summary of the Middle English stress system, especially as our picture of it does not coincide in all points with the one found in the handbooks.

We begin by considering two separate issues:

i)   the rules for stress subordination in compounds and other sequences larger than a single word
ii) the rules for stress assignment in a single word

With regard to the former we assume that in compound nouns, verbs, and adjectives the main stress of the second element is lower than that of the first. We shall assume that Chaucer stressed *brymstoon*[1][2], *greyhound*[1][2], *cartwheel*[1][2]. On the other hand, in the constituents that are not nouns, verbs, or adjectives and that contain more than one word, such as noun phrases composed of an adjective followed by a noun, we shall suppose that stress subordination does not occur. Thus a phrase such as *the first prize*[1][1] or *a useful book*[1][1] we shall treat as having "level stress." It is important to note that in this regard we are departing from contemporary American practice in which stress subordination does occur in such phrases, yielding patterns like *the first prize*[2][1], *a useful book*[2][1] (see note 2). These principles of stress subordination account for the fact that (a) the first syllable of compounds consisting of two monosyllabic words commonly occupies an even position, whereas (b) any constituent of a syntactic unit that is not a compound noun, adjective or adverb may be found in an even or an odd position. Examples illustrating (a) are:

1. Out of the *donghil* cam that word ful right!

    PF.597

2. Men clepen hym an *'outlawe'* or a 'theef'

    H.MCP.234

3. In al the toun nas *brewhouse* ne taverne

    A.MIL.3334

4. Twelve spokes hath a *cartwheel* comunly

    D.SUM.2257

Examples illustrating (b) are:

1. Oold fish and yonge flessh wolde I have fayne

    E.MCH.1418

2. His eyen caste on hire, but in sad wyse

    E.CL.237

   3. The Millere was a stout carl for the nones

A.PROL.545

   4. A good Wif was ther of biside Bathe

A.PROL.445

The traditional view concerning the rule for stress assignment in simple words has been that Middle English possessed two kinds of words, native words and Romance words. Similarly, it was supposed, Middle English contained two stress rules, one for the native portion and one for the Romance portion. The rule for the native portion was assumed to be identical with that for the bulk of Germanic languages, including Old English, namely a rule which assigned primary stress to the initial syllables of words, excluding prefixes and the like. By this rule $\overset{1}{father}$, $\overset{1}{mother}$, $\overset{1}{become}$, $\overset{1}{coming}$, received their stress. The rule for the Romance portion of the Middle English vocabulary was assumed to be the Old French stress rule which was essentially like that for classical Latin, though with certain modifications:

Romance stress rule:

1. Assign primary stress to the final vowel of a simple word if that vowel is long.
2. If the vowel is short and followed by any number of consonants, including none, then look at the next to the last syllable.
3. If the penultimate syllable is strong, that is, contains a long vowel, or any vowel followed by two consonants, then assign major stress to the vowel of that syllable.
4. If the penultimate syllable is not strong, then stress the antepenultimate syllable.

Part 1 of this rule is responsible for the stress in $lic\overset{1}{o}ur$. Part 2 and Part 3 are responsible for the stress in $arrer\overset{1}{a}ge$ rhyming with $\overset{1}{a}ge$. (A.Prol.601). Part 4 of this rule is responsible for the stress in words like $t\overset{1}{a}ffata$ or $P\overset{1}{a}ndarus$.

It is commonly believed that a speaker of Middle English like

Chaucer possessed both rules and that he systematically applied one rule for the native portion of the vocabulary and one for the foreign. Since modern English clearly does not have both rules, a change must have occurred. And it is believed by many that the direction of that change was toward complete acceptance of the Germanic rule and rejection of the Romance rule. A typical example of this view is expressed in the following comment by Henry Sweet (*A New English Grammar* [Oxford, 1891], §786):

> In Old French the stress generally fell on the same syllable as in Latin, as in *na•ture* = Latin *nā̆•turam*. Through the dropping of the final Latin syllables many French words thus came to have the stress on the last syllable, as in *o•nour ho•nōrem, pi•te pie•tātem*. When first introduced into ME French words kept their original stress: *nā̆•türe, o•nur, pi•tē;* but such words afterwards threw the stress back on to the first syllable by the analogy of the native E. words, such as • *fader,* • *bodi* becoming • *nā̆türe,* etc.

We have argued elsewhere[9] against the traditional view. We have proposed that at the stage of Middle English when the Romance words first entered the language there must obviously have been two stress rules, but that quite soon the Germanic stress rule dropped and the Romance stress rule predominated. We shall not present here the details of our argument; rather we shall touch upon the major points.

To begin with, given a stage of English in which both stress rules were operative, it is crucial to note that the majority of Middle English words from the native portion of the vocabulary were either monosyllabic words or else dissyllabic words but with a short final vowel. As a consequence, the Romance stress rule would assign precisely the same stress to these words as would be assigned to them by the Germanic stress rule, namely initial stress. Thus a word like *father, mother,* or *bodi* would receive initial stress by either rule. On the other hand, ultimate or penultimate stress could only be assigned in words like *pilgrimāge, pitē, mercī, nature,* etc., by the Romance stress rule. Thus, of the two rules, the Germanic stress was largely dispensable; the Romance stress rule was not.

It must be recalled that besides final stressed *licŏur,* for example, with a long final vowel, there was also a second variant with initial stress and short final vowel. In the light of this, it becomes obvious that the initial stress of words like *lícŏur, píte*, *mercí, natŭre,* is not due to these words being treated as if they were native words, but rather is due to the fact that the long final vowel in these words was simply shortened prior to the operation of the Romance stress rule. Indeed, if we suppose that the shortening of long final syllable vowels was an optional rule in Chaucer's language, then both *licŏur* and *licŏur* receive stress by the Romance rule, the latter form having first undergone optional shortening of the long final syllable vowel.[10]

A similar systematic alternation among certain words in Middle English has been noted by many scholars, among them Ten Brink.[11] Specifically, Ten Brink noted that initial stress in words like *manēre, banēre* was often accompanied by loss of final *–e*. He assumed that the loss of final *–e* was due to initial stress and that initial stress was due to these words being stressed according to the Germanic stress rule. Let us suppose, however, that the loss of final *–e*, like the shortening of final long vowels, was an optional rule in Chaucer's Middle English. Let us further suppose that this rule, like the final vowel rule, applied to a word before the stress rule applied. Then we may account for the initial stress in these words as well. Thus *manēre* and *banēre* receive their stress by Part 2 and Part 3 of the Romance stress rule. If, however, the final *–e* dropping rule were to apply to these forms first, then the rule which shortens long vowels in final syllables could operate next to yield *banĕr* and *manĕr* which would then receive initial stress by Part 2 and Part 3 of the Romance stress rule, thus *banĕr* and *manĕr*. In a similar fashion *natūre* would become *natūr* by the final *–e* dropping rule, then *natŭr* by the final syllable shortening rule and finally *natŭr* by the Romance stress rule.

Thus not only is the assumption that the Germanic stress rule operated in late Middle English unnecessary, but the assumption that the Romance stress rule was operative in Middle English in conjunction with the final *–e* dropping rule and the vowel shortening rule now explains the systematic correspondence between initial stress and short final syllables and between initial

stress and lack of final –*e*, a correspondence which, in the traditional view, is accidental. Finally, when one considers that it is
necessary to postulate the rule which drops final –*e* and the rule
which shortens long vowels in final syllables in any case, then it is
clear that the assumption that the Germanic stress rule continued to operate in Middle English after the Romance rule
entered the language is unnecessary. The facts of Middle English
are equally well accounted for without the assumption.

At this point, however, there are certain facts about alternations in Chaucer's line which become quite important. Notice
that a word like *cominge* could only receive initial stress, according to our view, if the final –*e* first dropped. Thus a form
like *cominge* would be stressed *cominge* by the Romance stress
rule, but *coming* if the final –*e* is optionally dropped prior to
the operation of the Romance stress rule. Thus we have a
systematic alternation between initial stress in a dissyllabic word,
and penultimate stress in a tri-syllabic word. This puts certain
severe constraints on certain lines in Chaucer. That is to say,
if we find a line in which the scansion requires that a word like
cominge be tri-syllabic, then it must be the case that such a line
also requires that *cominge* receive penultimate stress. Otherwise,
our theory of stress placement would lead us to suppose exceptional lines in Chaucer. And the supposition of exceptional
lines must always be the last resort of the prosodist.

For example, a line like:[12]

> But now thi coming(e) is to be so swete
>
> TC.4.507

clearly requires that *coming* be initially stressed and dissyllabic.
Thus this line is perfectly straightforward. But consider lines
such as the following:

> The cause of his comynge thus answerde
>
> TC.2.1102

> The cause y-told of hir comynge, the olde
>
> TC.4.141

The nexte houre of Mars folwynge this

Ther maistow seen cominge with Palamón

In these lines the meter demands that *comynge* be tri-syllabic and penultimately stressed.[13] The view that the Germanic stress rule operated in Middle English could not possibly account for the necessary penultimate stress in these native words. The view that the Romance stress rule operated supplies precisely the desired stress to render these lines regular.

Rhymes such as *cominge* and *springe* further support the view that these words were stressed *cominge* : *springe*.[14]

Moreover, the existence of stress doublets such as *comyng* beside *comynge* provides Chaucer with a metrical resource which he puts to use in passages such as the following:

Gret sweryng is a thyng abhominable,
And fals swerynge is yet moore reprevable.
The heighe God forbad swerynge at al,
Witnesse on Mathew, but in special
Of sweryng seith the hooly Jeremye
"Thou shalt swere sooth thyne othes, and nat lye,
(4)   And swere in doom, and eek in rightwisnesse"
But ydel sweryng is a cursednesse,
Bihoold and se that in the firste table,
Of heighe Goddes heestes honurable
Hou that the second(e) heeste of hym is this:
"Take nat my name in ydel or amys."
Lo, rather he forbedeth swich swerynge
Than homycide or many a cursed thynge;

The alternation from one line to the next of the variants
$\overset{1}{sweryng}$ and $\overset{1}{swerynge}$ (for elision see pages 395ff. below) offers
a striking example of the way in which Chaucer makes use of
these linguistically given variants for poetic effect. Indeed, without the recognition of such variants operating here, this passage
loses both its metrical form and its poetic effect. (Note also
other alternations operating here, such as that between *swere* as
a stress maximum (see page 378 above) in the seventh line but
not in the sixth and the internal off-rhyme in the first line of
$\overset{1}{sweryng}$ and $\overset{1}{thyng}$ over against the feminine rhyme $\overset{1}{swerynge}$:
$\overset{1}{thynge}$ in the final lines of the passage.)[15]

In summary, then, the theory of stress placement which is entailed by the theory of prosody to be outlined below contains
the following three rules:

1. Final *−e* may be optionally dropped at the end of a word.
2. A long vowel in a final syllable may be shortened.
3. The Romance stress rule.

In this brief excursus we have been necessarily informal.
Nevertheless the preceding pages embody the major points of the
theory of stress placement which accounts for the data provided
by Chaucer's poetry.

Before we leave this topic and proceed to a detailed discussion
of the theory of prosody which accounts for Chaucer's verse, assuming this theory of stress placement, an interesting and quite
independent result of this theory is worth mentioning. Elsewhere it has been shown that the rule which governs placement
of stress in modern English words is essentially the Romance
stress rule stated above, although with several modifications due
in large part to the great influx of learned words in the 16th and
17th centuries. The fact that our assumptions lead us to postulate
the Romance stress rule for Middle English as well can hardly
be a coincidence. Rather it seems that, in the course of the
development of English, the Germanic stress rule was rendered
superfluous by the large influx of Romance words into English
after the Conquest. This rule dropped out and the Romance
stress rule remained from Middle English into present day English as the dominant rule for the assignment of stress in simple
words.

THE THEORY OF CHAUCERIAN PROSODY

We have characterized above the strict iambic pentameter interpretation of Chaucerian verse by means of a set of principles or rules. These principles taken together constitute a theory of prosody, albeit an inadequate one. The principles assume and arrange in various patterns certain theoretical entities, such as the foot, which nowhere appear in the actual line of verse. Prosodists have, in general, recognized the theoretical nature of their entities. Thus, Paull Baum (p. 11) asserts that "Chaucer's line is a series of five iambs," and then adds in a footnote, "For this flat statement there is to be sure only deductive evidence. If it must be regarded as in the first instance an assumption or an hypothesis, it can be tested in the usual ways of corroboration and accounting for apparent exceptions."

The theory that we propose for the Chaucerian iambic pentameter is framed in terms of metrical constructs which are, to a certain extent, familiar and relates these in a particular manner to the sequences of speech sounds that make up a given line:

Principle 1.
The iambic pentameter verse consists of ten positions to which may be appended one or two extra-metrical syllables.
Principle 2.
A position is normally occupied by a single syllable, but under certain conditions it may be occupied by more than one syllable or by none.
Condition 1.
Two vowels may constitute a single position provided that they adjoin, or are separated by a liquid or nasal or by a word boundary which may be followed by *h–*, and provided that one of them is a weakly stressed or unstressed vowel.
Condition 2.
An unstressed or weakly stressed monosyllabic word may constitute a single metrical position with a preceding stressed or unstressed syllable.
Principle 3.
A stress maximum may only occupy even positions within a verse, but not every even position need be so occupied.

Definition.

A stress maximum is constituted by a syllable bearing linguistically determined stress that is greater than that of the two syllables adjacent to it in the same verse.

Each principle embodies several alternatives, and the possible employment of Condition 1 and/or 2 increases further the number of alternatives. The order in which the alternatives are given is significant. Thus the first alternative within each principle represents what we shall consider the most neutral actualization of the metrical pattern. The subsequent alternatives yield lines which are perfectly regular in that they violate no rule. However, they represent a more complex actualization of the metrical pattern. Thus a line in which each position is occupied by a single syllable and in which each even position is actualized by a stress maximum is deemed neutral. Lines, however, which exhibit even positions without stress maximum, or lines which exhibit polysyllabic (or empty) positions are considered to be more complex actualizations of the metrical pattern.[16]

Differences in complexity of an analogous sort are found in syntax. For example, a sentence such as *The man who casts the first stone is innocent* is as regular as *The man the first stone is cast by is innocent,* though it is obviously less complex than the latter.

With respect to metrics, differences in complexity have traditionally been viewed as instances of metrical tension. The difficulty with this view, however, is that it confuses the essential distinction between more complex and less complex lines with the distinction between regular and irregular lines.[17]

SCANSION

Let us turn, then, to the examples. To begin with, the most neutral actualization of the iambic pentameter line is, as we have stated, one in which each syllable occupies one metrical position and in which each even position is occupied by a stress maximum.

The following lines are typical:

$$\overset{\prime}{}\quad\overset{\prime}{}\quad\overset{\prime}{}\quad\overset{\prime}{}$$
Hir brighte heer was kembd, unstressed al
A.KN.2289

(5)   And, sóoth to séyn, vitaílle gréet plentee

B.ML.443

Ye shál be déed, by mýghty Márs the réde!

A.KN.1747

In these lines we use the / to indicate that the syllable so marked is a stress maximum; that is, it has greater stress than the surrounding syllables. Thus this mark expresses a relationship between the syllable and its environment. It says nothing whatsoever about the degree of stress of the syllable, merely that, whatever it is, it is greater than that of the two neighboring syllables.

Notice that as a consequence of our definition of stress maximum we find that in the first two lines of (5) the tenth position is not occupied by a stress maximum since the environment to the right of the tenth syllable contains no syllable. In the last line of (5), however, the extra-metrical syllable renders the first syllable of *réde* a stress maximum. The occurrence of a stress maximum in the tenth position will depend on whether there is an extra-metrical syllable added since Chaucer normally places a stress bearing syllable in the tenth position. This is related to Chaucer's rhyming practice which requires that only syllables bearing some degree of stress may rhyme. As a consequence, the stress maximum in the tenth position is without interest, and we shall ignore it in all subsequent scansions.

It should be obvious, however, that in the same way that a stress maximum does not occur in the tenth position of a line without an extra-metrical syllable, so, too, a stress maximum may never occur in the first syllable of a line. A consequence of this is that lines in which the first syllable bears stronger stress than the second syllable are as metrically regular as those in which the stronger stress falls on the second syllable. Examples of such lines are:

Greyhoundes he hádde, as swíft as fówel in flight

A.PROL.190

(6)   Képte hir estát, and bóth of yónge and old

                                            TC.1.130

           I, your Alcéste, whílom quéne of Trace

                                            LGW.432

The lines in (6), so-called "inverted first feet," are extremely common in Chaucer, so common in fact that prosodists have been forced to allow for them as being, not wholly iambic as are the lines in (5) but, nonetheless, "permissible deviations." In terms of the theory presented here, the lines require no special comment. They are a natural consequence of a theory which bases its prosodical analysis on stress maxima and even position occupancy. Indeed, this theory provides a natural explanation for the occurrence of lines such as these, while, in terms of a modified strict iambic pentameter theory, there is no more reason to expect to find this particular deviation than one, say, in which the second and fourth feet are occupied by trochees.

It was observed by Jespersen in his "Notes on Metre" that while iambic lines may have an inverted first foot, trochaic lines may not. Thus, for instance, Longfellow's

           Life is but an empty dream

is rendered unmetrical if the initial trochee is replaced by an iamb, as in

           A life's but an empty dream

or

           To live's but an empty dream

The reason for this asymmetry between iambic and trochaic lines is clear once it is realized that trochaic verses have stress maxima only on odd positions in the verse and that an initial iambic foot locates a stress maximum on the second (i.e., on an even) position in the line, in direct violation of the trochaic principle.

A further consequence of the rules, in particular of Principle 3, is that one would expect to find lines in which several even positions, namely, the 2nd, 4th, 6th, and 8th, are not occupied by stress maxima. Indeed, one ought to find lines in which this is true of only one even position per line and also of more than one. The only constraint is that a line in which all the even positions are unoccupied by stress maxima is highly unlikely in view of the natural stress patterns of the language. (We will see below, however, that such lines do occur.)

The lines in (6) already provide examples of verses without a stress maximum in the second position. To turn then to examples in which other even positions are not actualized by a stress maximum, we may cite the following lines:

Examples in the fourth position are:

$$\text{And wéddede the quéene Ypolita}$$

A.KN.868

(7) $$\text{In ármes, with a thóusand shíppes, wente}$$

TC.1.58

$$\text{To préye for the péple, and dó servyse}$$

D.SUM.1897

Examples in the sixth position are:

$$\text{Was sént to Córynthe in ful gréet honour}$$

C.PARD.604

(8) $$\text{That whílom jápedest at lóves péyne}$$

TC.1.507

$$\text{That Í wol létte for to dó my thynges}$$

B.NP.4279

Examples in the eighth position are:

$$\text{And whén he cám, hym háppede, par chaunce}$$

C.PARD.606

(9)   Of yónge fólk that haúnteden folye

C.PARD.464

The dróghte of Márch hath pérced to the roote

A.PROL.2

The careful reader may, at this point, wonder about the first line in (7). Thus the proper name *Ypolita* is not shown above with a stress maximum on the antepenultimate syllable so that, in effect, this line is actually an example of a line without stress maxima in the fourth and eighth positions. Our position on this question must remain open. It strikes us as reasonable that *Ypolita* would contain a secondary stress on the antepenultimate syllable. Indeed, in polysyllabic words in general one would expect to find in Middle English as in contemporary English secondary stress placement elsewhere in the word. The difficulty is that our only source of stress in words is the Romance stress rule (see above) which supplies primary stress only. Therefore, it is impossible to say with certainty (though quite possible to conjecture) that words like *citrinacioun, superfluytee, abhominable, Ypolita,* etc., had two stressed syllables, perhaps by some rule similar to the rule which distributes two stresses in modern English in words like $\overset{2}{O}kla\overset{1}{h}oma, M\overset{2}{i}ssiss\overset{1}{i}ppi,$ or in words like $\overset{1}{h}urric\overset{3}{a}ne, \overset{1}{a}dvoc\overset{3}{a}te$ (verb). In view of this limitation on our knowledge of secondary stress placement in Middle English we shall take the conservative (and no doubt artificial) position that simple words are supplied with only a single stressed syllable. It should be pointed out, however, that if secondary stress placement is assumed to have been similar to that in contemporary English, this will not result in exceptional lines; rather lines supplied with secondary stress will simply require reclassification.

Consider, for example, the following line:

(10)   So dúl ys of his bestialite

TC.1.735

In terms of our convention this line exhibits a stress maximum in the second position only. If secondary stress were supplied, the word would be *bestiālite*. This would not make (10) a counter-example, but rather a line which exhibits stress maxima in the second, sixth, and eighth positions. In general, then, we shall ignore such alternative analyses especially since we have been unable to uncover lines which, when supplied with secondary stress, provide counter-examples to our theory.

We mentioned earlier that within the space of a verse the likelihood of finding phrases which contain only one linguistic stress is extremely small, and so with two stresses. As a consequence, lines lacking three stress maxima are not very common. The line in (10) above is a possible example of a line without a stress maximum in the fourth, sixth, and eighth positions.

Examples without stress maxima in the second, sixth, and eighth positions are:

By superfluytee abhominable

C.PARD.47

(11)   Of thy religioun and of thy bileeve

G.SN.427

And of oure silver citrinacioun

G.CY.816

(Notice that if *superfluytee* is stressed *superfluytee,* a possible option in Chaucer, then the first line in (11) will be reclassified as exhibiting no stress maxima in the second, fourth, and eighth positions.)

Lines without stress maxima in only two even positions are far more common.

Examples without stress maxima in the sixth and eighth positions are:

Nis nat to yow of reprehencioun

TC.1.684

(12)   And how this town come to destruccion

TC.1.141

In so unskilful an oppynyon

TC.1.790

Examples of lines without stress maxima in the fourth and eighth positions are:

In Southwerk at the Tabard as I lay

A.PROL.20

(13)   The ravysshing to wreken of Eleyne

TC.1.63

The smyler(e) with the knyf under the cloke

A.KN.1999

Examples of lines without stress maxima in the fourth and sixth positions are:

Cucurbites and alambikes eek

G.C.Y.794

(14)

As licour out of alambik, ful faste

TC.4.520 [18]

Examples of lines without stress maxima in the second and eighth positions are:

And for the trouthe I demed in his herte

F.SQ.563

(15)   And by his sýde a swérd and a bokeler

A.PROL.112

And on the daúnce he goóth with Canacee

F.SQ.277

Examples of lines without stress maxima in the second and sixth positions are:

"Nabugadónosor was gód," seyd(e) he

B.MK.3752

(16)   This Pandarús so desiroús to serve

TC.1.1058

Whan that Aprílle with his shoúres soote

A.PROL.17 [19]

(Notice that in the second line of (16) one might want to read *Pandarus* with initial stress, but this reading would spoil the internal rhyme *Pandarus* : *desirous*.) [20]

There is a second issue with respect to secondary and lower stress raised by the examples in (15) as well as the last two lines in (7), the last line in (9), the last two lines in (11), and the last line in (16). All of these lines contain a preposition or pronoun which has not been treated as a stress maximum. It is clear that there is a fundamental distinction between major categories like Noun, Adjective, Adverb, and Verb on the one hand, and minor categories like conjunction, preposition, pronoun, article, and certain verbs like *to be* on the other. It is also clear that major category words always bear stress. But the facts are not so clear when we deal with the minor categories. Thus the rhyme evidence of Chaucer suggests that certain words like *the* and *a* never bear stress, while certain other words like *to, so, by,* and *he* do bear stress, at least in certain circumstances.[21] Since we do not at the moment see any way in which a definitive judgment can be made with respect to the relative stresses among words which belong to the minor categories, we have assumed that all of them bear the same degree of stress, whatever that may be.

Needless to say, further research may require that our views be modified. It is also true that contextual factors may provide a guide as to stress of minor category words. In all of the examples cited above, however, the context of the lines seems to be quite neutral with respect to the relevant minor category items. But it is worth mentioning here that a modification which demands that *to,* under normal stress, be given a greater linguistic stress than *and* or *the* (as in the last line in (9) above) does not render the lines in question exceptional; instead the lines need be only reclassified.

In the lines in (6) through (16) we have not found certain combinations of even position without stress maxima by virtue of linguistically determined weak or unstressed syllables being adjacent to one another. There are fourteen possible combinations of even positions 2 through 8 being occupied and/or unoccupied by stress maxima. We have been able to find examples for eleven of those possible combinations. The combinations for which we have been unable to find examples are: (a) lines without stress maxima in positions 2, 4, 6, and 8; (b) lines without stress maxima in positions 2, 4, and 6; (c) lines without stress maxima in positions 2 and 4. The absence of (a) and (b) type lines is probably due to their rarity in the language. That is, in a space of ten syllables one is likely to find at least three stresses but rarely less. The absence of (c), however, is suggestive. It may be accidental. On the other hand, it may be that Chaucer consciously avoided lines in which the 2 and 4 positions were both unoccupied by stress maxima, perhaps because of the weak onset imparted to such lines. In this case the absence of all three types would be explained as violations of this added constraint. We shall merely suggest the possibility of incorporating some such stipulation into Principle 3.

Up to this point we have dealt with even positions occupied by unstressed or weakly stressed syllables rather than by stress maxima. There is, however, a second way in which even positions may be unoccupied by stress maxima; namely, when a major syntactic boundary intervenes between two metrical positions.[22] We shall say that neutralization of stress takes place when two main stresses are separated by a major syntactic boundary, and we shall attempt to demonstrate that, like the so-called inverted first foot, neutralization is also a consequence of the theory presented here while it gives rise to a host of examples which, in terms of the strict (or modified) iambic pentameter theory must be treated as deviations. We shall begin by citing examples of neutralization.

Examples of neutralization between the second and third positions are:

$$\overset{1}{\text{By}} \overset{1}{\text{God}}, \text{right in my} \overset{/}{\text{litel}} \overset{/}{\text{closet}} \text{ yonder}$$

(17)   TC.3.663

$$\overset{1}{\text{And}} \overset{}{\text{seyd(e)}}, \text{``} \overset{1}{\text{Here}} \text{ at this} \overset{/}{\text{closet}} \overset{/}{\text{dore}} \text{ withoute}$$

TC.3.684

An example of neutralization between the fourth and fifth positions due to a preceding parenthetical phrase is:

(18) $$\text{Therfore, as frend,} \overset{1}{\text{fullich}} \overset{1}{\text{in}} \overset{}{\text{me}} \overset{/}{\text{assure}}$$

TC.1.680

Examples of neutralization between the sixth and seventh positions due, respectively, to the major break between an introductory adverbial clause and the following (elliptical) main clause and between two coordinate sentences are:

$$\text{And} \overset{/}{\text{whan}} \text{ youre} \overset{/}{\text{prey}} \text{ is} \overset{1}{\text{lost}}, \overset{1}{\text{woo}} \text{ and penaunces}$$

(19)   TC.1.201

$$\text{Love hath} \overset{/}{\text{byset}} \text{ the} \overset{1}{\text{wel}}; \overset{1}{\text{be}} \text{ of good cheere!}$$

TC.1.879

Now notice that whereas all of the above are treated as "acceptable complications of the norm" in the strict (or modified) view of iambic pentameter, they are perfectly regular in terms of the view presented here.

Thus Principle 3 asserts that a stress maximum may only occupy an even position within the verse, but that *not every even position need be so occupied*. And in all of the above this requirement is met. Consider, for example, the second line in (19):

Love hath byset the wel; be of good cheere!

In this line the seventh position is occupied by a strongly stressed syllable. But our theory states not that odd positions may not be occupied by strongly stressed syllables, but only that odd positions may not be occupied by stress maxima. And in the above line we see that the strongly stressed syllable in the seventh position is not a stress maximum since it is not preceded by a syllable of lesser stress. The important point here, however, is that the reason that the seventh position is preceded by a position containing a syllable with equal (that is, neutralizing) stress is that there is a major syntactic boundary intervening between the two positions.

What Jespersen termed "pauses" (see note 22) are, in fact, major syntactic breaks within the line. More often than not they are represented orthographically by commas, semi-colons, or colons. Further, it is a fact about the rules of English stress placement that they operate within but not across major syntactic breaks. Thus stress subordination will be found within major categories but not across major syntactic breaks. For this reason, it is only at "pauses" that one will find two equal stresses back to back, i.e., absence of stress subordination. Examples of major syntactic breaks are the breaks between an interjection and the following phrase as in (17), or between a phrase of direct quotation and the following direct quote as in (17), or between a parenthetical expression and the following clause as in (18), or between the clauses in a complex sentence such as, for example, the sentence we have just considered.[23]

A particularly striking case of neutralization due to lack of stress subordination across major syntactic breaks is items in a series. Consider, for example, the following well-known line in Chaucer:

(20)   As ook, firr(e), birch, asp(e), alder, holm, popler

A.KN.2921

which is reminiscent of the following line from Milton:

(21)   Rocks, caves, lakes, fens, bogs, dens and shades of
death.

In both of these lines the linguistic stresses in the even syllable positions are neutralized by the preceding and following stresses in the first six positions so that the first six positions contain no stress maxima. These lines are precisely like those in (6) and (16). Thus (20) like all of the preceding lines with internal neutralization is a perfectly regular though more complex consequence of the theory of prosody presented here.

Other examples which may be added to (20) are:

That hot, cold, hevy, lyght, moyst, and dreye

(22)   PF.380

Yong, fressh and strong in armes desirous

F.SQ.23

(The first of these is a headless line, for which see below.)

Examples of neutralization between the first and second positions which are, more often than not, due to initial interjections are:

Lo, he that leet hymselven so konnynge

TC.1.302

(23)   O, Salamon, wys and richest of richesse

E.MCH.2242

O wombe! O bely! O stynking cod

C.PARD.534

There is, however, an environment in which neutralization may come about without the intervention of a syntactic boundary. We noted earlier (see note 2) that, unlike American English which exhibits subordination in noun phrases composed of an adjective + noun, contemporary British English shows level stress in these constructions. Assuming, then, the absence of stress subordination in adjective + noun phrases in Chaucer, one ought to expect to find lines in which either member of such constructions may occupy an even or an odd position in the line. (This is so since, given a sequence *old man* with level stress, namely $\overset{1}{old}\ \overset{1}{man}$, neither word may be a stress maximum.) And, indeed, we find this to be the case.

Examples of neutralization in noun phrases are:

$$\text{The M}\overset{/}{\text{i}}\text{llere w}\overset{/}{\text{a}}\text{s a st}\overset{1}{\text{o}}\text{ut c}\overset{1}{\text{a}}\text{rl for the nones}$$

A.PROL.545

$$\text{A g}\overset{2}{\text{o}}\text{od W}\overset{2}{\text{i}}\text{f w}\overset{/}{\text{a}}\text{s ther of bis}\overset{/}{\text{i}}\text{de Bathe}$$

(24)   A.PROL.445

$$\text{All}\overset{/}{\text{a}}\text{s! a f}\overset{2}{\text{o}}\text{ul th}\overset{2}{\text{y}}\text{ng }\overset{/}{\text{i}}\text{s it, by my feith}$$

C.PARD. 524

$$\text{A w}\overset{2}{\text{y}}\text{s w}\overset{2}{\text{o}}\text{mman wol b}\overset{/}{\text{i}}\text{sye hire }\overset{/}{\text{e}}\text{vere in oon}$$

D.WB.209

Lines such as those in (24) are quite common in Chaucer. Further, making the natural assumption that level stress was characteristic of British English from Chaucer to the present, it ought to be the case that such lines occur throughout English poetry and this, too, seems to be true.[24]

We have seen that all of the lines discussed in (5) through (24) are regular lines in terms of our principles. We have also seen that whereas (5) contains the most neutral actualization of the metrical pattern, (6) through (24) exhibit more complex actualizations of the pattern. These are lines characterized by even positions which are not actualized by stress maxima, either because of neutralization or because of the adjacency of syllables with linguistically determined weak stress. The number of metrical lines of this type is extremely large. We have already seen examples of many of them above. A particularly good example of the interaction of these phenomena is the following line which, from the point of view of the strict (or modified) iambic pentameter theory, would be wildly deviant:

(25)   "Knowe ich hire aught? For my love, telle me this.

TC.1.864

This example as well as those in (6) through (24) should be sufficient to illustrate the manner in which a variety of complex lines may result from the alternatives provided by our principles.

METRICAL POSITIONS

Up to now we have focussed our attention on the character of the stress maxima in Chaucer's iambic pentameter line. We have in general chosen as our examples lines in which there is a one to one correspondence between syllables and positions. But there are other mappings possible. Thus Principle 1 states that the iambic pentameter line consists of ten positions, and Principle 2 states that a position, normally occupied by a single syllable, may, under certain conditions, be left vacant or, under yet different conditions, be occupied by more than a single syllable. Let us turn to the condition under which a position may be occupied by no syllable.

HEADLESS LINE

A zero syllable may occur only in the first position in a line. Such a line is called a headless line. An example of such a line is:

(26)   Twenty bookes clad in blak or reed

A.PROL.294

In this line the first phonetically realized syllable is, in fact, in the second metrical position. The first position has been realized by zero. Notice also that in this line the second metrical position is realized by a syllable which does not constitute a stress maximum since it is not surrounded by syllables of lesser stress.

An example of a headless line with the second position occupied by a weakly stressed syllable in contrast to (26) above is:

(27)   Of that wórd took héde Troilus

                                                    TC.1.820

An often cited line of Chaucer which is relevant here is the well-known Parson's adage:

(28)   That if gold ruste, what shal iren do?

                                                    A.PROL.500

A possible reading is to treat *ruste* as dissyllabic. The stress contour of *gold ruste* would be $\overset{2}{gold}\ \overset{1}{ruste}$ and the line would be a straightforward example of the Chaucerian iambic without a stress maximum in the second position. But this violates the sense of the line and the clear contrast implied between *gold* and *iren*. Thus, without dealing here with the mechanism whereby emphatic stress may be assigned to any word in a line,[25] we shall simply assert that $\overset{1}{gold}\ \overset{2}{ruste}$ is what the line requires. We shall read (28) as follows:

               That if góld rust(e), whát shal íren do?

That is, we take it as a headless line without a stress maximum in the second position. (We assume *ruste* to be monosyllabic by operation of the final –e dropping rule.)

DISSYLLABIC POSITIONS: CONDITION 1

No discussion of the Chaucerian line can be complete without a discussion of the metrical status of several lines which are, in traditional terms, viewed as undergoing various processes of syllable reduction such as elision, apocope, aphesis, syncope, etc. What is essentially at issue in dealing with these lines is the question of what constitutes a metrical position for Chaucer. To begin with, notice that the strict iambic pentameter view described earlier is quite explicit about this question. It states that a metrical position must be occupied by a single syllable. As a consequence, when faced with lines like:

(29)

> With a thredbare cope, as is a povre scoler
>
> A.PROL.260
>
> And leyde it above upon the myddeward
>
> G.CY.1190

it is necessary to recognize them as hypermetrical lines since a mapping of unstressed syllables and stressed syllables into the iambic foot results in an extra syllable being left over. In the first line in (29) the strongly stressed syllable position of the iamb is actualized by the first element of *thredbare*. Thus the weakly stressed position of the iamb must be supposed to consist of two syllables, namely *with a*. But because this violates the canon of one position, one syllable, scholars have either treated the line as irregular or, as did Ten Brink, emended it to read *with thredbare cope*.

The important point to keep in mind, however, is that the one position, one syllable doctrine is an hypothesis and no reasons are given why it should be honored. There is, however, a suspicion that the reason for its widespread acceptance is due to a prior assumption. The effect of this doctrine is essentially to allow there to be a one to one mapping between the theoretical entities proposed and the phonological entities which actualize them. But there is no reason why there should be such a relationship between observables and the theoretical constructs which explain their behavior. In fact, in the spoken language the assumption of such a relationship is clearly false.[26] One consequence of assuming a one to one relationship between constructs and their phonetic realizations is to confuse two issues which ought to be kept clearly apart. The first issue is what constitutes the metrical structure of a given line. The second issue is how a given line should be performed. Thus when Paull Baum (*Chaucer's Verse* [Durham, N.C.] p. 65) comments on a line like:

(30)   Wyd was his parisshe and houses fer asonder

A.PROL.491

asking whether it is better to "squeeze *parisshe* down to one syllable than to welcome the anapest," he is confusing the issues. The question of squeezing *parisshe* down is a question of performance. We shall say nothing here about how this and similar lines are to be performed. Rather we shall consider only the first issue, namely whether there is some systematic way of determining what syllables may occupy a single position from a metrical point of view.[27]

We have already seen that the realization of a position as zero is possible only when that position is the initial position of a verse. We have also asserted that any position may be occupied by a single syllable. Using the symbol ⌒ to mark the domain of a position, we see that the third line of (5) has each of its metrical positions actualized by a single syllable, thus:

(31)   Ye shal be deed, by myghty Mars the rede!

A.KN.1747 [28]

But now consider:

And bathed every veyne in swich licour
(32)   A.PROL.5

O, Salamon, wys and richest of richesse

E.MCH.2242

Here if we could treat the last two syllables of *every* and the last two syllables of *Salamon* as occupying a single position, these lines would be quite regular. Otherwise they would have to be treated as exceptions since they would exhibit stress maxima in odd positions. Notice that in these lines the relevant sequences are *–ery* and *–amon;* that is, an unstressed vowel followed by an unstressed syllable.

Other lines which would be quite regular if there were a principled way of assigning such sequences to a single position are well-known. Among them are:

Of Éngelónd to Cáunterbúry they wende

A.PROL.16

(33)   To Cáunterbúry with fúl devóut coráge

A.PROL.22

A líkerous móuth moste hán a líkerous tayl

D.WB.466

If the lines could be treated with *–bury* and *–erous* constituting single positions then again the lines would be restored to regularity.

We mentioned earlier that there were certain conditions according to which a sequence of syllables was assigned to a single metrical position. As a first approximation of one of these conditions, we formulate the following:

CONDITION 1

Within the same word an unstressed vowel followed by a liquid or nasal followed by another unstressed vowel may constitute a single metrical position.

By *Condition 1* all of the examples in (32) and (33) are rendered regular. Thus, *–ery, –amon, –ury,* and *–erous* constitute single metrical positions by *Condition 1.* But now consider the following set of examples:

And spécially from évery shíres ende

A.PROL.15

(34)   Of thy religíoun and of thy bileeve

G.SN.427

O háteful hárm! condícion of poverte

B.ML.99

In these lines we have in words like *specially, religioun,* and *condicion* sequences of unstressed vowels but without an intervening liquid or nasal; thus –*io*– and –*ia*–. If these sequences could be assigned to a single position (in the fashion indicated in (34) above), then regularity would be restored to these lines as well. We can do this by making a simple adjustment to *Condition 1.* Where it now specifies that two unstressed vowels must be separated by an intervening liquid or nasal, we simply stipulate that two unstressed vowels may but need not be separated by an intervening liquid or nasal. Thus the condition now appears as:

CONDITION 1¹

Within the same word an unstressed vowel followed by an optional liquid or nasal followed by another unstressed vowel may constitute a single metrical position.

There is, however, a strong similarity between *Condition 1¹* as now stated and the traditional concept of vowel elision. Since the latter deals with final vowels in words which are followed by vowel initial words, all that needs be done to *Condition 1¹* is to drop the requirement that it may only apply within the same word and sequences like *many a, glori(e) and,* etc., may be analyzed as *many a* and *glori(e) and,* etc. Since elision may also occur before an *h*– initial word, a sequence like *contrari(e) hire* would be analyzed as *contrari(e) hire.* Indeed, that *Condition 1¹* should be so altered is suggested by the following lines which require analyses like the above:

And many a breem and many a luce in stuwe

A.PROL.350

(35)   With múchel glóri(e) and greet solémpnytee

A.KN.870

        To eschúe, and by hire contrári(e) hire opprésse

G.SN.4 29

Notice that by extending *Condition 1¹* to operate across word boundary, a line like the following is rendered perfectly regular:

        Of hire comýnge and eek of his also

TC.3.1675

In this line a final *–e* on *comynge* is necessary in order to achieve penultimate stress by the Romance stress rule ,while the fact that the final *–e* is followed by a vowel initial word insures that *–e and* will be assigned to a single position by *Condition 1¹*.[30]

    In a line like:

        And sétten týme of métyng éft yfeere

TC.3.1712

the initial stress on *metyng* indicates that the final *–e* has been dropped prior to the operation of the Romance stress rule. Thus, in this line, there is no final *–e* which can occupy a single position with *eft*. Notice that *tyme of* is ambiguous since it may represent *tym(e) of* with the prior operation of the rule which drops final *–e* or else *tyme of* without the prior operation of that rule with *–e of* assigned to a single position by *Condition 1¹*.

    Condition 1¹ is almost in final form. There are, however, certain lines which indicate that it must be modified still more. Consider the sequence *to eschue* in the last line of (35). *Condition 1¹* requires that an unstressed vowel be followed by another unstressed vowel. But we have already seen earlier that *to* may indeed bear a certain degree of stress. Thus, it is possible that some condition other than lack of stress is sufficient for the assignment of more than one syllable to a single position. Consider, for example, the following lines:

(36)

And where they engendred and of what humour

A.PROL.421

To eschue, and by hire contrari(e) hire oppresse

G.SN.4

In the first line we should like our condition to treat *they engendred* as *they engendred,* and *to eschue* as *to eschue.* As *Condition 1¹* now stands it will not provide these analyses since *they* and, very likely, *to* have some stress. But notice that in each case the sequences to be analyzed do not involve stress maxima.

Thus, if we were to drop the requirement in *Condition 1¹* that both relevant vowels must be unstressed, then the sequences discussed above will automatically be assigned to a single position. We shall reformulate *Condition 1¹,* therefore, as:

CONDITION 1

Two vowels may constitute a single position provided that they adjoin, or are separated by a liquid or nasal or by a word boundary which may be followed by *h–* and provided that at least one of the vowels is a weakly stressed or unstressed vowel.

As now stated, *Condition 1* will not only handle the sequences discussed in (32) through (35), but it will also account for those in (36). In particular, *they en–* and *to es–* are single positions by this condition.[31] Note also that neither position is occupied by a stress maximum since neither syllable of the dissyllabic positions is surrounded by syllables of lesser stress.

Since *Condition 1* allows an optional sonorant, word boundary, and *h–* to intervene between two vowels, the sequence *–er his* constitutes a single position, neither syllable of which is a stress maximum, in the following line:

(37)   Withoute bake met(e) was never his hous

A.PROL.343

Up to now the examples have dealt with *Condition 1* producing dissyllabic positions composed of syllables which were not stress maxima. It is equally possible, of course, to have such dissyllabic positions occupied by stress maxima. That is to say, there are lines in Chaucer which illustrate the operation of *Condition 1* to yield dissyllabic even positions occupied by a stress maximum. Consider, for example, the following:

And his comynge unwist is to every wight

TC.3.912

And Phyllis also for Demophoun

BD.727

(38)   Trille this pyn and he wol vanysshe anon

F.SQ.328

The cause y-told of hir comynge, the olde

TC.4.141

Wyd was his parisshe and houses fer asonder

A.PROL.491

In the first line of (38) *to ev–* constitutes a single position by *Condition 1* and, since *ev–* contains greater stress than the surrounding syllables, it constitutes a stress maximum. Thus, the eighth position is both dissyllabic and occupied by a stress maximum. The line also requires penultimate stress on *comynge* which can only be achieved if the final *–e* has not been dropped. But since *–e un–* constitutes a single position by *Condition 1* which does not contain a stress maximum, this causes no difficulty. Finally, the sequence *–ery* in *every* is also a single position by *Condition 1,* which is not occupied by a stress maximum so that the first line is quite regularly iambic.

In the second line in (38) *Demophoun,* rhyming with *Jasoun,* bears final stress. But *Demo–* constitutes a single position by *Condition 1* not occupied by a stress maximum.[32] The third line in (38) contains a zero first position and is, therefore, headless. But notice that by *Condition 1 vanyssh(e)* constitutes a single position. Moreover, the position contains a stress maximum. (Whether the final *–e* was dropped by the final *–e* dropping rule or whether it is to be treated as a single position with the following *a–* does not matter here.)

The fourth line in (38) requires a final *–e* in *comynge* in order to yield the appropriate penultimate stress in *comynge* which will preserve the iambic character of the line. But notice that the *–e* is not subject to *Condition 1.* However, the sequence *the olde* is a single position and *olde* is a stress maximum.

The fifth line in (38) contains the word *parisshe* which may be treated as a single position by *Condition 1* and the first syllable of which constitutes a stress maximum, regardless of whether the final *–e* has been dropped or not since a vowel initial word follows.

One final example of a line which contains a dissyllabic position should suffice. Consider the last line in (36) above:

To eschue, and by hire contrari(e) hire oppresse

We have already seen that *to es–* is a single position by *Condition 1.* But now consider *contrarie hire.* We must first assume that the final *–e* has dropped in order to yield initial stress on *contrari* and maintain the iambic character of the line. But the sequence *–i hire* may also constitute a single metrical position by *Condition 1.* Finally, since *hire* is surrounded by completely unstressed syllables, and since it very likely bears some degree of stress, it is probably a stress maximum. Thus *–i hire* constitutes a single metrical position by *Condition 1* and is occupied by a stress maximum.

DISSYLLABIC POSITIONS: CONDITION 2

There is one more condition for position assignment. The evidence for this condition is contained in the following lines:

"But we were lever(e) than al this toun," quod he

A.MIL.3751

Turne over the leef and chese another tale

A.MIL.3177

(39)   The cook yscalded, for al his longe ladel

A.KN.2020

Thow hast translated the Romauns of the Rose

LGW.225

In many places were nyghtyngales

RR.657

In these lines an unstressed or weakly stressed monosyllabic word is preceded by an unstressed syllable; in particular, *–er,* the past tense *–ed,* and the plural *–es.* We can set up a second condition for position assignment which would say something like the following:

CONDITION 2[1]

An unstressed or weakly stressed monosyllabic word may constitute a single position with a preceding unstressed or weakly stressed syllable.

So stated, *Condition 2[1]* accounts for *–er, than, –er the, –ed for, –ed the, –es of,* and *–es were* as constituting a single position. Moreover, all the positions are without stress maxima. Without *Condition 2[1]* the lines in (39) would have to be treated as ir-regular. But there are other lines which *Condition 2[1]* also renders regular. Thus the following illustrate the assignment of the verbal endings *–eth* and *–est* to a single metrical position along with the following weakly stressed monosyllabic word:

And Émely(e) hym lóveth so téndrely

A.KN.3103

(40)

No man háteth his fléssh, but in his lyf

E.MCH.1386

If thou lóvest thyself, thou lóvest thy wyf

E.MCH.1385

In these lines *–eth so, –eth his,* and *–est thy* occupy single metrical positions by *Condition 2¹* which do not contain stress maxima.

Condition 2¹ now specifies that any unstressed or weakly stressed monosyllabic word may constitute a single position with a preceding unstressed or weakly stressed syllable. But notice that the preceding syllable may in fact be a monosyllabic word and not necessarily an unstressed syllable which is part of a word. Thus *Condition 2¹* not only accounts for the examples in (39) and (40) but it also accounts for the following:

Of a sólempn(e) and a gréet fraternitee

A.PROL.364

As wél of this as of óther thýnges moore

D.WB.584

For hym was léver(e) háve at his béddes head

A.PROL.293 33

(41)

And álso wár him óf a significavit

A.PROL.662

And saugh his visag(e) al in an other kynde

A.KN.1401

I ne saugh this yeer so myri(e) a compaignye

A.PROL.764

And is also fair and fresh of flour

R.R.4333

This is al and som, he heeld virginitee

D.WB.91

The sequences of *a, as of, at his, of a, in an, I ne, And is,* and *This is* all constitute single metrical positions by *Condition 2¹* which are not occupied by a stress maximum. Thus all of the lines in (41), as well as those in (39) and (40), are regular.

Let us now return to the lines in (29). *Condition 2¹* will account for the first of these lines since it may assign *with a* to a single metrical position which is not occupied by a stress maximum. Thus:

With a thredbare cope as is a povr(e) scoler

is quite regular. (The adjective *povr(e)* is monosyllabic by operation of the final *-e* dropping rule.)

But now consider the second line in (29). As it now stands *Condition 2¹* will not apply to *leyde it* since *Condition 2¹* requires that the syllable preceding the weakly stressed word, in this case *it,* be unstressed or weakly stressed. But suppose we were to drop that requirement. Then *leyde it* would constitute a single position and, since *leyde* is a stress maximum, the position would be actualized by a stress maximum. Since this alteration in *Condition 2¹* does no violence to the examples discussed up to now, we shall adopt this modification. *Condition 2¹* now reads:

CONDITION 2

An unstressed or weakly stressed monosyllabic word may constitute a single metrical position with a preceding stressed or unstressed syllable.

By *Condition 2* the second line in (29) is treated as:

$$\overset{/}{\text{And}}\ \widehat{\overset{/}{\text{leyde it}}}\ \overset{/}{\text{above upon the}}\ \overset{/}{\text{myddeward.}}$$

Thus we see that *Condition 2*, like *Condition 1*, may operate to produce polysyllabic positions which may but need not be occupied by stress maxima.

Two lines which appear in every discussion of hypermetrical lines in Chaucer bear some comment. These are:

(42)

$$\widehat{\text{Pekke hem}}\ \overset{1}{\text{up,}}\ \overset{1}{\text{right as they}}\ \overset{/}{\text{growe, and}}\ \overset{/}{\text{ete hym in}}$$

                                          B.NP.4157

$$\widehat{\overset{/}{\text{Seven(e) hennes}}}\ \text{for to}\ \overset{/}{\text{doon al his pleasaunce}}$$

                                          B.NP.4056

In the first line the phrase *Pekke hem up* is the relevant phrase. Note, first, that *up* very likely bears greater stress than the preceding words just as it does in the modern English equivalent $\overset{2}{\text{pick}}\ \overset{3}{\text{them}}\ \overset{1}{\text{up}}$. By *Condition 2 hem* may be assigned as a single metrical position with the preceding *pekke* just as was done with *leyde it* in (29) above. But what of the stress maxima assignment? A major syntactic break exists between *up* and the following adverb *right*. Thus neutralization occurs and the *up* is not a stress maximum. But notice that *Pekke* also is not a stress maximum since it is not surrounded by syllables of lesser stress. Thus the line exhibits an interesting example of a polysyllabic first metrical position, occupied by *Pekke hem,* and neutralization between the second and third positions. The line is perfectly regular.

Now let us consider the second line in (42). The relevant phrase is *seven(e) hennes*. By *Condition 1* the sequence *–en henn–* may be assigned as a single metrical position since the two vowels are separated by a sonorant, a word boundary, and an *h–*. Moreover, *henn–* is a stress maximum. Thus the second position is occupied by a stress maximum and the line is regularly iambic. (We assume prior operation of the final *–e* dropping rule in *sevene*.)

One final line is worth noting. The single example of the proper name *Attilla* occurs in the line:

(43)   Looke, Attilla, the grete conquerour

C.PARD.579

If we suppose a single *–l–*, then the Romance stress rule provides initial stress as $\overset{1}{A}ttil(l)a$. In this case the line would exhibit neutralization between the first and second positions and is quite regular. If, on the other hand, the *l* is geminate, then the Romance stress rule provides penultimate stress as $A\overset{1}{t}tilla$. In this case *Condition 1* may not assign *–illa* to a single metrical position since it requires that there be a single intervening sonorant. However, *Condition 2* will assign *–a the* to a single metrical position and the position will not be occupied by a stress maximum. By this latter interpretation, the line is *headless*. Since we have no way of judging whether *Attilla* contains *–l–* or *–ll–*, we cannot choose. But both alternatives are regular within the framework of our principles.[34]

PHONETIC CHARACTER OF THE CONDITIONS

At this point the reader will have noticed that *Conditions 1* and 2, while explicitly non-phonetic, nonetheless bear a strong resemblance to certain optional phonetic rules of contemporary spoken English. Thus the sequence *I wol* which constitutes a single position by *Condition 2* may well have been pronounced as *I'll* by a contemporary reader of Chaucer. Similarly, the sequence *–ery* in *every* which constitutes a single metrical position by *Condition 1* is quite normally pronounced as a dissyllable in contemporary English. Indeed, in every example in the *Concordance* with the word *every* it is necessary to invoke *Condition*

1. On the other hand, there are occurrences of forms, such as *Canterbury,* in which the relevant sequence is sometimes a single position and sometimes not. Thus we have the following lines:

Of Éngelónd to Cáunterbúry they wende

(44)   A.PROL.16

That tóward Cáunterbúry wólden ryde

                                                                 A.PROL.27

Examples such as *every* and *–bury* indicate that it would be wrong to suppose that *Condition 1* and *Condition 2* had no phonetic counterparts in Middle English. On the other hand, examples such as *parisshe, vanisshe, Demophoun,* and *Phyllis* (see (38) above) indicate that it would be too strong to suppose that *Condition 1* and *Condition 2* were, in fact, phonetic conditions.[35] We shall not attempt to indicate which of the metrical options specified by our conditions were also phonetic options in Middle English.

Notice that we keep quite distinct cases of syncope in Middle English which, as indicated by the spelling, entail bonafide phonetic variants. Thus we suppose the phonetic doublet *comprende* beside *comprehende* in view of the following lines and their spellings:

As muche joie as herte may comprende

(45)   TC.3.1687

Than they kan in hir lewednesse comprehende

                                                                 F.SQ.223

Similarly, the following lines require doublets:

The god of love, a benedicitee

(46)   A.KN.1785

What! lyveth nat thy lady, bendiste?

                                                                 TC.1.780

Further, the well-known *bileeve* : *bleeve* and *coroune* : *croune*
doublets clearly indicate that we must suppose phonetic doublets
in dealing with lines containing these words.[36]

EXCEPTIONS

We mentioned earlier that the fundamental distinction which
a theory of prosody must make is that between metrical and
unmetrical lines. The theory which we have discussed does this.
Thus in terms of our theory the preceding sentence is unmetrical. However, one need not construct hypothetical exceptions. There are lines in Chaucer which, in terms of our theory,
must be deemed unmetrical. For example, consider the following
lines:

$$\text{Ful we}\acute{\text{e}}\text{l she so}\acute{\text{o}}\text{ng the servi}\acute{\text{c}}\text{e dyvyne}$$

(47)   A.PROL.122

$$\text{Arsenyk, s}\acute{\text{a}}\text{l arm}\acute{\text{o}}\text{nyak and br}\acute{\text{i}}\text{mstoon}$$

G.CY.798

In the first line of (47) the penultimate syllable of *servīce* is
stressed by the Romance stress rule. But observe that with this
stress the syllable becomes a stress maximum which occupies the
seventh position in violation of Principle 3. The alternative of
supposing that to the underlying form *service* the final *–e*
dropping rule and the vowel shortening rule have applied to
yield *servĭce(e)* which is stressed *servĭc(e)* by the Romance stress
rule does not help. This alternative requires that the line be read
as headless, but in this case, too, the first syllable of *servic(e)* is a
stress maximum occupying the seventh position in violation of
Principle 3.

In the second line in (47) we find the compound noun *brimstoon*. Its stress assignment, in accordance with English stress

subordination in such units, requires that we suppose a stress maximum in the ninth position in the line. Again this is a violation of Principle 3.

What these lines make clear is that there is a sharp line drawn, in terms of our theory, between metrical and unmetrical lines. (Indeed, the very concept of an exception to a theory has meaning only in terms of the theory itself.) From our point of view the lines in (47) are unmetrical. From some other point of view they may be perfectly regular. The crucial question, of course, is the number of exceptions which a theory must presuppose. The inadequacy of the strict iambic theory is that it must suppose a significant portion of lines in Chaucer to be unmetrical. Indeed, it is precisely for this reason that the theory is modified in order to avoid this intolerable supposition. But the modification assumes the form of a list of "permissible deviations" which fails to capture the features that these deviations have in common. For this reason we have rejected the modified iambic pentameter theory in favor of that presented here. But now we see that this theory also entails exceptions. The question is, whether the exceptions entailed comprise a significant portion of the lines in Chaucer. The answer is that they do not. Thus a random selection of one thousand lines in Chaucer yielded less than 1.0 percent exceptional lines. Such a percentage of exceptional lines seems tolerable in view of the exigencies of manuscript transmission, scribal error, and, finally, the possibility of poetic oversight, though, in principle, the latter seems to us a last recourse since it fails to do justice to the craftsmanship of a great poet.[37]

It would exceed the scope of this article and also be premature, to attempt to show how various poets throughout the history of English literature have made use of the set of principles outlined above. It is our contention, however, that these principles, first adhered to by Chaucer, have provided the system of prosody for a major portion of English poets. One of the things which a study of later poets would show is the way that these principles have been modified by a given poet. Thus one might expect to find that some poet used the same schema but allowed a stress maximum in, say, the ninth position, or else modified Principle 2 to exclude an initial zero position. Indeed, one would not be surprised to find a poet experimenting with several such modifications of the system.

CHAUCER'S ART POETICAL

We have seen that the language of Chaucer provides him with several stress doublets and that he utilized these for poetic effects (see pages 409–410 above). Additional examples of stress doublets in Chaucer are *dívers* beside *divḗrse, creatóur* beside *créatour, sécree* beside *secrḗe*. Chaucer makes use of these variants within the same line, balancing one variant, within the iambic pattern, against the other. Examples in which he manipulates the stressed variants within the line are:

In dívers árt and in divérs(e) fígures

D.FRI.1486

(48)

The créatour of évery creatúre

G.SN.49

Is of the sécree of secrées, pardée

G.CY.1447

O, Sálamon, wýs and ríchest of richésse

E.MCH.2242

Examples in which he makes use of stress for purposes of internal rhyme are also found:

(49)

Thanne spák Alcéste, the worthýeste queene

LGW.G.317

This Pándarús tho desiróus to serve

TC.1.1058

In these examples the rhyming syllables within the line all bear 1 stress regularly according to the rules of Middle English accentuation. (Notice, by the way, that the first line in (49) is not hypermetrical since *Condition 1* and Principle 3 allow us to treat *–yest* as a single position occupied by a stress maximum. Alternately the line may exhibit a dissyllabic fifth position without a stress maximum.)

An example of the fashion in which Chaucer manipulates stress, syntax, and phonology is contained in the following passage:

> Men reden nat that folk han gretter wit
> Than they that han be most with love ynome;
> (50)   And strengest folk ben therwith overcome,
> The worthiest and grettest of degree:
> This was, and is, and yet men shal it see

> TC.1.241–245

In the first line the comparative *grétter* is followed in the next three lines by superlative forms, namely *most, strengest, worthiest,* and *grettest*. The first two are clearly stressed *móst* and *stréngest*. But, as is often the case in Chaucer when he uses the same word or syntactic form in adjacent lines, he makes use of stress options to vary and make more interesting the repetitions. Thus the fourth line in (50) may be read as:

> The worthíeste and gréttest of degree

with Chaucer opposing stress variants in the same lines as in (48) above. Finally, notice the repetition of the consonant features of the superlative ending *–este* in the final line of (50), thus:

> This was, and is, and yet men shal it see.

and the obvious play between *worthiest* in the fourth line and *was and is* in the fifth line.

(Another example of his making use of stressed variants for purposes of variety and interest is contained in the passage (4) from the *Pardoner's Tale* cited earlier.)

Finally, consider the following stanza from Chaucer's *Complaint of Venus* in which he varies syntax and stress not only for interest but also as a subtle reinforcement of sense. The stanza appears in Robinson's edition of Chaucer in the following fashion:

> Now certis, Love, hit is right covenable
> That men ful dere abye thy nobil thing
> As wake abedde, and fasten at the table,
> (51)   Wepynge to laughe, and singe in compleynyng;
> And doun to caste visage and lokyng,
> Often to chaunge hewe and contenaunce
> Pleyne in slepyng, and dremen at the daunce,
> Al the revers of any glad felyng.

We propose first to read the seventh line as:

> Pleye in slepyng, and dremen at the daunce.[38]

Now, however, we notice a certain symmetry developing in the stanza. Thus in the same way that the seventh line begins with an infinitive followed by a prepositional phrase consisting of a preposition and a gerund, so, too, we find the fourth line ending in just that fashion, namely *singe in compleynyng*. Now we may ask whether the symmetry goes further. Thus the first part of the fourth line begins with a participial adjective *wepynge* followed by the infinitive *to laughe*. But when we look at the end of the seventh line we find *dremen at the daunce;* the symmetry is thus broken.

If, however, we look closely at the manuscript readings we find that one of them. MS.Arch.Seld.B.24, does, indeed, have a participial adjective in the second half of the seventh line. It reads:

> Pleye dremyng and slepyng at the daunce

With this as authority we may further modify the seventh line to read:

> Pleye in slepyng, and dremyng at the daunce.[39]

Now symmetry (chiasmus) is restored to the verses. Thus the fourth line begins as the seventh line ends and the fourth line ends as the seventh line begins. Indeed, the parts of the lines can be interchanged along the diagonals of an X.

Chaucer has developed, however, an even deeper symmetry among these lines. He has accomplished this by means of balancing infinitives against participial adjectives and gerunds in *–inge*. Thus both line four and line seven are not only reversals of one another, but they are also internally reversed as well. Line four begins with a participial adjective and an infinitive and ends with a reversal of this sequence, namely an infinitive and another *–ing* form, this one a gerund. Schematically it appears as:

adjective *–ing* plus infinitive . . .
infinitive plus gerund *–ing*

In line seven the mirror image is also retained with an infinitive followed by a gerund and ends with a gerund followed by a prepositional phrase. Its schematic structure is:

infinitive plus gerund *–ing* . . .
adjective *–ing* plus noun

Thus the symmetry which balances line four against line seven, also balances each line against itself.

Consider now the fifth and sixth lines of (51). These lines are identically constructed. Each contains an adverb and a compound infinitival phrase consisting of an infinitive and two nouns. But notice that the placing of two identical lines between four and seven is precisely the same sort of device as that of constructing lines four and seven as mirror images of one another. In other words, line four and line five are mirrored in this verse by line six and line seven, in the same fashion that the first halves of line four and line seven are mirrored by their second halves.[40]

Next let us turn our attention from the syntactic to the phonetic devices exhibited in these verses. We have seen above that Chaucer opposes stressed variants in the same line for the sake of variety. Here, too, we find such opposition. Thus in line four the form *wepyng* is clearly dissyllabic and must therefore be stressed *wepýng*. It is opposed, however, by the gerund *compleynýnge* which, because of its rhyme with *thýnge* and *lokýnge* is to be stressed *compleynýnge*. Thus the phonetic opposition of *wepýng* versus *compleynýnge* complements the syntax of this line whereby the first half opposes the second. In other words, in precisely the same way that the line is a syntactic mirror image, so too is it a phonological mirror image with respect to stress. It is scanned as:

$$\overset{/}{\text{We}}\text{pyng to }\overset{/}{\text{la}}\text{ugh and }\overset{/}{\text{si}}\text{nge in comple}\overset{/}{\text{y}}\text{nynge}$$

But now consider line seven in which the same phenomenon occurs, only this time with the *–inge* forms at the center of the opposition rather than at the extremes. It is scanned:

$$\overset{/}{\text{Ple}}\text{ye in }\overset{/}{\text{sle}}\text{pynge and }\overset{/}{\text{dre}}\text{myng at the }\overset{/}{\text{da}}\text{unce}$$

Not only is the stress pattern identical with line four, but it also opposes precisely the same elements, namely the *–inge* forms.

Thus, this stanza offers a complicated example of the way in which Chaucer manipulates the linguistic givens of his language for a poetic purpose. The obvious characteristic of these syntactic and phonological manipulations is that of opposition and, indeed, opposition of a special sort, namely reversal. And when one considers the sense of the stanza, Chaucer's intention becomes apparent. In these lines he is saying that the pride one pays for Love is that the normal world in which one lives is topsy turvy. Thus because of Love, one lies awake in bed, fasts when he should be eating, cries when he wants to laugh, sings when he wants to cry, plays while he is sleeping, and, at the dance, dreams instead of playing. Indeed, as Chaucer sums up at the end of the stanza, he suffers:

$$\text{Al the re}\overset{/}{\text{ve}}\text{rse of }\overset{/}{\text{a}}\text{ny }\overset{/}{\text{gla}}\text{d fe}\overset{/}{\text{ly}}\text{nge}$$

In other words, in this stanza Chaucer is manipulating sound, syntax, and sense by means of the devices available on their respective levels, to reinforce the central theme of the stanza, namely the reversal of feeling brought about by love, the familiar Petrarchan paradox.

If, then, we were to edit this stanza in terms of the theory of prosody, stress assignment, and the interpretation just presented, the stanza would appear as follows:

> Now certis, Love, hit is right covenable
> That men ful dere abye thy nobil thinge
> As wake abedde, and fasten at the table
> Wepyng to laughe, and singe in compleynynge,

And doun to caste visage and lokynge
Often to chaunge hewe and contenaunce
Pleye in slepynge and dremyng at the daunce,
Al the reverse of any glad felynge.

Appendix

The principle stated above may be formalized in the following fashion:

Branching rule

1. $V \rightarrow \# P_1 P_2 P_3 \ldots P_n \# (s\ (s)\ )$

    where V = verse
    P = position
    s = syllable
    \# = verse boundary
    ( ) = elements enclosed thus are optional; that is, may or may not be present
    n = the total number of positions in the line; in the pentameter line n = 10; in the tetrameter line n = 8, etc.

Substitution transformations

1. SD: $\# P_1 X$
    SC: $1\ 2\ 3 \rightarrow 1\ \emptyset\ 3$
    (optional transformation)

2. SD: $X P_n Y \# Z$

    SC: $1\ 2\ 3\ 4\ 5 \rightarrow 1 \begin{Bmatrix} S \\ S_a \\ S_b \end{Bmatrix} + (s)\ 3\ 4\ 5$

    where n = 2, 4, 6, and/or 8
    S = stress maximum
    S_a = neutralized syllable
    S_b = weakly stressed syllable equal to adjacent syllables in stress
    (s) = extra syllable assigned to P_n under *Conditions 1* and *2*.
    { } = one of items so enclosed must be substituted
    (obligatory transformation)

(For significance of this formalism see reference in note 25.)

We mentioned in the beginning of this article that a meter was an abstract pattern which the poet uses as a basis of selection to choose out of the infinitely many sentences of natural language those which qualify for inclusion in the poem. In the light of the above rules we now restate this view. The abstract pattern is defined by the branching rule. In particular there are three possible metrical patterns; one with no extra-metrical syllable, one with one such syllable, and one with two such syllables.

The substitution transformations state the conditions which any sentence or part of a sentence must meet in order to qualify as a realization of one of the patterns and therefore as a possible candidate for the iambic pentameter line.

Different branching rule and/or substitution transformations define different meters and metrical styles. Iambic tetrameter, for example, requires that $n = 8$ in the branching rule. A change in the second substitution transformation will change the podic composition of the line. Thus, for instance, by allowing stress maxima to occupy odd, rather than even, positions we obtain a trochaic rather than an iambic line. On the other hand, dropping the first substitution transformation eliminates headless lines. This substitution transformation may, therefore, be said to characterize the metrical style of the poet.[41]

NOTES

1. While this article deals primarily with iambic pentameter, we have quoted on occasion relevant examples from certain of Chaucer's works written in iambic tetrameter, in particular the *Romaunt of the Rose* (RR), the *Book of the Duchess* (BD), and the *House of Fame* (HF).

Abbreviations of titles throughout follow those of *A Concordance to the Complete Works of Chaucer and to the Romaunt of the Rose* compiled by John S. P. Tatlock and Arthur G. Kennedy (The Carnegie Institution of Washington, 1927). All quotations come from the *Concordance* from *The Complete Works of Geoffrey Chaucer*, ed. F. N. Robinson (Boston, 1933).

2. In American English the normal stress pattern in adjective + noun phrases is 2 1, thus *black bird, old man,* etc. Commentators on British stress, however, observe that in such syntactic units the stress distribution is level, *black bird* as opposed to *blackbird*. Thus Daniel Jones, *Outline of English Phonetics,* 9th ed. (Cambridge, 1960), §959 observes, "Foreign learners should note particularly the case of one word qualifying another. Both the

words have as a rule strong stress." In the ensuing examples of adjective +
noun phrases, he makes no distinction between the level of stress on either
constituent. This suggests that the subordination of the adjective stress to
the noun stress in noun phrases is a peculiarity of American English. In
what follows, then, we shall assume stress subordination in compounds but
level stress in noun phrases and the like. It will be seen below that this
assumption is consistent with the metrical practice of Chaucer and other
English poets. The assumption of the (American) 2 1 stress pattern in these
phrases renders a number of regular lines metrically deviant. Examples of
such lines will be found on pp. 385–386.

3. These facts are intended to convey a picture of English stress under
neutral emphasis. Thus in American English the noun phrase *black bird*
in a sentence such as "I saw a black bird" has the pattern 2 1. This is
not to say that the noun phrase could not, in such a sentence, receive a
1 2 stress pattern, prompted, for example, by a request for clarification:
"*What* color bird?" But such an emphatic stress pattern departs from the
normal distribution of stresses in simple declarative statements. In general,
we shall assume neutral stress distribution in the lines of verse which follow
unless there are strong contextual reasons for supposing otherwise.

4. See B. Ten Brink, *The Language and Metre of Chaucer*, 2nd ed. rev.
F. Kluge, trans. M. Bentinck Smith (London, 1901), §279.

5. For a discussion of this point see Morris Halle and Samuel Jay Keyser,
The Evolution of Stress in English (forthcoming).

6. For elision of *–e* before an *r* which separates unstressed vowels in
Milton, see Robert Bridges, *Milton's Prosody* (Oxford, 1921), pp. 29ff. See
also pp. 395ff. below for our treatment of such sequences in Chaucer. In the
matter of vowel elision as well as in certain others, Bridges arrived at
conclusions that are substantially identical with those presented here.

7. In this connection we cite the following passage from Robert Bridges'
A Letter to a Musician on English Prosody which, in our view, captures
precisely the role of prosody in poetry: "What, then, exactly is Prosody? . . .
it denotes the rules for the treatment of syllables in verse, whether they are
to be considered as long or short, accented or unaccented, elideable or not,
etc., etc. The syllables, which are the units of rhythmic speech, are by nature
of so indefinite a quality and capable of such different vocal expression, that
apart from the desire which every artist must feel to have his work consistent
in itself, his appeal to an audience would convince him that there is no
chance of his elaborate rhythms being rightly interpreted unless his treatment
of syllables is understood. *Rules must therefore arise and be agreed upon for
the treatment of syllables, and this is the first indispensable office of
Prosody*" (italics ours MH/JK). The essay from which this passage is drawn
is reprinted in a useful anthology edited by Harvey Gross entitled *The
Structure of Verse: Modern Essays on Prosody* (Greenwich, Conn., 1966), pp.
86–101.

8. As is frequently done; for example, by Seymour Chatman, "Robert
Frost's 'Mowing': An Inquiry into Prosodic Structure," *Kenyon Review*,
XVIII (1956), 421–438. "The present analysis attempts to describe the verse
line as it is actually 'performed.' It avoids the unfortunate assumption that
performances involve 'exceptions' to some kind of norm. In fact, it suggests
that the poem as document may be lifeless until it is actualized into sound
pattern. The analysis starts with the performance, not the norm; and it
suggests that the metrical tension of much successful verse lies in the poet's
subtle modification and evasion of the expected, *plus* the performer's keen-
ness in interpreting the poet's intentions."

9. Halle and Keyser, *The Evolution of Stress in English* (forthcoming).

10. The precise environment for shortening of long vowels in final syllables is slightly more complicated. Thus a long final vowel or a long vowel before a single final consonant may optionally shorten. A long vowel before more than one final consonant will not shorten, however. Thus *merci* and *licour* are subject to shortening; *servaunt* is not.

We argue in *The Evolution of Stress in English* that this rule was a native English rule which already existed in the language prior to the influx of Romance words. It is responsible for the short final vowels in words like *wisdŏm, stirrŏp* and *wurthlĭche* (from earlier *wisdom, stigrap,* and *wurthlic*). Romance words which entered the language simply fell within the domain of this rule.

11. Ten Brink, §257.

12. The enclosing of *e* in parentheses indicates that the rule which drops final *–e* has applied. Thus orthographic *coming(e) is* is phonetically *coming is.*

13. In the line *Ther maistow seen cominge with Palamon* the meter also requires that *Palamon* be treated as occupying two metrical positions. That this is permissible in Chaucer will be shown below (pp. 395ff.). The alternative which treats *cominge* with initial stress renders the line exceptional.

14. There are two other conceivable explanations for rhymes like *–inge* : *springe.* One is to deny the assumption that in Chaucer only stress bearing vowels may rhyme. But then the absence of rhymes like *the* : *he, an* : *man,* etc., would be merely a coincidence. The assumption that only stressed vowels ryhme offers a principled explanation for the absence of such rhymes.

The second possibility is to suppose that *–inge* bears a 2 stress. This is itself based upon the hypothesis that *–inge* bore 2 stress in OE. It seems to us that the view of 2 stress in *–ung* in OE is questionable. But even if one accepts that position, it is noteworthy that the ME reflex of OE *–ing/–ung* is *–ing (e).* The shift from $u \rightarrow i$ is commonly explained as due to alterations of vowel quality in unstressed syllables. (See Bruno Borowski, *Zum Nebenakzent beim altenglischen Nominal-kompositum* (Halle, 1921); Joseph Wright, *Middle English Grammar,* 3d ed. (Oxford, 1925), §134; Sievers-Brunner, *Altenglische Grammatik* (Halle, 1951), §142; Anm. and Alistair Campbell, *Old English Grammar* (Oxford, 1959), §§204.8, p. 383.) Thus the supposition that OE *–ung,* even if it did bear a 2 stress, became unstressed in ME accounts quite naturally for the shift from *–ung* to *–ing(e).* Otherwise the shift in vowel quality is quite inexplicable.

Yet a further argument against 2 stress in *–inge* is that it implies that the metrical behavior of *cominge*, etc., would be identical to compound nouns like *brimstoon*. This prediction, however, is not borne out. (See Halle and Keyser, *The Evolution of Stress in English,* chap. 1, forthcoming.)

15. The passage from the Pardoner's Tale constitutes a variation on Robinson's text based upon our view of the operation of final *–e* and its effect on stress placement. The reader will notice that in certain instances, in particular *thynge*, we assume a final *–e* which was not present in the nominative and accusative in Old English. We base our assumption of a final *–e* in *thynge* on the well-known occurrence in Chaucer of forms with inorganic *–e* extended to the nominative and accusative cases from the oblique cases. The evidence for such forms is cited in Ruth Buchanan McJimsey, *Chaucer's Irregular –E* (New York, 1942). With respect to *thynge,*

she states that no *–e* is required in 374 "easy scansions" and in 154 rhymes. She adds, however, that in 16 other scansions a reasonable metrical variation would allow a final *–e* and she also notes the *springe* : *thynge* rhyme in RR 2627 with *springe* in the infinitive. She further notes the line *Thynge that is to reprove* RR 7546 which is deviant without a final *–e*. Because she finds only 16 examples requiring final *–e*, she concludes that the statistical evidence legislates against *thynge* with an inorganic *–e*. This seems to us overly hasty in view of two facts. The first is the existence of inorganic *–e* in Chaucer in other nouns (for a list of which, see McJimsey, pp. 19–20). The second is the need for an optional *–e* dropping rule. If it were the case that every example of an *–ynge* rhyme could only be explained, according to us, by the assumption of an inorganic *–e* in the rhyme word, then our position would indeed be weakened. But a large number of *–ynge* rhymes are paired with infinitives and finite verb forms where the *–e* is historical. Thus the assumption of an inorganic *–e* does not seem at all implausible.

16. We have omitted the constraint that Chaucer's lines rhyme because it plays no role in what follows, though a complete list of Chaucer's principles must clearly include rhyme, as well as stanza construction, etc. The one aspect of rhyme in Chaucer which we have called attention to (see note 14) is that for two sequences to rhyme they must bear some degree of stress (as well as share a sequence of identical segments to the right of the stress bearing segment).

It will be seen that the principles outlined above may be readily formalized; cf. Appendix [above], where a formal statement of the principles may be found.

17. The concept of a more or less neutral actualization of a line is closely related to the concept of markedness in linguistics. (Cf. Noam Chomsky and Morris Halle, *The Sound Pattern of English* [New York, 1968].)

18. We assume a basic form *alambīk* which receives final stress by the Romance rule alone. Notice that the vowel shortening rule, if applied, would yield *alambĭk* which would be stressed *alambik* by the Romance stress rule.

19. Robert O. Evans, "Whan that Aprill(e)?" *Notes and Queries,* new series, IV (1957), 234–237, presents the results of an extensive manuscript comparison of the various readings for the first line of the Canterbury Tales. He points out that 8 mss. support the reading *Apríllĕ* but that this is by no means conclusive. He says (p. 237), "As there is no conclusive textual evidence, I submit that there is a strong possibility, even a probability that Chaucer intended the initial lines of the Prologue to be read as a regular decasyllable, perhaps with a trochaic substitution in the first foot." Moreover in Northern dialects of English the word is pronounced [a|prail] (cf. e.g., W. Grant and T. M. Dixon, *Manual of Modern Scots* [Cambridge, 1921], p. 62) pointing towards a historical antecedent with a tense ī.

20. Since *desirous* has a long ī (the simplex *desīr* rhymes with *shīre*, etc.), there are only two possible stress patterns, namely *desīrous* by the Romance rule alone, or *desĭrous* by the prior operation of the vowel shortening rule in final syllable before no more than a single segment. Only the former is possible in this line and this suggests that of the two stress options for *Pandarus*, the end stressed one is correct in view of the internal rhyme produced. (For a discussion of the stress options in proper nouns, see Halle and Keyser, *The Evolution of Stress in English* [forthcoming].)

21. Consider the three examples in the *Concordance* in which *to* occurs in rhyme. These are:

To do al that a man bilongeth to (E.Mch.1459)
That on a tyme seyde his maister to (G.Cy.1449)
And ful devoutly I prayed hym to (BD.771)

The most obvious fact about these three lines is that each ends with an inverted prepositional phrase. Thus the normal *bilongeth to a man* has become *a man bilongeth to, to his maister* has become *his maister to,* and *to hym* has become *hym to*. It is perfectly possible, then, that *to*, normally without stress, received stress as a result of this special inversion. Indeed, a phenomenon precisely like this occurs in modern English in a special construction in which inversion is quite regular. Consider, first, the sentence *John ate up the apple*. In this sentence the normal stress contour is some-

thing like *John ate up the apple;* that is, with *ate* receiving less stress than the adverbial *up* and *up* receiving less than the object noun *apple*. But notice that it is quite normal in English to invert the object noun phrase and the adverbial preposition to yield a sentence like *John ate the apple up*. Such an inversion also changes the stress contour, which is now something like

John ate the apple up. The important point here is that inversion has provided the adverbial preposition *up* with greater stress than it would have received without inversion. Without attempting to delineate the rules whereby stress is assigned in these two sentences in modern English, we draw attention to the fact that a rule which would provide a word with greater stress under inversion than it would normally receive is not without parallel. That *to* in each of its rhyming occurrences in Chaucer is the result of inversion is clear. That it receives stress as a result of inversion is plausible. Therefore, while we may take *to* to have a linguistically determined stress in Middle English, it is by no means clear that the evidence of rhyme forces us to do so under normal occurrences. The fact that prepositions were subject to the Great Vowel Shift lends further support to the assumption that *to* was stressed, since only stressed vowels were subject to Vowel Shift.

22. See Jespersen, for example, "Notes on Metre," *Linguistica* (Copenhagen, 1933), p. 255: "This leads us to another important principle: the effect of a pause: If I hear a syllable after a pause it is absolutely impossible for me to know whether it is meant by the speaker as a strong or as a weak syllable: I have nothing to compare it with till I hear what follows. And it is extremely difficult to say with any degree of certainty what is the reciprocal relation between two syllables separated by a not too short pause."

23. Wimsatt and Beardsley (p. 596) comment on the line *Wondring upon the word, quaking for drede* (E.Cl.358) as follows: "Here is a very special relation of phrase to meter. The double inversion, at the start of the line and again after the caesura, gives the two participial verbs a special quiver. But this depends on the fact that there *is* a meter; the inversions otherwise would not be inversions."

In terms of the principles outlined above, this line is perfectly regular. Indeed, it is precisely like the second line in (19) above. It exhibits a strongly stressed syllable in the first position and neutralization between the sixth and seventh positions. In other words, this line is a normal iambic line. Moreover, both lines are distinguishable from unmetrical, i.e., exceptional lines, such as, for example, the sentence on p. 368 above. The difference in complexity between the above line and neutral lines like those in

(5) is reflected in the fact that this line is derived by the later alternatives of Principles 1 through 3.

24. Several examples of lines from later poets are cited in Jespersen's "Notes on Metre" which indicate level stress. To quote just one from Shakespeare: *The course of true love never did run smooth* (Mids. I.I.134). Here, level stress in *true love* renders the line regular.

25. See, for example, Noam Chomsky, "A Transformational Approach to Syntax," *The Structure of Language,* ed. Jerry A. Fodor and Jerrold J. Katz (Englewood Cliffs, 1964), pp. 227ff.

26. A similar assumption about the relationship between the sounds of language, the phones, and the theoretical entities to which they correspond, the phonemes, has been assumed by many linguists. For a discussion see Noam Chomsky, "Current Issues in Linguistic Theory," in Fodor and Katz, pp. 93ff. Note also the statement by Bridges above "whether . . . [syllables] . . . are to be considered as . . . elideable or not . . . " (see note 7).

27. Notice, then, that it is no accident that the processes which scholars have assumed to make unruly lines regular have been phonetic processes, such as syncope, apocope, elision and the like. The reason for this is to preserve a one to one mapping between the phonetic line and the metrical structure, and this, as we have suggested, results in confusing the performance of a line with the structure of the line. In what follows we shall attempt to describe the conditions whereby syllables may participate in metrical positions.

We shall try to demonstrate that certain principles were used by Chaucer which determined the constituency of metrical positions in much the same way that analogous principles determined metrical constituency in classical poetry. The phonological and morphological constraints will be quite different, of course, but the conditions will function similarly. In precisely the same fashion as a weak position in a classical dactyl can be occupied by one or two syllables ($-= \smile \smile$), so a metrical position in Chaucer's pentameter can be occupied by one or two syllables. This, however, does not mean that in Chaucer's recitation a two syllable position was pronounced as a monosyllable any more than it means that two syllable positions in classical verse were pronounced as monosyllables.

28. In this line we have marked the domain of each position. In general this will not be necessary. In the lines which follow we shall only mark the domain of those positions which, by virtue of the conditions under discussion, are occupied by more than a single syllable. All positions occupied by a single syllable will be left unmarked.

29. In a count of the various elisions of final –*e* before a vowel or *h*– initial word in the prologue to the *Canterbury Tales,* Alexander Ellis, in his *Early English Pronunication,* V (London, 1869–1889), pp. 341ff., lists 315 as the total number of elisions of final –*e* before a following vowel initial word and 147 as the total number of final –*e* elisions before a following *h*– initial word. Thus it seems that *Condition 1* should be altered so as to apply across word boundaries.

30. For discussion of *also* see note 32.

31. The similarity between *Condition 1* and the classical conditions of elision, echthlipsis, and synaloepha is obvious.

32. There is some evidence which suggests that *also* might bear a 2 1 stress pattern in Middle English. Without attempting to resolve the issue here, note that even assuming a 2 1 stress pattern the line is regular since *Phyllis* may also constitute a single position (by *Condition 1*) occupied by

a stress maximum. Thus under the assumption of 2 1 stress in *also*, the line is scanned as:

And Phyllis also for Demophoun

33. This reading seems preferable to one which would treat *lever(e) have* in this fashion.

34. A great many of our examples have been drawn from commentaries by many scholars on Chaucerian prosody. The commentaries that we have examined include A. H. Licklider's *Chapters on the Metric of the Chaucerian Tradition* (Baltimore, 1910), Baum's *Chaucer's Verse* (Durham, N.C., 1961), as well as the studies by Ten Brink and A. J. Ellis cited above.

35. Licklider (p. 56) introduces a principle of "Resolution after development of liquid or nasal" to account for the lines in which these words occur. We have seen that *Condition 1* will account for these lines and a good many others besides. It is interesting to note, however, that Licklider does not treat the reduction in these words as phonetic. Thus, he is setting up conditions for position occupancy implicitly. He says of these forms, "Whether the atonic vowel ever completely disappears or not is hard to determine; it probably remains as a very light touch" (p. 56).

36. For further discussion of such doublets, see Licklider, pp. 71ff.

37. The difficulty that recourse to this principle can have is illustrated by Yvor Winters' comment on the Keats' line *Bright star, would I were steadfast as thou art:* ". . . however, in this line the stressing of *would* would result in an inverted foot in the second position, and although inversion is possible in this position, it is difficult and generally unlikely, so that we naturally expect the stress to fall on *I*, which likewise is the natural recipient of the rhetorical stress . . . but if, as in this line, the comparison is completed, an actual stress should fall on the second pronoun; but since this pronoun also is coupled with a verb which is mechanically its equal and on the basis of its inherent nature could as well take the accent, and since the foot ends the line, and a rhymed line at that, the accent must fall on *art*. *This blunder by Keats could scarcely have occurred as a result of his reading poetry in a dramatic fashion . . . and had he read the line dramatically he would have noticed the error*" (emphasis added). "The Audible Reading of Poetry," reprinted in the Gross volume (see note 7), p. 139.

But notice that the "unlikely inversion" which Winters rules out is precisely what the line requires since it allows for the natural comparison between *would* and *art*. Notice, also, that a stress on *would* is not difficult since it is neutralized by the syntactic boundary that separates it from immediately preceding main stress on *star*. Thus the line may be scanned as:
  1   1   1   /   1
Bright star, would I were steadfast as thou art with neutralization between the first, second, and third positions and with a stress maximum, the only one, occurring in the sixth position.

38. This proposal is, in fact, merely a restoration of the original manuscript readings. The line as restored appears, for example, in *A One-Text Print of Chaucer's Minor Poems,* ed. Frederick J. Furnivall (Chaucer Society, First Series 24, 61, London, 1868–1880). In 1888 the line is printed in this form in *Chaucer, the Minor Poems,* ed. W. W. Skeat (Oxford, Clarendon Press, 1888). In 1890 M. Piaget in his article "Oton de Grandson et ses Poesies," *Romania,* XIX (1890), 414, prints the original Granson ballads from which the *Compleynt of Venus* was freely translated by Chaucer. He

prints Chaucer's rendition alongside the French following ". . . l'excellente edition du Rev. W. Skeat . . . ." In 1892, however, Paget Toynbee in his *Specimens of Old French Poetry (IX–XV Centuries)* (Oxford, Clarendon Press, 1892) included the Granson ballads, and in a footnote on p. 492 he comments, "*Plaindre en dormant,* the reading, 'Pleye in sleping,' in the printed editions of Chaucer's version of this line, is an evident error for 'Pleyne in sleping,' the mark over the y in MS. (ŷ = yn) having been disregarded."

Toynbee's suggestion was duly noted by Skeat who, in his *Complete Works of Geoffrey Chaucer, Romaunt of the Rose and Minor Poems* (Oxford, Clarendon Press, 1894) alters his earlier reading and comments in a footnote on p. 561, "The French text shows that we must read *Pleyne,* not *Pleye; besides,* it makes better sense. This correction is due to Mr. Paget Toynbee; see his *Specimens of Old French,* p. 492."

Evidently the Toynbee suggestion has been followed ever since. Indeed, Robinson in his edition of Chaucer (p. 1038) lists the manuscript authorities, of which there are nine, and observes that all manuscripts (save one in which the first 44 lines are missing) contain the reading *pleye in slepyng.* Nevertheless, he reads *Pleyne in slepyng* on the basis of the French *Plaindre.*

The logic of this escapes us for two reasons. First, Chaucer's version is by no means a literal translation. Thus the fifth line of Granson's ballad is, "Baisser les yeux quant on doit regarder" but it appears in Chaucer as, "And doun to caste visage and lokyng." Similarly Granson's refrain, "Tout a rebours de ce qu'on vuelt trouver" is rendered by Chaucer as "Al the revers of any glad felyng." Thus the argument that the French contains *Plaindre* seems to us not a very strong one when applied to a poem so freely rendered by its translator.

Secondly, when one considers that every manuscript reading contains *pleye* and not *pleyne,* it seems impossible not to follow the manuscript readings. Indeed, since the nine manuscripts are not derived from the same stemma but are, in fact, seen as descending from three separate stemmata, the probability of supposing the same error to have appeared in all manuscripts is remarkably small. It seems to us, then, that we have no recourse but to restore the original manuscript readings *pleye in slepyng.* Moreover, as will be seen below, the original manuscript reading makes much the better sense.

39. The manuscript basis for this emendation is considerably weaker than for *Pleye in sleping.* If the emendation is accepted it will be seen that this passage illustrates a syntactic and semantic parallelism not unfamiliar to students of medieval rhetoric. If this emendation is not accepted, then the semantic parallel is the only one to be found in the passage. We shall opt for the full parallelism on the grounds that so slight an emendation, albeit with only meager manuscript support, yields an extremely complicated pattern which one cannot reasonably suppose is due to chance.

40. It is worth noting that, in order to achieve this effect, Chaucer has seriously altered the French original. Thus Granson's fifth line, "Baisser les yeux quant on doit regarder" appears in Chaucer as "And doun to caste visage and lokyng." Indeed, it seems reasonable to suppose that the resultant symmetry provides a natural explanation for the changes Chaucer incorporated into his translation.

41. This work was supported in part by the Joint Services Electronics Program under Contract DA36-039-AMC-03200(E): in part by the National Science Foundation (Grant GP-2495), the National Institutes of Health (Grant MH-04737-05), the National Aeronautics and Space Administration

(Grant NsG-496), and the U.S. Air Force (ESD Contract AF 19(628)-2487). The authors gratefully acknowledge the helpful comments of their colleagues, J. V. Cunningham, A. Grossman, Paul Kiparsky, and Haj Ross who have read earlier versions of this study. We would also like to give special thanks to M. Bloomfield, Angus McIntosh, and James Sledd.

22. *A GRAMMAR*
OF PROSODY

Joseph C. Beaver

In "A Grammar of Prosody," Joseph C. Beaver proposes stress
rules based upon Seymour Chatman's "syllable types" (see Selection 18) to complement the general metrical theory propounded
by Halle and Keyser in "Chaucer and the Study of Prosody," and
argues that the theory and the rules associated with it constitute claims about the poet's "metrical competence." Professor
Beaver suggests that trochaic meter is always more regular than
iambic meter because it is commonly written in shorter lines
(tetrameter or trimeter) which, whether iambic or trochaic, tend
to have a greater percentage of actualized stress maxima than
longer forms. He shows that a tendency to place actualized
stress maxima in certain positions in the line is an important
characteristic of metrical style. Joseph C. Beaver is professor
of American English and linguistics at Northeastern Illinois
State College.

In their recent study of Chaucerian meter, Morris Halle
and Samuel Jay Keyser propose a theory of prosody which they
hope may serve as a framework for the study of "a major portion
of English poets." [1] The rules of stress assignment and meter
they have discovered for Chaucer's iambic pentameter appear
to me quite convincing (with some minor reservations to be
discussed later), and metrical rules of this sort should be of considerable help in stylistic analysis, whether for individual poets
or for different periods of poetry. But I think the major role of

Joseph C. Beaver, "A Grammar of Prosody," *College English* XXIX
(January, 1968), pp. 310–321. Reprinted with the permission of the National
Council of Teachers of English and Joseph C. Beaver.

the Halle-Keyser rules (or, ultimately, more refined rules of this kind) will be to constitute essentially a grammar of meter, comparable to the generative grammarian's "rules of competence," which will determine (i.e., provide a metrical description of) what are metrical and what are unmetrical lines. And in this role, in addition to providing a basic framework for stylistic analysis, which may have to be supplemented with something comparable to "rules of performance," [2] such rules should be useful in providing explanations for metrical phenomena, and in determining various prosodic questions, some of major importance. For example, why has the decasyllabic line (iambic pentameter) been the overwhelmingly predominant vehicle for English verse? Or, alternatively, in what way does it provide the freedom and flexibility the poet obviously finds there? Why do shorter line lengths (tetrameter, trimeter) in duple meter appear to be so much more "rhythmic" than pentameter, exhibiting always a more insistent beat or accent? Why does trochaic meter appear more inflexible than iambic (i.e., why does it seem peculiarly beat-insistent, or, why does it show such a low tolerance for "irregular feet")? The purpose of the present article is to explore, in a preliminary way, some of these questions, to examine possible extensions of the rules Halle and Keyser have proposed, to suggest a different set of stress rules to use in conjunction with the Halle-Keyser principles of meter (for purposes of analysis of English poetry of the past three centuries), and to provide a critical commentary on the new prosodic system.

Two sets of rules are essential to the system: rules of stress, and rules (Halle and Keyser use the word "principles") of meter. It is the rules of meter Halle and Keyser think may have provided the system of prosody for a major portion of English poets, and I reproduce them here.

Principle 1

The iambic pentameter verse consists of ten positions to which may be appended one or two extra-metrical syllables.

Principle 2

A position is normally occupied by a single syllable, but under certain conditions it may be occupied by more than one syllable, or by none.

Condition 1

Two vowels may constitute a single position provided that they adjoin, or are separated by a liquid or nasal or by a word boundary which may be followed by *h-*, and provided that one of them is a weakly stressed or unstressed vowel.

Condition 2

An unstressed or weakly stressed monosyllabic word may constitute a single metrical position with a preceding stressed or unstressed syllable.

Principle 3

A stress maximum may only occupy even positions within a verse, but not every even position need be so occupied.

Definition

A stress maximum is constituted by a syllable bearing linguistically determined stress that is greater than that of the two syllables adjacent to it in the same verse.[3]

For purposes of this article, I assume that these three principles are in fact the principles of all English regular-metered verse, and extend them, as Halle and Keyser suggest, to embrace different kinds of meter in obvious ways:

1A. A tetrameter iambic or trochaic line consists of 8 positions, a trimeter line of 6, etc.

3A. For trochaic verse, stress maxima may occupy only odd positions, though not every odd position need be occupied.

Turning now to rules of stress (which are needed to determine stress maxima—see "Definition" under 3), it could be argued that a different set would be needed for every period of verse (and every dialect). But I think that a set can be constructed—perhaps somewhat primitive, but adequate to our purpose—sufficient to provide a working tool for most English verse of the last three centuries. We adopt Seymour Chatman's distinction of five types of syllables for purposes of arriving at linguistically determined "lexical stress," and we identify stress maxima from certain configurations of these syllable types.[4] The five kinds of syllables are:

a) full-voweled monosyllabic words with non-reducible vowels (*e.g.,* "straight," "bright," etc.)
b) reducible full-voweled monosyllabic words ("a," "to," "shall," "you," "it," "can," etc. In general, most non-lexical monosyllabic words can reduce the vowel coloring to /ɨ/.
c) stressed syllables of polysyllabic words
d) full-voweled unstressed syllables in polysyllabic words
e) unstressed syllables in polysyllabic words with reduced vowels

We now assume that a syllable of type a or c, preceded and followed by syllables of types b, d, or e will constitute a *stress maximum,* unless a syntactic juncture intervenes—for, following Halle-Keyser, we will maintain that if a major syntactic boundary intervenes between two metrical positions, neutralization occurs, which is to say, the adjacent positions cannot carry stress maxima.[5]

The center syllable, then, of any sequence of three syllables which meets this description is a stress maximum:

$$
\begin{array}{ccc}
\text{Syll.} & \text{Syll.} & \text{Syll.} \\
\left[\begin{Bmatrix} b \\ d \\ e \end{Bmatrix}\right] & \left[\begin{Bmatrix} a \\ c \end{Bmatrix}\right] & \left[\begin{Bmatrix} b \\ d \\ e \end{Bmatrix}\right]
\end{array}
$$

In essence, what is proposed for the determination of stress maxima is a rule which is *lexically* based, but which operates as a determinant of *underlying* stress in any phrase segment of three sequential syllables.

Since it is *capacity* for reduction that determines the membership of "b," rather than whether the monosyllable is in fact reduced in a given instance, and since the rule deals with only two stresses (stress and unstress), the system proposed here will find a somewhat different set of stress maxima than any alternative system that assigns four (or even three) degrees of stress, or that assigns phrasal and clausal stress on a basis of syntactic order.

To briefly illustrate the use of the Halle-Keyser rules of prosody in combination with the rules of stress I propose, consider the familiar lines from Hamlet:

<pre>
    1   2   3   4   5   6   7 8   9   10
    Oh that this too too solid flesh would melt,
    1   2   3   4   5 6 7 8 9   10
    Thaw, and resolve itself into a dew.
</pre>

Both lines have ten positions occupied with syllables, and there are no problems of extra-metrical syllables. The lines are iambic pentameter, and our rules call for stress maxima, if there are any, to fall only on even-numbered positions.

The syllables that could, by virtue of their linguistically determined stress, conceivably carry stress maxima are: "Oh," the first syllable of "solid," "flesh," "melt," "thaw," the second syllables of "resolve" and "itself," and "dew." These are either the accented syllables of polysyllabic words (*so*lid), or else they are non-reducible full-voweled monosyllables (*melt*):

$$
\begin{array}{cccccccccc}
1 & 2 & 3 & 4 & 5 & 6 & 7 & 8 & 9 & 10
\end{array}
$$
Oh that this too too *so*lid *flesh* would *melt*,
$$
\begin{array}{cccccccccc}
1 & & 2 & 3 & 4 & 5 & 6 & 7 & 8 & 9 & 10
\end{array}
$$
Thaw, and re*solve* it*self in*to a *dew*.

The unitalicized syllables are of types b, d, or e. Most of them are type b, reducible full-voweled monosyllables. For example, "too" is a full-voweled syllable (/tuw/) but it frequently reduces to a neutralized vowel (/tɨ/), as in "too much" said rapidly, with stress on "much." It is important to note that it is this capacity for reduction, rather than how the word may actually be said in a particular instance, which determines its classification.

Let us now examine the italicized syllables, those with linguistically determined stress. The first syllables in both lines carry linguistic stress (they are type a: non-reducible full-voweled monosyllables). However, neither "Oh" nor "Thaw" is a stress maximum, and for two reasons. First, no syllable precedes them in their respective lines, and they thus cannot be thrown into relief by unaccented syllables on each side. For this reason, neither the first nor the last syllable of a line (unless an extra-metrical syllable follows) may be a stress maximum. So "melt" and "dew," though both are linguistically stressed (they are non-reducible full-voweled monosyllables), also do not constitute stress maxima.

But there is a second reason why neither "Oh" nor "Thaw" can be a stress maximum, namely, that these syllables are followed by major syntactic junctures, which have the effect of neutralization: neither the syllable before nor the syllable after major syntactic juncture may carry stress maxima.

This leaves five candidates for stress maxima, positions 6 and 8 in line one (*so*lid *flesh*) and positions 4, 6, and 7 in line two (re*solve* it*self in*to). The second syllable of "itself" and the first of "into" have linguistically determined stress (they are type c— accented syllables of polysyllabic words), but they are back to back. Thus each keeps the other from being a stress maximum: neither can be bordered on both sides by non-stressed syllables.

This leaves then only three linguistically stressed syllables to consider: "flesh," the first of "solid," and the second of "resolve." In each of these cases, unstressed syllables are to be found on both sides, without intervening juncture. These three syllables, then, do constitute stress maxima. Further, they fall on even positions, so the two lines are metrical by our rules, the first showing positions 6 and 8 occupied, and the second showing only position 4 occupied (not every even position need be occupied):

1　2　3　4　5　6　7　8　9　10
Oh that this too too *solid flesh* would melt,
1　　2　　3　4　5　6　7　8　9　10
Thaw, and re*solve* itself into a dew.

These metrical rules, or principles, may be regarded as claims about the metrical competence of the poet.[6] It could be said that it is claimed the poet internalizes, not a poetic foot (some recurring pattern of stress and unstress), but a sequence of positions to be occupied by syllables; it is claimed that he is aware somehow of whether a given syllable Y occurs in an arithmetically even or arithmetically odd position; it is claimed further that the poet is metrically conscious only of stress maxima(linguistically determined lexical stress sandwiched by unstressed syllables, without intervening major syntactic boundary); it is claimed that he allows these to occur, or accepts their occurrence, only in even positions for iambic meter and only in odd positions for trochaic meter.[7] His grammar, *per se,* is not concerned with mere "accent" (though possibly his rules of performance might register cognition of these and other refinements).

Let us turn now to such matters as the greater rhythmic regularity of short-line verse (tetrameter and trimeter), and the long noted and frequently debated difference in character between iambic and trochaic verse. Otto Jespersen, for example, contends that trochaic meter is characterized by a "falling" rhythm, and iambic meter by a "rising" rhythm; in the former, there is a tendency to "linger" on the stressed syllable.[8] This suggests that the trochaic "foot" might be quantitatively longer than the iambic. No measurements of performance that I know of have established this,[9] but even those who do not accept the foot (Chatman, and Jespersen himself, in part—p. 74) unite in finding a more regular and insistent beat to trochaic verse.

If we assume, however, that the difference attributed to trochaic verse is in fact a difference to be found generally in *all* short-lined verse whether trochaic *or* iambic, there can be found an explanation for the assumed difference. Since most trochaic verse in English is in short lines, and since our impressions of iambic verse are derived almost entirely from pentameter, it would seem entirely possible that the issue has been falsely formulated—that the differences of rhythm encountered are attributed not to the type of foot, but to the length of line in which the foot characteristically appears. And it will be argued below that the more regular beat of short-lined verse is accounted for by the fact that a much higher percentage of positions available for stress maxima are occupied than is the case in decasyllabic verse.

In English, most trochaic poems are in tetrameter, or trimeter.[10] Here, for example are two ten-line passages from Longfellow's "The Song of Hiawatha," the syllables carrying stress maxima, in accordance with rules here adopted, printed in italics.

> Till at *length* a small green *feat*her
> From the earth shot slowly *up*ward,
> Then a*no*ther and a*no*ther,
> And be*fore* the *Sum*mer *end*ed
> Stood the *maize* in *all* its *beauty,*
> With its *shin*ing *robes* a*bout* it,
> And its long, soft, yellow *tres*ses:
> And in *rap*ture Hia*wa*tha
> Cried aloud, "It is Mon*dam*in!
> Yes, the *friend* of man, Mon*dam*in!"

> "THE SONG OF HIAWATHA,"
> SECTION V

> Straight be*tween* them *ran* the *path*way,
> Never *grew* the *grass* up*on* it;

> Singing birds, that *utter falsehoods*,
> Story-*tellers*, mischief-*makers*,
> Found no *eager ear* to *listen*,
> Could not breed ill-will be*tween* them,
> For they *kept* each *other*'s *counsel*,
> Spake with *naked hearts* together,
> Pondering *much* and *much* con*triving*
> How the *tribes* of *men* might *prosper*.

"THE SONG OF HIAWATHA,"
SECTION VI

A tetrameter line has available only three positions (2, 4, and 6 for iambic; 3, 5, and 7 for trochaic) for occupancy by stress maxima—a trimeter line only two. Pentameter has four. In the lines quoted from "The Song of Hiawatha," 46 of 60 available positions are occupied by stress maxima, for a 77 percent occupancy. Various randomly selected passages in "Hiawatha" show an average 75 percent occupancy.[11] By contrast, an analysis of 10 of Shakespeare's sonnets (where there are four available positions per line, or 56 per sonnet) show an average of only 27.7 stress maxima per sonnet, or 49 percent occupancy.[12]

But the high occupancy ratio in Longfellow's trochaic verse is matched by that in various randomly sampled short-lined *iambic* poems. A. E. Housman's ballad stanzas show about 75 percent occupancy; even so varied a poem, metrically, as "Loveliest of trees, the *cherry* now" (the first line with only one stress maximum) shows 27 out of 35 positions occupied, or 77 percent.

Nor does the type of poet, or the type of verse (e.g., sonnet, or blank verse) seem ordinarily to affect the density of stress maxima. Edwin Arlington Robinson's blank verse dramatic monologues show about the same occupancy as Shakespeare's sonnets, and so do Robert Frost's blank verse and e. e. cummings' sonnets and other pentameter poems.[13] (The condition indeed appears so general that when we find poetry departing significantly from the pattern, the occupancy ratio and distribution provide a basic tool for initial stylistic analysis, as we shall see a little later.)

It appears then that the often noticed difference between trochaic and iambic verse, if understood as actually a perceived difference between poems of different line length, may be correlated with the much greater density of stress maxima in short-lined verse: about 75 percent occupancy for short-lined verse, contrasted to 50 percent occupancy for decasyllabic verse. Put another way, there is 50 percent greater density of occupancy in short line verse.

Such an explanation follows naturally upon the concepts of positions and stress maxima. But the concept of feet does not explain it, for in fact just as high a percentage of iambs is found in pentameter as in shorter lines (or trochees in trochaic lines). Shakespeare's Sonnet 89, for example, which shows only 27 stress maxima in 56 available positions, shows 66 iambic feet out of a possible 70 (defining an iambic foot for this purpose as one which can be read, by any reasonable stretch of performance rules, as a lesser stressed syllable followed by a more greatly stressed syllable). For purposes of direct comparison, here is Sonnet 89, with stress maxima italicized, and with only those "feet" which do *not* seem, to me, susceptible to an iambic reading printed in capital letters:

> SAY THAT thou didst for*sake* me for some fault,
> And I will *com*MENT UP*on* that offense.
> SPEAK OF my *lame*ness, and I *straight* will halt,
> A*gainst* thy *rea*sons *mak*ing no defence.
> Thou canst not, love, dis*grace* me *half* so ill,
> To *set* a *form* up*on* de*sired* change,
> As I'll my*self* disgrace, KNOWING thy will.
> I will ac*quain*tance *strang*le, and look strange,
> Be *abs*ent from thy walks, and in thy tongue
> Thy *sweet* be*lov*ed *name* no more shall dwell,
> Lest I, too much profane, should *do* it wrong
> And *hap*ly of our *old* ac*quaint*ance tell.
>   For thee, *against* my*self* I'll *vow* debate,
>   For I must ne'er love him whom thou dost
>   hate.

I have designated 28 stress maxima here, but count only 27 that fall in an even position, since the stress on the second syllable of "upon" in line 2 falls on position 7, thus making that line unmetrical. The point is that there are 66 syllables in even position capable of some kind of stress, but only 27 of these are stress maxima.

Glancing now at English triple meters, anapestic and dactyllic, it might at first appear that the insistent beat in these meters is at odds with our assumption that the phenomenon is associated with "short-line verse," for most triple meters are in lines longer than decasyllabic. Indeed, the percentage of occupancy of available positions by stress maxima in anapestic verse appears to run higher than for the short line verse examined earlier. Byron's "Destruction of Sennacherib" and "On the Day of the Destruction of Jerusalem by Titus" show 96 stress maxima out of a possible 117 positions, for somewhat over 80 percent occupancy.

But in this case I think we must look for a different explanation of the rhythmic insistency. If the phenomenon in short line duple meters is to be accounted for—as I think it must—by a relative numerical scarcity of available positions as these relate to the syntactic units that normally comprise a line, in triple meter verse I think it is to be explained by the fact that the poet has to rely excessively on preposition-determiner-noun sequences, and other set syntactic patterns of English, to throw the stress always on the third syllable. It is worth noting, however, that complete lines without any stress maxima are possible in triple meter, as witness Byron's "When the blue wave rolls nightly on deep Galilee," where each potential stress maximum is cancelled by an adjacent non-reducible full-voweled monosyllabic or accented syllable of a polysyllabic.[14]

Certain aspects of the Halle-Keyser principles of meter may provoke attack, and there remain some formal problems to be solved. For one thing, there is the claim—if I am right in postulating that their first principle in effect makes a claim—having to do with internalizing in some manner a sequence of positions (up to 10, in the case of decasyllabic verse) and identifying within this chain those positions which may be legitimately occupied with stress maxima. At first consideration, this might appear counterintuitive. The claim asks nothing of rhythmic or temporal considerations. It is quasi-arithmetic, and on the face of it seems harder to believe than what amounts to the traditional claim that what is internalized is a recurring rhythmic pattern consisting of stronger and weaker pulses (which claim, of course, has support from psychological research).

To this objection, it might be answered that counting is the basis of all rhythm, musical as well as poetic. But how much counting (up to what number, without assistance of metrical grouping) is another question. In music, for example, one does not "count" higher than four in most cases—indeed, it can be argued that one does not have to internalize a count higher than three, since the various quadruple meters lend themselves to subdivision so easily. Herein lies the strength of the foot concept, since it hypothesizes only a recurring pattern of stress and unstress that never exceeds three (in English). The stress maximum concept on the other hand (at least in its unsupported version) implies that we can internalize 10 positions and be satisfied—to use Jespersen's word—by an event in the 8th position (which may not have occurred in 2, 4, or 6); or dissatisfied by an event in the 7th, even though we have no other occurrences anywhere in the line to use as an interval or distance estimate. Such observations suggest that rules for stress maxima should be supplemented by rules perhaps of another sort.

A quite minor detail is that fact that the rules of meter indicate that a position may under certain conditions be unoccupied, though the conditions are not specified in the rules. In fact, the only position which may be unoccupied appears to be the first position in iambic pentameter, though as I have suggested (note 14) provision for other empty positions would probably have to be made in other meters.

On this point, note that if we postulate a set of rules governing trochaic verse exactly parallel to those generating iambic verse (including the conditions of position occupancy by more than one syllable, and the possibility of zero occupancy), we have no way to distinguish consistently beheaded iambic verse (zero initial position) from consistently catalectic trochaic verse (zero final position). Thus, Tennyson's "Locksley Hall" and many others of this form:

> Comrades, leave me here a little, while as yet 'tis
> early morn;
> Leave me here, and when you want me, sound
> upon the bugle horn.

Tennyson's poem continues in a precisely similar metrical manner for 194 lines, with stress on the first and last syllables of each line. An obvious solution to this problem is to view such poems or portions of poems as metrically ambiguous in their surface structure, and postulate that they are, in their deep structure, either iambic with initial position always unoccupied, or trochaic with final position always unoccupied.[15] As a matter of fact, many poets have capitalized on this ambiguity. In "To a Skylark," Shelley chooses a stanza form which maintains the ambiguity through the first four lines of each stanza, resolving it in the iambic hexameter fifth line. And much of the charm of John Donne's "Go and catch a falling star" consists in precisely this ambiguity, which he maintains unresolved throughout the three stanzas.

Finally, it might be argued that the principles appear to offer no way of dealing with the reality of run-on lines—that is, if a line is in fact run on (proceeds without major juncture into the next), why then cannot the tenth syllable of the first line (or the first syllable of the second line, in trochaic verse) be considered occupied by a stress maximum? The major difficulty is that if this be admitted, we will be forced in some cases to find stress maxima in initial position in iambic verse, thus losing the strength of our position (see next paragraph) that an initial stress does not make an irregular or unmetrical line. However, it must be remembered that our principles postulate a verse line as *a sequence of positions only:* the verse line is taken as a primitive, so to speak, and in this light, the foregoing objection loses some of its force.

Far more than offsetting these present possible inadequacies is the explanatory power of the principles. Initial "trochees" in iambic verse pose no problem at all: to say a line begins with a trochee is to say that the first position contains a stress greater than the second position, but no more: in our view, the first position cannot contain a stress maximum. And in fact, more of the lines in Shakespeare's sonnets begin on accented than on unaccented syllables: in the ten sonnets studied, only 52 of 140 lines had stress maxima in position 2. More common are lines like this one from Sonnet 2:

Proving his beauty by succession thine.

Traditional prosody finds itself in the uncomfortable position, here, of saying that the most common occurrence is the allowable exception. In our view, an initial "trochee" is entirely regular—all that matters is that stress maxima occur, when they occur at all, in even positions.

In a similar vein, the absence of bona fide iambs in various feet other than the first poses no problem. The fact that "by" in "Proving his beauty by succession thine" is unstressed does not embarrass the metrical theory. Traditional prosody, on the other hand, must say that in some sense "*bý* sŭccéssiŏn thíne" occurs.

Our acceptance of strong accent after internal juncture also demonstrates the explanatory power of the rules. The following line shows an accented syllable in the wrong position, but it is not a stress maximum (because it is neutralized by juncture), and we intuitively feel that its occurrence does no violence to the meter.

As I'll myself disgrace, *know*ing thy will

"SONNET 89"

We readily accept also special intonations which might appear to violate the meter, if meter is taken to be based on performance. But our principles and our stress rules say nothing at all about how lines may happen to be read. Stress maxima are defined in terms of linguistically determined stress (i.e., not performance determined). In the present study, a syllable is one of the five kinds[16] distinguished by Chatman, and it belongs in that class *regardless of how it is performed.* The following lines may be performed with unusual stress on the italicized syllables in odd positions, but it does not make the lines unmetrical:

1 Say that thou didst forsake *me* for some fault
[7 above "me"]

"SONNET 89"

2 As he would add a shilling to *more* shillings
[9 above "more"]

Robinson
"BEN JONSON ENTERTAINS A VISITOR FROM STRATFORD"

$$\overset{5}{3 \quad \text{Oh, that this too } too \text{ solid flesh would melt}}$$

HAMLET

In 1, "-sake" is the stressed syllable of a polysyllabic word, and "me" is a reducible full-voweled monosyllabic (as are most pronouns). The fact that "me" may be said louder (perhaps to indicate that in the past the reverse had been true) or higher than "-sake" does not alter the linguistic fact. In 2, which has an extrametrical syllable after the tenth position, "more" is a prenominal adjective and subject to reduction (even though it may not be so performed in this instance), and therefore is not a stress maximum. In each case, the performance cannot alter what as native speakers we know, and our knowledge of inherent linguistic stress overrides performance. Ictus in our sense is not synonymous with what is phonetically higher or louder or with what is more carefully enunciated. Therefore we need no performance records to determine the meter of the poem—though we need a knowledge of "performance" (i.e., a corpus) from which to derive our rules of stress in the first place.

And, as Halle and Keyser have demonstrated, our principles explain the otherwise unexplainable phenomenon that while iambic lines can accept initial trochees, trochaic lines frequently cannot accept initial iambs. In "Proving his beauty by succession thine," the initial accent on "*Prov*ing" cannot be a stress maximum, and thus its occurrence on an odd position in iambic verse does not alter the meter. But if, to parallel Jespersen's illustration, we change Longfellow's trochaic line

Straight between them ran the pathway

to read

Be*tween* them straight ran the pathway

we have created a stress maximum in an even position, thus violating the rule of trochaic meter.

So the Halle-Keyser prosodic system is first of all a grammar of verse: it is a set of rules which enables us to say that certain lines are metrical, and certain lines are not metrical. Beyond this lies the question of whether the rules can be used significantly for stylistic analysis. This article has not for the most part concerned itself with this question. The distinction drawn between short line and long line verse (75 percent density of stress maxima in the former, 50 percent in the latter) is not fundamentally a stylistic distinction. Rather, it would appear that the language mechanics of verse lines shorter than decasyllabic linguistically requires the higher percentage of occupancy because of the relatively fewer available positions for stress maxima in each line to correlate with normal syntactic units.

Perhaps we should look for stylistic devices to emanate from something corresponding to rules of performance, rather than to metrical competence. In effect performance—but in an oral production sense—is what earlier structuralist analyses of metrical stress dealt with.[17] If efforts are made to supplement rules for determination of stress maxima with rules showing how phrase accent and clause accent, etc., may be appended, these might have more to do with metrical performance (not oral production) than with metrical competence.[18]

However, certain basic stylistic determinations may be derived from the rules. Relative density of stress maxima occupancy comes first to mind as a stylistic determinant. I have said that most of the decasyllabic verse examined shows about 50 percent occupancy, and have suggested that this ordinarily obtains, irrespective of poet or period. But individual poems may show significant variance; and individual efforts in different verse forms may exhibit differences. An analysis of the first ten of John Donne's "Holy Sonnets" shows 236 of 560 positions occupied, for 42 percent density of occupancy, as compared to the 49 percent found for ten of Shakespeare's sonnets.

Predilection for placing stress maxima in certain positions would appear to be, potentially, a more telling stylistic determinant. My study of the sonnets of Shakespeare and Donne shows distribution of stress maxima in the four available positions (140 possibilities for each position) as follows:

Position	Number Stress Maxima		Percentage Stress Maxima	
	S.	D.	S.	D.
2	52	65	37	46
4	76	50	54	36
6	65	47	46	33
8	83	74	59	53

Shakespeare uses position 8 most, followed by 4, then 6, then 2. Donne also uses 8 most, but favors next position 2 (last with Shakespeare), then 4, then 6. This suggests, in Donne, a metrical structure tending to support stability at the extremities of the lines, somewhat like a suspension bridge, perhaps at the expense of medial stability. Shakespeare, on the other hand, tends to provide anchors at half way points. This possibly subjective interpretation might be represented in this manner:

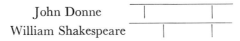

Distribution of the stress maxima does appear to provide the richest source for stylistic analysis. Many more possibilities suggest themselves. For example, if a poet has employed positions 6 and 8 in one or two lines, how long will it be till he balances by placing maxima in 2 and 4? What overall distributional patterns of occupancy present themselves, and what is their significance? What lines show total occupancy? What show none? In the ten sonnets of Shakespeare, there were 10 lines with no stress maxima; in the sonnets of Donne, there were 11. The following are typical:

> Some glory in their birth, some in their skill
>
> Shakespeare
> "SONNET 91"

> My worlds both parts, and (oh) both parts must die
>
> Donne
> "HOLY SONNET 5"

The particular uses—and the frequency—of *un*metrical lines is another potential stylistic consideration. There is always the possibility of a lapse on the part of the poet, and occasionally a poet may be a poor metrist (see note 14), but some lines unmetrical by the rules seem calculated for effect. In the ten sonnets of Shakespeare I found only one clearly unmetrical line (which, incidentally, is about two-thirds of 1 percent as compared to the 1 percent of unmetrical lines Halle and Keyser found in Chaucer), but four in Donne. The unmetrical line of Shakespeare's occurs in Sonnet 89:

> And I will comment up*on* that offense.

As pointed out earlier, a stress maximum falls on position 7, rendering the line unmetrical. This would seem to be merely a lapse.

John Donne's unmetrical lines, however, occur with sufficient frequency to suggest deliberation. He appears to seek the device which will capture attention, by departing from the usual (note that he does not attempt to achieve novelty—which would not have been novelty—by low frequency use of position 2, and the attendant stress in initial position). One of the ways of doing this is by deliberately placing stress maxima in off positions. In Sonnet 1, we find:

> Thou hast *made* me, and shall thy *worke* decay?

where the very first stress maximum occurs in position 3, perhaps underscoring the conflict, the contradiction in the two thoughts Donne contemplates. An unmetrical line in a passage that interests because of its use of double position occupancy occurs in Sonnet 4:

> line 5 Or like a thiefe, which till deaths doome
> be read,
>
> 6 Wisheth him*selfe* deli*ver*ĕd from prison;
>
> 7 But *damn'd* and *hal'd* to exe*cu*tiŏn,
>
> 8 Wisheth that *still* he might be imprisonĕd.

Here "wisheth" is used in positions 1 and 2 of line 6, and the line is metrical (but the extra-metrical syllable at the end, the second of "prison," is made to carry the rhyme). Then in line 8, the two syllables of "wisheth" both occupy position 1, which places the stress maximum in position 3 for an unmetrical line. Alternatively, if "wisheth" occupies two positions, "still" carries stress maximum in position 4, but now the stress maximum in "imprisoned" falls in position 9, for an unmetrical line. One could assign "be" and "im-" to the same position by condition 1 of the rules, and, with other adjustments, argue that the line is metrical. The other two unmetrical lines are printed without comment:

To where they're bred, and would *presse* me, to
    hell

Makes sinnes, else equall, in mee more *heinous?*

It may be noted in passing that Donne's experiments in position occupancy by more than one syllable are most interesting, and is another aspect which lends his verse its rough-hewn effect.

In summary, the Halle-Keyser principles of prosody appear to bear a relationship to traditional prosody somewhat akin to that which transformational grammar bears to traditional grammar. Their approach represents an attempt to make explicit what had been only implicit. Pursuing the analogy, the principles appear also to represent certain claims about the nature of metrical competence, and though the claims may at first pose something of a credibility gap, in fact they stretch the credulity no more than the failure of implicit claims in traditional prosody to account for what would otherwise be an intolerable percentage of unmetrical lines. The principles, together with the stress rules here suggested, offer a unified explanation for the fact that the majority of iambic lines begin with trochaic feet; for the absence of regular feet at various other positions in the line; for our acceptance of strong stress before or after juncture, even in odd-numbered positions; for the fact that special intonation features do not appear to violate the acceptability of metrical lines; for the rejection of iambs in trochaic verse; for the fact that poetry in duple meter in verse lines shorter than decasyllabic appears to be more irresistably metrical. Finally, they offer a well-defined procedure for basic metrical-stylistic analysis.[19]

NOTES

1. Morris Halle and Samuel J. Keyser, "Chaucer and the Study of Prosody," *College English*, XXVIII (1966) [reprinted in this volume].

2. For those unfamiliar with generative terminology, Chomsky has distinguished between rules of competence (in effect, these are the grammar of the language; they are the rules which will generate grammatical sentences), and rules of performance (stylistic rules, which will allow grammatically deviant sentences, or place certain restrictions upon the use of what would be, technically, grammatical sentences). See Noam Chomsky, *Aspects of the Theory of Syntax* (Cambridge, Mass., 1965), pp. 8–15 and *passim*.

3. Halle and Keyser, p. 197. The *stress maximum* is reminiscent of Jespersen, who, in "Notes on Metre," points out that the initial syllable of a verse cannot be judged to bear ictus until the second syllable occurs—because there is nothing preceding the first syllable for purposes of comparison. For this reason, an initial trochee in iambic verse disappoints only in the second syllable, not in the first. If this is the only disappointment in a decasyllabic line, and if the third syllable carries even less stress than the second (Jespersen uses four degrees of stress), the line will show only 10 percent disappointment, as compared to 20 percent occasioned by an initial iamb in a trochaic line. The recognition of stress relationship to adjacent syllables and the concomitant notion that stress next to nothing cannot be optimum stress are key elements of the Halle-Keyser rules. See Otto Jespersen, "Notes on Metre," in *Essays on the Language of Literature,* ed. Seymour Chatman and Samuel R. Levin (Boston, 1967), pp. 71–90.

4. Seymour Chatman, *A Theory of Meter* (The Hague, 1965), pp. 123ff. Note that one could also evolve a theory of phrase and clause accent to supplement lexical stress. One could for example postulate that in prepositional phrases the head word bears phrase accent, that in determiner-adjective-noun phrases the noun bears phrase accent (in American English, if not in British English), that in NV-terminal juncture clauses, the V bears clausal accent, that in NV-adverb clauses, the adverb bears clausal accent, and so forth.

The supplementing of rules of lexical stress with accent rules of this kind would yield some additional stress maxima, specifically where two back to back lexically stressed syllables would otherwise cancel each other out. Halle and Keyser do propose to include rules of this kind in their theory on the grounds that one should make as strong a hypothesis as the facts will support (personal communication). I do not employ such rules in the present exploratory article. Like lexical secondary stress (which I also do not use in the present article), it is not at present clear to me that such rules need be a part of the metrical rules determining stress maxima, even though they are clearly a part of the phonological rules of the language.

5. Halle and Keyser, pp. 203, 204. Notice that for the same reason (incapacity for stress subordination) a syllable at the beginning of a line cannot bear stress maximum, no matter what the meter; nor can the syllable at the end of a line, unless there is appended an extra-metrical syllable.

6. It would be useful to have a word comparable, in this metrical context, to "native speaker" in the more general linguistic situation. The claims in any event are of the competence of the poet and of those attuned to poetry in some metrical sense, but I shall use the world "poet," in this situation, to refer to both. By "competence" is meant what the poet and the attuned reader know (though not necessarily what they can articulate) about the rules of meter.

7. Or, obviously, some other pattern of position occupancy in the cases of dactyllic or anapestic verse.

By way of comparison, it could be said that traditional "schoolroom" prosody also may be reduced to a set of claims: namely that the poet internalizes a recurring group of stressed and unstressed syllables in a certain sequence—this is essentially the claim of the "foot" concept.

8. Otto Jespersen, "Notes on Metre," in *Essays on the Language of Literature,* pp. 86–88.

9. One, in fact, shows the iambic foot as longer: Ada Snell, "An Objective Study of Syllabic Quantity in English Verse," *PMLA,* XXXIII (1918), 396–408; XXXIV (1919), 416–435. Though this was not her principle objective, her measurements did show the average iambic foot to be of .69 seconds duration, and the average trochaic foot to be .55 (XXXIV, p. 433).

However, her tabulations on p. 432 show the average short syllable (unstressed) of the trochaic foot to be .35 seconds, and the average long syllable (stressed) as .20! Obviously, from an examination of the other figures, the two columns were accidentally reversed in the printing, a fact which may possibly have contributed to what seems to me Chatman's misleading conclusion that her figures "demonstrated clearly that syllable length was not necessarily an indication of metrical ictus, that indeed unstressed syllables could last longer than adjacent stressed syllables" (Chatman, p. 80). On the contrary, Snell's figures, to me, suggest that there is a clear general correspondence between the classical prosodist's length and ictus, so far as performance is concerned.

10. Poe claimed that he wrote "The Raven" in trochaic "octameter acatalectic" alternating with "heptameter catalectic" but the heavy internal junctures after the fourth foot in most lines, and the internal rhyme, clearly suggest that the poem is in fact tetrameter.

> Once up*on* a *mid*night *drear*y
> While I *pond*ered *weak* and *wear*y
> Over *many* a *quaint* and *cur*ious
> Volume (of) for*got*ten lore

Note in the four lines (as I have rearranged them) that ten of the eleven available positions carry stress maxima, which are indicated by italics. The position not occupied is enclosed in parentheses.

11. The lowest percentage of occupancy I found in Hiawatha was 64 percent, in a thirteen-line passage, also from section V. Four of the thirteen lines contain only one stress maximum each: "Sorrowing for her Hia*wa*tha," "He meanwhile sat weary *wai*ting," "Till the sun dropped from the *heav*en," and "As a red leaf in the *au*tumn."

12. The following sonnets were analyzed: 1, 2, 29, 55, 58, 73, 89, 90, 91, 107.

13. I am indebted to Helen Tulsky for work with e. e. cummings' poetry.

14. These comments on triple meter are based on the assumption of a set of rules that would provide, in anapestic tetrameter, for a 12-position verse, with stress maxima allowed to occupy only positions 3, 6, or 9, and with provisions for empty initial positions, and for extra-metrical syllables. In actuality, I think the framing of rules for triple meters in English poses difficulties not encountered in duple meters. Conditions for empty medial positions where there are terminal junctures would have to be set for most poets who employ the medium.

15. "Locksley Hall," like "The Raven," seems to me misleadingly arranged with respect to line length. A major syntactic break occurs in the middle of each line; instead of rhyming octameter couplets (as Tennyson arranged it), these seem to me to be tetrameter quatrains, with lines 2 and 4 rhyming, and —as Poe would have put it—tetrameter trochaic acatalectic alternating with tetrameter trochaic catalectic.

16. In fact four kinds, for in this analysis I do not distinguish between his types d and e: between full-voweled unstressed syllables in polysyllabic words and unstressed syllables in polysyllabic words with neutralized vowels.

17. Though Seymour Chatman has now shifted his position substantially, *A Theory of Meter* is still performance-oriented in this sense.

18. See note 4. For a full "grammar of prosody," further refinements might be needed, but I think their necessity would have to be demonstrated. For example, I have not used secondary stress in polysyllabic words as stress maxima. Thus, Poe's line

1   2   3 4 5 6 7 8   9 10 11 12 13 14   15
To the tintinnabu*la*tion that so *mus*ically wells

would show stress maxima in positions 7 and 11, but not in 3 or 5 or 13, all of which are occupied by syllables that possibly have secondary stress of some kind. A glance at several dictionaries will show how divided opinion is on the question of secondary stress. And the fact that secondary stress can be subordinated to primary stress seems to me to eliminate it from stress maximum status. Observe the behavior of the third syllable of "refugee" in the following triple meter:

The ré̆fū̆geē cáme tŏ thĕ vílla̋ge hĕ knéw.

Additional conditions for occupancy of a position by more than one syllable might be needed, though I have so far encountered few situations that are not encompassed by those in the Halle-Keyser principles.

19. I should like to acknowledge the valuable assistance of Don Seigel, who read two versions of this paper and whose criticism has been most helpful.

I am indebted also to Morris Halle and Samuel Jay Keyser for a detailed commentary. I have adopted some of their suggestions, but responsibility for the entire paper is my own.

George Hansen, Elsa Atkins, and Leonard Stenson have helped in various ways.

23.   ON THE PRIMES OF
METRICAL STYLE

Donald C. Freeman

At the end of "Chaucer and the Study of Prosody," Morris Halle and Samuel Jay Keyser suggest that aspects of their metrical theory are relevant to the study of metrical style. The following article proposes that large-scale studies of metrical style—periods, genres, forms—can be organized around new kinds of information elicited by the Halle-Keyser theory. Patterns of actualization of stress maxima (linguistically determined stress contrasts), incidence of stress neutralization, reversed initial feet, and number of actualized stress maxima per line are seen to be among the "primes" of metrical style. The shift in metrical style during the sixteenth century from the stiffly formal pentameters of Gascoigne and Grimald to the more flexible verse of Marlowe and Kyd can be characterized, it is argued here, as a shift in the metrical ideal from a line with four actualized stress maxima to a line with three. The Halle-Keyser theory also is shown to lend itself to metrical analysis of individual poems, and provides evidence for a characterization of metrical foregrounding.

Since the time of Saintsbury, Anglo-American students of prosody have concerned themselves chiefly with the enumeration of meters and an inventory of metrical effects. Most prosody handbooks have stated the abstract metrical pattern for a given form, and then proceeded directly from abstract description to detailed consideration of how the inevitable "exceptions" or

Donald C. Freeman, "On the Primes of Metrical Style," *Language and Style,* I (1968), 63–101. Reprinted by permission of Southern Illinois University.

"allowable deviations" may be appropriate in the context of a given poem or the work of a given poet. As a consequence, such studies have failed to separate those aspects of meter as a percept which inhere in the *language* from those aspects which exist as a consequence of *form*.[1] Left unconsidered in this work are the issues which lie between the abstract metrical pattern and its actualization in an individual poem: that is, the structure of what J. V. Cunningham has called "metrical language." [2]

Paralleling the theoretical inadequacies have been inconsistencies and deficiencies in the study of metrical style. Most studies have proceeded from extremely broad theoretical statements about the nature of metrical forms—or even of meter itself—to particular statements about local effects, without consideration of a period's metrical traditions or a poet's typical metrical practices. Adequate statements about metrical style depend upon an adequate theory of meter. The business of this paper will be to propose some approaches to metrical style from a linguistic point of view.

Recent work in linguistics has spurred the use of its findings and methods for metrical study.[3] While linguistics has provided some useful insights into English metrics, the use in literary explication or criticism of a methodology not originally intended for these purposes has brought with it some difficulties, chiefly exaggerated claims of accuracy and relevance, incisively catalogued recently by Stanley B. Greenfield.[4]

A more difficult if less obvious problem with linguistic studies of meter has been their failure to establish a unified methodology and an order of priorities. The chief question generally has been the relative linguistically assigned strength of a syllable used to fill a given "metrical point," to use Seymour Chatman's term. This method has been useful for the study of small bodies of text,[5] but is not well adapted for more general statements. Abercrombie,[6] on the other hand, is more concerned with the physical characteristics of metrical language than with the structural units of meter. More recently, Fowler[7] has concentrated upon higher-level relationships of similarity and contrast between syntactic and metrical patterns. But none of these theories has offered a basis for broad stylistic statements based upon clear and replicable evidence.

1

In a recent study of Chaucer's prosody,[8] Morris Halle and Samuel Jay Keyser have presented a theory of English meter which, in a subsequent paper by Keyser,[9] is extended to cover the mainstream of English prosodic development. This theory makes the minimum claim as to aesthetic consequence, and depends upon the simplest possible linguistic methodology. It provides easily replicable evidence for prosodic analysis. Most important, the Halle-Keyser theory suggests an articulated and organized methodology for considering questions of metrical style from broad generalizations about the metrical practices of a period to the metrical structure of an individual poem.

Briefly summarized, the theory is as follows for iambic pentameter, the form to which I shall limit this discussion. An iambic pentameter line has ten positions plus up to two extra-metrical syllables. The odd positions are "weak"; the even are "strong." A position usually is occupied by one syllable, but synaloepha may occur under certain stated conditions. The first position may be actualized as zero (headlessness). Stress maxima may occupy only strong positions. A stress maximum is a syllable which carries more linguistically assigned stress than its immediate neighbors in the same syntactic constituent in a line of verse. (Therefore, neither the first nor the last metrical position in any line can be a stress maximum.) Synaloepha—the actualization of *one* metrical position by *two* syllables—may occur optionally over two contiguous vowels, irrespective of word boundaries, or over two vowels separated by a sonorant consonant. Finally, a single metrical position may be actualized by an unstressed or weakly stressed monosyllabic word *and* a preceding stressed or unstressed syllable.

Such a theory proposes, in effect, that in English meter, which is syllabo-tonic (that is, which depends both upon syllable-count and upon stress), the minimum metrical unit is the *stress contrast,* the percept created by the actualization of a stress maximum. The neutral actualization of a given syllabo-tonic meter is a certain number of actualized stress maxima. The syllabic content can be complicated in certain ways—by synaloepha and diaeresis, and by headlessness. The structure of stresses also can be complicated: certain stress maxima can be unactualized (because words without assigned linguistic stress occur at contrast-points dictated by the metrical form; the theory says only that stress maxima must *not* occur in odd positions), or the effect of stress contrasts created by the stress maxima can be obliterated by stress neutralization—the occurrence of two contiguous linguistically assigned main stresses, either as a result of their being separated by a major syntactic break or in sequences consisting of a monosyllabic Adjective and a monosyllabic or initially stressed Noun. In a metrical line, the *stresses* can be moved, but the *potential stress contrasts* cannot.[10]

This theory makes the appropriate distinctions for syllabo-tonic meters. In a tonic, or stress-timed, meter, for example, only a given number of stresses must be actualized.[11] Any stress-contrast thus is irrelevant to considerations of metricality. In Old English poetry, for example,

/   / × \ ×
weorc wuldorfæder

"CAEDMON'S HYMN," 3

is as metrical as

×   / × \ ×
mid wuldorfæder

MENOLOGIUM, 147

even though there are contiguous main stresses in the first example. These are different verse-types[12] and hence stylistically dissimilar. It is stress *contrast,* not stress alone, which is crucial for syllabo-tonic meter. Within the constraint of the metrical form (that is, pentameter, tetrameter, etc.), it is not the number of stresses but their disposition that is important for a syllabo-tonic meter.

The theory thus formalizes the intuitive notion that syllabo-tonic meter is somewhat freer than tonic or syllabic meters in that its global rules are primarily proscriptive rather than prescriptive. Accordingly, we might expect to find a more complex set of possible stylistic effects arising from the meter. We might expect to be able to trace changes in metrical taste, broad historical trends, in terms of the theory. And the theory implies that metrical stylistics is generally a more important question in syllabo-tonic meters than in other meters.

The Halle-Keyser theory offers a logical progression for the study of metrical style in English. Such study must begin with a general theory for syllabo-tonic meters and a description of the typical realization rules for a given period of genre, that is, particular variations of the basic "mapping rules," setting the context for the consideration of metrical style. Studies of metrical style then should assess the typical practices of a poet with respect to certain primes of metrical style elicited by this theory. These primes are a poet's preference for actualization of stress maxima, the disposition of these stress maxima, stress neutralization, headlessness, synaloepha, and diaeresis. Not all of these primes are necessarily relevant for every poet or period. Finally, the study of metrical style should proceed from these general backgrounds to consider how the metrical structure created by the disposition of actualized stress maxima and the complications of the neutral pattern works in conjunction with other structures—of rhetoric, of images, of sounds—in an individual poem.

Stylistic study organized in this fashion proceeds from questions which are chiefly factual (e.g., the actualization of stress maxima) to questions which are chiefly interpretive (the interaction of metrical structure with other kinds of structure); at the same time, the movement of the analysis is from linguistics (e.g., the determination of linguistically given stress on a certain syllable by an explicit set of rules such as those proposed in Noam Chomsky and Morris Halle, *The Sound Pattern of English*[13]) to literary criticism (the affective nature of a given metrical pattern). An ordered procedure of this kind is one of the most important contributions which linguistics can make to literary studies.

The Halle-Keyser framework satisfies the first and theoretically most important demand which we must make upon a theory of meter: that it distinguish in a principled way between metrical and unmetrical lines. The questions which follow this basic inquiry, however, are, if less important, more difficult. What are we to ask beyond metricality? What does such a theory allow us to say about metrical style? What are appropriate criteria for the description of metrical styles? To what extent are such criteria valid for informed critical judgments?

2

An appropriate historical locus for the consideration of these questions is the early English Renaissance, when modern English blank verse first flowered—that crucial half-century between, very roughly, the mid-1540's and the mid-1590's, between the rough-hewn but assured pentameters of Surrey's translation of the *Aeneid* and the polished, versatile brilliance of "Marlowe's mighty line," which established blank verse as the medium of the English drama for the next fifty years. The limitation of this study to blank verse will enable the comparison of the broadest possible range of poets during this period writing in the same form.

We must consider first what modifications of the Halle-Keyser rules must be made in order to deal with the period in question. Their rules for Chaucer's prosody hold good generally for most early Renaissance blank verse in English.

The Halle-Keyser rules of complex actualization center upon synaloepha, realization of one metrical position by two syllables. For sixteenth-century verse, the list of consonants over which synaloepha can occur (limited by Halle and Keyser to sonorants) must be extended to include at least /v/ and /ð/ (and perhaps /z/, though the evidence here is shaky) to account for lines such as these:[14]

O Gáveston, it is for thée that Í am wronged

> Marlowe
> EDWARD II, V, ii, 41

And sáw she was not ótherwise to be won

> Kyd
> SPANISH TRAGEDY, IV, i, 116

That thús hath pént and méwed me in a príson

> EDWARD II, V, i, 18

Elision of /v/ for metrical purposes apparently begins during this period, and is common in later poeticisms such as "o'er" and "e'en." Interestingly enough—although it may be pushing the evidence too far to suggest a direct relationship—this poetic convention is consistent with the vocalization of intervocalic Middle English *v* from Old English *f* in *hlaford > levered > lord. Over, even,* and *heaven,* the words most frequently elided in this fashion, have Old English *f*. It is at least possible that this metrical theory makes visible the relationship of certain poetic conventions—that is, metrical options—to basic phonological processes in the language.[15]

Synaloepha of this sort clearly is optional in order to make a line metrical; against lines like

Scarce can I name salvation, faith or heaven

Marlowe
DOCTOR FAUSTUS, v, vi, 19

are such lines as

O sacred heavens may it come to pass

SPANISH TRAGEDY, III, vii, 47

There are instances in which synaloepha occurs over other voiced fricatives, but these can be explained under the Halle-Keyser rules of synaloepha for other syllables in the line (however, see note 16).

More important for complex actualization in sixteenth-century verse is diaeresis, the actualization of *two* metrical positions by one syllable. This phenomenon takes a variety of forms, but the most interesting is the use for metrical purposes of pronunciations which are either archaic or obsolete with respect to realization of vowels. Hence there occur lines such as the following, with one vowel "phoneme" actualizing two metrical positions:

To summon me to make appearance
w   s   w   s   w   s   w   s   w   s

SPANISH TRAGEDY, III, xiii, 153

Those bloody wars have spent my treasure
w   s   w   s   w   s   w   s   w   s

And with my treasure my people's blood.
w   s   w   s   w   s   w   s   w   s

SPANISH TRAGEDY, I, iii, 35–36

Then issued she, backed with a great rout
w   s   w   s   w   s   w   s   w   s

Surrey
AENEID, IV, 12

Three alternatives are open: the lines can be dismissed as un-metrical; we can postulate the realization of a now-silent "e"; we can suppose that for *metrical* purposes the underlying long vowels in "treasure," "great," and "appearance" count as two positions. The first solution is unlikely. Each of the lines from *Spanish Tragedy* comes from a "set" speech in which Kyd is even more careful than usual to write metrical lines. The second alternative forces us, in the first example, either to do violence to the long-established pronunciation of "appearance,"

make appearance,
w   s   w   s

or to place stress upon the final "silent" vowel,

make appearance.[16]
s   w   s   w   s

The second objection holds of the second example as well. The third alternative is by far the most economical and consistent.

There are many instances in which the actualization for metrical purposes of a "silent" *e* is the only way in which a line can be made metrical. There are at least two examples of actual-ized final *e* in *Tamburlaine, Part I*:

And kill as sure as it swiftly flies
w   s   w   s w s w   s   w   s

Thy words assure me of kind success.[17]
w   s   w s   w   s   w   s   w   s

II, iii, 59–60

There are also instances of syllabification of plurals following consonants:

Injurious villains, thieves, runagates
w s w s w   s   w   s w   s

I TAMBURLAINE, III, iii, 225

Like to the shadows of Pyramides
w   s w   s   w s w s w s

I TAMBURLAINE, IV, ii, 103

Then must these daemones that haunt that place
w   s   w   s   w s   w   s   w   s

Greene
FRIAR BACON AND FRIAR BUNGAY, IX, 40

That, while they brought about the nighte's chare
w   s   w   s   w   s w   s   w   s

Sackville
INDUCTION to the MIRROR FOR MAGISTRATES, 48

Finally, there are several cases of syllabification of liquids and nasals which are not reflected in the orthography but required by the meter:

Some made your wives, and some your children
w   s   w   s   w   s w   s w s

I TAMBURLAINE, V, i, 27

A hundred and fifty thousand horse
w s w s   w s w   s   w   s

I TAMBURLAINE, IV, iii, 53

As monstrous as Gorgon prince of hell
w s w s w   s   w   s   w s

I TAMBURLAINE, IV, i, 18

And from their shields strike flames of lightning
w   s   w   s   w   s   w   s   w   s

I TAMBURLAINE, III, ii, 81

Shall blast like plants and the young saplings
w   s   w   s   w   s   w   s   w   s

SPANISH TRAGEDY, IV, ii, 17

Once again these lines could simply be considered unmetrical. But Kyd and Marlowe very rarely write unmetrical lines; we must exhaust all possible motivation for these lines before dismissing them. The words in question—"children," "hundred," "monstrous," "lightning," and "sapling"—all have archaic pronunciations which would account for the apparent unmetricality of the lines in which they appear.[18] While we by no means need assume that these lines actually were pronounced with the syllabic consonant (unless we are to postulate some kind of *Bühnesprache* for English drama of this period, since I have not as yet found any examples outside the drama), the notion that poets made use of older phonological forms for metrical purposes is given further support.

A more difficult problem is analysis of lines such as the following pair:

And scorns the powers that govern Persia
w   s   w   s   w   s   w   s w s

I TAMBURLAINE, II, vi, 40

And govern Persia in her former pomp
w   s   w   s w   s   w   s   w   s

I TAMBURLAINE, II, v, 19

The facts are clear enough. Derivational affixes and place-names like "Persia," "Asia," etc., have optional syllabic /i/. But accounting for the facts is not as simple. There is a general tendency for the actualization of /i/ in these affixes to take place at the end of the line:

And add more strength to your dominions
w   s   w   s   w s w s w s

I TAMBURLAINE, V, ii, 385

And by profession be ambitious
w   s   w s w   s   w s w s

I TAMBURLAINE, II, vi, 14

I take thy doom for satisfaction
w s   w   s   w   s w s w s

I TAMBURLAINE, II, iii, 5

And he that would not strain his conscience
w   s   w   s   w   s   w   s   w s

SPANISH TRAGEDY, III, iii, 8

Was English Robert, Earl of Gloucester
w   s   w   s w   s   w   s   w s

SPANISH TRAGEDY, I, v, 26

To visit Delos, his mother's mansion
w   s w   s   w   s   w   s   w s

Surrey
AENEID, IV, 21

Medially, however, the shorter option usually occurs:

His resolution far exceedeth all.
w   s w s   w   s   w s   w   s

I TAMBURLAINE, IV, i, 39

With all the legions Europe doth contain
w   s   w   s   w   s   w   s   w   s

FRIAR BACON AND FRIAR BUNGAY, II, 64

The contrast is reinforced by the occurrence of two contiguous lines in which the option is exercised:

Hath ravish'd Delia of her senses clean,
w   s w   s w s w s w   s

And she forgets that she is Delia.
w   s   w   s   w   s   w s ws

George Peele
THE OLD WIVES TALE, 693–694

There is occasional syllabification of /i/ in derivational and inflectional affixes medially:

Be satisfied and the law discharg'd
w   s ws w   s   w s   w

SPANISH TRAGEDY, III, vi, 36

Infortunate condition of kings
w s   w   s   w s ws   w   s

SPANISH TRAGEDY, III, i, 1

The marriage of thy beloved niece
w   s w s   w s   w s   w   s

SPANISH TRAGEDY, III, xiv, 28

A rare exception to the rule of two-syllable *-ion, -ience* affixes at line-endings where the alternative is available is

You hope of liberty and restitution
w   s   ws ws   w   s ws w

I TAMBURLAINE, V, ii, 147

and that, if one synaloepha is allowed, could very well be ruled out (but see note 16).

It appears that this particular method of "justifying" a decasyllabic line occurs fairly late in the period. There are some instances of it in Surrey's translation of the *Aeneid* (c. 1545), but none in *Gorbuduc,* the first blank-verse play (c. 1561). We find it first in Kyd. But this same alternation evidently occurred in Chaucer. Halle and Keyser cite

      /   /   /
Nis nat to you of reprehencioun
w   s   w   s   w s   w   s   w s

p. 200

but

    /   /   /
Of thy religioun and of thy bileeve
w   s   w s   w   s   w   s   w   s

p. 208

In the Renaissance, however, the option is not, for some reason, available until late in the sixteenth century. Why this should be so is difficult to say with certainty; one possibility is that alternation of this sort is foreign to strictly syllabic meters (there was also a prejudice against using polysyllabic words for metrical effects early in the period) and to rhymed forms. Although Sir Philip Sidney cites words with disyllabic -*ion* affixes (motion: potion) as examples of *sdrucciola* (three-syllable rhymes) and praises them as a part of the native rhyming flexibility of English, I know of no examples of this optional lengthening in his major poetry.[19] Even Marlowe, who uses it frequently in his dramatic blank verse, has only two instances of this actualization in *Hero and Leander,* a long poem in iambic pentameter couplets:

Nor is't of earth or mold celestial
w   s   w   s   w   s   w s w s
Or capable of any form at all.
w   s   w   s   w s w   s   w   s

I, 272–273

Till she, o'ercome with anguish, shame, and rage
w   s   w   s   w   s   w   s   w   s
Danged down to hell her loathsome carriage.
w   s   w   s   w   s   w   s w s

II, 333–334 [20]

No principled explanation has yet been offered as to why the longer pronunciation variants of the derivational affixes should occur at the end of the line. However, in terms of the Halle-

Keyser theory, common three-syllable adjectives such as "ambitious" would be automatically unmetrical when they occurred at line-endings because they would create a stress contrast in the ninth position. If the four-syllable option is exercised,

ambitious,
w   s w   s

the unmetricality is removed. Such a hypothesis, if true, would provide further empirical support for the Halle-Keyser theory.

These alternate realizations for metrical purposes did not necessarily have anything to do with the way in which the lines actually were spoken (any more than, in an acceptable reversal in the first foot, we do violence to the native English pronunciation of a word in order to make it fit the abstract metrical pattern). These alternants, as well as those mentioned earlier and those put forward by Halle and Keyser, constitute a poetic dialect—in the case of the -ion alternation, a dialect for unrhymed iambic verse.

The Halle-Keyser rules of synaloepha, then, with slight modifications for certain voiced fricatives, serve to account for most of the complex realizations of underlying iambic pentameter in Renaissance blank verse. Another set of rules of diaeresis accounts for a class of apparently unmetrical lines: optional actualization of underlying *e* plus sonorant consonant (the resemblance to the Halle-Keyser conditions for synaloepha here is interesting), and optional actualization of underlying /i/ with accent on the ultimate syllable in certain Romance derivational affixes.

3

In considering how this metrical theory can assist studies of metrical style, we must consider first what distinctions we wish the theory to make and what stylistic categories we wish it to establish. But beyond "rough" and "smooth" and "fast" and "slow" meter, there is no such set of categories; earlier studies of metrical style have turned immediately to local effects, to the question of the "appropriateness" of a given meter to the poem in which it occurs. This terminological lack is in large part attributable to an inadequate descriptive framework for metrical style. No new terms are proposed here, but the differentiae postulated in the course of this paper may suggest some.

Let us begin, then, by considering some lines in which we have fairly good evidence of what a poet was trying to do with his meter. As this discussion will show, a most important "counter" in metrical style is frequency of stress neutralization, the occurrence within the line of contiguous syllables which receive main stress. What effect does a high frequency of stress neutralization have upon metrical style in a passage of poetry? As a beginning, we can examine a couplet of Pope's which Seymour Chatman has analyzed:[21]

When Ajax strives some rock's vast weight to throw
1   2 3   4   5   6   7   8   9   10

The line too labours, and the words move slow
1   2   3 4   5   6   7   8   9   10

ESSAY ON CRITICISM, II, 370–371

Using the Trager-Smith[22] four-level system of stress, Chatman argues that "the reverse effect [from that of speed] is achieved by filling metrical zeroes [i.e., odd-numbered metrical positions, in the sense proposed above] with syllables capable of secondary stress." [23] He scans -jax, vast, too, and move as having secondary stress, yet in the analysis of the "fast" line

Not so, when swift Camilla scours the plain
1   2   3   4   5 6 7   8   9   10

in which it is argued that the effect of speed is "produced by using light phonemic stresses to fill the metrical points," Chatman scans so and swift as having tertiary stress (compare vast and too, said to have secondary stress). The inconsistencies in the analysis are difficult to reconcile.[24]

I stress this point only to suggest that a theory of meter adequate for the study of metrical style must provide consistent and verifiable results. Chatman's analysis and the Trager-Smith stress system fail to provide an adequate interpretation of Pope's attempts to write exaggeratedly "fast" and "slow" meter. What is involved here is not the filling of "metrical zeroes" with secondary stresses (an analysis which is open to question, as we have seen), but stress neutralization or its absence:

Not so, when swift Camilla scours the plain
w   s   w   s   w s w   s   w   s

When Ajax strives some rock's vast weight to throw
w   s w   s   w   s   w   s   w   s

The line too labours, and the words move slow.
w   s   w   s w   s   w   s   w   s

Stress neutralization is at work even more clearly in another of Pope's deliberately and exaggeratedly "slow" lines:

And ten low words oft creep in one dull line.
w   s   w   s   w   s   w   s   w   s

The line is perfectly metrical, but the monosyllabic adjective-noun and adverb-verb combinations create so much stress neutralization that no stress maxima, or at most one, are actualized in the line.[25] The effect thus created is one of great deliberation; in its phonological (but not its syntactic) aspect it is analogous to the effect created by another frequent instance of stress neutralization, when major stresses occur across a major syntactic boundary:

Love hath byset the wel; be of good cheere![26]

Poetry with a high percentage of stress neutralizations thus can have a "slow" metrical style, but stress neutralization may also be used for other stylistic effects. Moreover, it is not sufficient to attribute a deliberate metrical style merely to a smaller number of actualized stress maxima; it may be that even-numbered positions are frequently filled by words of minor categories which do not receive main stress and hence cannot constitute stress maxima. The effect in these cases is the reverse; in fact, blank verse with a *high* percentage of lines in which only one or two stress maxima are actualized and a *low* incidence of stress neutralization probably would have a "fast" or "light" metrical style, although lines of this sort are rare:

In which he can win widdowes, and pay scores.[27]
w   s   w   s   w   s   w   s   w   s

Let us consider another "extreme": poetry which has a high percentage of lines in which all four stress maxima are realized.

We must consider first what possible syntactic and lexical combinations might produce such lines. It is likely that there would be a preponderance of disyllabic words, since monosyllables would create more possibilities for stress neutralization. More derivational affixes and function words, which do not take primary stress, would be in evidence; this characteristic would be balanced by the necessity that enough words which can take primary lexical stress be present for the actualization of stress maxima. The result would be a great many verb auxiliary-main verb combinations, prepositional phrases, participial clauses, and the like.

As the most nearly neutral actualization of an iambic pentameter, the line with four stress maxima might be considered as some sort of aesthetic ideal. Yet for modern prosodic tastes, poetry which has the highest percentage of lines in which nearly every stress maximum is actualized very quickly lapses into doggerel:

> For Tullie, late, a toomb I gan prepare:
> When Cynthie, thus, had mee my labour spare.
> Such maner things becoom the ded, quoth hee:
> But Tullie liues, and styll alyue shall bee.
>
> Nicholas Grimald (c. 1550)

At the other extreme from the four-stress-maximum line, the one- and two-stress-maximum lines appear to be stylistically marginal. There are two significant variations, one high, one low, in the data, which will be discussed later.

Another important axis in metrical style is weak and strong onset, that is, whether the stress maxima in positions 2 and 4 are actualized. There is no significant high variation with respect to strong-onset lines in the data gathered for this study. This finding is consistent with Halle and Keyser's failure to find any lines in Chaucer lacking stress maxima in these positions; during the Renaissance, poets retained this convention, if somewhat less rigidly. They normally actualized stress maxima in at least one of these positions; consistent failure to do so probably was either a metrical solecism or a deliberate local stylistic device.

Verse which shows a high percentage of lines with unactualized stress maxima in positions 2 and 4 can be said to have a weak onset, as Halle and Keyser point out. There are, however, two quite different kinds of weak onset, depending upon whether the stress maxima are unactualized because of stress neutralization (in which two linguistically determined primary stresses obscure one another) or because linguistically unstressed syllables occupy the even-numbered positions. In essence, weak-onset lines such as

Stand still, you ever-moving spheres of heaven
w   s   w   s w   s w   s   w   s

DOCTOR FAUSTUS, V, ii, 133

Such hope, such fortune have the thousand horse
w   s   w   s   w   s   w   s   w   s

I TAMBURLAINE, I, ii, 118

are different in their stylistic effect from lines such as the following (which are much rarer):

So is it not with me as with that Muse

Shakespeare
"SONNET 21"

A more delicate level of stylistic analysis should make visible this distinction.

Let us return to the question of metrical "regularity," raised earlier in connection with lines that have four actualized stress maxima. Our intuitive expectation that verse which showed a high degree of such lines would be more "regular" did not work out in practice; consider the sharp stylistic distinction between these lines and those which tend to actualize only *three* stress maxima:

And say they racke their rents and ace too high,
When they themselves, do sel their landlords lambe

For greater price, then ewe was wont be worth
I see you Peerce, my glasse was lately scowrde

Gascoigne
THE STEELE GLAS

Come, lady, let not this appall your thoughts;
The jewels and the treasure we have ta'en
Shall be reserved, and you in better state
Than if you were arrived in Syria,
Even in the circle of your father's arms,
The mighty Soldan of Egyptia.

I TAMBURLAINE, I, ii, 1–6

The clattering lockstep of Gascoigne's verse arises from a too-perfect actualization of the ideal metrical pattern. When every stress maximum is actualized, we become aware of the form itself rather than the substance of the poem expressed in the form. There are no instances of stress neutralization or complex realization (these characteristics are not as strong in all of Gascoigne's poetry). Despite the presence of a fairly strong enjambment,[28] the reader is led to set off each line as a unit of thought, rather than thinking in larger terms.

If lines of this sort are not, then, ideally "regular" lines, as most modern prosodists and critics grant,[29] we might then inquire into the linguistic characteristics of a meter which we perceive as "regular," particularly since—with one important exception—the data underlying this study show a fairly narrow range in the incidence of lines with four actualized stress maxima. The distinctions, in terms of the metrical characteristics elicited by this theory, between "hypermetrical" and regular English blank verse constitute an important historical watershed in the history of English metrical taste and for the possibilities for English metrical stylistics.

For the style of the passage from *Tamburlaine* just cited is quite different. The dramatic blank verse of the eighties and nineties shows a low percentage of weak-onset lines, a high percentage of lines with three stress maxima (again with one important exception which I shall discuss), a low percentage of lines with reversed initial first feet, and a low percentage of stress neutralization.

In the passage cited, there is considerable metrical variety within even the narrow scope of six lines: stress neutralization, two kinds of synaloepha, a reversed-foot line, and two instances of enjambment. Yet we have a greater sense of regularity.

The causes for this sense are difficult to elucidate clearly. Part of the problem may be the question of modern tastes. In the modern view, a great deal of the beauty of poetry is its strategic "ungrammaticality" [30]—chiefly with respect to syntax. To say this is to state a commonplace of stylistic study. But poetry strains "metricality" in certain strategic ways as well.[31] As I have suggested, the ultimately "metrical" blank-verse line in the Halle-Keyser framework is the line with four actualized stress maxima. Yet poetry which displays a high degree of this consistent actualization—such as the passage from Gascoigne—seems mechanical, stiff, and choppy.[32]

The dominant English metric thus changes as blank verse becomes more established; it is not the syllabism of Gascoigne, but the freer style of Marlowe, with its complex actualizations of the ideal patterns, which finally takes over as the norm. The form is subordinated to the sense; typically, in Marlowe, the unit of thought is at odds with the structure of the line: the major units, after the apostrophe to Zenocrate, are $1\frac{1}{2}$ lines, $1\frac{1}{2}$ lines, and 2 lines in length. The Gascoigne passage does not allow for the rhetorical "crowding" of actualized stress maxima, because all of them are actualized, whereas Marlowe uses complex actualizations to dispose the stress contrasts for the greatest rhetorical effect, especially in lines 3–4, where the rhetorical sweep of Tamburlaine's dismissal of Zenocrate's protests is heightened by the enjambment. Yet this rhetorical manipulation is achieved within rather narrow scope; only one of the lines has fewer than three actualized stress maxima. The three-stress-maximum line thus retains the guise of regularity; four, and the verse soon begins to sound like doggerel; fewer than three, and a "roughness" sets in, particularly if it is achieved by stress neutralization:

Batter my heart, three-person'd God, for you
As yet but knock, breathe, shine, and seek to mend;
That I may rise and stand, o'erthrow me, and bend
Your force to break, blow, burn and make me new.

Donne
"HOLY SONNET XIV"

For the Renaissance, regularity, which I oppose to "strict metricality," or, in Halle-Keyser terminology, "most neutral actualization," depends to a considerable degree on the proportion of
lines in a passage or writer in which three stress maxima are
realized. The three-stress-maximum line is important in the study
of metrical style for this period, but the exact place of this loosely
defined metrical "regularity" in stylistic analysis is by no means
settled. A useful task for the future would be the construction
of a framework for "degrees of metricalness" analogous to Chomsky's proposals for "degrees of grammaticalness." [33]

A secondary consideration for this strict metricality/regu-
larity axis of metrical style may be a certain range of density of
lines with reversed initial feet, although my own data is incon-
clusive on this point. A high percentage of initially reversed lines
in a passage would begin to obscure the form of iambic pentameter and create the same sense of "roughness" mentioned above,
as in the following sestet from Sidney:

Rich in the treasure of deserved renown,
Rich in the riches of a royal heart,
Rich in those gifts which give the eternal crown;
Who, though most rich in these and every part
Which make the patents of true wordly bliss,
Hath no misfortune but that Rich she is.

Sir Philip Sidney
ASTROPHEL AND STELLA, 37, 9–14

So far, at least, the reverse does not hold; it is not necessarily
true that a low percentage of these lines will lead to "strict
metricality" in the absence of other confirming characteristics.

The foregoing discussion has isolated the salient characteristics of iambic pentameter verse in terms of the metrical theory outlined earlier, and has related these characteristics—stress neutralization, weak and strong onset, number of actualized stress maxima, and reversed initial feet—to certain stylistic idiosyncrasies. An attempt has been made to consider several different kinds of questions within the broader limitations of metricality in order to derive some linguistic parameters for the study of style.

These parameters need not necessarily be given a name at this point, chiefly because the traditional names do not apply. We can, using this framework, isolate what I have called strictly metrical verse, and perhaps "rough" and "smooth" verse as well (although, as was suggested, there are different kinds of "roughness" arising from different causes). We may ultimately have to speak of "neutral" or "unmarked" lines (that is, lines with no complex actualizations). Lines with weak and strong onsets probably form a category of their own. And, although this technique has not been used here, another proposal for use of the Halle-Keyser theory in stylistics suggests that a significant factor is the percentage of lines with different patterns of actualized stress maxima (that is, lines with positions 2, 6, and 8 actualized, or 2, 4, and 8, etc.).[34]

4

These parameters will be used not to differentiate a broad range of metrical styles—although the theory would be suited to such analysis—but to trace by way of example the characteristics and historical development of an important change in metrical style in English blank verse of the Renaissance. This study is in no way intended to be definitive, for the focus of this essay is not upon the data but upon the theory which underlies the data, and the generalizations drawn from it have been deliberately and severely limited. Approximately four hundred lines of dramatic blank verse were taken from each of the following plays: Sackville and Norton, *Gorbuduc* (c. 1560); Thomas Kyd, *The Spanish Tragedy* (c. 1585); Robert Greene, *The Honourable History of Friar Bacon and Friar Bungay* (c. 1589); Christopher

Marlow, *Tamburlaine, Part I* (1587), and *Edward II* (c. 1592). For comparison, the study includes the fifty-seven lines of Faustus' last speech in Marlowe's *Doctor Faustus,* and some non-dramatic blank verse by early practitioners of the form: George Gascoigne, Nicholas Grimald, and Henry Howard, Earl of Surrey.

These passages were analyzed according to the Halle-Keyser framework with the additions discussed earlier, and the results appear in Table 1.[35]

TABLE I

	STRESS NEUT.	ENJAMB.	REV. FT.	1 and 2 SM	3 SM	4 SM	X NNN	XX NN	N XXX	NN XX
Surrey	40	40	26	23	38	39	29	15	75	65
Grimald	40	20	17	22	37	40	11	7	83	69
Gascoigne	27	11	17	17	31	52	20	6	81	77
Gorbuduc	22	25	15	21	40	37	21	7	78	69
Kyd	27	7	7	22	46	30	29	7	71	59
Greene	29	12	16	25	45	30	20	8	82	67
Tamb.	15	15	15	15	48	34	18	4	77	71
Dr. Fau.	65	10	18	42	22	34	32	16	68	52
Edw. II.	34	11	12	24	44	33	22	9	78	67

ABBREVIATIONS
Stress neut.: stress neutralizations
Rev. ft.: reversed initial feet and headless lines
1 and 2 SM: lines with one or two actualized stress maxima
3 SM: lines with three actualized stress maxima
X NNN: lines with unactualized initial (position 2) stress maximum
XX NN: lines with positions 2 and 4 unactualized
N XXX: lines with position 2 actualized
NN XX: lines with positions 2 and 4 actualized

Note that all figures are percentages expressed as fractions of the number of lines in the passage selected, and are rounded off to the nearest whole number.

Data of this sort are best used with extreme caution: nonetheless, absolute prohibitions against statistical studies of literature are in ways unrealistic (although statistics have been abused, of course). When we make a judgment of an author's style, we are saying that certain characteristics predominate over others, and in doing so we are implicitly and imprecisely counting the occurrences of these features. Numbers are no substitute for sound thinking and critical sense, but they often provide a confirmation of intuitive perceptions. In the case of these data, the statistics make visible some salient aspects of Tudor metrical style which hitherto have not been shown. I emphasize the word "salient"; there are other potentially important stylistic features which do not vary significantly.

1. Both the highest and the lowest incidence of stress neutralization—from 15 per cent to 65 per cent—are found in one writer, Marlowe.

2. One passage from Marlowe (Faustus' death speech) shows an extremely large percentage of lines with but one or two actualized stress maxima, and an extremely small percentage of lines with three actualized stress maxima. Yet another Marlowe play, *Tamburlaine, Part I,* shows the smallest percentage of one- and two-maximum lines. The incidence of these lines in the other poets stays fairly constant, as does the percentage of lines with four actualized stress maxima, except in the poetry of George Gascoigne.

3. As well as showing the largest percentage of four-maximum lines, Gascoigne shows the smallest total of one- and two-maximum and three-maximum lines.

4. Generally speaking, the percentage of lines with three actualized stress maxima decreases as we move forward historically from Surrey to Gascoigne, and then increases as we approach the time of Marlowe, whose plays, except for the speech from *Faustus,* show the highest percentage of these lines.

5. The highest percentages of lines with unactualized stress maxima in the first two positions occur in *Doctor Faustus* and Surrey's translation of the *Aeneid.*

6. The passages from Surrey show the highest percentages of enjambment, and lines with reversed first feet. They are second only to the short passage from *Doctor Faustus* in their employment of stress neutralization.

7. The dramatic blank verse of Thomas Kyd is lowest in lines with reversed initial feet, enjambment, and (along with that of Greene) lines with four actualized stress maxima.

Now let us consider these poets in an historical framework. As the previous discussion suggested, there is a constant tension in English prosodic taste between strict syllabism and stress regularity on the one hand and accentualism and more complex rules of metrical actualization on the other,[36] inherent to a certain extent in the nature and history of English verse.

For the early Renaissance, the observable origins of this tension reside in some important critical work after the middle of the century, in which it is possible to see—even though its views in the main did not prevail—what the later poets were using as a point of departure. The characteristics which this critical work suggests—which are more validly accounted for by the Halle-Keyser theory than by any others now extant—are the primes of metrical style at least for the blank verse of this period, and probably for other forms in this and later periods.

There are aspects of Surrey's verse which, in terms of our earlier discussion of linguistic characteristics of meter and their stylistic consequences, can fairly be described as crudities. There is a high incidence of reversed-foot lines, stress neutralization, and weak onset—lines with unactualized stress maxima in the first two even positions—making Surrey's blank verse a rough affair indeed:

> Then from the sea the dawning gan arise.
> The son hoist vp, the chosen youth gan throng
> Vnto the gates: the hayes so rarelie knitt,
> The hunting staves with their brode heddes of yron,
> And of Massile the horsemen, furth thei breke;
> Of senting howndes a kennell huge likewise.

IV, 165–170, MS. Hargrave 205

One trait of Surrey's verse, however, suggests what is to come. His poetry is among the three highest in lines with four actualized stress maxima, and among the lowest in those with three. In 1557, ten years after his death, there occurred an important event for the history of English prosody—the publication of *Tottel's Miscellany*. This volume, which included republication of some of Thomas Wyatt's poems, some new Wyatt poems, and poetry by, among others, Grimald and Surrey, provides some evidence of metrical tastes at the time, particularly in the revisions made by the editor of Wyatt's poems. These have been outlined

in detail by Thompson;[37] as he points out, the editors attempt
to regularize Wyatt's poems toward regular syllable counts and
stress alternation. From the point of view of the Halle-Keyser
theory, they attempt to reduce stress neutralization and complex
actualization. Some examples follow:

/   /   /   ⌒

They sang sometime a song of the feld mowse

Wyatt

/   /   /

They sing a song made of the feldishe mouse

Tottel

/   /   /   ⌒

She thought herself endured to much pain
w   s   w   s   w   s w   w   s

Wyatt

/   /   /   /

She thought, [sic] herselfe endured to greuous
w   s   w s   w   s   w   s w

payne
s

Tottel [38]

It is clear that the editors of *Tottel's Miscellany*, which went
through at least eight editions in thirty years[39] and was, for its
day, a very successful publishing venture, were attempting to
shape Renaissance critical tastes toward syllabicity and regularity
of stress alternation, or, more accurately, toward more neutral
actualization of the underlying metrical pattern, reducing complex realization and stress neutralization.[40] The line with four
actualized stress maxima is carried forward from Surrey as the
norm; preference for strong-onset lines and avoidance of weak
onset are added as hallmarks of what I have called strict metricality.

The characteristics predominate in the verse of Grimald, one
of the editors of Tottel, which appears in the *Miscellany*. He
still has not quite mastered the form, however, for his verse, like
that of Surrey, has quite a high incidence of stress neutralization.

As a consequence, we sense in his verse not only a cramped articulation but a crude one as well:

> O monstrous man (quod he) whatso thou art,
>
> I praye thee, lyue: ne do not, with thy death
>
> This lodge of lore, the Muses mansion marr.
>
> That treasure house this hand shall neuer spoyl:
>
> My swoord shall neuer bruze that skylful brayn,
>
> Longgathered heapes of science soon to spyll.
>
> O, how faire frutes may you to mortall men
>
> From wisdoms garden giue?

Grimald
"ZOROAS," 71–78

Gascoigne's poetry is a bit more palatable than Grimald's amateurish verse. Like Grimald, he practices the principles of strict metricality, particularly in his avoidance of weak-onset lines, and there is far less incidence of stress neutralization in his poetry. But his insistence upon rigidly controlled verse was greater: more than half of his lines have four stress maxima actualized. Clearly Gascoigne implicitly perceives this characteristic as the hallmark of metrical verse, for he is near the bottom in both three-stress and two-stress lines. For Gascoigne, either a line fulfills the ideal metrical pattern or it does not.

That this practice was deliberate is shown in his *Certayne Notes of Instruction,* published in 1575. In *Certayne Notes,* Gascoigne argues, in effect, for strict syllabicity and regular stress alternation. Poets are not to violate English word or phrase accent ("You shall do very well to use your verse after th[e] English phrase, and not after the manner of other languages."). The craft of poetry is in fitting the "given" of the language's stress-patterns to the requirements of the meter. Gascoigne urges that polysyllabic words be avoided, because they "do cloye a verse and make it unpleasant, whereas woordes of one syllable will more easily fall to be shorte or long as occasion requireth, or wilbe adapted to become circumflexe or of an indifferent sounde." [41]

The last observation, repeated and emphasized in another important critical document, George Puttenham's *Art of Poesie,* published fourteen years later, is particularly interesting in view of the Halle-Keyser theory. Gascoigne is attempting to account intuitively for a plain fact of English poetic language from Chaucer's time to ours:[42] stress neutralization does not disrupt metricality. Two adjacent lexically stressed monosyllables can be fitted to the metrical pattern by the stress-reduction rules, or they can be equal in stress and create stress neutralization. As we have seen in the lines from Pope, English poets have had this intuition for centuries.

Gascoigne's verse clearly establishes the four-maximum line as a hallmark of strict metricality. His critical contribution was the explicit formulation of what has now become known as stress neutralization. Gascoigne's career marks the high point of what C. S. Lewis has called the Drab Age. Lewis, who takes *Tottel's Miscellany* to be a Drab Age anthology, maintains that "the grand function of the Drab Age poets was to build a firm metrical highway out of the late Medieval swamp." [43] The way out of the swamp, the Drab Age poets evidently felt, was by the establishment of a strictly regular norm for English blank verse. If the result of their efforts is a bit dry for modern tastes, it must still be granted they are the first poets in English to pay serious attention to the art of prosody, and the character of their verse is a consequence of what they took to be the rules of English prosody. With regular stress alternation, native word- and phrase-stress, and high frequency of monosyllables as goals, it is hard to see how the Drab poets could have written otherwise than their rather choppy, singsong style.

But change begins to make itself evident with the dramatic blank verse of Sackville and Norton in *Gorbuduc.* Their tendency to avoid stress neutralization and their apparent relaxation of Gascoigne's insistence upon the four-stress-maximum line as the metrical norm adumbrates the freer metrical practices of Marlowe and his followers. Still, Sackville and Norton avoid the weak-onset line.

Kyd continues this development, for it is with his verse that we see the first clear signs of the established shift in taste. Kyd abandons the four-stress-maximum line as a metrical norm—his verse is among the lowest in incidence of these lines, and his poetry is higher in three-maximum lines than the earlier poets. The same characteristics are to be found in Greene, for whom the three-maximum line also is more frequent. Kyd and Greene mark the beginning of a new age in English blank verse, which henceforth has far more freedom and greater stylistic possibilities.

The causes for this shift are difficult to discover, and in any event are beyond the scope of this paper. Thompson attributes it to the experiments with classical meters during the 1580's and 1590's, which made poets aware of the distinction between the strict metrical pattern and the accents of speech.[44] My own view is that the clearest cases we have of the new freedom are in the blank-verse drama, which by its very nature has a far greater need for metrical variation.

But whatever the cause, the historical lines of the period are clear: from the rough beginnings of Surrey, whose crude variations from a fairly neutral actualization of the form are without stylistic warrant, through the gradually increasing regularity of Grimald to the strict syllabicity and stress regularity of Gascoigne, who followed his own metrical principles practically to the letter.

The mainstream of English poetry then turns away from the strict metricality of Gascoigne toward what eventually becomes "Marlowe's mighty line," as Ben Jonson later was to call it. Marlowe's line was strong, not "regular" in Gascoigne's sense; beginning with *Gorboduc* just after mid-century, writers of blank verse increasingly see the line with three rather than four stress maxima as the norm.

English poets come to learn a more flexible blank verse line, in which one of the basic stress contrasts normally is left unactualized, and the position of the unactualized contrast is shifted for rhetorical effect and metrical variation. Marlowe himself quite unmistakably announces the New Metric in the prologue to *Tamburlaine, Part I*, a *tour de force* meant to shock in every possible way.

> From jigging veins of rhyming mother wits,
>
> And such conceits as clownage keeps in pay,

We'll lead you to the stately tent of war,

Where you shall hear the Scythian Tamburlaine

Threat'ning the world with high astounding terms

And scourging kingdoms with his conquering
  sword.

View but his picture in this tragic glass,

And then applaud his fortunes as you please.

Marlowe parodies the now outmoded prosody of the Drab Age,[45] and goes on to define in practice the new prosody which is to be the mainstream of English verse until the Restoration. As we move forward from *Gorbuduc* to Kyd and the early Marlowe, the strong line gradually comes to the fore as stress neutralization and one- and two-stress-maximum lines, with their weakening effects, diminish.

But as Marlowe himself must have realized, one voice, one style, one meter, is not enough for the drama. The "high astounding terms" of *Tamburlaine, Part II,*

> Holla, ye pampered jades of Asia!
> What, can ye draw but twenty miles a day,
> And have so proud a chariot at your heels,
> And such a coachman as great Tamburlaine . . .
>
> IV, iv, 1–4

moved Shakespeare to parody:

> Shall pack-horses
> And hollow pampered jades of Asia,
> Which cannot go but thirty mile a-day,
> Compare with Caesars, and with Cannibals,
> And Trojan Greeks?
>
> HENRY IV, PART II, II, iv, 148–152

In his later plays, Marlowe varies his meters for dramatic effect to differentiate characters and states of mind. Observation of those metrical characteristics which Marlowe chooses to vary in order to achieve these differentiations can yield insight into what metrical traits were considered important during this period. While the bravado of Faustus and Edward, Marlowe's two self-deceived heroes, finds issue in terms as "high and astounding" as Tamburlaine's, stress neutralization and weak-onset lines increase markedly in the periods of their despair and misery. This variation does not exist for Bajazeth, Tamburlaine's foil—Marlowe gives him lines which are just as strong as his victorious opponent's. Marlowe is the first writer of English dramatic blank verse for whom the poetic form becomes a working part of the artistic medium.

Marlowe's perfecting of blank verse liberates English dramatists from the rigid metrical conformity inherited from the rhymed forms with which the modern English drama began. He is the chief architect of that metrical tradition which enables Shakespeare to employ these metrical primes for such telling rhetorical effects as Macbeth's almost fatalistic determination:

> To-morrow, and to-morrow, and to-morrow
>
> Creeps in this petty pace from day to day
>
> To the last syllable of recorded time,
>
> And all our yesterdays have lighted fools
>
> The way to dusty death. Out, out, brief candle!
>
> Life's but a walking shadow, a poor player
>
> That struts and frets his hour upon the stage
>
> And then is heard no more.

MACBETH, V, V, 19–26

The actualized stress maxima on the stressed syllables of the three "tomorrows"; the monotonous regularity as they creep "in this petty pace" to the neutralized "last syllable" and then continue, again regularly, to "dusty death"; the sharp break in tone achieved by the stress neutralization on "out, out, brief candle"—

these variations in metrical style are not possible until a tradition is created for them. In the sixteenth century, the disposition of stress maxima and stress neutralization become an important device for *metrical foregrounding*.[46]

After Shakespeare, Marlowe's chief metrical legatee, English verse continues its movement between the metrical innovations and freedom of such poets as Donne and Milton, and the more conservative syllabicity and stress regularity of such poets as Ben Jonson:

> Thou art not, Penshurst, built to envious show
>
> Of touch or marble, nor canst boast a row
>
> Of polished pillars or a roof of gold;
>
> Thou hast no lantern whereof tales are told,
>
> Or stair, or courts, but stand'st an ancient pile,
>
> And these grudged at, art reverenced the while.
>
> Thou joy'st in better marks, of soil, of air,
>
> Of wood, of water; therein thou art fair.
>
> "TO PENSHURST," 1–8

Perhaps in response to Milton's strikingly irregular (but not unmetrical) blank verse, stress regularity begins to be enforced in the late seventeenth century in the poetry of Dryden and those whom he influenced. The movement of English verse between these poles continues—from the strict regularity of Pope and Swift to the true accentualism of Coleridge's *Christabel*; from the freedom of metrical practice typical of much Romantic verse to the more formal meters of Tennyson and Arnold to the radical departures from the mainstream of English metrical tradition to be found in modern poetry. Detailed study of each of these periods in terms of this framework is needed, and it is not the purpose of this discussion to provide it. It is important to realize, however, that these primes of metrical style are still salient in the poetry of our own day:

Light breaks where no sun shines;

Where no sea runs, the waters of the heart

Push in their tides;

And, broken ghosts with glow-worms in their
heads,

The things of light

File through the flesh where no flesh decks the
bones.*

Dylan Thomas
"LIGHT BREAKS WHERE NO SUN SHINES"

5

The phrase "primes of metrical style" has dominated this discussion, and I should like to conclude by returning to an issue
raised at the beginning of this paper: an appropriate framework
for the study of metrical style.

The basic mapping rules proposed by Halle and Keyser for
the iambic pentameter of Chaucer carry through, with modification for each period and form, for all of the subsequent iambic
verse forms in English poetry. Their work needs to be carried
forward for different periods and forms, and the first part of
this paper is an effort to propose slight modifications for Tudor
blank verse.

Subsequent to the construction of these rules is the question
of which of them and the kinds of lines they produce are stylistically significant first for a given period, then for a given author,
and finally for a given poem. Hence for Tudor blank verse, stress
neutralization, lines with four actualized stress maxima, lines
with three actualized stress maxima, and weak- and strong-onset
lines were found to be stylistic primes; the changes in metrical

---

* Dylan Thomas, *Collected Poems.* Copyright 1939, 1946 by New Directions Publishing Corporation. Reprinted by permission of New Directions
Publishing Corporation, Inc. Also by permission of J. M. Dent & Sons Ltd.
and the Trustees for the Copyrights of the late Dylan Thomas.

style which occur in the period were found to turn upon these characteristics. Notice that enjambment, headlessness, synaloepha, and diaeresis were *not* found to be stylistic primes for this period—for another era they might well be crucial (in fact, for the heroic couplet in the eighteenth century weak and strong onset probably are far less important than the type of disyllabic actualization of a single metrical position).

I suggest that the *deep properties* of English meter[47] are characterized by the evidence which this theory elicits. As Halle and Keyser have shown, basic questions of metricality are explicitly and exhaustively answered by analysis of this sort. As has been argued in the foregoing, the fundamental historical contrast in the mainstream of English metrics—that between strict stress alternation and more complex realization of the metrical pattern—can be demonstrated, and its development in early modern English rather precisely traced, in the blank verse of the Tudor period. The most crucial distinction for metrical style is the disposition of *linguistically given stress contrasts.*

But evidence of this sort by no means exhausts the question of metrical style. Beyond these deep properties of English meter are what can be termed its surface properties. These can be roughly divided into syntactic and phonological effects. The syntactic properties of surface metrical style in English include (but are by no means limited to) the relative strength of the stresses which are used by the poet to fill the actualized stress maxima, the "fit" of the poem's syntactic structures with its line structures, and the nature of unactualized stress maxima (that is, whether attributable to heavy use of function words or to stress neutralization).

Such work as Chatman's on the relative strength of stresses filling the "metrical points" does not permit us to consider the stylistic effects of complex realization and stress neutralization in as systematic a fashion as the present theory. Having once settled the question of deep metrical style with respect to disposition of actualized stress maxima, however, we can make more delicate stylistic distinctions through analysis of stress assignment.

The matter of the "fit" between a poem's syntactic structures and its metrical structures has been examined in detail by Fowler. The stylistic consequences of this feature depend upon the fact that "the grammar of a poem may reinforce or subtly resist the division into lines which is implied by other features —number of syllables, end rhyme, arrangement on the printed page." The most obvious result of such a "resistance" is enjambment—the run-on line—but enjambment is very difficult to define, and there are "degrees of enjambment, degrees of tension between the metre, wanting to make a break, and the grammar, wanting to be continuous." [48] These degrees range from the very slight, as with Marlowe's compounding in "Is this the face that launched a thousand ships,/And burnt the topless towers of Ilium?" to the extreme, in e. e. cummings's "You/'ll see/an in/-ch/of an if . . . ," and it is difficult to know where to draw the line. Enjambment can be used as a foregrounding device in an otherwise regular passage for strong rhetorical effect (for example, Andrew Marvell's "Thus, though we cannot make our sun/Stand still, yet we will make him run" ["To His Coy Mistress"]) or it can be used to create rhetorical units which are larger than the line:

> Forgett'st thou that I sent a shower of darts,
> Mingled with powdered shot and feathered steel
> So thick upon the blink-eyed burghers' heads,
> That thou thyself, then County Palatine,
> The King of Boheme, and the Austric Duke,
> Sent heralds out, which basely on their knees,
> In all your names desired a truce of me?

> II TAMBURLAINE, I, ii, 14–20

Certain instances of enjambment may have consequences for deep metrical structure, for they cause the actualization of a fifth stress maximum in the blank verse line.[49] But in the absence of any clearly articulated "scale" for enjambment as proposed by Fowler, a systematic account of the effects created by this kind of enjambment is not yet possible.

A more delicate matter is the "fit" between smaller grammatical units (short phrases and words) and metrical feet. There are some difficulties in Fowler's discussion of this question—arising chiefly from the vagaries of the Trager-Smith stress-analysis employed and the problematic definition of the metrical foot in English—but it is clear that there is a stylistic distinction between (to use his examples) such lines as Spenser's "But if for me ye fight or me will serve," in which the stress patterns are naturally iambic, and "And all the way the wanton damsell found," in which, in the fourth and fifth feet, the foot-divisions cross the word boundaries. It may well be that effects of the sort created by the first example were what Gascoigne was seeking in *Certayne Notes* when he counselled poets not to violate native English stress patterns and to use monosyllables.

Some of the phonological aspects of surface metrical style are a subclass of what G. N. Leech has called "syntagmatic" figures of speech—that is, "where there is choice to be made at different points in the chain, the writer repeatedly makes the same selection." [50] Under this heading are classified such foregrounding stylistic elements as rhyme, both internal and external, alliteration, consonance, and assonance, when they support the metrical pattern.

This last limitation distinguishes lines such as Marlowe's "Black is the beauty of the brightest day" (*II Tamburlaine*, II, iv, 1), from Sir Philip Sidney's "Of those fierce darts Despair at me doth throw." [51] In Marlowe's line the poet orchestrates a number of phonological and syntactic devices in support of a strong metrical pattern: a reversed first foot, emphasizing *black;* alliteration of the initial syllables and both the actualized stress maxima (a frequent occurrence in Marlowe); and initial stops for all of the lexically stressed words in the line. Sidney's alliteration is more subtle, to use the word neutrally; it is part of a phonological substructure which works against the metrical pattern. The contiguous alliteration of *darts* and *de-* is obscured by the stress neutralization on *darts* and by the placement of *de-,* the only unstressed syllable in the line surrounded by lexically stressed syllables, following stress neutralization. The alliteration of *doth* also is obscured; it is not a stress maximum, and as an auxiliary its stress is subordinated to *throw.* Questions of the sort raised by this line from Sidney lie outside the limits of strictly *metrical* style; with such traits as consonant clusters and vowel quantity they belong to the phonology of poetry, an area of stylistics which has not been systematically explored.

There remains the question of rhyme, which is difficult to consider under this theory. In certain kinds of poetry rhyme certainly is organic, and must be considered as a part of the deep

properties of meter. Rhyme is not merely incidental to a couplet
such as:

> Here thou, great Anna! whom three realms
>   obey
> Dost sometimes counsel take—and sometimes
>   Tea.

Alexander Pope
RAPE OF THE LOCK, III, 7–8

The case is not so clear, however, when we consider forms other
than the heroic or octosyllabic couplet. The question is further
complicated by the general requirement in English poetry that
there be lexical stress on the rhyming syllables, a requirement
which may affect the distribution of actualized stress maxima
in the line. Looser rhymed forms such as rhyme royal, Spenserian
stanza, and various *abab* forms cannot be said to have rhyme at
their very center to the same extent as the closed couplet, but
it is difficult to state with any confidence whether one ought to
consider rhyme as an element of metrical style, and if so where.

An ancillary contribution which metrical analysis of this sort
makes to literary studies is in the editing of modern texts. I do
not know of a single modern text of Renaissance verse or drama
which takes systematic account of the metrical pronunciation
variants suggested in the first part of this paper. Our tendency
might be, for instance, to think of the octosyllabic line "My
bottle of salvation" (Sir Walter Ralegh, "The Passionate Man's
Pilgrimage") as a forced accommodation to the metrical pattern,
and to think the less of the poet's skill, until we become aware
that disyllabification of the *-ion* ending is an acceptable metrical
alternative throughout the period in question. This particular
line is so marked in an anthology chosen at random,[52] but a
decasyllabic line by the same author which exercises the same
option is not so marked ("What is our life? A play of passion.")
Inconsistencies such as this are common in modern editions, and
suggest that sound editing of poetry depends in no small part
upon an adequate theory of meter.

The issues raised in this paper have centered upon a linguistically determined question—metricality—which leads immediately to questions of literary taste. As Cunningham points

out in a number of pungent examples, a linguistically metrical line is not necessarily a poetically metrical line. The poetic context for

I'll have a cúp of cóffee and a roll,

a perfectly metrical iambic pentameter line with two actualized stress maxima, is difficult to imagine. The separation of matters of fact from matters of taste and from interpretation applies equally to the stylistic features postulated in this study. Stress neutralization, for example, was not found to have any consistent thematic effect; it does function as a very clear device of foregrounding, and it is perhaps to just such neutral terminology that linguistically oriented studies of literature initially should limit themselves.[53]

A still more important question implicit in the study of meter is the nature of poetic language—or, more accurately, the nature of a poet's *faculté de langage*. Part of this subject is approachable through the study of meter, as is suggested in the hypotheses advanced here and in other work about poets' use of deep phonological processes. The question of "metricality" is part of the larger question of "poeticality," of the intellectual mechanism which arranges a scale from "I'll have a cup of coffee and a roll" (not poetry) to

> Last steps Abbreviation, bold and strong,
> And leads the volant trains of words along,
> With sweet loquacity to *Hermes* springs,
> And decks his forehead and his feet with wings.[54]

(bad poetry) to

> Thy firmness draws my circle just,
> And makes me end, where I begun.

Donne
"A VALEDICTION FORBIDDING MOURNING"

The proposal of an abstract theoretical structure for such differentiations is the logical province of linguistics and would constitute an important contribution to literary studies. If there is a scale of acceptability within "grammaticality," [55] it is reasonable to suppose that there is a scale of "poeticality" as well.

The syntax of poetic language has been the subject of much recent work, but the major difficulty in the general linguistic study of poetic language hardly has been approached: the theoretical juncture of a "grammar of prosody" (i.e., the phonological component of poetic language) and a syntax of poetry. For metrical structure belongs to the deep, rather than the superficial, structure of poetic language; in strictly metrical poetry, at least, it is a constraint on the syntactic structure of poetic language. The structure which the formalization of such a theory would take is difficult to predict. But a linguistic theory of poetic language which does more than catalogue the history of tastes— which is, in short, mentalist and generative rather than empiricist and taxonomic—is a crucial future task for linguistics. A generative theory of poetic meter and its consequences for major periods of literature is the first necessary step.[56]

NOTES

1. See S. J. Keyser, "The Linguistic Basis of English Prosody," in *Modern Studies in English*, ed. David Reibel and Sanford Schane (Englewood Cliffs, N.J., 1969), pp. 379–394.

2. J. V. Cunningham, "How Shall the Poem Be Written?" *Denver Quarterly*, II (1967), 45.

3. The major studies have been Harold Whitehall, "From Linguistics to Criticism," *Kenyon Review*, XIII (1951), 710–714; Edmund Epstein and Terence Hawkes, *Linguistics and English Prosody*, Studies in Linguistics, Occasional Papers, No. 7 (Buffalo, 1959), and Seymour Chatman, *A Theory of Meter* (The Hague, 1965), and earlier work cited therein.

4. Stanley B. Greenfield, "Grammar and Meaning in Poetry," *PMLA*, LXXXII (1967), 377–387.

5. E.g., Seymour Chatman, "Comparing Metrical Styles," *Style in Language*, ed. Thomas A. Sebeok (Cambridge, Mass., and New York, 1960), pp. 149–162.

6. David Abercrombie, "A Phonetician's View of Verse Structure," *Studies in Phonetics and Linguistics* (London, 1965), pp. 16–25.

7. Roger Fowler, " 'Prose Rhythm' and Metre," *Essays on Style and Language*, ed. Fowler (London, 1966) [reprinted in this volume].

8. Morris Halle and Samuel J. Keyser, "Chaucer and the Study of Prosody," *College English*, XXVIII (1966) [reprinted in this volume].

9. Keyser, "The Linguistic Basis of English Prosody."

10. The theory allows for the common reversed initial foot and for a weak line-ending because linguistically assigned stress contrast—and hence an actualized stress maximum—is impossible in the first and tenth metrical positions (for iambic pentameter). For discussion of stress neutralization on

Adjective-Noun sequences, see Halle and Keyser, "Chaucer and the Study of English Prosody" [pp. 389–393 in this volume].

11. See Keyser, "Old English Prosody," *College English,* XXX (1969), 331–356, for discussion.

12. Da and C verses, according to the analysis presented by Robert P. Creed in "A New Approach to the Rhythm of *Beowulf,*" *PMLA,* LXXXI (1966), 23–33.

13. New York, 1968.

14. Texts cited are as follows: Christopher Marlowe, *Tamburlaine, Part I,* I, ii–II, ii; *The Tragical History of the Life and Death of Doctor Faustus,* V, i, 130–187; and *The Troublesome Reign and Lamentable Death of Edward the Second,* V, i–V, iii, in *The Complete Plays of Christopher Marlowe,* ed. Irving Ribner (New York, 1963). Thomas Kyd, *The Spanish Tragedy,* I, i–I, iii; Robert Greene, *The Honourable History of Friar Bacon and Friar Bungay,* Scenes I–IV, in *English Drama 1580–1642,* ed. C. F. Tucker Brooke and Nathaniel Burton Paradise (Boston, 1933). George Gascoigne, *The Steele Glas* ("The Plowman" and "Epilogus") and *Certayne Notes of Instruction in English Verse,* in *English Reprints,* ed. Edward Arber (Birmingham, England, 1868); Henry Howard, Earl of Surrey, *Aeneid,* Book 2, 1–71, in *The Poems of Henry Howard, Earl of Surrey,* ed. F. M. Padelford, rev. ed., 2 vols. (Seattle, 1928); Nicholas Grimald, "The Death of Zoroas" and "Marcus Tullius Ciceroes Death," in *Tottel's Miscellany,* ed. Hyder E. Rollins, rev. ed. (Cambridge, Mass., 1965), pp. 115–120; Thomas Sackville and Thomas Norton, *The Tragedy of Gorbuduc,* I, ii, in *Chief Pre-Shakespearean Dramas,* ed. Joseph Quincy Adams (Boston, 1924).

The scansion notation is as follows: / is an actualized stress maximum; ͟ indicates stress neutralization; a bar over two syllables (pri͡son) indicates synaloepha. Some passages have w-s-w-s subscripts; these indicate metrical positions (weak, strong).

15. For /v/, at least, the option evidently was longer lived, for we find in Milton the following line, pointed out to me by Dudley L. Hascall of Harvard:

$$\text{Made g\'oddess of the ri}\overline{\overbrace{\text{ver}}}\text{; still she retains.}$$

COMUS, 842

The possibility that meter may be patterned on underlying phonological forms was first raised by V. J. Zeps in "The Meter of the So-Called Trochaic Latvian Folksongs," *International Journal of Slavic Linguistics and Poetics,* VII (1963), 123–128. See also Paul Kiparsky, "Metrics and Morphophonemics in the Kalevala," *Studies Presented to Professor Roman Jakobson by His Students* (Cambridge, Mass., 1968) [reprinted in this volume, Selection 10]. I am grateful to Professor Kiparsky for discussion of this issue.

16. This question raises another issue: some order of priorities for patterns of realization through the rules. At present, we are in effect saying that if a line can find more than one path through the rules, any path will do. The result is to make many lines metrical by the general rules that indeed *are* metrical, but are so, intuitively at least, not by the general rules but by the operation of a special "realization rule" of the form proposed here for Renaissance verse. At issue are such lines as "Speak, shall he presently be despatched and die?" (Marlowe, *Edward II,* V, 44). In the present formulation of the Halle-Keyser theory there are at least two paths through the rules:

1. φ Speak shall he presently be despatched and die
 w   s   w   s w s w s   w s

2. Speak shall he presently be despatched and die
 w   s   w   s w s w s   w s

Notice that the analysis cannot be:

° Speak shall he presently be despatched and die
 w   s   w s w   s w s   w s

This analysis would assign an actualized stress maximum on position 3, thus making the line unmetrical.

If there were some kind of simplicity measure which might, for example, assign the highest value to an analysis which preserved metricality with the fewest allowable complications, and an order of realization rules which made, let us say, synaloepha over contiguous vowels less marked than synaloepha over sonorants, the case would be considerably strengthened for new metrical alternants such as synaloepha over voiced fricatives, which was discussed earlier. A simplicity measure and ordered realization rules also would lend more precision to discussion of metrical style. For discussion of the notion "simplicity measure" see Noam Chomsky, *Aspects of the Theory of Syntax* (Cambridge, Mass., 1965), pp. 37–47. [On metrical position, see Donald C. Freeman, "Metrical Position Constituency and Generative Metrics," *Language and Style*, II (1969), 195–206.]

17. These may be cases of disyllabification of the internal vowel, however. In *English Pronunciation, 1500–1700* (London, 1957), E. J. Dobson cites (p. 761) Peter Levin's *Manipulus Vocabulorum* (1570) as having *sure* with final glide. For further discussion see Bror Danielsson, *John Hart's Works on English Orthography and Pronunciation 1551, 1569, 1570*, Part II, *Stockholm Studies in English*, XI (Stockholm, 1963), 185.

18. There is some evidence from spelling in support of this assertion: *OED children*, from earlier *childeren*, and cf. Dobson, *English Pronunciation*, pp. 908–909; *OED hundered*, and cf. Dobson; *OED monsterous; OED lightening* (no date); *OED sapelynges* (from Middle English). Danielsson's analysis of Hart's work on pronunciation (p. 179), while not entirely clear on this point, suggests that the three-syllable pronunciation of *children* required by the meter in the first example is archaic or nonexistent in normal speech by the time of Marlowe: "In 1551 Hart states that the words are sometimes written *bretheren* and *childeren* with the penultimate *e* mute, and thus he then pronounced them with -*r* followed by a glide-vowel and -*n*. When, in 1570, he does not use a glide-vowel in these words, this clearly indicates that he wanted to denote a pronunciation with syllabic n."

19. See *The Defense of Poesie*, in *The Prose Works of Sir Philip Sidney*, ed. Albert Feuillerat (Cambridge, 1962–1963), III, 45. In the Eleventh Song of *Astrophel and Stella*, Sidney in fact chooses the shorter alternative at a line-end, although the fact that the poem is trochaic weakens the force of the example:

What if you new beauties see
 s w s w   s w s

Will not they stir new affection?
 s w   s   w   s w s w

I will think they pictures be,
 s w   s   w   s w   s

Image-like, of saint's perfection,
 s w s w   s   w s w

Poorly counterfeiting thee.
s   w   s   w   s   w   s

20. It may be, too, that Marlowe is using the metrical option to heighten the mildly ironic tone that pervades the poem. See Paul M. Cubeta, "Marlowe's Poet in *Hero and Leander,*" *College English,* XXVI (1965), 500–505.

21. See Chatman, "Comparing Metrical Styles," p. 160, and *A Theory of Meter,* pp. 199–200ff. I have reproduced Chatman's scansion which, for the purposes of his analysis at this point, is concerned with the strength of the stresses on the odd-numbered metrical positions.

22. George L. Trager and Henry Lee Smith, *Outline of English Structure* (Norman, Okla., 1951). Their system has been criticized by Noam Chomsky, Morris Halle, and Fred Lukoff, in "On Accent and Juncture in English," *For Roman Jakobson* (The Hague, 1956), pp. 65–80, and in later work of both Halle and Chomsky. I shall be taking the Chomsky-Halle position throughout this paper: that the most significant opposition is accented vs. unaccented, rather than the four-level "phonemic" opposition proposed by Trager and Smith and those who use their system for metrical studies.

23. Chatman, "Comparing Metrical Styles," p. 160.

24. The principles of this analysis are set out to better advantage in Chatman's *A Theory of Meter,* pp. 127–141. But the validity of his analysis still is limited by the inconsistencies of the Trager-Smith system.

25. Halle and Keyser do not argue for level stress (and hence stress neutralization) on monosyllabic verb-adverb or adverb-verb combinations. Yet in these and other cases (notably monosyllabic verb-adjective-noun-object constructions) it is required if the line is to be metrical. In the ensuing analysis and discussion, I have assumed stress neutralization on verb-adverb combinations only where required to make a line metrical.

26. Chaucer, *Troilus and Criseyde,* 879, quoted by Halle and Keyser.

27. Donne, *Satire IV*; cited by Chatman, "Comparing Metrical Styles," p. 155.

28. In " 'Prose Rhythm' and Meter," [see Selection 20 in this volume], Fowler discusses the different degrees of enjambment and their stylistic effects.

29. Cunningham (p. 58) remarks that "the theoretical iambic norm . . . is a very uncommon pattern."

30. There has been much discussion of this notion recently, most of it from a transformational point of view. See, e.g., Samuel R. Levin, "Poetry and Grammaticalness," in *Proceedings of the Ninth International Congress of Linguists,* ed. Horace G. Lunt (The Hague, 1964), pp. 308–314, and J. P. Thorne, "Stylistics and Generative Grammars," *Journal of Linguistics,* I (1965) [reprinted in this volume, Selection 11] for discussion and further references. These issues are considered in a more theoretical context by Manfred Bierwisch, in "Poetik und Linguistik," *Mathematik und Dichtung,* eds. Helmut Kreuzer and Rul Gunzenhäuser (Munich, 1967), pp. 49–65 [reprinted in translation in this volume].

31. This statement is not intended to support the argument postulated by Chatman and others for "tension" between the two-level system of meter and the four-level system alleged to underlie English stress. It is difficult for me to understand how there could be "tension" between a line of verse (which is not the same thing as a performance) and an "on-off" pattern which is rarely actualized in quite that sense. Rather, it appears to me more consistent to postulate an abstract metrical pattern of potential stress contrasts, a set of realization rules, and a hierarchy for their operation. (This last part of the theory is not worked out in this paper.) There is thus no "tension"; there are simply different patterns of actualization and hence different metrical styles.

32.   This tradition of strict metricality dominated in the eighteenth century, as the scholarly account of Augustan prosody by Paul Fussell, Jr., has shown in detail: *Theory of Prosody in Eighteenth-Century England,* Connecticut College Monograph no. 5 (New London, Conn., 1954). The Renaissance aesthetic is more akin to our own as regards metrical regularity; strict metricality had a very short vogue during this period, but soon fell from fashion for a time.

33.   Chomsky, *Aspects of the Theory of Syntax,* pp. 148–153. The issues raised in note 16—the question of an ordered pattern for realization rules in the meter—also are important here.

34.   Joseph C. Beaver, "A Grammer of Prosody," *College English,* XXIX (1968) [reprinted in this volume; see Selection 22]. Working independently, Beaver arrived at some of the same generalizations about deep metrical structure as are raised at the end of this paper. Somewhat the same method was employed by Andrej Belyj in 1910 (*Simvolizm*) in his studies of Russian prosody. For discussion see V. Žirmunskij, *Introduction to Metrics,* trans. C. F. Brown (The Hague, 1966), pp. 37–48.

35.   The principles used in scanning this verse are generally those set forth by Halle and Keyser (pp. 381–394) with the additional rules discussed earlier in this paper. Occasionally, where the rhetorical structure of a line seems to require it, I have allowed pronouns to carry major stress.

36.   This contrast is discussed at length in Fussell, *Theory of Prosody, passim.*

37.   John Thompson, *The Founding of English Metre* (New York and London, 1961), pp. 18–28.

38.   Cited in Thompson, *The Founding of English Metre,* p. 19.

39.   Hyder E. Rollins, ed., *Tottel's Miscellany (1557–1587),* 2 vols., rev. ed. (Cambridge, Mass., 1965), I, 263. See also II, 36–37.

40.   The editors of the *Miscellany* also printed Book IV of Surrey's *Aeneid,* with similar "revisions" as compared with MS. Hargrave 205, which is a later (c. 1550–1575) manuscript. We do not know from what manuscript the editors of Tottel might have worked. See Padelford, pp. v and 260, for discussion.

41.   Gascoigne, *Certayne Notes,* pp. 37, 35.

42.   Harvey Gross's scansion of the final lines of Robert Frost's "Out, Out—" (*Sound and Form in Modern Poetry* [Ann Arbor, 1964], p. 67) shows, in effect, that stress neutralization operates in Frost's prosody:

$$\overset{/}{\text{And they, since }} \overset{/}{\text{they}}$$

$$\overset{/}{\text{Were }} \text{not the } \overset{/}{\text{one}} \overset{/}{\text{dead,}} \overset{/}{\text{turned}} \text{ to } \overset{/}{\text{their}} \overset{/}{\text{affairs.}}$$

In the Halle-Keyser scansion, stress neutralization would occur over the three linguistically and metrically stressed syllables "one dead, turned."

43.   C. S. Lewis, *English Literature in the Sixteenth Century, Excluding Drama* (Oxford, 1954), p. 237.

44.   See Thompson, *The Founding of English Metre,* pp. 128–138.

45.   It is true, of course, that Marlowe's polemical prologue has two targets: the earlier rhymed verse forms in the drama and the strictly metrical prosody which accompanied these forms and later inhered in unrhymed dramatic verse as well. But the chief butt of the parody is the "jigging"; the shift in style occurs as Marlowe loosens the form so as to be able to pattern stress contrasts for greatest effect.

46.   The term "foregrounding" with respect to the language of poetry was proposed by Jan Mukařovský in "Standard Language and Poetic Language," *A Prague School Reader on Esthetics, Literary Structure, and Style,* ed. Paul L.

ON THE PRIMES OF METRICAL STYLE   491

Garvin (Washington, 1964) [reprinted in this volume]. (Garvin translates as "foregrounding" the Czech term "aktualisace.") For the purposes of this essay, the following passage is perhaps most relevant: ". . . for poetry, the standard language is the background against which is reflected the esthetically intentional distortion of the linguistic components of the work, in other words, the intentional violation of the norm of the standard. . . . The more the norm of the standard is stabilized in a given language, the more varied can be its violation, and therefore the more possibilities for poetry in that language" (p. 42 in this volume). For metrical analysis, I am arguing that the "standard language" is precisely the "most neutral actualization" (in Halle-Keyser terminology) of the line. Metrical foregrounding can be viewed as an ascending scale, from failure to actualize one or more stress maxima to synaloepha, diaeresis, reversed initial feet, headlessness, and stress neutralization (but see note 16). In this historical period it is likely that the great variety of metrical styles in the latter part of the century is attributable in part to the earlier enforcement of the strictly metrical norm. The stability effected in metrical language allows for varied violation.

47. Beaver reaches conclusions very similar to these. What I have called "deep properties" he terms the poet's metrical "competence." I hesitate to use such a term because of its psycholinguistic implications, but the difference is not a great one.

48. Fowler, " 'Prose Rhythm' and Meter" [Selection 20 in this volume].

49. This statement has not yet been formalized, and may be open to question or modification. But if syntax is to play a role in metrical analysis, consistency would demand that a stress maximum be actualized on metrical position 10 of a line where there is no syntactic break between position 10 and position 11 (i.e., position 1 of the next line), if position 10 bears greater linguistically determined stress than positions 9 and 11. Somewhat similar issues may be involved in rhyme, which is not well handled by this theory in its present form.

50. G. N. Leech, "Linguistics and the Figures of Rhetoric," *Essays on Style and Language,* p. 145.

51. *Astrophel and Stella,* 39, cited in another context by A. L. Binns, " 'Linguistic' Reading: Two Suggestions of the Quality of Literature," *Essays on Style and Language,* p. 131.

52. Fred Englis, ed., *English Poetry 1550–1660* (London, 1965).

53. In part to obviate the general criticisms of contributions made by linguistics to literary studies. Most of these criticisms arise from the excesses of a few. Despite Greenfield's relevant and accurate remarks on this subject, however, I must point out that most of the excesses have been committed by literary critics in their enthusiasm over what they take to be the new techniques of linguistics. Most *linguists* of my acquaintance are very conservative on this point.

54. Erasmus Darwin, *The Temple of Nature* (1802).

55. See Chomsky, *Aspects of the Theory of Syntax,* pp. 148ff., and John Robert Ross, "Constraints on Variables in Syntax," unpublished M.I.T. dissertation, 1967, pp. 51–80.

56. This work was supported in its early stages by grants from the research committee of the Academic Senate, Santa Barbara Division, University of California; from the American Council of Learned Societies, and from the National Science Foundation. The major portion of the work was done at the Massachusetts Institute of Technology under a National Science Foundation Postdoctoral Research Fellowship and an appointment to the Humanities Institute of the University of California. For discussion and criticism I am grateful to Morris Halle and Samuel Jay Keyser.